JAMES WHITEY BULGER

1428-AZ

The Last Interviews

AS TOLD TO

MICHAEL ESSLINGER

INTRODUCTIONS BY

James "Whitey" Bulger
and **Robert Schibline**, Alcatraz Prisoner, 1355-AZ

For information contact:

Ocean View Publishing
P.O. Box 2303
Marina CA 93933
www.HistoryArchive.com

ISBN: 979-8-9867443-2-2 (Paperback)
ISBN: 979-8-9867443-7-7 (Hardback)

Library of Congress Catalog Card Number: 2022914839

Interviews, photographs, and/or commentary of persons (or their likeness) shall not imply or represent their endorsement or as being a contributor to this work. The narratives included herein have not been validated for accuracy, including those extracted from the official Bureau of Prisons inmate case files. The views expressed in the interviews, letters, narratives and other commentary are solely those of the individuals providing them, and do not necessarily reflect the opinions of the author, publisher, contributors to this work, or any others. James Bulger, his family, friends, associates, and/or any other person interviewed or named were not compensated for interviews, photos, or any materials included in this work. This work does not claim any accuracy of the accounts provided herein.

Please note that the formatting of passages, merging, editing, rephrasing, and paragraphing changes specific to the author interviews and other quotations have been made to improve readability. In some cases, textual passages were recreated and not verbatim to the original interview transcript in an effort to combine a variety of source materials. Some historical photographs have been restored or enhanced. An abbreviated version of this work, including various interviews and select inmate biographies first appeared in *Letters from Alcatraz*, by Michael Esslinger, © 2015. Brief passages from William Bulger's 2003 testimony before the House Government Oversight Committee investigating the FBI handling of informants was used along with other interviews and material. The Scorsese narrative was weaved together from three interviews that include a brief excerpt from Warner Bros. *The Departed*, and a short passage from Richard Schickel's *Conversations with Scorsese*, courtesy of Knopf Doubleday Publishing Group.

The interviews in this collection were conducted by Michael Esslinger between 2011 and 2018. All rights are protected under domestic and international copyright laws. The official inmate case files included in this collection are held as United States Public Records in the National Archives and Records Administration, United States Library of Congress, FBI, Department of Justice, and the Bureau of Prisons. Brief passages of correspondence with Bulger were also reprinted by permission from former Alcatraz associates Robert Victor Luke and Charlie Hopkins.

Book Design and Composition by John Reinhardt Book Design
Cover Design by Jim Zach
Editor: Kelly Rabe

No biographies or narratives within this book have been authorized or endorsed, implied or otherwise, by those persons named or associated. All people accused of crimes are considered innocent until proven guilty in a court of law.

This book contains graphic depictions and photographs of extreme crime and violence. Additionally, there is extreme language including derogatory and negative racial slurs and comments provided in descriptions of historical events transcribed from interviews. This content may be offensive, disturbing, and is not suitable for all readers.

CONTENTS

"Redemption can be found in hell itself,
if that's where you happen to be…"

—LIN JENSEN

"No matter how much you change, you still have to pay the price
for the things you've done…"

—DOUG MACRAY
(As portrayed by Ben Affleck in The Town)

Jim Bulger 1428 AZ James Bulger James Bulger Jim Bulger

James J. Bulger James Bulger 1428AZ Jim Bulger Jim Bulger Jim Bulger

James Bulger 1428AZ Jim Bulger Jim Bulger Jim Bulger James Bulger

James J. Bulger AZ 1428 Jim Bulger Jim Bulger James Bulger

Jim Bulger 1428 AZ Jim Bulger Jim Bulger Jim Bulger AZ 1428 Jim Bulger

Jim Bulger 1428 AZ Jim Bulger 1428 AZ James Bulger Jim Bulger

Jim Bulger 1428 AZ James Bulger Jim Bulger Jim Bulger Jim

Jim Bulger James Bulger James Bulger Jim Bulger James Bulger James Bulger

Jim Bulger AZ 1428 James Bulger James Bulger James Bulger James Bulger

James J. Bulger AZ 1428 James Bulger Jim 1428 AZ James Bulger Jim Bulger

Jim Bulger AZ 1428 Jim James Bulger Jim Bulger 1428 AZ James Bulger

Jim Bulger 1428 AZ Jim 1428 AZ Jim Bulger AZ 1428 Jim Bulger 1428AZ

James Bulger Jim Bulger 1428 Jim 1428 AZ James Bulger Whitey 1428 AZ

James Bulger 1428AZ Jim Bulger 1428AZ Jim Bulger 1428 AZ James Bulger

Whitey 1428 AZ James Bulger James J. Bulger James Bulger 1428AZ

James Bulger Jim Bulger 1428 AZ James Bulger James Bulger Jim

James Bulger James Bulger Jim 1428 AZ Jim Bulger 1428 AZ

James Bulger Jim 1428 AZ Jim 1428AZ James Bulger James Bulger

James Bulger Jim Bulger Jim 1428 AZ James Bulger James J. Bulger

James J. Bulger James Bulger James Bulger Jim Bulger 1428 AZ James Bulger

James J. Bulger Jim Bulger 1428 James Bulger James Bulger James Bulger

James J. Bulger James Bulger Jim Bulger 1428 AZ Jim 1428 AZ

Jim Bulger 1428 AZ James Bulger Jim Bulger 1428 James Bulger 1428

Jim 1428AZ James Bulger James Bulger James Bulger

AUTHOR'S PREFACE

"Michael is thorough and follows all leads to the final truth.
Glad he wasn't hunting me. I never would have
made it 16 years…"

—JAMES "WHITEY" BULGER (In a letter to journalist Jon Forsling)

HISTORY ISN'T ALWAYS a pleasant picture. Sometimes it's dark; void of triumphs and heroes, but no less important. And when it comes to retelling history, no one can tell a better tale than those who lived the experience. I've spent decades sifting through archival records and have interviewed a wide range of historical figures, but I was especially intrigued by the legendary status Bulger had risen to in American culture. In the 1930s and 40s era, sharp dressed gangsters like Al Capone, John Dillinger and Machine Gun Kelly—men who Bulger later said he idolized during his youth—dominated national headlines as famous figures in crime, and he'd later follow in their footsteps… There were many in his old neighborhood who saw Bulger as a folk hero of sorts, but few ever got close enough to know the true depth of his ventures in crime. The headline announcing his death in *The New York Times* read: "A Murderous Mob Boss—As Mythical as He Was Elusive." There was always an essence of mystery surrounding Bulger and his criminal past…

The book you are holding is the result of more than seven years of interviews and correspondence with Bulger, and it works to strip away some of that mystery. The goal of any memoir or biography is to get a good sense of what the person was like; the essence of who they were as a human being—to feel like you're sitting with them and listening to stories about their life, in their own words. This book isn't intended to be a biography about the life of Whitey Bulger. In fact, those unfamiliar with Bulger and his crimes would benefit from reading some of the more comprehensive accounts in advance of this work, including one written by his crime partner and close associate, Kevin Weeks. This book is certainly not a balanced or unbiased representation of his life. It's rather a collection of stories weaved together from interviews, using his own pen and written from inside a prison cell; transcribed from his own voice, or culled from the actual inmate case files. It is a scrapbook of memories about his early and later parts of life, and about many of the famous and not-so-famous men of Alcatraz, as Whitey Bulger remembered them; like a voice from beyond the grave. Represented are his memories; a freedom he was provided

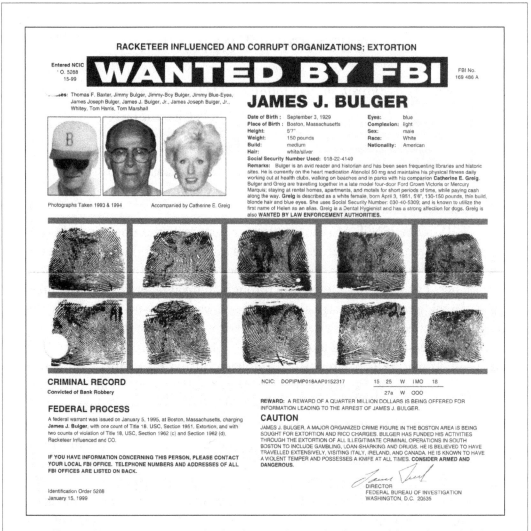

to offer unfiltered accounts which ultimately resulted in a self-made and debatable sympathetic portrait. The obvious absence of perspectives from all sides of these stories will impede objectivity and be a bridge too far for many.

In bookstores, true crime sections are typically dominated with works chronicling his life and criminal past, and in movies, he is depicted as a hands-on enforcer who ruled the streets of Boston and beyond. Despite the numerous books and movies on Bulger's life, what's often overlooked are the formative years he spent on Alcatraz closely watching Mafia moguls like Mickey Cohen, Frankie Carbo and Bumpy Johnson. For the young Bulger, it was an influential period, and he learned the criminal trade from some of the best; all of them housed together under a single roof.

The folklore and dramatic depictions of life on Alcatraz are still very much alive, but for men like Whitey who lived the experience, time served on Alcatraz was not a glamorous existence. In his own words, "It was all very human, very lonely and a place that offered plenty of time to think…On Alcatraz, our lives were frozen in time…." Society continued forward, while the men lived an existence of fierce monotony and limited contact with the outside world.

The interviews I conducted with Bulger ranged from only weeks after he was first captured in 2011, until just months before his own brutal murder in 2018. It's what makes this collection so interesting. These reflections were weaved together over the course of several years while sitting idle in his prison cell, alone with his memories…a lifetime looking back. It was all he had left, his memories and a pen.

While Bulger wrote many people following his capture, he frequently made it clear that he despised the media (he felt his family had been unfairly ridiculed and targeted by journalists) and except in rare cases, sternly refused to engage in any lengthy or structured interviews. He received a lot of mail and responded if he felt their interest was sincere or their project was interesting, or more commonly those seeking an autograph and/or answering questions of certain aspects about his past. There were a lot of people he enjoyed corresponding with. They included old friends, men he served alongside at Alcatraz, as well as some of their relatives, and even one of the jurors from his trial.

Bulger received letters from people in all walks of life: academics, criminologists, journalists, writers, researchers, crime enthusiasts, autograph seekers and those who were simply curious. He'd send me copies of their letters with his handwritten comments, usually asking if I knew the authors writing him, had any thoughts as to whether he should respond to certain requests, or to simply offer his own commentary.

He also kept a keen pulse on the media and public interest in his story, despite his status in isolation. About a year before his trial, I did an interview with Bill Whitaker, a correspondent on the CBS News program *60 Minutes*. To my complete shock, Bulger reached out to me immediately after the feature aired to compliment the interview. At one point I received a flurry of correspondence inquiring on Hollywood actor Johnny Depp (who at the time was preparing to play Bulger in the film Black Mass). Bulger was contemplating meeting with him, but after much deliberation, he ultimately decided against it. He realized it wouldn't have any influence on the film and felt the accuracy of the book that the movie was based on was seriously flawed and surmised the on-screen portrayal of him wouldn't be any different. He was also aware that Ben Affleck and Matt Damon had been engaged in tackling a project about his criminal past. The same was said relating to Mark Wahlberg, who he'd been told had expressed interest in meeting him while in prison, but that never came to fruition; and lastly, Martin Scorsese's fictional depiction of him in the epic motion picture *The Departed*. He felt Scorsese was a great storyteller, but

the portrayal of him as an informant and how he treated women was in his own words, "Inaccurate, extreme and inexcusable." He commented that both he and his girlfriend Catherine watched the film at a theatre in Santa Monica while on the run, and it immediately became clear the Frank Costello character was based on him (director Martin Scorsese officially confirmed this and is described herein). He was always aware of the public interest in his story. This in itself was fascinating to him.

Keeping all the above points in mind, I think it's important to be crystal clear on a few bold points. Bulger belonged in prison, as he was an elite class of criminal that admitted to committing horrific crimes. He confessed this, more than once, without apology and you'll find that callousness here in his own words. There were debates over which crimes he committed and those he would firmly state to which he was innocent. Even one of his own attorneys, Jay Carney, didn't hold back about Bulger's coldness toward his crimes during their pre-trial meetings. He described Bulger as "mercurial," stating that at one point he laughed about the memory of shooting one of his victims in the head.

I admit that I grappled with the idea of giving someone with such a notorious past a voice. Through the dusty lens of history, James "Whitey" Bulger has emerged as a legendary figure with a complicated legacy. As much a symbol as a man, he rose from the tough Irish South Boston projects to become a master of one of the most powerful organized crime rings in the United States. Bulger was a political powerhouse that corrupted the FBI's Organized Crime Squad and his influence leaked deep into various branches of law enforcement and government. So powerful was he in his reign that he successfully acquired intelligence about rivals, top secret information about covert surveillance operations, and all had been secretly secured from key law officials. Decades later, even after his own murder, Bulger's shadow over Boston remains. His life in crime is as intriguing as it is complicated to disentangle. It's a yarn cloaked inside a thick blanket of corruption, clandestine relationships, betrayal, and power.

The publication of these interviews is not in any remote way to be considered as an endorsement or glamorization of his crimes or views. I would never want to trivialize the suffering and tragic losses of the families. His own family and girlfriend, Catherine Greig, also suffered immensely despite having no involvement in his criminal past. Over the course of several years, I shelved this project many times knowing both the controversy and criticism that would follow, but I finally came to the conclusion that attempting to bury the history of any historical figure would be a greater mistake. I once spent a year looking through archival records and personal letters from Al Capone. I had engaged on a formal endeavor to reconstruct his years on Alcatraz, but finally surrendered the project as there was not enough in his case file records that adequately represented his personal views. It made the interviews with Bulger seem that much more important as he was one of a small group of men who served on Alcatraz—one of America's most historical landmarks—who could offer key perspectives of that experience. I felt he should have a right to tell his own story; to frame his own words, and to the extent possible, review the interview and case file transcripts. The residue of grief resulting from crimes tied to Bulger was something he was unable to soften with words, even when he offered a sense of regret.

Whitey Bulger frequently admitted his violent past, but it's not to say he was without a conscience. Maybe it was the result of many years of reflecting on his criminal ventures during his quiet years with Catherine while living in Santa Monica. Many times, he offered remorseful comments and went as far to acknowledge that some innocent people had become casualties in a war that was not their own. When talking about the innocent victims, his tone would change, and he seemed genuinely remorseful for those who died undeservingly. He repeatedly made clear that never in his life had he ever hurt a woman. He explained that the women from his past were all living proof of this and it was not part of his fabric. He made a comment specifically about Debra Davis, who was murdered in 1981. Bulger would firmly state that he was innocent of her murder, and it was alleged by more than one source, that his crime partner Stephen Flemmi had a clear motive, as she was leaving him for another man, and he'd felt she knew too much about his criminal associations. Bulger commented that those thoughts weighed heavy on him...We may never know the real truth, and Flemmi was not interviewed for this work or given the opportunity to defend himself against the allegations made by Bulger. Kevin Weeks, one of Bulger's closest associates, admitted he didn't know who killed Davis, but during an interview on WCVB-TV in 2006, he fingered Flemmi in the actual murder of Debra Hussey, stating he witnessed him choke her to death using a rope. Weeks later implicated Bulger and he was convicted of her murder by a jury in 2013, although he remained firm as to his innocence. Their deaths were terribly sad and tragic. Both were completely innocent victims who met horrific fates. It's important to remember these were real people and their families suffered immensely.

Bulger often spoke of his own family and their suffering because of his life in crime. His tone was always heartfelt when he spoke of his siblings. His brother William, the former President of the Massachusetts Senate and once the most powerful politician in the State of Massachusetts, lost his prolific career over allegations he had been in contact with his brother while he was on the lam. The brothers, who had grown up in the same household, both rose to the pinnacle of their professions and power. Their younger brother Jack, who also had a prominent career as a clerk magistrate in the Boston juvenile court system, was later reportedly convicted of lying under oath and forced to resign. He admitted to having had contact with his brother and lying out of "brotherly concern and not criminal intent." It was a dilemma that would have been difficult for any family to face and cost his siblings not only their successful

Debra Davis, the girlfriend of Stephen "the Rifleman" Flemmi was a completely innocent victim and was brutally murdered at the hands of a coldblooded killer. Bulger remained adamant that Flemmi had motive and claimed that he was solely responsible. He would go on record to state that he never hurt any women in his life and this was not part of his fabric. Flemmi later testified that Bulger strangled her because she knew they were both FBI informants, but Bulger fiercely denied any involvement and the jury during his trial ruled there was no finding that he had killed Davis. Regardless, her death was horrific and heartbreaking.

careers in public service, but also their pensions. Both men had dedicated their lives to public service and upholding the laws and ethical principles of society, and both would later fall from grace under intense scrutiny of the press.

There was another side that was much darker. When it came to the subject of Bulger's criminal adversaries, it was a completely different story. For those he claimed were his rivals in the dark underworld of crime, he never showed regret or shame for any of his actions. He felt justified in that they were criminals who sought deadly vengeance against enemies. He was direct and unremorseful. We rarely spoke about his recent crimes or murder charges that eventually landed him back in prison. He never gave up names, never any information that would be incriminating to anyone, and even spoke of his enemies with a sense of reverence which I hadn't expected. Once when he brought up the Italian Mafia, he spoke of them as being "Intensely smart, well organized, keen in business, understanding of honor and loyal to the death…" His respect was genuine, and he was careful to never divulge details that could land even a former enemy back in prison. He commented that it was against their code, and any lingering issues were handled among themselves.

In March of 2012, Hank Brennan, Bulger's trial attorney, contacted me and stated that the FBI and federal prosecutor had secured copies of our correspondence and much of what is included here. Bulger not only trusted Hank, but he admired him and stated more than once that he couldn't have asked for better counsel. Hank wanted me to be aware that our exchanges would be used in their investigation and could surface during his trial. Hank explained that for whatever reason, Bulger hadn't realized the letters he had written were being opened and copied for inclusion into his inmate case file. He had apparently assumed that since he was allowed to seal his own letters, he had a legal right to confidentiality and his mail would be forwarded without review from a censor. I was somewhat surprised since this practice went back to his years on Alcatraz and Bulger must have at least considered this. I had never thought anything otherwise...Regardless, this seemed to have no bearing on Bulger. Even with the knowledge that the FBI now went on record that they were scanning our correspondence, he never softened his words. Bulger knew that anything he wrote would be used as evidence, and during closing arguments in his trial, a passage was read from one of the letters, basically acknowledging he had come to the end of the line and that he would die in prison. It marked a bitter end to a storied life in crime. Bulger weighed in:

> Feds can read, add and subtract from anything written here and I don't care. For them my whole trial will be for one purpose, to uphold the lies and try to sabotage my reputation. The hope of the prosecutors is to fast track my trial and get me into the State Courts of Florida and Oklahoma for execution—Fuck them—they know I'm innocent on several of the charges, but they made a big deal saying they wanted to solve these cases, yet the killer in both is free. He wrote a book, is working to get a movie, his deal involves the hanging of me. If I prove he lied, then his plea deal is vacated and he's on trial for first degree murder. The prosecutors want him to hang me literally so not to expose the system of deal making.

Looking back on his early years, James Bulger was no ordinary criminal. When he arrived on Alcatraz as 1428-AZ in November of 1959, the soft-spoken bank robber known simply as "Jimmy" to fellow cons, didn't stand out as the man who would become the Al Capone of his era. After completing his sentence and being released from federal prison in 1965, he would rise to become one of the most notorious crime moguls in the United States. He sustained as the head figure of Boston's most powerful criminal syndicate for nearly three decades, never once receiving a single indictment for even a misdemeanor. Whitey Bulger was seen by many in Boston as a Robin Hood-style outlaw dedicated to protecting the neighborhood and its residents. Kevin Weeks, his longtime crime associate, later indicated that Bulger led his crime schemes with a code of ethics that did not allow his criminal affiliations to blur the lines of law-abiding people who were not involved in any of the underworld commerce. He recounted that Bulger was always eager and generous towards people in need. There were stories of Whitey buying families major appliances, televisions and even cars. "Jimmy's loyalty to friends had no limits" and Weeks further noted in a brief excerpt from his memoir, *Brutal: The Untold Story of My Life Inside Whitey Bulger's Irish Mob*:

> As a criminal, he made a point of only preying upon other criminals, as opposed to legitimate people. And when things couldn't be worked out to his satisfaction with these people, after all the other options had been explored, he wouldn't hesitate to use violence...He'd get especially angry when he heard about someone in Southie being robbed by residents of the town. "Don't rob people who have less than you," he'd tell the thieves.
>
> If you crossed him, then that side would come out...but he didn't deal with a lot of people, really. You had to get through three to four layers before you could ever get to him. I didn't see much of that side. For the most part, he was respectful—he was a businessman.

Whitey allegedly masterminded a protection racket that targeted drug kingpins and those running illegal gambling operations. In 1995, Bulger fled Boston after his FBI handler, John Connolly, tipped him off that a warrant for his arrest would be forthcoming on an impending racketeering indictment. For his ability to evade the law, Bulger rose to the top of the FBI's Ten Most Wanted Fugitive list, until he was finally captured in Santa Monica, California, on June 22, 2011.

Long before Bulger's capture, I had already met and interviewed several men who had served time with him on Alcatraz. They all had their stories, but it was an article written in 1998 and published in *The Boston Herald* that captured my attention and intrigue. The article talked about his relationship with Clarence "Joe" Carnes, the youngest prisoner to ever serve time on the Rock. Carnes had spent nearly his entire adult life behind bars. At only sixteen years of age, and living in near poverty, Joe and young accomplice Cecil Berry attempted to rob a gas station in Oklahoma. As the youths demanded money from the cash register, the attendant failed to take their threats seriously and attempted to grab the gun. In a struggle that lasted only seconds, the gun fired and forever changed the course of their lives. In October of 1943, still only sixteen, Carnes was found guilty of first-degree murder and sentenced to life in prison.

After two escapes (one included taking a hostage and transporting him across a state line), Carnes was sent to Alcatraz at only eighteen years of age. Less than a year later, he would play a role in the brutally violent 1946 Battle of Alcatraz, where two correctional officers were killed and several others who had been held hostage were injured so severely, they'd never return to work on the Island again. There were six men including Carnes identified as being principals in the failed break. Three convicts died in the attempt and his two other co-defendants were given the death penalty; they were later executed sitting side by side in San Quentin's lethal gas chamber. Carnes's life was spared as a result of his youth and the leniency he extended to the officers after being instructed by an accomplice to kill them and not leave any witnesses. The hostage guards later testified that Carnes had spared their lives. They overheard Carnes take an order from the ringleaders to finish them off, but as they held their breath attempting to fake death, he walked in front of the cells and showed mercy by reporting he had confirmed they were all dead. He later admitted that he knew they were still alive. Carnes was pardoned from the death penalty and received an additional life sentence for his role in the deadly failed escape attempt.

More than a decade later, on November 16, 1959, James Joseph "Whitey" Bulger arrived on Alcatraz as 1428-AZ. Clarence "Joe" Carnes, now in his early 30s, would be the first convict he'd meet, standing outside his cell, C-145, on the west side of Broadway. Having now been imprisoned on Alcatraz for fourteen years, Carnes provided him crucial insight to the dissident politics needed to survive the cloak and dagger underworld of the Rock. This same favor Bulger would later pass along to John Anglin, who would famously escape from Alcatraz in 1962, never to be seen or heard from again.

The Boston Herald article stated that following Carnes's death in 1988, believing he had no surviving relatives, prison officials buried him in a pauper's grave at a Catholic cemetery in Springfield, Missouri. Carnes's obituary was syndicated in newspapers nationwide when Bulger came across the obscure, brief commentary located on one of the back pages. When he learned of his friend's fate, he couldn't be at peace with the fact they had buried him in a pauper's grave. Bulger paid to have his friend's body exhumed, placed into an expensive bronze casket, then shipped nearly 280 miles to Daisy, Oklahoma, where he would be laid to rest in a proper grave on Native Indian land. He placed a bronze tombstone that included an engraved crest of pinecones symbolizing immortality, the ability to overcome difficulties, and a strong will to survive against the odds. At least, that was the story. To me, it sounded more like another myth, but this story circulated around Alcatraz like the fierce watery currents that gave the island its inescapable reputation. It was a story that was retold and debated time and time again by staff of the National Park Service and other aficionados of Alcatraz.

There was some irony relating to his friendship with Carnes. I too had been introduced to Alcatraz by "Joe." I'd met him during my first visit to Alcatraz as a tourist in the mid-1970s. Carnes had served on Alcatraz from July of 1945, until only a few months before its closure in 1963. Ten years later he was paroled on Christmas Eve, and by the time of his release, Alcatraz had just opened for public tours by the National Park Service.

As our tour group departed Fisherman's Wharf, our boat was in a flurry over its celebrity guests, but the person that everyone was most focused on wasn't Joe. It seems so random today, but on the date of my visit, Joe's guest was Hollywood actor Art Carney; well known for the 1950s television series *The Honeymooners* and his most recent role in the motion picture *Harry and Tonto,* which had earned him an Academy Award for Best Actor. I had no idea who Art Carney was back then, but as I had bought a few books in the days before my tour, I knew exactly who Carnes was and his role in the 1946 escape attempt.

I owe my interest in Alcatraz to Joe Carnes. As the group focused most of their attention on Art and plagued him with questions related to his Hollywood career and Oscar win against Al Pacino in *The Godfather: Part II,* and Jack Nicholson who starred in the Roman Polanski film *Chinatown,* I remained pensive and stayed close to Joe, careful not to miss a single word. I was too nervous to approach him, so I stayed back and just listened. I was completely fascinated that he knew men like Mickey Cohen, Alvin Karpis, and Frank Lee Morris, and celled next to the Birdman of Alcatraz with whom he'd played chess into the late hours of the night. I was in awe when he commented he had also been part of the plot in the '62 escape and pointed out specific areas of the prison where certain events took place, and the cells where some of the more notable prisoners lived. But still, he was evasive as far as sharing the grittier details. When someone would ask a question, he only pointed to where it happened, without giving a detailed answer. The Park Ranger would share in the story and Carnes would nod his head and then walk away from our group as if to be in deep thought. Carnes winced when the park ranger slammed shut one of the doors in D-Block. He said, "When the doors slam shut, it echoes in my brain…It's depressing…I think of all the men I knew. What happened to them…The dead ones…I also pictured myself here, growing older, with no hope."

Alcatraz had been his home for almost two decades, and it was a harsh reminder of a lifetime lost…My most vivid memory of Carnes was when we stood in A-Block looking at the old military cells, then Joe and Art stood at the top of the staircase that led into the dungeon. Joe said he had never once seen beyond the darkness of the descending staircase. He had heard stories of what lurked below, a darkness so deep, it pressed heavy against your eyes. I overheard him comment to Art that following the '46 escape attempt, he feared he would be thrown into the dungeon and left to perish in the darkness. I watched from above as he slowly walked step by step down a cement staircase to get a glimpse of what had haunted him for so many years.

A few hours later, after the boat had delivered our group back to the pier, I noticed Carnes sitting at a vendor's booth signing books. I tried to muster the courage to introduce myself and ask him a few more questions about what had happened in 1946. But just as I approached him, he got up, motioned to the vendor that he was hungry, and walked away. Keeping a safe distance, I followed him through Fisherman's Wharf, finally arriving at a food concession stand. Carnes purchased a hot dog and soft drink, then walked over to the telescopes located at the end of Pier 45, which advertised a close-up view of Alcatraz Island for only ten cents. He dropped a dime in the first one and looked through it for about a minute. Noticing me, he turned and motioned to the eyepiece, inviting me to have a look. He said that if I looked quickly, I might be able to catch a glimpse of a tour group walking down the stairs from the recreation yard. Cautious, I accepted the invitation, and watched him carefully as I positioned myself. Eventually, I was able to use the eyepiece to navigate and explore the scenery. Carnes started walking away, gazing casually at the island every few seconds. I finally found the courage to approach him and introduce myself. I explained that I had learned who he was from two books I had read about the prison. Gracious, he shook my hand and allowed me to ask some unsophisticated questions about his long incarceration on Alcatraz and the tragic events of 1946. That day stayed with me, and I never forgot meeting him.

In 1984, while I was attending the College for Recording Arts, a now defunct tech school that was located on Harrison Street in San Francisco to study film and audio science, I searched out Joe to see if I could film him discussing his memories of Alcatraz for a class project. As it was before the days of the internet, I ended up seeking the help of a parole office to locate him. It was tragic to learn that he had violated his parole and was back in federal prison. I spoke to him by phone, and he declined to be filmed or even interviewed, but offered others that he thought could be interesting to talk with. What intrigued me was after almost a lifetime in prison, he was so well spoken. When I attempted to see if I could change his mind, he responded with a respectful no and wished me luck. A little over a year later and completely out of the blue, I received an autographed photo of him wearing a ball cap during a time when he was free from prison. That was the last contact we ever had, but it was only the beginning of my study of Alcatraz.

In the late 1990s, while searching newspaper articles on grainy microfiche reels in a San Francisco library that might mention Carnes, I came across an article. The opening lead read: "Fugitive Irish Mob Boss James J. 'Whitey'

Bulger paid to have the body of one of Alcatraz prison's most infamous inmates exhumed from a pauper's grave and brought home for a proper Indian burial in the Eastern Oklahoma hill country..." Believing he had no surviving relatives, prison officials buried him in an unmarked community grave at the Catholic Cemetery of Springfield, Missouri. That fact was written into obituaries of Carnes that ran in newspapers nationwide and caught the attention of Bulger. The article indicated that Bulger was a former Alcatraz convict and currently a fugitive of the FBI. I mailed a letter to the Department of Justice to see if I could secure any public records on Bulger, but all I received back was a small WANTED BY FBI poster folded in thirds with a mailing label affixed to it, and no other info. Despite this, there was something on the poster that caught my interest. The first line of the remarks section read: "Bulger is an avid reader and historian and has been seen frequenting libraries and historic sites." There was also a surveillance photo I came across years later where Bulger was clearly wearing an Alcatraz belt buckle, and it seemed clear, he must have had at least some appreciation for its history. In 2006, Bulger's close associate, Kevin Weeks, published a riveting memoir about his life inside Whitey Bulger's Irish Mob, and confirmed the legend of Bulger exhuming Carnes to provide him a proper burial. I knew there had to be an important story here...

When I first started researching his life and crimes, I couldn't find much info, other than he'd spent time on Alcatraz and had risen to become a top fugitive on the FBI's "Ten Most Wanted" list. I knew very little about what landed him as one of America's most sought-after fugitives. In November of 2008, when Bulger's FBI handler John Connolly was found guilty of second-degree murder for having served as an accomplice and providing protected information to Bulger and his other close associates, based on what I'd read in the media, I believed that sealed the deal and he would never be captured. It seemed he'd probably have too much dirt on the FBI and stay in hiding until the end of his days... I'd felt confident the FBI had given him a 'get out of jail free card' and that would be the last we'd ever hear from him. In fact, there was an alleged joke that circulated around the FBI offices that Bulger was on the "Least Most Wanted List" since it had seemed that there had been minimal effort to locate him.

There had been several alleged sightings, including at least one that seemed credible. In September of 2007, photos of a couple seen strolling in a seaside resort town in the south of Italy were being circulated by the FBI as a probable sighting. At a book signing on Alcatraz, I met one of the producers from the popular television show *America's Most Wanted*, and she went as far to say that they were attempting to confirm the sighting with credible sources, but she'd felt it was 'highly likely' Bulger and his girlfriend Catherine Greig... This along with many other leads eventually turned cold and the search finally went stale. His former crime partner Kevin Weeks and several others even theorized that after the 9/11 terrorist attacks in 2001, Bulger was likely trapped in Europe as a result of the heightened international security measures.

As the ranks changed in the FBI and Bulger's case had remained unsolved for what was now approaching two decades, a new group of agents aggressively tackled the search and, using new modern tactics, finally brought him to justice in 2011. My phone rang off the hook as the news of his arrest flooded broadcasts. He was found living in a modest Santa Monica apartment complex with his girlfriend, Catherine Greig, under the assumed names of Charlie and Carol Gasko. They had blended into the tranquil neighborhood and took daily walks down an ocean side trail with beautiful views of the Pacific Ocean, located only a few miles south of Malibu on the coast of California. U.S. Marshals and the FBI located more than $800,000 cash hidden in the walls of his apartment, and numerous firearms that included assault rifles and handguns. Bulger and Greig were immediately flown to Massachusetts where they were held to stand trial.

After about a week of debating, I finally wrote him asking if he would be willing to meet for an interview. I mailed him a few transcripts with former Alcatraz convicts to give him a sense of my past projects and style of the content. I included a variety of questions about whom he associated with during his time on Alcatraz. It didn't take long to get a response, and it wasn't at all what I had hoped for. One of the questions I'd asked him had struck a nerve. The question focused on how he spent his time and whether he kept friends at Alcatraz. There was a lot of men who kept to themselves and chose not to interact with other cons. As an example, Alvin Karpis, once identified as Public Enemy #1, was known to keep to himself and often walked the yard alone. Bob Luke, 1117-AZ, shared a cell directly next to him. Despite nearly two years being celled side by side, just feet apart, Luke stated they rarely spoke. When they would come out of their cells, they would nod to each other and stand quietly side by side. In the dining hall, they sat next to each other and only occasionally commented on something superficial like the weather, but that was the extent. Luke once said, "We were side by side for a little more than two years and spoke a little more than two words a day in all that time." I sent Bulger the passage below extracted from a project I did with Luke the same year:

> Alcatraz was like any other small city, or perhaps a better term would
> be a neighborhood. One block long with around 280 people living
> there. Some of your neighbors would be friendly and have the same
> interests, while others would be more standoffish with outside friends
> and family, or with completely different opinions and lifestyles. Some

were quiet and minded their own business. That is the way it was on Alcatraz. Just because we were all prisoners, doesn't mean that we had anything in common. We had different backgrounds, and the crimes we were convicted of were as different as car theft is from murder.

There were only a few that were compatible, and most were either ignored or detested. But there was still a modicum of civility, which was necessary for survival. An example of this was the two years I lived in the cell next to Alvin Karpis, J. Edgar Hoover's and the FBI's #1 nemesis. He was serving a life sentence for the crimes he committed while part of the Barker gang. Arthur 'Doc' Barker was shot and killed while trying to escape Alcatraz in 1939. Karpis was a prisoner there for more than twenty-five years, the longest sentence served on the island, so no one knows his frame of mind at any time during that period. It's impossible to have a closer neighbor. We were separated by 6-inches of concrete and could hear everything that went on in the adjoining cell. But I learned to close my ears to outside sounds for my own sanity. Because of the strict regimen, Karpis and I moved everywhere together, with me following him as he was in Cell B-300 and I was in B-302. Three times a day to the mess hall and sitting next to each other. Two times a week, I followed him down the stairs to the shower room, where we took showers next to each other with another forty prisoners close by. Even with that close proximity there was no conversation, and aside from a quick nod as we emerged from our cells to stand until given the signal to walk in single file to the dining hall for meals, there was rarely any acknowledgement of each other. He was a loner and so was I. All I was interested in was doing my time quietly.

There was another part of the population that didn't maintain as much of an isolated existence. They spent time in groups during weekends on the yard, selected common work assignments and requested cells next to one another. This was common on Alcatraz. Where you celled and who was next to you was important. It dictated who you would sit next to during meal periods. Friendships were also struck with those who knew each other on the outside, having served together at other prisons, or simply from being from the same city or state. There was a lot of camaraderie between men serving time together on the Rock. Frank Sprenz, a close friend of Bulger's who was a skilled pilot and bank robber dubbed the "Flying Bandit" by J. Edgar Hoover, later commented, "Alcatraz wasn't all hard time and grim faces. There were many humorous happenings to blunt the loneliness and isolation... I still consider many of those I served with as good friends, and Jimmy was one of them..."

I wasn't sure what category Bulger fell into and was eager to learn whether he had friends or kept to himself, how he occupied his time, and of course his association with Joe Carnes. I had endless questions…When Bulger finally responded, his reply was harsh and direct:

> I am most suspicious of people who write books and reporters—for just cause. Did I have friends on Alcatraz? Insulting question. I was on Alcatraz because I was a friend. I didn't give up a friend for a sentence shave. I owned the time. I didn't have a reason to avoid other cons or look over my shoulder. I conducted my time inside prison the way I did outside of prison. I want to read what you've written about Alcatraz. That will speak volumes.—James Bulger, 1428-AZ.

And that was it…Richard Sunday, a former Alcatraz con and a close friend of Bulger, once told me "Jimmy said what he meant, and meant what he said." I assumed it was pointless to attempt to make any further contact, but went ahead and mailed him a couple of books I'd written previously on the island's history to follow through on my promise. I expected the myths would remain myths, and he'd likely take his memories to the grave.

More than a month later, I was startled to find a large envelope in my mailbox. It was from Bulger and included a thick bundle of pages that were all handwritten in a fine cursive style penmanship. In the opening letter, he thanked me for sending books and apologized for the tone of the initial letter. He appreciated the format by "allowing the men a voice" and "using their own words" to tell the story. It had brought back some good memories of his years on Alcatraz. He commented "I spent hours looking through it and long periods just looking at the roster. It was really like a trip through an old cemetery. I had flashbacks seeing the names of many good friends. Many I knew for years; how they lived and how they died. I'm pretty sure Boston and its suburbs were well represented on Alcatraz. I also had friends from New York City, Chicago, etc…When I put the book down, I had to jump up and pace my cell. I felt deeply depressed thinking back to so many good friends lost." Most significant was that he felt I was fair to Joe Carnes on paper, and because of this, he'd help me.

Bulger went on to explain that he knew he had reached the "end of the line" and regardless of the outcome of the trial, he'd never see freedom again. He said so many states had retainers on him, his life as a free man had come to an end, and with that, he wanted to "set the record straight" on some issues, and offer help in documenting both his memories of Alcatraz, and the friends who served alongside him.

This is how it all began. While our relationship was strictly professional, from that day forward we were on a first name basis. I received numerous letters each week that generally ranged from four to twelve pages in length. He wrote in a fine cursive style penmanship that I became adept at reading, and with paper and the real estate of space at a prime, he used every inch and the fine ink always overflowed into every margin. No space on the paper was ever spared.

In December of 2013, following his trial, he was transferred from the Plymouth County Correctional Facility in Massachusetts to the Metropolitan Detention Center in Brooklyn, New York, and then to a federal prison in Tucson, Arizona. It was around this time that I'd finally have the opportunity to talk with Bulger. Despite his years on the run and sixteen years of life in California, his Boston accent came through. He was soft-spoken and his speech patterns were eloquent, with a clear command of the English language. That was also the case in his writing. You could tell that he was well read, and he seemed to encompass a level of education that couldn't come just from the street. Only once was there a hint...

To help alleviate any reservations about contributing to this work, and though he didn't have any formal association to the project, I asked Bulger if he'd feel more comfortable signing an agreement that would allow him to feel safe in what he shared during the more detailed interviews. I explained that I intended to remain within the provisions of the 'Son of Sam' law and that I couldn't compensate him in return for his stories, but I offered to put in writing that he could reframe anything he didn't feel was accurately reflective of his memories. He seemed frustrated, not understanding what I was specifically asking. Finally, he uttered sharply "Paper? You want to do paper? Fuck the paper. You gave me your word, that's the fucking paper. I want truth, not revenge. Just write the truth, that's all I'm asking. I'm so sick of all the lies. I don't care if you print everything that's in my file and let others say what they will, but I want to tell my side too. That's all I ask. All these other guys are singing 'Whitey told me to do it' and I just want to set the record straight. I want my side of the story on record." The tone of the conversation quickly reverted back to his soft but even paced voice, and we spent the remaining time talking about his years on Alcatraz, his crime partners, how many cons might still be living, life in Santa Monica with Catherine, and the hope of seeing her when she was finally released from prison. He said he would spend his final years remembering their talks while sitting on a bench in Palisades Park. He would tell her stories of Alcatraz and the men he knew in his early years. The memories with her in Santa Monica were what he treasured most. He said those conversations were golden to him. We also shared a few good laughs. At one point, as I was buying him various Alcatraz memoirs written by other convicts for help in my research, his address was set up as the primary shipping address in my profile. I purchased a copy of the children's book *Dogzilla*, which I had planned to have sent to my home address, but the book was inadvertently shipped to him. The book parodies Godzilla as a giant canine. We both got a big laugh out of this.

I expect he always was careful about what and how he shared his memories. What he shared was carefully crafted as he knew it would help define him beyond his passing. At least, that is my opinion. There were often questions I'd ask that he'd remained silent to or offer an unrevealing answer. There are things he undoubtedly took to the grave following his own murder in 2018. He read most everything here. Our interviews were always very structured, but it was Bulger who ultimately provided the framework and the stories. The book evolved into a scrapbook of sorts. I'm not claiming any of the materials are historically accurate, or even true. They are simply the stories he provided, or what was documented in the inmate case files.

About a year following Whitey's capture, Richard Tuggle (screenwriter of the classic motion picture *Escape from Alcatraz*) and I met with Josh Bond, the manager of the apartment building of where Bulger was captured. Josh had lived in the apartment next door, and he had also been persuaded (though very reluctantly) by the FBI to help in the arrest by luring Bulger in the garage area of the complex. Tuggle and I shared a curiosity to see where and how he lived while as a fugitive. Ironically, Tuggle had frequented many of the same places in Santa Monica as Bulger and Catherine, and Bulger later wrote that he clearly remembered seeing him in passing on several occasions walking the path in Palisades Park. After we went to see Bulger's apartment on the third floor, we stood in the hallway listening to Josh share his memories of living next to the "Gasko" couple and the details of the arrest. Following in Bulger's footsteps, we entered the elevator, and I immediately noticed the worn buttons on the panel. Bulger had once told me that only moments before his capture, he had stared intently at the buttons while gathering his thoughts as he was being lured to the apartment building garage. Unknown to him, when he pressed the button to descend down into the garage, it transformed Charlie Gasko back into the legendary Boston criminal Whitey Bulger.

In closing, his memories tell an important part of history. Historical places like Alcatraz are important to our society. They offer the rare ability to stand where important historical events took place and see it as it was. At the time of this writing, the chipped paint in Bulger's old cell on the top tier of C-Block is still the original coat from when he lived there more than a half century ago.

There is an obligation we all have in preserving our museums, historic sites, and the voices that connect them. They all perform valuable services. They preserve history…They educate…They often help us to understand past struggles, to appreciate how far we've come, to plan a better future. I would like to emphasize that while Alcatraz is an important chapter in American history, it is essential that you not glamorize or forget that the men who were incarcerated there were not victims, as they're often portrayed in Hollywood. Most all of them had sordid and violent pasts. They belonged there. It's important to humanize them, but not glamorize or portray these men in a light that implies any valor as a criminal. Most all were deserving of the punishment they received by the courts, and nearly all of the former convicts I interviewed acknowledged this. This included Bulger himself. He recognized the need for prisons, but was intensely critical of the current penal system:

> I'm the first to admit prisons are necessary, but know that the tougher the prison, the tougher the prisoner. He's much more dangerous when released. I don't have a solution or answer, but prison life changed me for the worst and hopefully our country can find better ways to reform those who will eventually be released.
>
> Prison life is rough. Hard time makes hard people…Life inside today's prisons embody a different code of ethics than what was represented on Alcatraz during my years there. Prisons have turned into sewers and these guys steal and rat on each other. The observation that Alcatraz was a spirit of a different era is all very true. Prisons are populated by society's killers, thieves, losers, and mental cases. Most of these men are dangerous and will be harder to stop the next time around. Prison teaches one thing to perfection: Hate.

Guys find that it helps to harden and get through the days and nights. And in some cases (most cases) innocent people suffer. I don't have a solution or answer, and I'm the first to admit prisons are necessary. I always admired the men who broke free from crime and went on the straight line and didn't look back. There wasn't many, but some of them pulled it off.

That was the contrasting element. There were a considerable number of men who earned their release back to free society and turned their lives around. They learned meaningful skills in work programs on Alcatraz that translated to meaningful employment in free society. For many men, Alcatraz was the end of the line in crime...For Bulger, it didn't take long for him to return to a criminal trade. He was mentored by some of the most powerful criminal minds. When the young Whitey Bulger came to Alcatraz, he was a bank robber who was very different than the mafia men he would observe and learn from. Fellow con Bob Luke (and also a fellow bank robber) offered more on this perspective. I later connected Luke with Bulger and the two corresponded for a brief period. Luke offered a view outlining the stark contrasts of mob bosses and outlaws, and their mixing on the Rock:

Al Capone was certainly treated like any other prisoner on the island. The same rules and regulations. He also had cons that he talked to and got along with, but he could not have been treated with the same fear and respect he had when he was a mob boss in Chicago. He was sent to Alcatraz because of his notoriety, and because there were no con bosses on Alcatraz, Capone was treated the same way as any other prisoner. He probably arrived with an air of superiority, but soon learned that he was just another con. Not only did he realize this from the prison administration, but almost certainly from the other cons. We all learned this fact of prison life quickly or we learned it the hard way. I think Al Capone had to learn this lesson the hard way because Jimmy Lucas in 1936 tried to kill him with half a scissor. All Capone's injuries were defensive. The shower room was probably the most dangerous place on Alcatraz, and we were all capable of inflicting all types of injuries to any other prisoner. And to do this without any warning or remorse.

Alcatraz was a very harsh environment with no soft spots or soft people. Capone's life experience was as different from mine as night is from day. We were raised in a completely different environment; religion, family ties, early friendships that set our later activities, and our relationship with politicians/law enforcement. Al Capone believed in cooperation with these people for business reasons, whereas my view of that was completely opposite, absolutely no cooperation. So, Al Capone looked at my type of criminal as a 'cowboy', who was not under anyone's control. 'Cowboys' and 'Gangsters' didn't mix. So, the only thing we had in common was wearing a number on our backs. The men who served time and are still living were all changed because of our experience there. The exception though is Alcatraz itself. Alcatraz hasn't changed at all... Even as a tourist site and National Park, it's exactly how I remember it. Concrete and steel... Boredom and regimentation... Cold and forbidding...

For the young Jimmy Bulger, Alcatraz provided not only a front row seat to watch the highest stratum of crime figures and how they conducted themselves walking among peers, but also allowed him to contribute to one of the greatest prison breaks of the 20th century. His role in the famed 1962 escape of Frank Morris and the Anglin Brothers (later portrayed in the classic film *Escape from Alcatraz* starring Clint Eastwood), would become a training ground for understanding what it would take to successfully disappear while on the run from authorities. Bulger later acknowledged that he admired men like Mickey Cohen and how he held himself in the company of fellow cons. Cohen occasionally spoke to the young Bulger as they passed each during meal periods and when he'd pick up his weekly issued clothing. He mostly kept to himself, but stood proud and was respectful to everyone, no matter of race or criminal affiliation, including officers. So while Alcatraz became an epiphany of sorts for men to change their lives following their release, it had the opposite effect on Bulger. He was taking mental notes to better hone his craft.

Decades after his release from prison, there was one trademark that one of his associates remembered about Jimmy Bulger: the Alcatraz belt buckle he always wore, ironically an alleged gift from FBI agent Nick Giantutco. It was a symbol of his past and the many friendships he held during some of the toughest years of his life. For many of the men who first stepped foot on Alcatraz, their criminal past had come to a close, but for James "Whitey" Bulger, it was only the beginning.

A FINAL NOTE: I am frequently asked my thoughts on Bulger and what was he like. It's important to keep in mind that I didn't know him during his criminal reign or much about the charges he faced for allegations of horrific violent acts. Over the course of several decades, I've sat with numerous convicts who served time on Alcatraz and Bulger proved to be one of the most interesting I've interviewed. He always seemed to offer memories that consistently matched up with information located in the Bureau of Prisons case files. It seemed like he never felt a need to insert himself into any of the grand stories or embellish beyond the facts. Without exception, every time I followed one of his leads relating to certain incidents that took place on Alcatraz, they always checked out.

I feel I got to know him extremely well and it all felt very genuine to me. Following Bulger's murder, his girlfriend Catherine commented to me in a letter "He considered you someone he could trust and that is a rarity…" I mention that because I feel that trust came through in the stories he shared and what is reflected in this work. Just as the FBI Wanted poster described him, his love for the history always seemed heartfelt and he was generous in sharing his memories on subjects I had studied for decades. Despite having conducted scores of interviews with former convicts and correctional officers from Alcatraz over the span of thirty years, there was no one who taught me more about the history than Whitey Bulger.

Again, I'm not defending him as a criminal, but his voice as a historical figure is important. He had a razor-sharp memory and helped frame a part of history that would have otherwise been lost had he not been willing to share his memories. Several men he served time alongside on the island and their stories would have also faded and been lost with time. In fact, while transcribing and stitching together some of the content from letters and interviews following his death, I remain completely astonished at his ability to remember names and events. As an example, he remembered the name of a clothing salesman who recognized Willie Sutton following a prison break and collected the reward. I decided to double check and validate the info and was amazed that despite his age and having no access to the internet, his memory was spot on down to the exact spelling of his name.

A key point to readers is that some of the case histories transcribed in this work might seem out of place in certain chapters, too extensive, or like materials that don't seem to belong in a scrapbook of his own memoirs. This is especially prominent in the sections on Cohen, Twining, Arquilla, Johnson and Kawakita. Bulger loved history, and even more importantly, Alcatraz history. He noted that the inmate case file narratives written by officials during that era were the most interesting to him and frequently encouraged not only their inclusion but including them in their entirety. I believe that including the era files worked as both a strength and a weakness. I made the decision to include them, as this was how he would have wanted those aspects of the story structured. In the end, these reports dominated our conversations and omitting them would take away from the essence of our interviews.

As a final thought, allowing Bulger his voice and to shape the content should in no way be interpreted as a way to trivialize the violence suffered by the victims of his crimes, whether it was by his own hand or one of his associates. It's important to underscore that he only wanted his voice to be heard and never attempted to discourage me from others' perspectives, even when they were critical or in conflict with his. At one stage, I explained that it was possible that I would write things about him that he may not agree with. I committed to allow him to edit his statements, but not the statements of others. As an example, I told him that I had seen his crime partner Kevin Weeks memoir *Brutal* (which became a *New York Times* bestseller), on his bookshelf from the FBI evidence photos taken inside his Santa Monica apartment and explained that there may be similar accounts I include which may be in direct conflict with his version. Not once did he ever ask to have anything pulled, and despite years of interviews, he rarely spoke about Kevin or his book, and his only request was that he be given an equal voice. That's what he asked for, and that's what's included here.

Was he a mafia mogul; brutal murderer; a bank robber; a criminal; a family man; a gentleman; a Robin Hood or an informant? He may have been none, or he may have been all of those things. However, one thing is clear: he was very human. Everyone has a right to their story. Even after his murder, I feel that I've kept my word without any compromise. These are the conversations and the stories he shared about his life, and memories of his years spent on Alcatraz.

Michael Esslinger

Robert Schibline, 1355-AZ

INTRODUCTION

I FIRST MET WHITEY BULGER on Alcatraz in 1959. Remember, this was 1959; Whitey was not the famous "kingpin" of Boston's "Winter Hill Gang," he was just another bank robber like me. As a matter of fact, one day on the yard we compared our lives together. It seems that we were both robbing banks in the mid-1950s, both got busted in 1955, and we both got sentenced in 1956. I got fifteen years and was sentenced to Leavenworth, Kansas; Whitey got twenty years and was sent to Atlanta, Georgia. I screwed up in 1958 while at Leavenworth. I was accused of being a ringleader and an 'Enforcer' in a strike, and got picked up along with twenty-two others, including Alvin 'Creepy' Karpis, 325-AZ (who was being railroaded back to Alcatraz). Whitey screwed up in 1959 and was sent to Alcatraz.

When Alcatraz closed in 1963, I was shipped back to Leavenworth, while Whitey was sent to Lewisburg via Leavenworth. We both got released from federal prison in 1965. I moved to Wisconsin and opened a scuba diving shop and became a dive instructor. My life took a positive path: I instructed on the sport, and set up scuba diving trips to the Bahamas and other places in the Caribbean Sea for the next thirty years through my dive shop, which I named Neptune's Dive Center. I later retired to Florida where I have been for the last few decades.

Now, Whitey, took an altogether different path... He used his Alcatraz 'diploma' as a resume to join the Irish Gang in Boston, and like me worked the next thirty years rising to the top of his profession. Around 1994, Whitey got word that an indictment was coming down and a warrant was to be issued for his arrest. Whitey had prepared well for such an event. He went on the run and successfully evaded the law for sixteen years. He had money and identifications in safe boxes around the world.

He was finally arrested in California in 2011, sent back for trial, received two consecutive life sentences plus five years, and was doing the majority of his time in the Max Federal Prison at Coleman II in Florida, before the final transfer to Hazelton. So, I guess you could say that he also retired to Florida, since this is where he served out his final years... One more point, Whitey was twenty-two years older than his girlfriend Catherine that he was on the run with. I was twenty-two years older than my late wife, Karen, but believe that I had more fun being retired in Florida than him. Just to prove my point... I just opened and drank a cold beer.

James "Whitey" Bulger

FOREWORD

I ARRIVED ON ALCATRAZ in March of 1959 and stepped behind the mythical steel curtain which was to become my new home. You may be surprised to find that I look back at Alcatraz with a sense of nostalgia. My life today would break most men. After fifteen years on America's Most Wanted list and living a quiet life on the California Coast, I'm back in a cold isolation cell and reflect often back to those years on the Rock.

The upper tier of C-Block was my home and many of the people that were considered America's worst in that era were not only fellow residents, but actually people I considered good friends. I knew and respected many of the famous and not so famous men who resided as fellow convicts. While I didn't know some of the earlier residents like Al Capone, or whether he actually lived up to his notorious reputation, there is something I do know about him just about better than any living person. I have a good idea of what thoughts he had while serving time on Alcatraz. Capone lived in the same section of C-Block for a period of time. We read from the same library, we worked some of the same jobs, and were counted by some of the same guards. We lived the very same routine, ate from the same menus, and both of us served time with some of the same men, under the same harsh conditions. We were all part of a unique band of brothers.

The myths and dramatic depictions of life on Alcatraz are still very much alive, but for the people who lived the experience, it was all very lonely and a place that offered plenty of time to think. Alcatraz was an iceberg...Our lives were frozen in time. The film versions of Alcatraz, while entertaining, fail to capture what life served on the Rock was really like. It was an existence of fierce monotony that in a flash could erupt into explosive violence.

When a man walked into the receiving gates of Alcatraz, his name, reputation, importance, wealth and all his eminence were stripped away. I was 1428-AZ. Every man became an equal. His name was exchanged for a prison number and no longer would he be recognized as unique individual. His power and ego had no place on the Rock. The humiliating absence of privacy, twenty-four hours a day, the constant surveillance by prison guards paired against a life set in slow motion was how all of us existed on a daily basis.

Make no mistake, Alcatraz was a tough prison. It was designed to house the rogues within the Federal prison system. It broke some, but for me I survived to see a better life. I'm sure that if men like Capone, Joe Carnes and

Foreword

I arrived on Alcatraz in March of 1959, and stepped behind the mythical steel curtain which was to become my new home. You may be surprised to find that I look back at Alcatraz with a sense of nostalgia. My life today would break most men. After fifteen years on America's Most Wanted list and living a quiet life on the California Coast, I'm back in a cold isolation cell and reflect often back to those years on the Rock.

The upper tier of C-Block was my home and many of the people that were considered America's worst in that era were not only fellow residents but actually people I considered good friends. I knew and respected many of the famous and not so famous men who resided as fellow convicts. It was like a small community, not much unlike any small town or city. While I didn't know some of the earlier residents like Al Capone, or whether he actually lived up to his notorious reputation, there is something I do know about him just about better than any living person. I have a good idea of what thoughts he had while serving time on Alcatraz. Capone and I lived in the same section of C-Block for a period of time (my cell was above his on the upper tier). We read from the same library, we worked some of the same jobs, and counted by some of the same guards. We lived the very same routine, ate from the same menus, and both of us served time with several of the same men; under the same harsh conditions. We were all each of a unique band of brothers.

The many myths and dramatic depictions of life on Alcatraz are still very much alive, but for the people who lived the experience time served on Alcatraz was all very human, very lonely and a place that offered plenty of time to think. Alcatraz was an iceberg... Our lives were frozen in time... The film versions of Alcatraz, while

All that remain on Alcatraz are our ghosts ... James Bulger 1428AZ

Jack Twining were alive today, we would reminisce over coffee, having a lot of the same memories of our years there. But with the legends and foggy myths still abound, the real history is lost behind the poetic license of Hollywood's carefully woven tales. There was an element of civility that existed against the backdrop of violent episodes, and though rare, unlikely friendships emerged between the keepers and the kept.

A.G. Bloomquist was a guard who started his Alcatraz career in the early 1940s. Of all the officers who worked on the Rock, Bloomie had a just reason to be bitter towards the prisoners. During the 1946 escape attempt known as the Battle of Alcatraz, he was struck in the back by a bullet during an episode where a fellow officer was shot and killed. But Bloomie didn't hold any grudges whatsoever. He looked upon the convicts as men who were paying the wages of their criminal past and treated every man with a high level of respect and consideration. The respect for Bloomie rose to such a level among the inmate population, that there was an unspoken code among the men that in the event of any escape attempt, Bloomie would not be harmed. For me, he became a trusted friend even following my release from prison. It's ironic, as the Hollywood depictions of the relationships between inmates and officers were often conflicted and full of strife, but Bloomie became an iconic figure to me. Looking back to my tenure at Alcatraz, I remember him with deep sense of admiration and reverence. Following my release, we met over several dinners, and we enjoyed talking about our families and both looked towards the future with great optimism.

Alcatraz is slowly coming back into focus as the voices from the past, through historical accounts like this, help recount time served on what was once termed Hell's Twelve Acres. Alcatraz is still a part of me and during my freedom, I was able to visit and walk the old cellblocks and think back to all of the memories and life inside. The muffled sound of a passing seagull, the bell of the small buoy just off the Alcatraz shore, or the sound of a cell door racking, now by a park ranger rather than a prison guard. All that remains on Alcatraz are our ghosts...

James Bulger, 1428-AZ

"James Bulger's story reads like the plot of a thousand mobster films. An Irish American boy grows up in the poor neighborhood of South Boston—Southie—turns to a life of crime and ends up leader of the Irish Mob. Smart, charismatic and generous to those he liked, Bulger—whose blond hair earned him the nickname Whitey—was both feared and revered. At the height of his power...he was allegedly taking a share of almost every drug and racketeering operation in Boston."

—Life Magazine

EARLY YEARS

I RECEIVED MY NICKNAME "WHITEY" when I was just a young kid. I had real white hair that started way back, long into my youth. The cops would see a few of us and chase us off the street corners. I was usually the most identifiable, and therefore became their focus. I grew up in a poor neighborhood, but our community was close, and we always made the best of our situation. During the Depression Era, we had the subway and street cars for transportation and at that age we never paid the fare, at least I didn't and all my friends. The exception was my brother who always did, but the small gang of friends in my circle figured out how to sneak past the ticket booth and ride for free. To show how much nerve we had, we

10371-DJC Document 1254-9 Filed

A young Jimmy Bulger during his teenage years. The photo was a reference in his Department of Justice case file.

would go down on the platform, jump down onto the tracks and walk from the Broadway Station, down to South Station through the tunnel. There was a live electric third rail that if contacted would kill you instantly. We moved swiftly through the tunnel, but before you could hear the train, you could feel the rush of forced air. We would squeeze into these depressions in the tunnel wall that were only about 9-inches wide. We would press in as tightly as possible and then the train would rocket by us and miss us by only inches. Looking back, it was chilling and would give us all such a big adrenaline rush. We'd come out at South Station and then make our way to the pool room where we would all hang out together.

Bulger seen in his early 20's, just as he was entering his criminal career as a bank robber. It was another reference photo included in his early DOJ case file.

The first time I was shot at I was around fourteen years old and then many, many more times over the course of my life. When I was young, when you ran from the cops, they shot at you...I always tried to escape if there was any chance. The neighborhood merchants would give these cops gifts for their efforts to keep us away from their storefronts. A bottle of whiskey was the usual gift. Boston had laws back then that it was illegal for stores to sell alcohol on Sundays and holidays. We were a close-knit community back in those days...When I was a little older, we drank in the streets on Saturday nights and then when the evening was winding down, we would all buy hot cups of chili to kind of sober us up before we called it a night.

The local druggist was my archenemy, and he often sold booze illegally. The cops were on the take; they were rewarded for looking the other way. This was good for the druggist as he had a brisk business. But despite this, he always had a big car, lived in a wealthy neighborhood, and offered "credit" to the poor folks (essentially everyone in the projects), then charged top dollar and cheated everyone that he could. As an example, if hard candy was two for a penny (few kids had as much as a penny during the Depression) and the kid was young, he would give the kid one piece. I caught him doing this more than once. Also, milk came in glass bottles and the cream would rise to the top. The druggist would take all of the cream off of each bottle and use the cream in a big stainless-steel machine to make ice cream, then sell the milk, less the cream, to people at regular price.

I could see all of this happening at a young age, and I deeply resented it. I felt that the druggist was a lowlife and was stealing from good people in our neighborhood. These were hard working people, and many were down on their luck. They didn't deserve the hand that they were being dealt and they didn't have any recourse. It was no wonder that the druggist could drive a new Buick Roadmaster. It was tragic, considering that only one person on my block had a car and it was an old beat-up Dodge. So, on top of this, he would chase the kids off the corner, like he owned the neighborhood. My friends and I would defy him, and his brother and wife would mutter slurs like "Dirty Irish." I was stubborn and would argue and engage with them.

James Bulger's brother William Bulger seen standing in front of the government housing building where their family was raised. The Old Harbor Village housing project was located at 41 Logan Way, in South Boston.

3

More than once, he paid cops to grab me and give me a beating. Two cops, one of whom was known as "Red," once grabbed me, put me in their police car, and then drove me over to the city dump. It's now the site of the John F. Kennedy library. They'd threaten me with a beating every time they saw me if I didn't stay off the corner, and proceeded to slap and punch me, and also inflict pain by using a club across my legs and deliver hard kicks. Then they'd drive off, leaving me to walk home.

I'd run back and then the other kids would tell me that Red came back, entered the drugstore, and went into the back room. His meeting was likely to deliver the news about what they did to me. He'd come out smiling, and we figured that he was rewarded for my beating. I later threw two bricks through the druggist's window and from that moment on, Red was always on the prowl trying to get me. We all ran from the cops because they would rough us up if they caught you.

Often the cops would park around my house and get me when I was coming in. I'd run or come over the rooftops, and it was a game for the cops. Years later, we would stone them from the roof. And if they saw five or ten of us, they would holler, "We'll get you Whitey," because my white hair stood out.

There were no rights for the poor back then. Cops would kick doors down, drag you down to the police station, and give you a good rough beating. In the rich neighborhoods, cops would knock on the doors gently, speak softly, and then look forward to their Christmas gifts. It's just like I've been quoted in the media many times with the statement "Christmas is for cops and kids." I watched many get clubbed down into a bloody pulp by cops for just being drunk and not moving fast enough. I personally saw cops kill young kids for no reason and know of others shot down by drunken cops on-duty. Victims were poor and the cops all got away with it; we feared the police.

On a hot summer night, my mother and her friends were sitting out on the doorstep; we witnessed cops chasing a "stolen car," shooting at it, and the kid driving was probably only fifteen or sixteen years old. He jumped out and started running, and then was shot in the back by his shoulder and then he collapsed into some bushes. The cops ran up and started clubbing and kicking him and all of the neighbors started screaming at them to stop. The kid's name was Red Crimmens.

On another occasion, I saw a little kid in a stolen pickup truck drive into Columbus Park. It was a really hot night, and the cops were stretched out sleeping on a park bench in the dark using their coats as

The Boston Police (seen here with one officer holding his pistol) had a daily presence patrolling the low income and rough neighborhood government housing project.

pillows. I know it sounds hard to believe, but this happened often in those days. It wasn't that unusual of a sight. The kid who went by the name of "Mousey," drove by at a high speed and the cops sprung up and started screaming "Stop!" and then they fired their guns into the back of a truck, hitting the kid in the back of the head and killing him instantly.

We ran up and looked inside the truck. We knew this little boy. He was undernourished. He was curled-up in a pool of blood with a little cardboard box full of french fries next to him. The cop was pulling on his jacket and pacing around while getting his alibi straight. When the others arrived, I overheard him comment, "He tried to run me over and I had to fire at him to save my life." He was a liar, but the cops ruled the streets in those days.

Later, they arrested me in an ice cream parlor with three of my friends, hollering inappropriate insults at me, and saying "Whitey you're under arrest!" for no other reason than they had seen me at the crime scene when they shot Mousey. They put me in a paddy

Brothers Jack, James and William Bulger in the early 1950s.

wagon and then a young couple came up and politely asked the cops if they could take me home as they knew my mother. The cops arrested the woman for assault because she touched the cop's arm to get his attention, and then if that wasn't bad enough, they arrested her husband for "interfering." Gallant was the name of the young couple.

When we got to Station #6 in South Boston, they let the couple out and kept me in the paddy wagon in the garage until after they were booked. They wanted them secure in their jail cells so they couldn't witness what was coming next. The cops formed a gauntlet and then said, "Come on Whitey." I was led out of the paddy wagon and then had to make it through them as they delivered kicks and punches— hardly any pain as they were eager to get in each other's way. They systematically delivered punches and kicks, and then struck me on the top of my head with a heavy phone book. Painful, but it left no marks. If you complained they'd tell the judge that you resisted arrest, and of course the judge was usually an ex-cop.

I have survived a few vicious beatings in the precinct basement, located in the projects when I was only about fifteen to sixteen years old. I was really thin back then and knew I was in for a bad beating when I was dragged down there, and it would be worse than what was handed out at the police station. The worst beating of my life was given by a drunken cop who took me down into the project's basement, where another cop was down there drinking booze at a desk around ten o'clock at night. It was only the three of us there. The cop's name was McDonough (he was a young guy) and he started to beat me with the club across my legs and with his fists. He put me down with his kicks, knees to the face, and then held me by my hair. McDonough was beating me fiercely, screaming and cursing, and I could smell the booze and knew that he was drunk.

The bastard spit in my face screaming "I'll kill you," which was the worst part of it. He took the polished hardwood club (made of a hickory wood which was a little over a foot long, thicker on one end with a hole drilled in it and then they poured lead into it to make it heavier and more deadly) and screamed "I'm gonna put your nose all over your face, pretty boy." As he came down with the club, I put my arm over to protect my face and I felt a sharp pain and a flash of white light in my head. I felt numb and he'd fractured my arm.

He was in a rage and then he took out his .38 revolver, put it in my mouth, shoving it down my throat, and pulled the hammer back. I swear I heard two clicks and then heard him screaming. "I will blow your fucking brains out!" I was choking and I felt I was going to die and because I wasn't in a police station, I thought this bastard was going to kill me. The other cop rushed over and hollered "Stop, you'll kill him…We've got to get him out of here…" At this point I was numb, and the cop straddled me on the ground and spit in my face again. I vowed then that I would kill him if I got out of there alive. I can still picture his face, how tall he was, and that whole night is still vivid in my memory.

From there they carried me out of the basement. They shoved and kicked me down through the back of the project (Old Colony) out onto the lighted street. I collapsed right in the middle of the street. The cops stayed in the shadows. A motorist picked me up and I wound up in the Boston City Hospital Emergency Room. A cop holding a clipboard walked in and asked me, "What happened?" I told him I was cutting through Columbia Park and was jumped by some guys who beat me up.

Things like that went on for a while. To rat out a cop was against the grain for most of the guys. I had a German Luger 9mm and looked for McDonough to take revenge on him, but I never saw him in Southie again. I suspect the other cop may have reported him or that

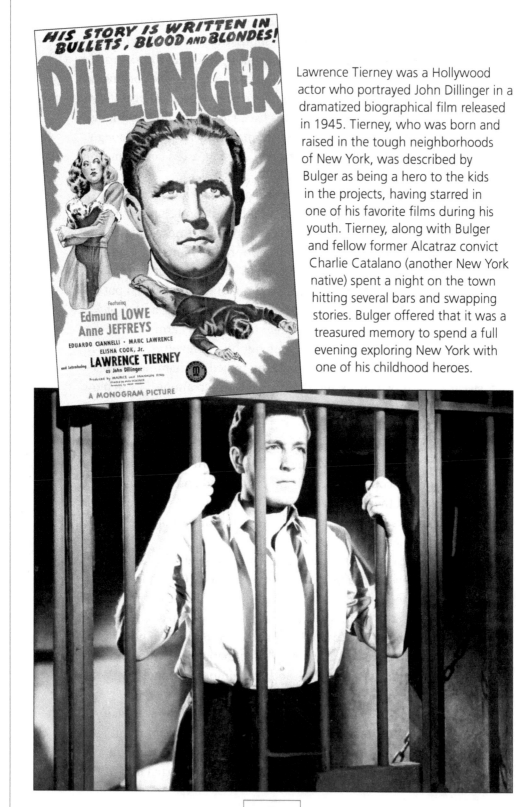

Lawrence Tierney was a Hollywood actor who portrayed John Dillinger in a dramatized biographical film released in 1945. Tierney, who was born and raised in the tough neighborhoods of New York, was described by Bulger as being a hero to the kids in the projects, having starred in one of his favorite films during his youth. Tierney, along with Bulger and fellow former Alcatraz convict Charlie Catalano (another New York native) spent a night on the town hitting several bars and swapping stories. Bulger offered that it was a treasured memory to spend a full evening exploring New York with one of his childhood heroes.

neighbors who lived upstairs in the building may have said something. I was too young then to be paying cops off. The local cops hated me and were always inflating the charges.

Of course, years later "money talked," and all the information could be purchased if the seller was convinced the buyer would never betray him. In fact, the cops all knew well who would and wouldn't talk, because they were put to the test in Station #6's famous "Blue Room," the name for their interrogation room. I had a serious session in there with two detectives whose specialty was working guys over and getting confessions. They failed in my case, even after causing me much pain and blood.

It's a long story, but from my earliest years I never trusted cops, and I hated them. Some of them in their alcohol rage proved to be capable of murder. We witnessed it… All those years were stressful… Years later when I rose up, they each wanted a piece of the action. And that's the system for you.

Another thing… when I was a kid, I loved all of those old crime movies and the "bad guys" like Cagney, Bogart, Edward G. Robinson, and George Raft. Those men were the heroes to kids my age in the

Hollywood actor Edward G. Robinson seen here in the film *Hell on Frisco Bay*. Alcatraz was a backdrop in many of the early gangster era films during the 1930s, 40s and 50's.

projects. The 1940's Dillinger film was one of my real favorite movies. Years later, my friends Charlie Catalano, Tommy Devaney and I hit the bars raising hell with Lawrence Tierney (who played Dillinger in the film and later played the bald headed old gruff gangster in the film *Reservoir Dogs*) all over New York City. It was a really memorable night for all of us. I liked him and he was a hero to all of us back then. I enjoyed seeing him later in *Reservoir Dogs*. I was still free in Boston when the film was released and seeing him brought back good memories. He was a great actor and as Dillinger, he seemed so convincing.

Looking back into my youth, I was always intrigued by those who lived criminal lives. I often hooked school and used to spend a lot of time at the courthouse where I would sit and watch trials for hours on end. Murder cases were rare back then and I remember sitting in on an entire trial where the guy held up a liquor store on State Street and shot someone during the robbery. Every day I sat in the courthouse and watched the proceedings. He was sentenced to death in the electric chair, and I remember he looked straight at me and bowed his head as he was led away in shackles...I confess that it's odd I chose this path as I didn't look up to anyone who killed or took advantage of innocent people. I was fascinated sitting in court watching all the drama I guess. The stories of these people were fascinating to me.

My father lost his arm in a work accident, and he did his best to provide for us. We were a poor family that suffered during the market crash of 1929 and during the worst depression of the 1930s. We had little food; the kids always ate first while my parents ate what was left over. We struggled with little hope, but we were a close family. We spent the winters together in our kitchen. We'd shut the doors around the house and use the heat of the stove to stay warm. The other parts of our house were freezing with ice formed along the window frame. I had a good family. I was loved. I made my own misfortune and accepted the price I had to pay.

I did take some legitimate employment during my youth, but things never seemed to work out. I went on the road with the Ringling Bros. and Barnum & Bailey Circus, and then another circus troupe for another short period. The job paid $10.00 a week with a place to sleep and free meals. They had a big top and good food. We ate free from any of the concessions we wanted and that was a big deal back in those days.

I primarily did jobs like painting and putting performers up on floats and circus vehicles when they made their spectacular entrance with the loud music. They'd go around and circle inside the tent, then exit, and I'd help pick performers off the vehicles. I was really young at the time. The Lilliputian family—real little people who had beautiful teen daughters—would dress up (the males in fine tuxedos) and then the females would holler for me to take them down. I always did little jobs like feeding the animals, moving wardrobes, trucks, and equipment.

There was always a big parade and a lot of fanfare into every town we'd arrive. The parades included large, themed floats on truck beds, and we rolled into town it was always a grand entrance and filled with excitement. I typically stayed close to the Lilliputian family who rode on a group of *Gulliver's Travels* themed floats. There were two Lilliputian brothers in their thirties or forties, and they'd be introduced

It is believed the brothers Bulger referred to were Mike & Ike Matina, a circus act that traveled with the Ringling Bros Circus and performed both comedy and magic skits. The twin brothers performed as 'Munchkins' alongside their older brother Leo in the classic 1939 film, *The Wizard of Oz*.

to the crowds as both having starred as munchkins in *The Wizard of Oz* movie. They were real popular with the crowds and had a comedy boxing act. I liked them both. Real nice guys and you could tell that their lives had taken a hard toll being on the road on and off for most of their lifetime. Few of the performers would spend time with the help, but the brothers always came out and sat with us. They did an act with a large man, bald head and curled mustache who would dress in a body builder outfit like something from the vaudeville era. They'd run circles around him all wearing boxing gloves and similar outfits. There was a young female contortionist who would also play in the act, and she'd roll up like a ball and knock him down like a bowling pin. When he'd get back up, the brothers would then run under his legs, stomping his toes, slap his backside, head-butt him in the groin (he'd bend over like he was in pain), then one would get on the other's shoulders, and

In the 1940s during his youth, Bulger traveled with the Ringling Bros and Barnum & Bailey Circus troupe as a stagehand. He had fond memories of a Lilliputian family that he spent time with during his circus adventures and their Gulliver's Travel themed float parade.

pretending to catch him off guard, tap him from behind and as he turned around, deliver a knockout punch. He would fall hard in the ring and the crowds would roar with cheers. The brothers would stand on his back and bow. This was my favorite act and I always laughed so hard every time they'd perform. Those were the best memories of the circus, but as I was only hired labor, they'd enter their trailers to rest while traveling and I'd be left in the idle company of the lowlifes, wanderers and whatevers of the circus troupe.

The circus workers were drunks, brawlers, ex-cons, fugitives from the law, thieves, perverts, and mental cases. They were the worst collection of flotsam and weirdos under one huge tent. The sleeping train was filthy, so I slept in a tent on the lot. I kept my clothes and boots on—I had metal cleats on my heels—and I also had a spade in the trunk with me to keep safe. As the train traveled from town to town, we were like a bunch of locusts grabbing anything and everything that wasn't nailed down. I finally hitchhiked home and went back to the streets.

AUTHOR'S NOTE: The references to the Lilliputian brothers was most likely the famous Mike & Ike brothers, but this has not been verified.

E XCERPTS FROM BULGER'S and Richard Barchard's FBI case files chronicle their criminal activities that landed both men their first federal prison sentences, and eventual transfers to Alcatraz:

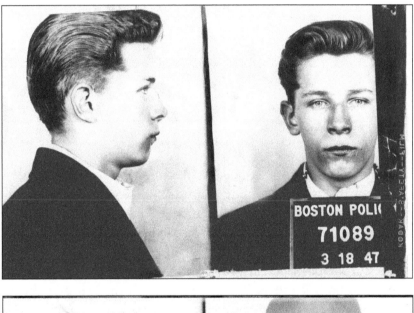

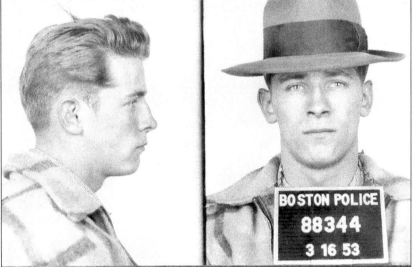

Early arrest photographs of Whitey Bulger from 1947 and 1953.

Ronald Dermody

The United States attorney indicates that on May 17, 1955, Bulger—together with Ronald Dermody and Carl Smith—participated in the armed robbery of the Industrial National Bank in Rhode Island. In participating in this robbery taking place in the early afternoon, Bulger carried a .22 revolver and forced two employees of the bank to lie on the floor. It was described that Bulger was the leader and was calm and collected as he gave orders. The getaway was accomplished by the use of a car stolen by the three participants just prior to the robbery. The amount stolen was $42,112.00.

On November 18, 1955, William L. O'Brien participated in the holdup of the Highland branch of the Melrose Trust Company, in Melrose, Massachusetts. Prior to the robbery they stole the car to be used in the getaway from an MTA parking lot in East Boston. They placed their switched cars in the parking lot of the Roosevelt School in Melrose and proceeded from there in the stolen car to the bank. Both O'Brien and Bulger were armed and took part in forcing the employees and customers in the bank to lie on the floor during the robbery. They left the bank in the stolen car and switched their own cars at the Roosevelt school in Melrose. The total amount stolen in this case was $5,035.

Then on November 23, 1955, Bulger, together with Richard Barchard (1251-AZ), participated in the holdup of the Woodmar Branch of the

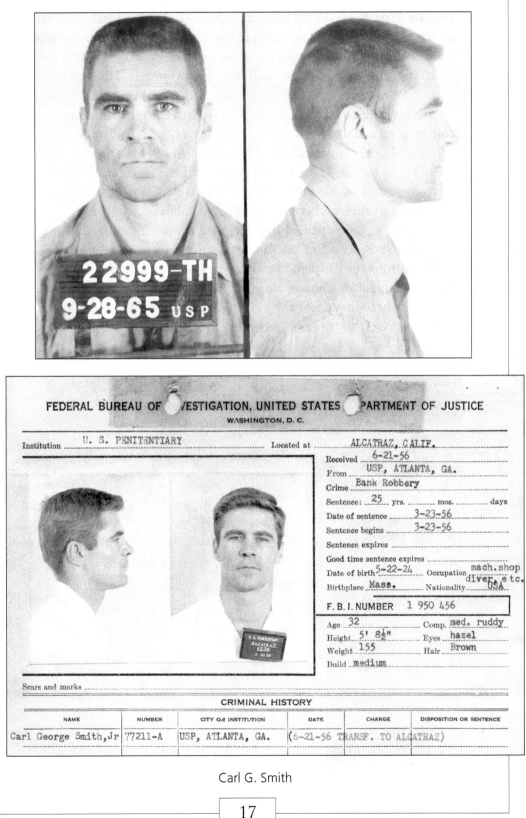

Carl G. Smith

Hoosier State Bank, in Hammond, Indiana. Bulger and Barchard set up the robbery of this bank earlier in the fall of 1955 and made the trip from Boston to Indiana for the expressed purpose of accomplishing this heist. They stole $12,612.28 in cash. They had approached the bank in a late model red and white Oldsmobile and fled in the same automobile.

This particular bank was selected by Barchard as a result of a previous conversation and discussion with Carl Smith (1238-AZ). Two banks in Hammond, Indiana were discussed by Smith and Barchard as the most likely banks to rob. Plans for the robbery of the other bank did not materialize and Smith made a trip to Oakland. Thereafter, Barchard called Bulger and together they planned the robbery.

They were accompanied by Barchard's wife, Dorothy "Dottie" Barchard, and Jacqueline McAuliffe Martin, a girlfriend of Bulger's. While en route to Chicago, the two girls learned of their plans. They stayed overnight in Chicago and from there proceeded to Hammond, Indiana, where they stole the Oldsmobile automobile to be used as a getaway car. The two girls remained in the car during the robbery.

The Woodmar Branch of the Hoosier State Bank, in Hammond, Indiana, and a money bag used to stash cash during the robbery.

Dorothy "Dottie" Barchard

Barchard maintained that Bulger carried two guns but he himself was not armed, and Bulger later verified this as a true statement. They wore identical clothing to confuse witnesses as to their identity. Both men wore dress suits with flannel shirts over the coats and visor type hunting caps. Their coattails tucked inside their trousers so that they could shed their outer clothing during the getaway.

Bulger held a gun in each hand and kept a steady aim on the employees while issuing orders. Methodically, Barchard moved to each teller station, dumping the cash drawers into a large money bag. After leaving the bank, they used the getaway car and drove directly to the parking lot where Bulger's automobile was parked. They abandoned the stolen auto, discarded the flannel shirts and hunting caps, and proceeded with the two girls back to Chicago where they evenly divided the proceeds from the robbery. They then traveled to St. Louis, where they ate Thanksgiving dinner and then parted company.

The investigation revealed that Barchard had visited Carl Smith in Indiana (Barchard and Smith had been fellow inmates in the

Massachusetts State Penitentiary) and lived with Smith and his wife for five weeks prior to the Hoosier Bank robbery. In October, Barchard and Smith traveled to Detroit, Grand Rapids, Chicago, and Milwaukee, looking for an appropriate bank to rob but claim they didn't find anything they considered ideal until their return to Hammond. In that city they "cased" the Mercantile National Bank and decided to rob it. Bulger was summoned to participate and traveled to Indiana.

Barchard admitted to planning the robbery of the Mercantile National Bank in Hammond on October 28, 1955, with Carl G. Smith and James Bulger. They made definite plans to rob this bank; however, after driving past several times, they observed what they believed was an undercover police officer entering the bank, and also noticed that the manager, three male tellers, and a woman teller were working in the bank at that point. They decided it was a police plant and decided not to rob the bank, and drove back to Gary, Indiana. Just over a month later, Carl Smith returned to commit the robbery along with other accomplices. He was ultimately captured and issued a twenty-five-year sentence to be served in federal prison.

Barchard was arrested by FBI agents in San Pablo, California, on May 14, 1956, and arraigned before the U.S. Commissioner in Oakland the next day. Barchard admitted he had planned to rob other banks with Bulger, Carl Smith, one "Fat" Carroll, Ronald Dermody, William Lawrence O'Brien, and others; however, the robberies did not materialize. Barchard admitted to helping plan the robbery of the Melrose Trust Company, Highland Branch, Melrose, Massachusetts, with Dermody and Carroll, however, they decided the bank was too close to home, etc. Later, in the first part of November 1955, they discussed robbing the bank again, and William O'Brien was also in on it.

They cased the layout but set no date for the robbery. Later, on November 18, 1955, the bank was robbed by Bulger and O'Brien without Barchard participating. Sometime after they offered Barchard $150 for helping set up the robbery; however, he declined, but borrowed $100 of the money and paid it back after they robbed the Hoosier Bank in Hammond, Indiana.

By way of mitigating circumstances, it might be pointed out that after apprehension and being confronted with the evidence against him, Barchard was very cooperative with the arresting agents. He made a complete admission and furnished details of the events for which he was charged and sentenced as well as his participation in planning the robbery of the Melrose Trust Company, Melrose, Massachusetts, and

A prison portrait of Barchard taken for his family while at Alcatraz.

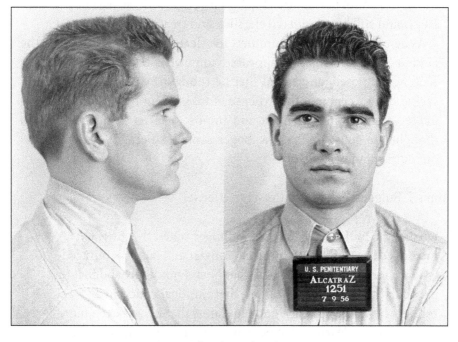

Richard Barchard

William L. O'Brien

the other plans for robbing Mercantile National Bank at Hammond, Indiana (two robberies he did not go through with, as narrated above). He should still be considered sly, slick and treacherous.

When Barchard was committed to Alcatraz on July 9, 1956, by the United States Marshal, he appeared somewhat depressed at the long sentence imposed, and stated that he thought by pleading guilty, and saving the government the expense of taking him back to Indiana, the judge would be more lenient and impose a lesser sentence. He also thought the court imposed a longer sentence because of his marital difficulties and past history.

James J. Bulger's Version of Present Offense:

During the initial social interview, Bulger stated that he was introduced to Carl Smith by an ex-convict and later encouraged to drive for Smith on some deal that he did not know about at that particular time. When he learned that this deal concerned a bank robbery he wanted to back out. He claims that he was even more afraid when he learned that he had to go into the bank and that two people previously involved had backed out.

Bulger stated that the bank robbery was successful, and that afterwards he was in on three more bank heists. Eventually Smith was caught, after he robbed a bank with two men in Tennessee, then returned home and spent the money extravagantly. Bulger said that Smith "squealed on us" after he was caught.

Bulger states that he was caught in a nightclub in Revere, Massachusetts after being a fugitive for two months. He believes that a friend walked him into a trap. He states that he had dyed his hair and started dressing in contrast to his previous style of dressing.

Personal History and Family Background (from his prison case file):

This man (James J. Bulger Jr.) is the second of six children and was born September 3, 1929, in Boston, Massachusetts. His father, James J. Bulger, Sr., was born in St. John, Newfoundland about sixty years ago. He is retired now, according to his mother, and is in good health. He was employed by the WPA until recently as a watchman. He's had no serious difficulty with the law. He was arrested for assault with a revolver in Roxbury, Massachusetts once, but the case was dismissed. The mother, Jean (McCarthy) Bulger, was born in Massachusetts about fifty years ago. She is in good health and is a devoted mother and housewife.

The probation officer's report indicates that this man has had very little to do with his parents. They were unable to control him during his early years. His companions were usually persons of poor reputation and far from a good influence upon him. He would associate with known thieves and ex-convicts.

His schooling consisted of attending both parochial and public schools in South Boston, Massachusetts. He had very little interest in school. He went for a short time to the Brandeis Vocational School in the ninth grade but then left to go into military service. While in the United States Military, he attended school and received a high school diploma.

As indicated above, this man has spent most of his time in local taverns, where he associated with known criminals. Although this was his first penitentiary sentence, it is indicated that he has always been willing to participate in any violations of the law, even if it meant using firearms to accomplish his goals. The police department records reveal episodes of juvenile delinquency and also that fines were paid as an adult for assault and larceny. This man was AWOL in the Army, but he received an honorable discharge.

Present Situation [1955]:

Bulger is a twenty-six-year-old single native of Massachusetts with a legal residence in Boston, Massachusetts. He is serving twenty years for the robbery of an FDIC Bank. He has a possible murder charge indictment against him pending by the State of Indiana. He denies his guilt, although he is accused by alleged eyewitnesses who are also his co-defendants in an Indiana bank robbery. Bulger wrote an anxious letter to his brother about this charge, but it was difficult to tell whether he was bragging or complaining. Under any circumstances, he appears deeply concerned that such a warrant would affect his adjustment here.

This man has close family ties and there are other persons in the community who have shown some interest in his welfare. He wants to have training and learn typing here and is thinking in terms of working his way into a clerical assignment.

Bulger remembered his arrest in Miami, Florida:

I first met Ronnie Dermody and Carl Smith in downtown Boston and had been introduced by an ex-con in Southie who served time with Ronnie in prison. Ronnie had just got married and was

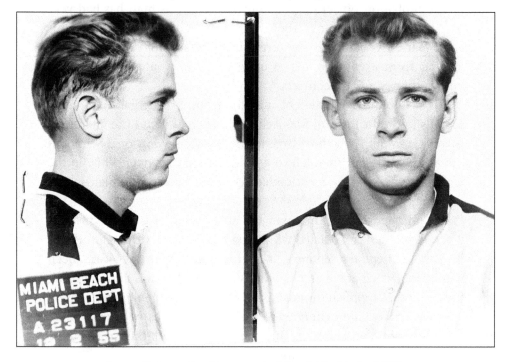

James Bulger after his arrest in Miami, Florida in 1955.

celebrating. They mentioned they needed a third man for a bank robbery and expected a big take in cash. They seemed confident as they had been casing various banks, but regardless, I knew it was a big mistake. I volunteered and after thinking it over, I knew I made the wrong choice, but it was too late, and I couldn't back out. The next day, we robbed the bank in Rhode Island. Carl was a strange guy, and I kept a distance.

Following the strings of bank jobs, I went to Florida with my girlfriend Jacquie to let things cool down. I knew the FBI was working to identify all the suspects in the bank robberies and Miami seemed like a good place to keep a low profile until things settled. The 1955 mugshot was from when I was picked up for a vagrancy charge. The cops used it as a means to hold anyone in custody from out of town that seemed suspicious or until they could pin other charges. They used this as a weapon, and when I was stopped by the police and asked what I was doing in Miami, they arrested me for the sole reason that I was driving a brand new 1955 Oldsmobile and had $5,000 in my possession.

I had been in a bank earlier that morning and a "Mrs. Berger" reported to police that I, along with a female companion, accessed a safe deposit box and when removing a leather pouch, several diamonds spilled out onto the floor. What spilled out was actually cash, not diamonds. They combed the beaches looking for me and I was arrested on the above charge. They put my girlfriend Jacqueline and me on the front page of the local newspaper as jewel thieves which was a completely jacked-up charge. It was completely untrue and something that always haunted me. When I was questioned for the Isabella Garner Museum heist, the detectives made comments about me being a jewel thief, and how jewel thieves often are associated with art theft.

I hired lawyers and was bailed out and then went to court. The charges were dismissed, and I was escorted out of Miami Beach and told not to return. In those days, all criminals had to register with police in order to live there legally. They would sweep the beach and pick up guys for no other reason than them having a tattoo or some other suspicious look. They were always aggressively searching for fugitives. They didn't respect anyone's rights back then.

On January 4, 1956, a federal warrant was issued for Bulger's arrest and all point bulletins were sent via teletypes across thirteen states. The FBI agent in

REFLECTS ON FLIGHT
Sits In 'Show Up' Room

LOOKS UP AT QUESTIONER
Composure Starts To Melt

TEARS BEGIN FLOWING
She Tries To Hold Back

Boston Blonde, Boy Friend Demand Freedom

Two Gem Suspects Defy Police Quiz

charge of the manhunt was Paul Rico, and he worked the streets of South Boston, leveraging his contacts with local informants to identify Bulger's whereabouts. An FBI report later noted that they attempted to arrest Bulger at the family residence at 41 Logan Way, but their attempts to locate him were unsuccessful. The report read in part "Our investigation to locate and apprehend Bulger proved unavailing. Contacts with all logical sources proved unproductive. His family and associates were hostile." On February 9, 1956, Ronald Dermody was arrested, and based on a tip by an informant a short time after, Bulger, surrounded by FBI agents, was finally captured while leaving the Reef Café in Revere.

Photos published in the Miami Herald in December of 1955, with Bulger and his then girlfriend Jacqueline McAuliffe Martin, following their arrest and questioning about their roles in an alleged jewel heist. Bulger vehemently denied any role even decades later.

No. 6513

United States District Court

District of R. I.

THE UNITED STATES OF AMERICA

vs.

JAMES J. BULGER, JR., alias,
ET AL

WARRANT
FOR ARREST OF DEFENDANT

James J. Bulger, Jr.

The official warrants issued for the arrest of James Bulger to stand trial on charges of conspiracy to commit bank robbery.

Warrant for Arrest of Defendant

District Court of the United States

FOR THE

DISTRICT OF RHODE ISLAND

DIVISION

UNITED STATES OF AMERICA

v.

JAMES J. BULGER, JR., alias John Doe
CARL GEORGE SMITH, JR., alias Richard Roe
RONALD PAUL BERMODY, alias John Moe

No.   6513

DISTRICT OF RHODE ISLAND
MARSHAL'S CRIMINAL
2/27/56

To¹ United States Marshal for the District of Rhode Island or
any United States Marshal

You are hereby commanded to arrest James J. Bulger, Jr., alias   and bring him

forthwith before the District Court of the United States for the   District of Rhode Island

in the city of Providence   to answer to an Indictment   charging him with

conspiracy in committing Bank Robbery

in violation of Title 18 U.S.C., Sec. 371.

RECEIVED

MAR 6 1956

Office of the United States Marshal
District of Massachusetts

February 27 1956.

Neale D. Murphy,   Clerk.

By   Deputy Clerk.

¹ Insert designation of officer to whom the warrant is issued, e.g., "any United States Marshal or any other authorized officer"; or "United States Marshal for   District of   "; or "any United States Marshal"; or "any Special Agent of the Federal Bureau of Investigation"; or "any United States Marshal or any Special Agent of the Federal Bureau of Investigation"; or "any agent of the Alcohol Tax Unit."

Bulger:

FBI Agent Paul Rico, who later proved to be a dirty agent and planned the murder of Roger Wheeler, was the one who laid a trap and captured me. I was the last man captured and the others were already doing time. I agreed to plead guilty to all crimes if they released my girlfriend Jacquie, who had no role other than being with me. I was a lucky guy, just like Catherine, she left everything behind to go on the run. I was not prepared, so it didn't last long. It was another world back then; the FBI never bothered my parents or family. They kept their word and when I signed a confession, they released my girlfriend. I

Bulger dyed his hair to a dark brown to evade authorities.

got a twenty-year sentence and felt it was worth it in exchange for her freedom. I had no regrets. I tried to do the same for Catherine, but they rejected every offer. They could seal me in a gas chamber or throw a big necktie party to hang me, but instead, they want everyone associated with me to suffer.

FEDERAL PRISON

On June 21, 1956, Bulger was convicted and sentenced to serve twenty years in a federal prison for armed robbery. He was sent to USP Atlanta. Bulger served hard time during his early years in federal prison, but quickly made friends and served alongside several of his criminal associates from South Boston. His case file shows that he was subjected to extreme medical testing through the Project MK-Ultra. MK-Ultra was the code name of a covert government research operation experimenting in the behavioral engineering of humans through the CIA's Scientific Intelligence Division. The program began in the early 1950s and employed many illegal activities; in particular it used unwitting convicts as its test subjects, which led to controversy regarding its legitimacy. MK-Ultra involved the use of many methodologies to manipulate people's mental states

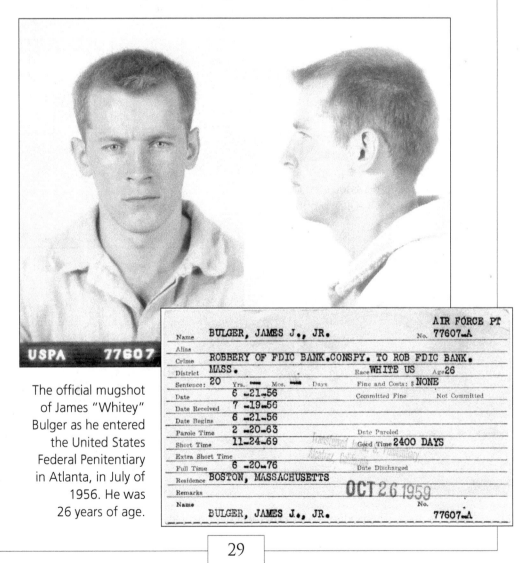

The official mugshot of James "Whitey" Bulger as he entered the United States Federal Penitentiary in Atlanta, in July of 1956. He was 26 years of age.

AIR FORCE PT

Name	BULGER, JAMES J., JR.		No.	77607-A
Alias				
Crime	ROBBERY OF FDIC BANK.CONSPY. TO ROB FDIC BANK.			
District	MASS.		Race WHITE US	Age 26
Sentence: 20	Yrs. — Mos. — Days		Fine and Costs: $ NONE	
Date	6 -21-56		Committed Fine	Not Committed
Date Received	7 -19-56			
Date Begins	6 -21-56			
Parole Time	2 -20-63		Date Paroled	
Short Time	11-24-69		Good Time 2400 DAYS	
Extra Short Time				
Full Time	6 -20-76		Date Discharged	
Residence	BOSTON, MASSACHUSETTS			
Remarks		OCT 26 1959		
Name			No.	
	BULGER, JAMES J., JR.			77607-A

and alter brain functions, including the surreptitious administration of drugs and other chemicals, hypnosis, sensory deprivation, isolation, as well as various forms of torture. Bulger and eighteen other prisoners—who had volunteered to lessen their sentences—were given LSD and other drugs and potent chemicals. Bulger later stated that he and the other convicts had been "recruited by deception." He remembered:

> I am cursed because I volunteered for those Medical Research Projects in the Atlanta Penitentiary, one of which was run by Dr. Carl Pfeiffer of Emory University. The doctor was allegedly searching for a cure for schizophrenia. Participating in these studies appealed to our sense of doing something worthwhile for society. I was on this project for one year, and it was the worst year of my life. I found out later that this project was financed and run by the CIA under the code name

The medical research wing at USP Atlanta. Whitey Bulger participated in a variety of medical testing programs in exchange for time credits off his prison sentence. The programs included test cures for malaria, whooping cough, and schizophrenia, the project later determined to be associated with the MK-Ultra program.

The United States Federal Penitentiary in Atlanta.

MK-Ultra. They would inject you with a syringe full of a chemical that would take you into an insane state that was very intense for seven to nine hours. The effects were both physical and psychological. It was pure trauma, and we were all naive as to how long the residual effects would last. There was never any follow-up and there were permanent effects for many of us. All of us feared it would damage us for the rest of our lives.

Two other volunteers went stark raving mad and psychotic. All of us feared it would happen to us. Since then, I have never had a good night's sleep; I don't sleep much and never longer than two hours straight. My sleep is filled with violent nightmares and restless nights. I sleep for an hour or so, have nightmares, wake up, doze off and on all night, and the same in the daytime while in my cell. Sleeping during

Dr. Carl Pfeiffer was a physician and biochemist of Emory University, and it was alleged that he led the convert MK-Ultra Project. Bulger, along with 18 other volunteers, were part of the medical research program at USP Atlanta to facilitate human studies related to the residual physical and mental effects of LSD. Pfeiffer, who was a pioneer in "orthomolecular psychiatry," allegedly solicited volunteers under the guise they were testing cure methods for schizophrenia. Several prisoners who participated in the program at Atlanta sued the government for effects they suffered from the extreme testing. Their complaints included many similar to Bulger's. The attorney for the Department of Justice on behalf of the CIA made the following admissions in a 1982 deposition: "MK-Ultra's purpose was the research and development of chemical, biological, and radiological materials [for use] in clandestine operations to control human behavior." The program was also "intended to develop an anti-interrogation drug to counter a Soviet truth serum, or possibly scramble a CIA agent's brain so that any confession to his captors would be useless." Dr. Pfeiffer later swore under oath that his only intent of the testing was to find a treatment for mental illness and that he never misled the convicts.

77607
Q F

CONTRACT BETWEEN
DEPARTMENT OF PHARMACOLOGY, EMORY UNIVERSITY SCHOOL OF MEDICINE

and

HUMAN VOLUNTEERS AT U. S. PENITENTIARY, ATLANTA, GEORGIA

Date 7-9-59

"I, _James J. Bulger_, the undersigned applicant, hereby apply for permission to participate in an investigation designed to study the hallucinatory effect of lysergic acid diethyl amide, LSD-25, and similar compounds which is being conducted by Emory University School of Medicine in cooperation with the Bureau of Prisons of the Department of Justice. I understand that I will be required to undergo a physical examination, including laboratory tests, in order to ascertain if I am a suitable candidate. I further agree to take the drugs offered me on the day of the experiment. The procedure, the potential benefits to humanity, and the risks to my health of participation in this study have been explained to me by Dr. _Carl C. Pfeiffer_, and I understand that there can be no guarantee that I will not become ill as a result of this experiment. I hereby freely assume all such risks of participation in the investigation."

"I further agree to cooperate to the fullest extent with the personnel conducting the investigation during the experimental period. I understand that upon completion of my participation in this experiment, the fact that I have thus voluntarily rendered outstanding service to humanity will be placed in my official record. In addition, I understand that each time I am used as a subject, a sum of $3.00 will be deposited in my trust fund account. No such deposit will be made until the Medical Officer has certified that my participation has been satisfactory."

"In consideration of the money referred to above, the other considerations referred to above, and for other good and valuable consideration, receipt of which in full is hereby acknowledged by me, I, acting for myself, my heirs, personal representatives, my estate and my assigns, do hereby release Emory University, the doctors, physicians, their assistants and all others participating in this experimental program from all liability of any kind or character, including claims and suits in law or in equity for damage, injury or death which may result to me or to my property from my participation in this experimental investigation."

"In witness whereof I hereunto set my hand and affix my seal this the ___9th___ day of ___July___, 1959."

___James J. Bulger___ L.S.
SIGNATURE OF INMATE APPLICANT

PRISON REGISTRATION NUMBER _77607_

Witnesses to signature:

"We approve of the foregoing agreement:"

_____
Warden

Carl C. Pfeiffer
U. S. Public Health Officer
JUL 9 1959

Date _____   Date _____

"I attest that the purpose of this study, its procedures, and inherent risk were fully explained to the applicant by the officer in charge of the experiment. I am convinced of the applicant's complete understanding and willingness to participate in this study. I am confident that no duress of any kind was present in these proceedings."

_____
(ASSOCIATE WARDEN)

The official contract signed by Bulger and Dr. Carl Pfeiffer, authorizing and agreeing to participate in the research of the hallucinatory effects of LSD. He would be repeatedly administered extreme dosages, which was later identified as a testing platform for the MK-Ultra program, the code name of a government covert research operation experimenting in the behavioral engineering of humans through the CIA's Scientific Intelligence Division.

Documents from Bulger's prison medical file illustrating the extensive and repeated chemical testing he was subjected to as part of the alleged MK-Ultra Program, later purported as being sponsored by the CIA.

the day is much easier because when I wake up, I know where I'm at right away and don't have as much anxiety and claustrophobia, and the hallucinations fade away faster. All of this I've dealt with for decades. In the beginning, I thought I was going crazy and said nothing—didn't want to wind up in a strip cell. When I first arrived on the Rock, I had bad nightmares and I'd wake up guys on Broadway and could hear the comments "That motherfucker is a mad man…" I'd never react and just lie still and hope they couldn't pinpoint it to me. I didn't want them to know it was coming from my cell. I admit that I felt at times I was going mad. At Atlanta, I saw Benoit and Jennings go insane and were carried away…I never seen or heard of them again. I later heard from a guy who said he'd seen both at Springfield in the mental unit and neither spoke to him nor would respond to his questions. I always feared insanity, but never spoke of it on Alcatraz. I feared if I mentioned it, I'd end up locked up in a mental unit or strip cell. I had terrifying hallucinations in my cell at night. I heard my mother's voice, saw ghosts, dead people, blood, and nights in prison were tough.

After I finally made it to a cell on the upper tier at Alcatraz, I always had a cell with light coming through the roof of the cellhouse, so that I could use the natural light that shined through the bars to read at night. I'd lie awake for hours on end. It's been so much a part of my life all these years it's become the norm. I get angry when I think back on this.

One of the worst experiences during the Project MK-Ultra experiments involved the death of a good friend named Jack Geary (456-AZ). As I recall, Jack's real name was Percy, and with a name like that, you learn to fight or become a punching bag. At a young age, after being arrested, a court official said to him "How could you commit these crimes? You have the face of an angel." Because of this comment, the press gave him the name "Angel Face" and the nickname was even listed on his FBI Wanted poster! He really got a laugh out of telling that story.

I met Jack through Henry Reddington, a friend in Atlanta. Henry was a jolly, overweight, non-violent guy. After getting out of prison, he was taken captive in his house and tortured by knife and then shot to death. I was in prison when this took place and there were a few men involved. Later, the main killer was shot a few times with a .38, which he initially survived; then he was gunned down with a machine gun and given a few pistol shots in the head for good measure. His death was one of the murders I was accused of. Another guy got life for a

Percy "Jack" Geary

Jack Geary being led from court in February 1937 on kidnapping and extortion charges.

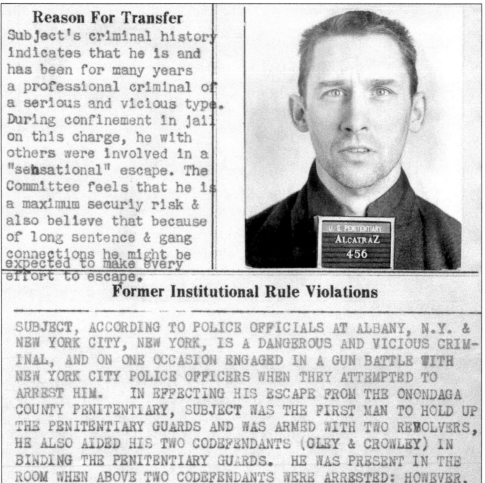

Reason For Transfer

Subject's criminal history indicates that he is and has been for many years a professional criminal of a serious and vicious type. During confinement in jail on this charge, he with others were involved in a "sensational" escape. The Committee feels that he is a maximum security risk & also believe that because of long sentence & gang connections he might be expected to make every effort to escape.

U. S. PENITENTIARY
ALCATRAZ
456

Former Institutional Rule Violations

SUBJECT, ACCORDING TO POLICE OFFICIALS AT ALBANY, N.Y. & NEW YORK CITY, NEW YORK, IS A DANGEROUS AND VICIOUS CRIMINAL, AND ON ONE OCCASION ENGAGED IN A GUN BATTLE WITH NEW YORK CITY POLICE OFFICERS WHEN THEY ATTEMPTED TO ARREST HIM. IN EFFECTING HIS ESCAPE FROM THE ONONDAGA COUNTY PENITENTIARY, SUBJECT WAS THE FIRST MAN TO HOLD UP THE PENITENTIARY GUARDS AND WAS ARMED WITH TWO REVOLVERS, HE ALSO AIDED HIS TWO CODEFENDANTS (OLEY & CROWLEY) IN BINDING THE PENITENTIARY GUARDS. HE WAS PRESENT IN THE ROOM WHEN ABOVE TWO CODEFENDANTS WERE ARRESTED: HOWEVER, HE SUCCEEDED IN EFFECTING HIS ESCAPE THE SECOND TIME BY JUMPING FROM BATHROOM WINDOW OF THE APARTMENT, A DISTANCE OF ABOUT TWENTY FEET.

An excerpt from Jack Geary's 1938 prison case file indicating he was a vicious criminal who once engaged in a gun battle with New York police officers during an attempted arrest. He was involved in a "sensational" jail break and following his capture (pictured), he was sent to Alcatraz during a period when some of the toughest conditions were imposed including the rule of silence. He committed suicide in July of 1959 at USP Atlanta.

murder he committed at a house party during a drunken rage where there were lots of witnesses, and the other guy is still hiding out or has already died of old age.

Geary and his gang—Jack Oley and John McGlone and a couple of others—kidnapped a guy from Albany, New York (John O'Connell, son of New York's most powerful upstate political family) for ransom. The family was friends of the then-Governor Franklin Delano Roosevelt. The New York State Police got the number on the gang, conducted a long torture session, put one of the gang members into a burlap bag, cuffed him into a rowboat, floated the boat to the middle of a lake in the dark and threw him in-and-out of the water. Another gang member was tied up and hoisted up a flagpole by his feet. Two of the other gang members committed suicide.

In another plot, Jack along with the Oley brothers, committed one of the biggest heists on record back in the 1930s; the robbery of a Brinks armored car carrying over $1 million on the streets of Brooklyn, New York. They netted about half that, but it was still a record haul back then. Jack was pushing a covered cart on the street (disguised as a street peddler) and when the armored car door opened, he pulled out a Thompson submachine gun and got the drop on them. The money was from their collection routes at Coney Island. A big score from the carnival and arcade deposits.

Jack ran many stories by me when he was a patient in the hospital (which is where I worked at USP Atlanta). I spent a lot of time in his cubicle-like room. I'd buy a cigar for him, and he'd cut it in halves and beam "Can't Beat This!" He was always making the best of it. He liked to talk about the good old days at the Hotsy Totsy Club in New York with Jack "Legs" Diamond and other old gangsters.

Then comes Dr. Brailler, a really incompetent swine and religious nut. He held services for the men in his office. Some cons played along by kissing ass, thereby hoping for an early parole. The doctor operated on Jack for gallbladder problems and screwed him up. He did a second surgery to correct it, but to no avail. Jack was left in deep pain and was vomiting. Dr. Brailler barred Jack from sick call; if he didn't see Jack, he could forget his mistake. One day I was coming out of the mess hall and Jack was waiting for me. He told me he wanted to say goodbye and commented that I was a good friend. He was assigned to one of the large eight-man cells and said "I'm real sick and it disturbs the guys in the cell. I don't like being a bother to anyone. I should have done this twenty years ago." He told me that he was going to kill himself. I told him not to talk like that and that my friends were going over the wall and that I'd put him in on it. He said he was too weak to make a break. I told him I'd carry him up the ladder and get him to the other side, but that he shouldn't talk about suicide. I had to rush to check in for the MK-Ultra project and couldn't stay another minute. I told him I'd be out in 24 hours and that we'd figure something out. I told him "Just hang on." He smiled and said, "I'll see you later." I rushed over to the hospital and was checked into the experiment room. I was injected with a syringe full of a chemical, which put me into a seven-hour schizophrenic state, which was very frightening. I saw blood dripping from the ceiling and the bars on windows turned into slithering snakes. Once, I looked over at the guy next to me and all of a sudden the flesh started melting away from his face and he turned into a skeleton.

The next thing that came into the hospital was a stretcher with blood soaking through the sheet and dripping onto the floor. I learned that Jack was under the sheet. He had thrown himself under the wheel of the giant earthmover that was working on a construction job on the prison grounds and crushed Jack to death [NOTE: It was later determined to be a prison laundry delivery truck]. I overheard Dr. Pfeiffer tell another doctor, "I'd like to examine a piece of his brain to check for substances." I grabbed Dr. Pfeiffer by the throat, screaming at the top of my lungs, and I started to choke him. It took me a long while to get over that, but by degrees, I felt that Jack was in a better place and finally free of prison and all his suffering. Most of my friends in prison died such violent deaths. I wish he had made it to freedom. He was a real nice guy. You don't meet many guys like Jack in one's lifetime.

The memories of the LSD testing and the beatings by police are still fresh in my mind, and once during the LSD tests, they hooked us up to polygraph machine. I remember the operator was in a suit out of Chicago (there's a good chance he was from the CIA) and while I was fully loaded with LSD, he asked the question "Do you hate cops?" He jumped because the needles/indicators came off the scale! I was thinking of that cop McDonough, and I can still picture his face, how tall he was and that whole night. I know that I've outlived that drunken cop and prefer my life and ending to his.

Charlie Catalano, 1381-AZ, was a close associate of Bulger's, both inside and outside of prison. He had suffered a litany of personal misfortunes and later killed his son—who was suffering from extreme drug abuse—and then turned the gun on himself. Catalano served alongside Bulger at both Atlanta and Alcatraz and was a conspirator in the November 1958 escape that earned Bulger, John Paul Scott and Louis Arquilla their ticket to Alcatraz. Catalano's official inmate case file provided the following biographical information written in February of 1959:

This white man, married, was sentenced August 16, 1955, at Brooklyn, New York to serve twenty-five years for robbery of an FDIC Bank. He together with two codefendants, Stephen Kritsky (1395-AZ) and a second codefendant unknown to prosecuting officials, obtained $24,459 from a bank in Forest Hills, New York, while masked and using guns. Committed to Atlanta July 19, 1956, he was transferred to Alcatraz on January 27, 1959 after his involvement in an escape attempt. Detainers are filed by the U.S. Marshal, Atlanta, Georgia—Attempted Escape; Clark, Queens County Court, Long Island, New York—Robbery and Grand Larceny.

He was reared in marginal circumstances in New York City. The family group was stable, and he remained in the parental home until age twenty-three when he married and there are two children by this union. The FBI reports his delinquency starting in 1934 when he was placed on probation for truancy. Two years later he was arrested in New York City for Grand Larceny, but the case was dismissed. In 1939, he was given an indefinite sentence for petty larceny, and he was paroled later that year. In April 1939, he was given an indefinite sentence for assault and was committed to the penitentiary at Rikers Island and was paroled the following year. Then followed arrests for disorderly conduct, attempted felonious assault, malicious mischief

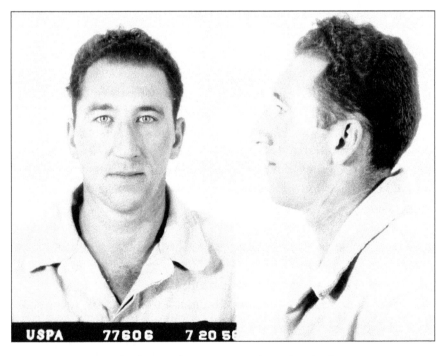

Charlie Catalano at USP Atlanta in 1956.

Stephen Kritsky

and in 1947, he was committed to the state penitentiary in Ossining, New York to serve two and a half to five years for assault and robbery. He has not received visits, but he corresponds with his wife Mrs. Mary Catalano, New York, N.Y.; and other family members.

At Atlanta there were two misconduct reports: October 22, 1956, possession for contraband; November 24, 1958, attempted escape as he together with other inmates made an unsuccessful attempt to scale the wall but they climbed to a roof where they were discovered and apprehended.

Because of this man's long sentence, the possibility of an additional sentence by Queens County, Long Island City, New York, his abortive escape attempt and the fact that upon interview with the warden, he stated that he was determined to escape confinement and would attempt to do so again in the future and that he did not fear being shot, it is the request of the Classification Committee that he be transferred to USP Alcatraz, California.

CATALANO Record Form No. 36 Rev. Oct., 1940 1381-AZ	ASSOCIATE WARDEN'S RECORD CARD	FPI—LK—5-1-56—55M—8414

Catalano arrived on Alcatraz in January of 1959.

Bulger reminisced:

Poor Charlie Catalano, he had such a hard life, full of disappointments. In prison, he made the best of it on the surface, but beneath, he was a volcano of anger and bitterness—he did a lot of time in his life. His mother was Irish, his father was Italian, and a singing waiter in an upscale restaurant. Charlie and I met in a federal holding facility in West State New York. It was like a huge warehouse full of cells and a recreation area up on the roof. Charlie and I were cuffed together for a long ride on a prison bus to Atlanta, with a stopover in Petersburg Prison in Virginia. Charlie was desperate to escape but we were surrounded by armed guards, and he was unable to get out of the cuffs. Charlie, Jack Twining (1362-AZ) and Louis Arquilla (1386-AZ) all had in common the plan to kill themselves if they were ever faced with capture again. All three eventually died from a bullet. I also knew Charlie's crime partner Stephen Kritsky, at Atlanta. Following the break, we were all housed together in segregation. After everyone landed at Alcatraz, Steve faded out of the picture, and I don't remember seeing him much on the island. He didn't mingle much with the Boston and New York crews.

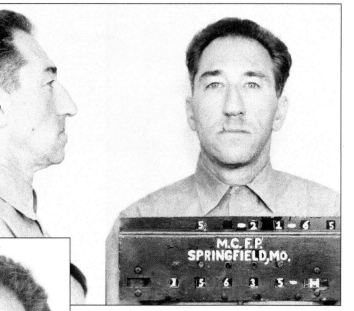

Later mugshots of Charlie Catalano at USP Lewisburg and USP Springfield Medical Center.

Once on Alcatraz during Christmas, they played Bing Crosby's *White Christmas* album over the loudspeakers which were located on top of the cellblocks. Charlie's cell was located at the very end of our section on the top tier, facing the library. His cell was located right below one of the speakers. I have a memory of Charlie singing to that music, probably reminiscing about his father performing for patrons and his family during holidays. One Christmas morning, like something out of a movie, Charlie imitating Bing's voice stood at the front of his cell, singing along to every song on the record. His voice echoed throughout the cellhouse. The guys cheered and cheered. He had such a good voice and knew every word! That was sure a special memory and all the guys, even a few officers, shook his hand thanking him. It was something I'll never forget and a good remembrance of Charlie.

I can't begin to express how profound that memory of Charlie singing and his voice resonating through the cellhouse is to me. It was the story that I shared at his funeral in New York, and how important it was to the guys that morning. The night before and after the Christmas Eve dinner, the warden allowed an extra hour before lights out. The cellhouse was somber as the men listened to Christmas and variety programs on the radio. When the lights finally went out, we heard something that shook all of us. I didn't know where it was coming from; I thought maybe the upstairs theatre. Although faint, we could hear beautiful voices singing Silent Night, and it sounded like a full, yet soft, choir of women and children in a calming harmony. It was the wives

and children of the guards singing Christmas carols. The men fell into a dark abyss of despair and depression. In that moment was the reminder of everything lost. The next morning, no one spoke during breakfast, and then it was back to our cells. When Bing Crosby's *White Christmas* record played over the loudspeakers and Charlie's voice echoed from the top of the cellhouse, the spirits of the men were lifted so high in that moment, their imagination went beyond the walls of the prison. We were all grateful to Charlie on that day...

In prison, Charlie usually smiled a lot and got along with everyone. Sadly, after prison, he drank quite a bit and was angry, but to his friends, he was a loyal guy. When he was captured on bank robbery, he never gave up his partner for a deal. I attended his wake, along with our mutual friend Tommy Devaney. Tommy had made the trip back to New York from Florida where he was keeping low. Afterwards, we went across the street for a drink (a custom) and "Mad Dog" Sullivan (a well-known mafia hitman) stepped in and shot Tommy to death on an order from "Fat Tony" Salerno. The murder took place at a bar named Dominick's, owned by Dominick Sicilia, an old timer from the Bronx who'd known Al Capone. We spent hours talking with him about the old neighborhoods. Lucky for Sullivan, I had already left the bar when he was murdered and didn't learn who'd made the hit until years later. I was armed and would have prevented it from happening, and then I would have avenged it … I've heard the hit was attributed to others from the Genovese crime family, but it was Tony who called the hit. Tommy and Charlie were part of Mickey Spillane's crew, and the grudges ran deep. Sullivan rubbed out Mickey about a year later. I was close to Devaney. Tommy, Charlie and I spent a lot of time in the Hell's Kitchen neighborhood at another bar called "Sonny's," located on the West Side of Manhattan in New York City. Eddie "The Butcher" Kaminski was a little guy and another close friend who on occasion helped me deal with problems, and he was always with us at Sonny's. He worked in the butcher shop at Rikers Island, New York's State Penitentiary, and used those skills on the outside. He had a

reputation for cutting up bodies and green bagging body parts and throwing them in a place called Hell's Gate, where the strong water currents wash everything out to sea. Devaney never joined us on Alcatraz, but we served together both in Atlanta and Lewisburg. Tommy and Charlie did a bank job together that landed Charlie in prison. Charlie was pinched for the robbery and never gave up Tommy. Sullivan killed a good Irishman paid for by Salerno for only

A newspaper photo clipping showing Bulger's crime partner Tommy Devaney (left) and Patrick Devine (right) being led from court.

crumbs. I didn't learn who was responsible for Tommy's death until years later when I was in Santa Monica. Sullivan spent the last decades of his life behind bars and he was fortunate I didn't hold the debt owed to Tommy.

The *New York Daily News* featured a story on Devaney's murder writing in part:

Police Hunting for Killer of Ex-Con—Police were searching yesterday for the murderer of an ex-convict who was gunned down gangland-style in a Lexington Ave pub Tuesday night shortly after attending a wake for an old prison pal. Thomas Devaney, 47, of Parsons Blvd., Queens, was shot in the back of the head, shortly after he walked into Dominick's Bar and Grill. He had just been to the Dimiceli and Son's funeral home for the wake of Charles Catalano, 56, who shot himself after critically shooting his son, Charles Jr., 31. Queens detectives said Catalano was angered by his son's drug problems. Witnesses described Devaney's murderer as a well-dressed blond man in his 20s. Police said Devaney and Catalano had criminal records going back 25 years.

Charlie's fate was hard for me to come to terms with. He was an emotional guy and faced much disappointment when finally released from prison. He ran with the Westies, an Irish American gang that operated out of the Hell's Kitchen neighborhood. He had a wife and two grown kids. His son had a bad drug problem and was stealing money to fund his heroin addiction. I could see how when he was released and returned home, he must have been in for a reality shock. They were living in near poverty conditions, and I expect alcohol only fueled his rage. His son apparently stole a television to sell to buy heroin and Charlie exploded, shooting him with a .357 magnum and putting him in a hospital intensive care unit. After he shot his son, he sat down at his kitchen table, wrote a suicide note, then shot himself in the head and ended his life. His son later died. I visited his wife in the Crown Heights neighborhood of Brooklyn. She told me all about it. It was a sad picture. She was weary and worn down...I tried to give her money, but she was too proud to accept anything, and I did my best to help her and her daughter with expenses. Charlie and I were such good friends. I considered him one of my closest associates in life. So many people from my past died so violently.

While he was a prisoner at Atlanta, Bulger—along with John Paul Scott (1403-AZ)—who made one of the most successful though short-lived escape attempts from the Rock—Charlie Catalano, Louis Arquilla, Charles "Jeep" Marcum (1407-AZ) and Stephen Kritsky plotted to escape from the prison hospital. Bulger refused to give up the name of a correctional officer who helped him acquire the hacksaw blades that were used to cut through the barred windows. This defiance earned Bulger his ticket to Alcatraz. Later, Bulger remembered:

> While at Atlanta, I worked in the prison hospital which was a key location as a starting point to bust out…I was asked to take part in an escape and help friends. I'd trained and worked as the physical therapist and liked the work. I agreed and helped plot how to get them checked into the hospital for various medical problems. They had a 40-foot ladder that Charlie, Louis, Scotty, and Jeep had built, and they were able to cut the bars of the hospital ward window. We used the hacksaw blades I'd received from a guard to saw through bars on a window in the hospital and make it outside. Using the ladder made from sections of piping, they attempted to scale a 45-foot wall, but the angle was too steep. At the weakest spot the ladder collapsed and they had nowhere else to go. Warden Fred Wilkinson came out with a shotgun, along with other guards, and all of them were demanding that the convicts surrender, or they would be shot. The cons told the guards "After we have this last cigarette, we will come down…We know that this will be our last cigarette for a long time." We were so close. Fortunately, I was the only person who knew who brought the blades in and never gave up the name.
>
> I was threatened with lots of time in the hole. I was stared down and given offers to reduce my sentence if I told who brought the blades. Just before the escape, I'd forgot that I was going to be given a test injection for a vaccine that was in development. I agreed to several different medical experiments and many of the cons believed they would help society while gaining good time credits. I had agreed to a test vaccine for Whooping Cough. At that time this was the number one killer of infants. It felt like a worthy project to be part of…Two hours after the injection, I felt like I was on fire as my body was fighting this foreign germ. I was so sick, and the warden pulled me into his office with a big guard standing behind me with a large pick handle who kept striking it into the palm of his hand. There was no violence used against me, just threats.…I expected the worst…I was stripped naked and thrown into a dark cell. I had a bad fever and was

really sick. They sent a medic to look at me and he urged the warden to send me back to the hospital and he said no…The warden says "He just tried to escape from the hospital…He stays in the hole…" The guard who slipped me the blades gave me some wet towels to bring down my temperature and I assured him I've forgotten everything, and he'd never have to worry. I spent weeks in the hole and finally was taken upstairs to the administrative segregation unit with the others. In a matter of only weeks, they started sending the guys out to Alcatraz. The last men standing

Louis Arquilla while a prisoner at USP Atlanta in 1962.

Charles "Jeep" Marcum

in segregation was Scottie and me. After they gave up and figured out that their efforts were useless, they shipped me to the Rock. Wilkinson was really angry and demanded me to name the guard who gave me the blades (they were top quality and came from the outside). I told him that I didn't know anything about it and never changed my story. He threatened me commenting, "I want that motherfucker's name. Next he'll be bringing in guns!"

I must admit, I expected physical torture or at least a severe working over, but all I got was long, hot, filthy sessions in the hole. Wilkinson's parting shot was "I should have sent you to Alcatraz years ago." I answered, "I wish you had!"

You know the rest.

January 6, 1959

To: Mr. F.T. Wilkinson, Warden

Bulger is serving a sentence of twenty years for bank robbery. Investigation discloses that this man furnished a hacksaw blade to three men in "B" Cellhouse who were attempting to escape from this institution.

Almost every time information is received about some escape plot, Bulger's name heads the list. When he was received, the state of Indiana had a pending murder charge against him. However, no detainer has been filed. It is my recommendation that Bulger be considered for transfer to Alcatraz as a serious escape risk.

W.H. York
Associate Warden
October 16, 1959

Director James V. Bennett
Warden F.T. Wilkinson, Atlanta
James J. Bulger
Registration Number 77607-A

Subject: Recommendation for Transfer to Alcatraz

The case of the above-named inmate is again being submitted to you with the recommendation that he should be transferred to Alcatraz. On January

Administrative Form No. 66
November 1938

UNITED STATES
DEPARTMENT OF JUSTICE
WASHINGTON

October 21, 1959

To the   Warden, United States Penitentiary, Atlanta, Georgia

WHEREAS, in accordance with the authority contained in title 18, sections 4082, 4085, and 4125, U. S. Code, the Attorney General by the Director of the Bureau of Prisons has

ordered the transfer of   James J. Bulger   #77607

from the   United States Penitentiary, Atlanta, Georgia

to the   United States Penitentiary, Alcatraz, California

Now THEREFORE, you, the above-named officer, are hereby authorized and directed to execute this order by causing the removal of said prisoner, together with the original writ of commitment and other official papers as above ordered and to incur the necessary expense and include it in your regular accounts.

And you, the warden, superintendent, or official in charge of the institution in which the prisoner is now confined, are hereby authorized to deliver the prisoner in accordance with the above order; and you, the warden, superintendent, or official in charge of the institution to which the transfer has been ordered, are hereby authorized and directed to receive the said prisoner into your custody and him to safely keep until the expiration of his sentence or until he is otherwise discharged according to law.

By direction of the Attorney General,

JAMES V. BENNETT,
Director, Bureau of Prisons.

FRANK LOVELAND
Assistant Director.

Closer custody

ORIGINAL.—To be left at institution to which prisoner is transferred

FPI—LK—6-11-59—400 pads—6779

Bulger's official transfer order from USP Atlanta to the United States Penitentiary Alcatraz Island issued on October 21, 1959.

28, 1959, I wrote to you about Bulger about his involvement with three other inmates to whom he furnished a hacksaw blade to assist them with their plans to saw their way out of B-cellhouse. As background, on November 24, 1958, the subject together with four other inmates, Charles Catalano, 77606, Stephen Kritsky, 77864, John Paul Scott, 78323 and Louis Arquilla, 78643, while quartered in the Institution Hospital managed to exit from the north side at about 9:30 PM and after an unsuccessful attempt to scale the wall, they climbed to the roof at the rear of the main institution where they were discovered and apprehended before they were able to complete any further escape plans. A full report of the escape is in the Central and Washington files. Two of these men were sent to Alcatraz, but it was decided to permit Bulger to remain here in hopes that he would settle down and become more favorably responsive to efforts by the staff here to help him.

On the basis of this decision, which had our heartiest endorsement, Bulger was released from administrative segregation and given an incentive assignment to the prison industries. He appeared to make a fairly good response to his program, at least superficially. He soon became actively affiliated with his former, undesirable associates here, and on August 24, 1959, he was returned to administrative segregation. This was after we received what we considered good information to the effect that he,

Thomas John Devaney, 79217-A, and one or two others whose identity we weren't able to establish, were again plotting an escape from this institution.

Notwithstanding our patient efforts to counsel Bulger towards constructive program participation, he is becoming more sullen, resistive, and defiant by the day. We do not believe we can return him to the population here without inviting further serious trouble. Accordingly, there appears to be no alternative to sending him to Alcatraz, where he can remain in the population under a closely supervised program.

*"The reminder of everything lost was always present at Alcatraz...
That made the nights tough..."*

WHEN ALCATRAZ OPENED IN 1934, America was suffering through a state of depression. The country was weathering a storm of criminal activity, spawned by the Prohibition in the teen years of the 1900s. Coined the "gangster era," the Federal Bureau of Prisons, established in 1933, was faced with the complex dilemma of housing and reforming criminals who had committed ruthless acts against society which instilled fear, and a loss of faith in the government's ability to keep their families safe.

Alcatraz became the prime solution to silencing these menaces. It was the melting pot for the cream of the criminal crop and would be the end of the line for the nation's more incorrigible and lawless individuals. A place where their stature in crime rings had no value, and escape was thought to be impossible. The prisoners sent to Alcatraz were considered the worst of the worst and represented less than one percent of the federal prison system population. They were comprised of the famous, infamous, unknowns, and were not only bank robbers and murderers, but organized crime figures who orchestrated complex crime syndicates where corruption was boundless. They infiltrated even the most sacred levels of law enforcement. Men like Al Capone, Alvin Karpis, Doc Barker, Machine Gun Kelly, Roy Gardner, Mickey Cohen, and Robert Stroud (the Birdman of Alcatraz) helped fuel the air of mystery that shrouded the island.

Alcatraz's first warden, James A. Johnston, commented that Alcatraz would remain reserved for only the Bureau of Prisons most troublesome prisoners: "The incorrigible gangsters whose associations must be disrupted; men with long criminal records; men with long prison records; men wanted by other jurisdictions for additional crimes and escape artists who showed ingenuity in securing weapons and instigating violence in escapes from other institutions." Conditions at Alcatraz changed little over the years, and even during the time Bulger called the Rock home, he was to experience one of the toughest regimens in the prison system. Joe Carnes, the youngest prisoner to ever serve on Alcatraz and a trusted friend of Bulger, described the state of mind: "Alcatraz—the stark, cold, reality of having to live there; the constant fight to retain your

United States Federal Penitentiary Alcatraz

Alcatraz was a forbidding island that was a focal point in the San Francisco Bay, and a symbol of America's solution to silencing the most notorious public enemies; men who were considered the "worst of the worst."

own sense of personal worth, your integrity, self-respect, the constant erosion of the environment on your sense of values, the constant awareness that a misstep can cost you your life."

Federal Bureau of Prisons Director, James V. Bennett wrote:

> Alcatraz was a tough, minimum privilege prison meant to deter the racketeers and those who tried to emulate them. Also, as Attorney General Homer S. Cummings put it, Alcatraz took the strain off the rest of the federal system. Once the troublemakers and the escape-prone had been sent to Alcatraz, it would be possible to ease the regimentation and set a freer climate in the mainland prisons. In a sense, I was the talent scout for Alcatraz. One of my jobs was to review the records of the men in the various federal prisons and decide who would be sent to "the Rock." I also had to supervise the performance of the men on Alcatraz and help determine who was ready to be sent back to prisons on the mainland.

A National Park study also provided an eloquent description of the Alcatraz model:

> Notorious or not, the policy on Alcatraz remained the same. Isolation from the outside world, so tantalizingly near, was enforced by strictly limited correspondence and visiting privileges. Only food, clothing, shelter, and necessary medical attention were given as a right. Everything else had to be earned by good behavior, including the chance to work at a prison industrial job. Before 1940, a rule of silence was enforced in the cellhouse to be relieved only at meals, while walking in the yard, and at industrial work. Prisoners remained on Alcatraz until their adherence to the rules demonstrated that they were candidates for transfer and then they were sent to another, lesser federal institution. Rarely were any released to the outside from Alcatraz. Specific information about the island prison was jealously guarded, seemed to enhance the aura of mystery, and contributed to the perception of Alcatraz as America's Devil's Island. The boredom of the routine, and the pervasiveness of the silence prompted one prisoner in the 1930s to exclaim that "they never give a break" on Alcatraz.
>
> Attorney General Homer S. Cummings announced that Alcatraz was to become a "special institution of maximum security and minimum privilege for the confinement of such ruthless individuals." The Bureau of Prisons...was given a legislative mandate to "assure the proper classification and segregation of federal prisoners according to their character, [and] the nature of their crime." Thus, Alcatraz became the ultimate prison within a nationwide system, and a safety valve that took the problem cases to allow rehabilitation and the chance of better treatment to continue elsewhere. Alcatraz would house the single percentage of America's most notorious, escape prone and unruly federal prisoners.

Bulger, who had grown up seeing Hollywood movies and reading about America's most infamous criminals, would find himself in the same spotlight. In November 1959, when he transferred from Atlanta to Alcatraz, the prison was in a state of transition. Warden Paul J. Madigan, who had worked under the first warden, the architect of the strict prison policies and security procedures that gave Alcatraz its reputation, was slowly easing away the harsh rudiments.

James "Whitey" Bulger was transported to the Rock aboard the prison launch, the Warden Johnston, named after the first warden of Alcatraz, James A. Johnston. It was from the boat window that he'd get his first glimpse of the notorious prison as they edged closer jetting across the choppy waters of the San Francisco Bay.

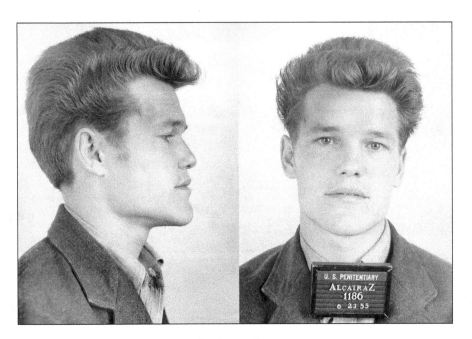

Charlie Hopkins

Charlie Hopkins, 1186-AZ, who arrived on Alcatraz in 1955 remembered:

The Rock started changing with the new warden, deputy warden and especially the new Attorney General, Robert Kennedy. During my years there, things were strict. The only sports in the recreation yard were handball and softball, and security was so tight you couldn't breathe. When I was in the Alcatraz hospital, at night I would look out to the Golden Gate Bridge and you could see the guard in the road tower always carrying a rifle, plus a guard patrolling the catwalk of the yard wall. These were closed by the time of the 1962 escape. The convicts would have been shot off the roof and every one of them killed. They would have never made it off the island.

Bulger offered memories of his transfer and life on the Rock as prisoner 1428-AZ:

I was flown on a TWA jet with around four or five Marshals from Baltimore, Maryland to San Francisco. I enjoyed the smell of the salt air and choppy water. I came over to Alcatraz on the Warden Johnston boat and was bolted in for security purposes. I remember it all so well. When I arrived, all of my old friends who I had served time with at

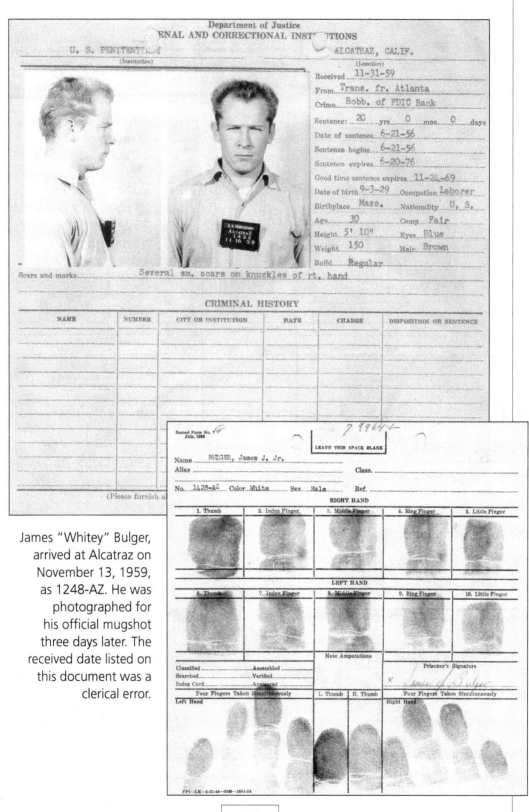

Department of Justice
ENAL AND CORRECTIONAL INST TIONS

U. S. PENITENT Y
(Institution)

ALCATRAZ, CALIF.
(Location)

Received 11-31-59
From Trans. fr. Atlanta
Crime Robb. of FDIC Bank
Sentence: 20 yrs 0 mos 0 days
Date of sentence 6-21-56
Sentence begins 6-21-56
Sentence expires 6-20-76
Good time sentence expires 11-24-69
Date of birth 9-3-29 Occupation Laborer
Birthplace Mass. Nationality U. S.
Age 20 Comp. Fair
Height 5' 10" Eyes Blue
Weight 150 Hair Brown
Build Regular

Scars and marks Several sm. scars on knuckles of rt. hand

CRIMINAL HISTORY

NAME	NUMBER	CITY OR INSTITUTION	DATE	CHARGE	DISPOSITION OR SENTENCE

(Please furnish a

James "Whitey" Bulger, arrived at Alcatraz on November 13, 1959, as 1248-AZ. He was photographed for his official mugshot three days later. The received date listed on this document was a clerical error.

Record Form No. 7
July, 1936

7 9964-L

LEAVE THIS SPACE BLANK

Name BULGER, James J. Jr.
Alias   Class.
No. 1428-AZ Color White Sex Male Ref.

RIGHT HAND

1. Thumb	2. Index Finger	3. Middle Finger	4. Ring Finger	5. Little Finger

LEFT HAND

6. Thumb	7. Index Finger	8. Middle Finger	9. Ring Finger	10. Little Finger

Note Amputations

Classified   Assembled
Searched   Verified
Index Card   Answered

Prisoner's Signature
James J. Bulger

Four Fingers Taken Simultaneously
Left Hand

L. Thumb   R. Thumb

Four Fingers Taken Simultaneously
Right Hand

FPI-LE-8-22-44-25M-1651-24

The main corridor known as "Broadway" would be Bulger's first place of residence when he arrived on Alcatraz in 1959. He was confined in C-145, a 5x9 foot cell, 23 hours each day, for 20 days straight until he was assigned a job in the clothing issue. His only privilege during this period was the ability to read books and magazines.

Atlanta gave me a big welcome. They were hollering from their cells as I walked down Broadway.

I often reflect back to those years on the Rock. Life there and then was not as described by Phil Bergen (former Correctional Officer and Captain of the Guards), etc. Guards viewed it from a very different perspective and have a tendency to view it like a Hollywood product. I'm kind of reluctant to describe it as I saw it, having served a few years of my life there.

A typical 5x9 foot Alcatraz cell. All general population cells located in the main cellhouse were of identical dimensions.

We had guys from all walks of life, and some were full of hate and quick to insult a guard. It was a mix of humor and acid tongue. Many guards were hated, and I saw it firsthand, but still, the culture was mostly one of respect and civility. The guards at Alcatraz were laid back and didn't go out of their way to make life hard. They saw us all as hardened convicts, but all of us were just doing time, trying to make the best of what life had dealt, and many were working to make things right.

Even though the city of San Francisco was always in close view, we felt so far removed from everything. It was like we were on the dark side of the moon. We saw the same faces all of the time, we had the same routine all of the time; everyone pretty much felt the same. I wouldn't say that again if I were there under the same conditions today. I'd be in the yard, sitting high up on the bleachers, taking in the warm sun, looking out across the bay, and watching the ships and the Golden Gate Bridge. It was the best view from any prison in the world.

When I first arrived on Alcatraz, I was assigned a cell on Broadway on the flats, where new men were kept until they were assigned a job and a regular cell. The guard who walked me to my cell was a big guy named Hart. He had a pleasant voice and as I came into the cellblock, a couple of guys (one was Catalano) started hollering my name, and other guys from Atlanta picked up that I had arrived on Alcatraz. I remember Hart turning to me and saying something like "You're real popular."

Al Capone and I didn't serve time on Alcatraz during the same era, but the prison hadn't changed much by the time I arrived twenty years later. There were a few guards still working from that era, as well as a few men like Karpis who knew Capone, and it wasn't uncommon to see old books, especially some of the classics that

Al Capone was one of the most infamous organized crime figures from the 1930s era. Capone would spend four tough years on Alcatraz among many other famous criminals including Alvin Karpis, Machine Gun Kelly, Doc Barker, and Floyd Hamilton (driver for Bonnie & Clyde).

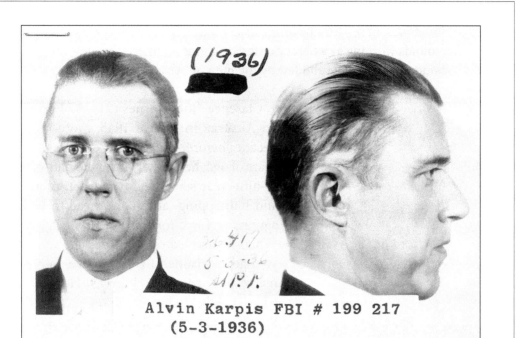

Alvin Karpis FBI # 199 217
(5-3-1936)

Alvin Karpis

had his register number, 85-AZ, on the checkout card. The reputation he carried on the Rock from those who knew him was that he was a pretty brutal guy. He'd beat a couple of his own guys to death with a baseball bat—pretty messy. He was a big figure when I was growing up and I remember the names Capone and Alcatraz were synonymous. I remember the first time seeing Alvin Karpis walk down Broadway and was really struck by it. I'd known his name since my youth and read about him and Capone serving time together on Alcatraz and now here I was, serving time alongside Karpis.

I met Joe Carnes after he introduced himself while he was making his rounds working as a library orderly. He was an interesting guy and considered one of the solid few by the men on Alcatraz.

Clarence "Joe" Carnes

Clarence "Joe" Carnes (714-AZ) arrived on Alcatraz in July of 1945, more than a decade before Bulger. At only eighteen years of age, he was serving a life plus ninety-nine-year sentence for murder, robbery and kidnapping, and had proved to be an aggressive force for the Bureau of Prisons. When he arrived on the Rock, he was the youngest prisoner to ever serve in what many had coined "Hoover's Heaven," a jab at J. Edgar Hoover (a key architect of the Alcatraz model). Carnes was a full-blooded Choctaw Indian who endured a tough childhood growing up in a poverty-stricken Oklahoma household. At only sixteen, Carnes and a school friend attempted to hold up a small gas station. Carnes remembered:

At the age of sixteen, I got involved with a fellow named Cecil Berry and we robbed a service station, and in the process of robbing the service station Cecil shot the attendant. It was more like a self-defense thing, there was a struggle for the gun and in the struggle the attendant was shot.

Both youths were quickly apprehended and locked up in the county jail and charged with first-degree murder. Not long after, they managed to overpower their jailer and escape, but both were recaptured within hours. In October 1943, Carnes was found guilty of first-degree murder and sentenced to serve life in prison. While at the Oklahoma State Reformatory in Granite, Carnes escaped once again. As part of a hard-labor chain gang working in a rock quarry, he and two accomplices escaped, stole a vehicle, kidnapped the owner and committed additional crimes. Their freedom was short-lived and following capture, Carnes received an additional ninety-nine years for larceny and abduction. He was sent first to Oklahoma State Penitentiary in McAlester, and then later to

Clarence "Joe" Carnes. At 18-years of age, he was the youngest convict ever incarcerated at Alcatraz as a federal penitentiary.

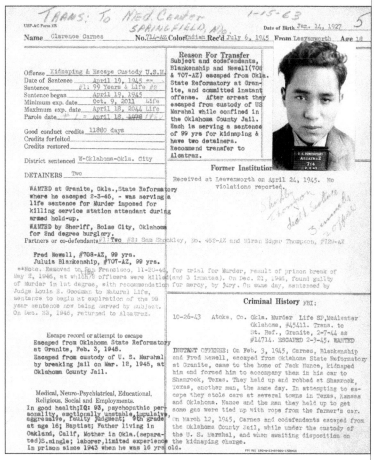

A young 19-year-old Carnes during the murder trial for his role in the 1946 Battle of Alcatraz. His co-conspirators, Miran Thompson and Sam Shockley were given the death penalty and executed sitting side by side in San Quentin's gas chamber. Carnes's life was spared based on his youth and acts of compassion he showed towards officers after being ordered by the ringleaders to finish them off.

Leavenworth. He became a serious disciplinary problem and the warden recommended that he be transferred to Alcatraz. When he first arrived, those who knew him described him as being out of place. He was quiet, easygoing, and rarely involved in altercations. But behind his quiet and easygoing disposition was the reality of a bleak future in prison. Carnes would take part in one of the bloodiest attempts to ever take place on Alcatraz.

The Battle of Alcatraz was one of the most violent escape attempts in the Rock's history. It was an extremely complex escape plan and it leveraged taking advantage of the routines by individual officers. The key element of this plan was to breach the gun gallery and acquire weapons to be used by the conspirators. It would be the only escape to successfully secure weapons and attempt to break out by using brutal violence against officers and taking hostages. On May 2, 1946, the Battle of Alcatraz took San Francisco by storm. All eyes would be focused on the island as the battle raged.

Bernard Paul Coy (415-AZ), was a forty-six-year-old Kentucky bank robber serving out the remainder of a twenty-five-year sentence on the Rock. Bernie, as he was known to friends, devised a clever scheme to climb and break entry into the west gun gallery using a crudely fashioned homemade bar-spreader. Once inside, he hid and ambushed the unsuspecting officer; violently choked and bludgeoned him into unconsciousness, then passed down high-powered weapons to fellow conspirators. Their hostile and murderous impulses became a toxic formula when the prospect of a successful escape faded, and the men decided it was better to be buried dead than buried alive; a metaphor for a life lost when sentenced to serve on Alcatraz.

Despite their complex and thorough planning, their escape was ultimately foiled by the ingenuity of officers, redundancies in security, and a little bit of fortuitous luck when an officer failed to return a key that the inmates needed to make their escape to the prison yard area. The Battle of Alcatraz ended in the deaths of two correctional officers, William Miller and Harold Stites, and the three primary conspirators Bernard Coy, Joe Cretzer and Marvin Hubbard, and later, the court ordered executions of Sam Shockley and Miran Thompson for their roles in the violent deaths of the officers. The jury was sympathetic towards Carnes based on his youth and testimony from officers that he helped spare their lives of those who had been left for dead by the principals. He covertly refrained from following orders to finish them off.... He later remembered:

> I didn't know if they were all alive, but I knew some of them were. I
> went back and said, 'they're all dead,' because at the age of nineteen I
> couldn't see any purpose in this. I'd never seen hate like this before and
> I couldn't see any purpose in hurting anybody—even before the siren

Scenes from the violent 1946 Battle of Alcatraz. Rocket grenades were launched into the cellblock by the United States Marines to battle the prisoners. The Battle of Alcatraz was one of the most vicious prison escape attempts ever recorded in United States history. Reinforcements were brought in from a variety of agencies to help gain back control of Alcatraz Island. They included personnel from the Bureau of Prisons, law enforcement agencies, and the military. Several officers were not only held as hostages, but two officers and three prisoners lost their lives in the bloody battle.

went off—unless it was necessary. Now, if you're struggling up there with a man for the gun and somebody got hurt, that I could see, but just to deliberately shoot and kill other human beings and to do it for no purpose, I didn't agree with that at all.

Carnes was given an additional life sentence to begin upon completing his first sentence, which ultimately would equate to three life sentences plus twenty-five years. He remained on Alcatraz until January of 1963, and many had believed he would serve out the remainder of his life there.

Bulger reminisced:

I came to respect Joe because he weathered the years of prison well … He was only two years older than me, but he seemed twenty years older and much wiser back then. When I first arrived and was assigned a cell on Broadway (C-145), Joe would hang around giving the new guys a run down on the system past and present, the usual stories of the '46 takeover—strikes—riots—escapes, etc. Joe lived on the third tier of C-Block, down the tier from where I'd end up living most of my years on Alcatraz. He'd say hello and deliver the library books from cell to cell. Joe was a good guy who would risk much for friends. I knew he had spent years in the hole and D-Block for his part in the past escape that went bad. He mentioned several friends of mine who were also serving time on Alcatraz, and Joe passed along their messages to say hello.

Bernard Paul Coy

Joseph Cretzer

Marvin Hubbard

Those first few weeks were grueling. I sat idle in my 5x9 foot cell, without any work and on lockdown. Those several weeks went by like years. I was only permitted to come out for three short meal periods and the remaining twenty-three hours lingered. I read whatever I could. Whatever Joe left for me, I read. Books, magazines, rules book; I read it all... At night, all the other cons had headphones to listen to radio programs, but whenever I asked for a pair, I was told they wouldn't be issued until I was given a work assignment. Until then, only reading would be allowed. It felt like a life in slow motion and my memory of sitting in my cell on Broadway remains vivid. The time passed so slowly. Every movement on the corridor caught my attention. The sounds of the

Miran Thompson   Sam Shockley

guards' footsteps, the cells being racked open and closed, counts and
more counts, the changing of guards that took place every eight hours,
on and on and on... Alcatraz was nothing like its reputation. During
the day hours when men were at work, it was quiet. At night the
cellhouse was saturated with the sounds of whispers, toilets flushing,
and guards yelling out their counts to the officer sitting at the desk at
the end of the cellblock. I could see the desk in clear view of my cell,
and the officers would walk over at the beginning of their shifts, grab a
pack of cigarettes, light one, and then sit at the desk reading magazines
from the library.

On Alcatraz, the library was sacred to the men. It was one of
the few means that afforded convicts the ability to mentally escape
their desolate life. As mentioned, I read everything Joe brought to
me. Books, magazines and sometimes pages carefully torn from
contraband articles that somehow made their way into the hands
of a convict. You see these documentaries with experts professing
that those books containing violent subject matter were banned
on Alcatraz. Completely false. I enjoyed westerns, thrillers, crime
mysteries, detective stories, science, and travel subjects; all readily
available in the library to check out. I don't remember any true crime
titles and they certainly didn't carry Sutton's autobiography, but they

had plenty of fictional crime works and everything else you could imagine, even romance novels.

I read for long hours every day. I read all of Mickey Spillane's crime thrillers (very popular among the cons). I lost myself in these books. I spent hours and hours escaping in the prose of so many greats. Several of the older titles had the library checkout label affixed to the inside cover. You'd see the numbers of men like Capone, Stroud and Kelly. Even then, I felt a nostalgic sense of history whenever I'd see Capone's number on the checkout list. Joe would always point out who'd read the book and if it had been checked out multiple times by someone he'd say, "This title endorsed by so and so…" I'd get a sense of getting lost in the same story, having read from the very same pages.

I read so many titles it would be impossible to list them, but Audie Murphy's *To Hell and Back* was a favorite, and of course many of Salinger's works. They had a big collection of Salinger's books and short stories bound from different digests. As Richard Sunday pointed out, I also enjoyed Zane Grey's works…Remarque's *All Quiet on the Western Front* is one I read probably a couple of times. Remarque was a veteran of WWI and the book dealt with the psychological effects of war and how it affected them trying to return to their normal lives after inflicting and suffering through so much violence. I think a lot of guys connected with those types of stories. Those books saved a lot of men. Books, radio and mail were the only things they had that connected them to the outside world.

On the weekends when the others went to the rec yard, they kept me locked down. Broadway was a busy corridor. Guards were constantly walking up and down, going between the main entrance and mess hall. I could see the visitation area from my cell and remember some of the men looked broken after their visits with their wives, kids and family. My family didn't have the financial means to visit, so my connection to home would only be through letters and photos.

"The apartment below mine had the only balcony of the house. I saw a girl standing on it, completely submerged in the pool of autumn twilight. She wasn't doing a thing that I could see, except standing there leaning on the balcony railing, holding the universe together."

From "A Girl I Knew…" — J.D. Salinger Published in The Best American Short Stories, a book carried in the Alcatraz prison library.

The Alcatraz Prison Library

List of library books submitted for approval to purchase -- 1951 supplement.

FICTION

AUTHOR	TITLE	PUBLISHER	PRICE
ADAMS, S.	PLUNDERER	RANDOM HOUSE	$3.00
AMBLER, E.	JUDGEMENT OF DELTCHER	KNOPF	3.00
Arnold, E.	THE COMMANDOS	DUELL	2.50
ARNOLD, E.	FISH AND COMPANY	MACMILLIAN	2.75
ARTHUR, B.	TROUBLE TOWN	DOUBLEDAY	2.50
ASCH, S.	MOTTKE, THE THIEF	PUTNAM'S	2.00
AUSUBEL, N.	A TREASURE OF JEWISH HUMOR	MACMILLIAN	3.00
BAGBEY, G.	COFFIN CORNER	DOUBLEDAY	2.25
BAYER, O.	AN EYE FOR AN EYE	AM. LEND. LIB.	1.50
BARTON, M.	BLOOD RED DEATH	"	1.25
BELLAMAN, H.	FLOODS OF SPRING	SIMON & SCHUSTER	3.00
BISSELL, R. P.	STRETCH ON THE RIVER	CLARKSON	2.25
BRADLEY, M.	MURDER IN MONTANA	DOUBLEDAY	2.50
BRAND, M.	FIGHT'IN FOOL	GROSSET	1.50
BRANDT,	COME HOT, LUCIFER	UNION LIB. ASSN.	1.00
BRICK, J.	THE RAID	FARRAR	3.00
BROWN, W.	DARK DRUMS	APPLETON	3.00
BRUNKER, R.	SHOCKING TALES	UNION LIB. ASSN.	
BUNZAN, J.	LONG DISCOVERY	FARRAR	
BURNETT, W. R.	LITTLE MEN, BIG WORLD		
CARR, J.	DEVIL IN VELVET		
CHRISTIE, A.	THEY CAME TO BAGHDAD		
CLARKE, H.	A LADY NAMED LO...		
CLOSS, H.	LOVE...		
COHEN, O. H.			
COLES, M.			
CONNOLLY, M.			
COXE, G.			
CRANE, F.			
CRANE, E.			
CROCKETT, J.			
DALY, B.			
DAVIS, D.			
DAVIS, F.			
DECKER, D.			
DEWEY, T. B.			
DOLPH, J.			
DRESSER, D.			
EBERHARDT, M. G.			
EGBERT, V.			
ELSTON, A. V.			
ROMINE, R.			
FALSTIEN, L.			
FAWU (LB), D.			
FARRELL, J. T.			
FENNER, E.			
FIELD, P.			
FISCHER, B.			
FORD, L.			
FOX, A.			
FOX, J. S.			
FREY, E.			
FULLER, R. B.	NINE CH...		

AUTHOR	TITLE	PUBLISHER	PRICE
O'DONNEL, E.	GREEN MARGINS	GROSSET	2.50
GELLAICHS, I.	DEATH OF A WHITE WITCH	DOUBLEDAY	1/50
O'MEARA, W.	GRAND PORTAGE	DODD	3.00
O'ROURKE, F.	BONUS ROOKIE	CLARKSON	2.00
PAIGETT, L.	A GNOME THERE WAS	DOUBLEDAY	2.00
PERSALL, F.	TOO HOT TO HANDLE	MORROW	2.50
QUEN, E.	THE ORIGIN OF EVIL	LITTLE	2.50
QUENTIN, P.	THE FOLLOWER	SIMON & SCHUSTER	2.00
RINEHART, M.	HAUNTED LADY	CLARKSON	1.00
RADIGUET, R.	DEVIL IN THE FLESH	UNION LIB. ASSN.	1.00
RING, A.	KILLERS PLAY ROUGH	AM. LEND. LIB.	1.50
ROBERT, C.	THEY WANTED TO LIVE	MACMILLIAN	2.50
NOMAINS, J.	THE DEATH OF NOBODY	AM. LEND. LIB.	2.00
RUMSEY, A.	CRY... THE LOCK	SIMON & SCHUSTER	2.00
SALINGER, J. D.	...IN THE RYE	LITTLE	3.00
SANDO...	...ER	AM. LEND. LIB.	0.50
		DOUBLEDAY	2.00
	...COMING	MAR.& HAR.	2.00
	...THE DON	UNION LIB. ASSN.	1.00
		DOUBLEDAY	2.00
		KNOPF	2.00
		"	2.00
		DUTTON	2.50
			2.50
			2.50
		SIMON & SCHUSTER	2.50
	...DOOR	DOUBLEDAY	1.50
		VIKING	2.00
			2.50
		BOBBS-MERRIL	3.50
		HARPER BRO.	2.50
		UNION LIB. ASSN.	2.50
		CLARKSON	3.00
		CRIME CLUB	2.25
		HARCOURT	2.50
		DIAL	3.50
		CLARKSON	3.00
		CLARKSON	3.00
		NELSON-HALL	2.00
		AM. LEND. LIB.	$0.50
		UNION LIB. ASSN.	1.00
		NELSON-HALL	3.75
		CLARKSON	2.50
		ILC	5.00
		DOUBLEDAY	3.00
		UNION LIB. ASSN.	1.00

AUTHOR	TITLE	PUBLISHER	PRICE	SUBJECT
McGivern, William P.	Heaven Ran Last	Little, Brown	$2.50	Mystery
Malte, Albert	Journey of Simon McKeever	Rinehart	2.75	Character
Mailer, Norman	The Naked and the Dead	Doubleday	4.00	War characters
Mason, F. Van Wyck	Dardenelles Derelict	Harper	2.75	Spy
McSorley, Edward	The Young McDermott	Clarkson	3.00	Character
Manning, Roy	Tangled Trail	Lippincott	.49	Western
Molloy, Robert	Best of Intentions	Am Lend Lib	3.00	Realistic
Mulford, Clarence	Tex	Farrar	.69	Western
Murray, Max	The Queen & the Corpse	Duell	2.50	Mystery
O'Farrell, William	Thin Edge of Violence	Clarkson	2.50	Suspense
O'Hara, John	Rage to Live	MacMillan	3.19	Realistic
Overholser, Wayne	West of the Rimrock	MacMillan	2.50	Western
Philips, James A.	Suitable for Framing	Crowell	2.50	Detective
Poole, Ernest	NancyFlyer	Duell	2.75	Pioneer
Putnam, George P.	Hickory Shirt	Clarkson	.49	Mystery
Queen, Ellery	Four of Hearts	Houghton	2.50	Western
Raine, Wm. MacLeod	Ranger's Luck	Morrow	2.50	Detective
Reach, James	Late Last Night	Random	2.50	Detective
Reilly, Helen	Staircase	Am Lend Lib	.69	Realistic
Reynolds, Quentin	70,000 to 1	Dodd	2.50	Detective
Rhode, John	Shadow of an Alibi	Am Lend Lib	.49	Detective
Ring, Adam	Killers Play Rough	Duell	2.50	Adventure
Rooney, Philip	Golden Coast	Houghton	3.00	Historical
Sabatini, Rafael	The Gamester	Doubleday	2.50	Western
Savage, Les	Doctor at Coffin Gap	Doubleday	3.00	Historical
Schenck, Earl	Weeds of Violence	Doubleday	2.00	Mystery
Scherf, Margaret	Gilbert's Last Toothache	Dial Press	3.00	Realistic
Schulman, Irving	Cry Tough	Clarkson	1.98	Realistic
Scully, Robert	Scarlet Pansy			

AUTHOR	TITLE	PUBLISHER	PRICE	SUBJECT
ALMAN, David	World Full of Strangers			
Carr, John Dickson	Below Suspicion			
Carey, Joyce	Horses Mouth			
Chandler, Raymond	The Little Sister			
Chase, Allan	Shadow of a Hero			
Clark, Walter Van Til.	The Track of the Cat	Do...		
Cumberland, Marten	Man Who Covered Mirrors	Do...		
Cumberland, Marten	Policeman's Nightmare	Dou...		
Cheney, Peter	Dark Wanton	Dodd		
Cheney, Peter	The Dark Street	An Le...		
Cheney, Peter	Try Anything Twice	Dodd		
Clarke, Donald H.	A Lady Named Lou	Am. Lend...		
Clarke, Donald H.	John Bartel, Jr.	"		
Clarke, Donald H.	Millie's Daughter	Clarkson		Character
Clarke, Donald H.	Louis Berretti	Clarkson	.49	Character
Cody, Al	The Big Corral	Dodd	2.00	Western
Cody, Al	Disaster Trail	Dodd	2.00	Western
Coles, Manning	Not Negotiable	Doubleday	2.25	Mystery
Corle, Edwin	In Winter Light	Duell	2.75	Navajo Ind.
Coxe, George H.	Inland Passage	Knopf	2.50	Mystery
Coxe, George H.	Lady Killer	Knopf	2.50	Detective
Crispin, Edmund	Buried for Pleasure	Lippincott	2.50	Mystery
Curtiss, Ursula	Voice out of Darkness	Dodd	2.50	Mystery
Davidson, David A.	Hour of Truth	Random	3.00	Psychological
Davis, Don	Death on Treasure Trail	Morrow	2.00	Western
Davis, H. L.	Beaulah Land	Morrow	3.00	Pioneer
Dawson, Peter	Royal Gorge	Dodd	2.00	Western
Denker, Henry	I'll Be Right Home, Ma	Crowell	2.75	Boxing

AUTHOR	TITLE	PUBLISHER	PRICE	SUBJECT
			.49	Mystery
			.49	Mystery
			.50	Mystery
			.50	Historical
				Romance
				Western
				Western
			2.50	Mystery
			2.50	Western
			2.98	Pioneer
		Farrar	2.50	Mystery
Halliday, Brett	Marked for Murder	Am Lend Lib	.49	Detective
Halliday, Brett	Murder and Married Virgin	Clarkson	.49	Detective
Halliday, Brett	Taste for Violence	Dodd	2.50	Detective
Haycox, Ernest	Rim of the Desert	Clarkson	.95	Western
Hayes, Alfred	Girl on the Via Flaminia	Harper	2.50	Character
Hendryx, James B.	Justice on Halfaday Creek	Doubleday	2.50	Western
Hemingway, Ernest	Men Without Women	An Lend Lib	1.25	Realistic
Hilton, James	Nothing So Strange	"	.89	Character
Hirsch, Richard	Crimes that shook the world	Duell	2.75	Mystery
Holmes, L. P.	Water, Grass and Gunsmoke	Doubleday	2.50	Western
Hopkins, Tom J.	Buzzard Tracks	Doubleday	2.50	Western
Hopkins, Tom J.	The Hard Riders	Doubleday	2.50	Western
Huggins, Roy	Lovely Lady, Pity Me	Duell	2.50	Mystery
Iams, Jack	Do Not Murder Before Christmas	Morrow	2.50	Mystery
Innes, Hammond	The Blue Ice	Harper	2.50	Suspense
Innes, Hammond	Killer Mine	Harper	2.50	Suspense
Jackson, J. H.	San Francisco Murders	Clarkson	2.85	Mystery
Jepson, Selwyn	The Golden Dart	Doubleday	2.25	Mystery

AUTHOR	TITLE	PUBLISHER	PRICE	SUBJECT
Daley, R.	Baxter Bernstein	Clarkson	$2.59	Character
Short, Luke	Ambush	Houghton	2.50	Western
Short, Luke	Fiddlefoot	Houghton	2.50	Western
Sherry, Edna	No Questions Asked	Dodd	2.50	Mystery
Skidmore, Hobart	On Careless Love	Doubleday	2.75	Realistic
Slaughter, Frank G.	Divine Mistress	Clarkson	2.50	Period
Slaughter, Frank G.	The Golden Isle	Am Lend Lib	.39	Historical
Slaughter, Frank G.	That None Shall Die	Doubleday	3.00	Historical
Stanley, Chuck	Off to Laramie	Phoenix	2.00	Western
Steen, Margaret	Twilight of the Floods		3.00	Historical
Sterling, Stewart	Dead Sure	Dutton	2.50	Mystery
Stewart, John Innes	Case of the Journeying Boy	Dodd	2.75	Detective
Stout, Rex	Trouble In Triplicate	Viking	2.50	Mystery
Summers, Richard	Vigilante	Duell	2.50	Real. Hist.
Sylvester, Robert	Dream Street	Am Lend Lib.	.49	Romance
Teilhet, Hildegarde T.	The Assassins	Am Lend Lib.	.49	Adventure
Thomas, Ward	Stranger in the Land	Houghton	3.50	Realistic
Thompson, James M.	Nothing More Than Murder	Harper	2.50	Mystery
Thompson, Thomas	Range Drifter	Doubleday	2.25	Western
Trimble, Louis	Case of the Blank Cartridge	Phoenix	2.00	Mystery
Van de Water, Fred.	Catch A Falling Star	Duell	3.00	Historical
Van Dyke, Tom et al.	Not With my Neck	Am Lend Lib.	.49	Detective
Vickers, Roy	The Whispering Death	Am Lend Lib.	.49	Detective
Weidman, Jerome	Too Early to Tell	"	.49	Character
Wheelwright, Jere	The Wolfshead	Scribners	3.00	Historical Adv.
White, Leslie T.	Lord Johnnie	Doubleday	2.50	Adventure
White, Max	Man who carved women from wood	Clarkson	2.59	Character
White, Max	Tiger, Tiger	Clarkson	.49	Character

NON-FICTION

AUTHOR	TITLE	PUBLISHER	PRICE	SUBJECT
Beebe, William	High Jungle	Duell	$4.50	
Benchly, Robert	The Early Worm	Am Lend Lib.	.49	Humor
	Blackstone's Card Tricks	Clarkson	.98	Magic
Bordeille, Pierre de	Fair and Gallant Ladies	Clarkson	2.49	Biography
Burke, Billie & Shipp, C.	With A Feather on My Nose	Appleton	3.00	Biography
Flesch, Rudolf	Art of Readable Writing	Harper	3.00	Expression
Forrest, Earle R.	Lone War Trail of Apache Kid	Trails End Pub.	3.25	Hist & Biog.
Elwood, Maren	Characters Make Your Story	Clarkson	3.37	Writing
Gilbreth, Frank	Cheaper by the Dozen	Crowell	3.00	Humor
Glick, Carl	I'm a Busybody	Crowell	3.00	Autobiog.
Golden, Francis Leo	For Doctors Only	Fell	2.95	Humor
Hall, Melvin Adams	Bird of Time	Scribners	3.50	True Adv.
Keyn, E. V. ed.	Book of True Stories	Clarkson	.75	Biog.
Jackson, Joseph H.	Bad Company	Clarkson	4.59	Biography
Leighton, Isabel	The Aspirin Age	Simon & Schuster	3.00	Collection
Mencken, H. L.	Mencken Chrestomathy	Clarkson	4.79	Best works
Mead, Margaret	Male and Female	Morrow	3.00	Contrast
Murphy, Audie	To Hell and Back	Holt	3.00	War exper.
Overstreet, H. A.	The Mature Mind	Norton	2.95	Psychology
Reid, Mildred	Make it Sell	Clarkson	1.89	Writing
Smith, H. Allen	Low and Inside	Doubleday	2.50	Sports Humor
Snow, Edward Rowe	Mysteries and Adventures along the Atlantic Coast	Dodd, Mead & Co.	4.00	Strange facts
Sonnichin, C. L.	Roy Bean	Clarkson	3.37	Biography
Spaeth, Sigmund	Music for Fun	Am Lend Lib	1.00	Music
Stern, Bill	Favorite Baseball Stories	Clarkson	.95	Sports
Stern, Bill	Favorite Football Stories	Clarkson	.95	
Stern, Bill	Favorite Boxing Stories	Clarkson	.95	

Despite the official Bureau of Prisons statement and news media reporting that subjects of crime and violence was banned in any form, Bulger's memory of reading materials in the Alcatraz library countered these claims. His perspectives on allowable reading materials lined up with the historical prison records and Alcatraz library catalog. Even a prisoner in a Bureau of Prisons press release photo was depicted reading a crime thriller title in his cell. In addition to a vast collection of reading materials that ranged from subjects such as travel, romance, adventure, suspense and history, the approval list also shows a variety of fictional crime and violence themed titles. Several actual example titles listed on the formal Alcatraz request list submitted by the Acting Alcatraz Warden in 1951, supports Bulger's memory. Titles included:

San Francisco Murders, An Eye for an Eye, Murder in Montana, The Widow had a Gun, Lullaby with Lugers, Book of Crime, Framed in Blood, Back Trail to Murder, Bleed Scissors, Murder is the Payoff, Murder Comes Home, Engaged to Murder, Guns of Arizona, Murder in the Outlands, Wine of Violence, Strangler's Serenade, Do Not Murder Before Christmas, Until You Are Dead, Murder Comes First, Do Evil in Return, Deadly Weapon, Torture Garden, Death of White Witch, Devil in the Flesh, Killers Play Rough, The Big Kill, Vengeance is Mine, Private Killing, Murder Gets Around, Death is my Lover, Murder Can be Fun, The Reluctant Murderer, Policeman's Nightmare, Buried for Pleasure, Lady Killer, Death on Treasure Trail, It's Raining Violence, Murder Up My Sleeve, This is Murder, Layout for a Corpse, Murder City, Taste for Violence, Crimes that Shook the World, Killer Mine, Framed in Guilt, The Base Derby Murder, Murder One, The Naked and the Dead, Killers Play Rough, Weeds of Violence, Vigilante, The Assassins, Nothing More than Murder, The Whispering Death, The Hanging Heiress, Date with Death, Show of Violence and Bad Company.

I looked forward to Joe's daily rounds. Whenever he stopped in front of my cell and offered me reading materials, he gave me the rundown on the routines; inside politics, who to avoid, who could get things, who could help with legal needs, best work assignments, backgrounds on the guards, etc. One day Joe mentions that he'd seen me visit the hospital and whether I'd met a man who was known by fellow convicts as the "Jap." The "Jap" was Tomoya Kawakita, 1059-AZ. I mentioned that I had been up to the hospital and met him, but knowing nothing about him or his crimes, I said "Yes," and that he seemed friendly. When I'd met Kawakita, he was dressed like a doctor in a white lab coat and asked about a con named Lovett, another Alcatraz alumnus who was at Atlanta for the murder of an FBI agent. He asked me how he was doing and whether I'd known him. It was all just friendly conversation.

Joe passed me a book titled *Southwestern Court Reporter* and remarked, "This will tell you all about that bastard." The book included a transcript from an appeal filed by Kawakita, as well as the crimes he'd been charged with and details of the horrendous acts he committed against our soldiers. It was the story of Tomoya Kawakita, AKA the "Meatball." Kawakita was American born but of Japanese ancestry. He was a student in Japan when Pearl Harbor was attacked. He joined the Japanese Army as an interpreter and eventually wound up in a prisoner of war camp for Americans in Japan, where our men were made slaves working in a tin mine. Kawakita was a cruel bastard. Our men were starving and most of them weighed in at about only 100 pounds. They were sickly, dying, and forced to hold heavy rocks and logs until they collapsed. As an example of the cruelty, our men were lined up facing each other and then Kawakita ordered them to fight or be killed. In another merciless act, he kicked two men into an open cesspool and then pushed their heads under with his boot. He would also select American soldiers to follow him into the woods, where they were never to come back or be seen again. Fellow prisoners had suspected that he had cut their heads off with a samurai sword.

The "Meatball" carried a torturous reputation among the American soldiers. He was known to strut around wearing putter style pants, knee-high perfectly shined boots, a short sleeve shirt with a thick belt, and a holstered samurai sword. He was given the nickname "Meatball" because of rumors he favored eating American rations confiscated from U.S. soldiers. He grew fat while our men starved. He would

Tomoya Kawakita

tell them "You bastards will never leave here alive; will never see the United States again, and we will kill all of you…"

When the war was over, Kawakita was listed and hunted as a war criminal. Following his capture and conviction of treason for committing horrific acts against American soldiers, he was directly committed to Alcatraz in 1953. Originally, I think he had been given the death penalty, but the president commuted his sentence to life in prison and he'd been sent to rot on Alcatraz. When I read his words in the appeal, I was sickened over it and all his lies to divert attention from the agony those men suffered while captive. Our family suffered immense pain because of acts similar to Meatball's. My sister Jean had married Joe Toomey, a very tall and fine gentleman who graduated from the U.S. Military Academy at West Point in 1949, and he'd been called to serve during the Korean War. Joe was from South Boston, and he was quickly accepted into our family. All of us liked him and my sister was heartbroken when he shipped off to war. It didn't take long for Joe to receive honors for his acts of bravery. I can still remember it all like yesterday when Jean received a telegram that Joe had been wounded and taken as a prisoner of war. Everything just stopped as we waited for any news of Joe's possible whereabouts and wellbeing. Jean was tortured by the long periods of silence, and when news finally came of his fate, it was horrible. Jean was completely devastated. We'd learned that Joe had been locked up, tortured and left to starve. The once powerful figure that our family admired had been left to waste away to malnutrition. The future with my sister he had probably dreamt of in his final hours were stolen from both of them. Whenever I saw Meatball, I thought of Joe and my sister's suffering by the hands of war criminals like him. At the war's end, Joe was never returned to his family for burial. In my eyes, Meatball was of the same cloth who tortured and murdered my brother-in-law. Joe was a hero and sacrificed everything for our freedom. We all owe him. He's still listed as Missing in Action. A terrible fate.

Kawakita's Alcatraz case file offered the following background:

This American born Japanese man is serving a life sentence for treason. Originally sentenced to death October 5, 1948, in Los Angeles, California, the sentence was appealed and on October 29, 1953, the sentence was reduced by a presidential commutation to life in prison. As an interpreter and foreman at an open pit nickel mine in Japan, he was charged with compelling American prisoners of war to labor in the mine and smelter thereby assisting the Japanese military forces. He beat, abused and attempted to destroy the morale and the physical well-being of members of the armed forces of the United

Bulger's brother-in-law, Joseph Toomey. He graduated from the U.S. Military Academy at West Point in 1949. Toomey was tragically captured during the Korean conflict and held as a prisoner of war. He remains listed as missing in action and was posthumously awarded the Silver Star and Prisoner of War Medals for heroism. Their family suffered immensely from his loss. The caption accompanying his West Point portrait read: "Joe, the M.I.T. Longshoreman with a bit of Boston in his Irish brogue, smiled on the Plain that first day and has been smiling ever since. No one could deny that his gregarious nature and sense of humor made the rough spots smoother and the high spots higher. He showed us a heart, too large for his 6-foot frame, and a determination to fill each day with his best, something superior."

States. He was committed directly to this institution on November 3, 1953, and becomes eligible for parole on October 28, 1968.

Reared in Calexico, California, he was the only son of a Japanese immigrant parentage but has three sisters who were born in the United States. His father and mother now both deceased, the father was a successful merchant, and the subject had an opportunity to complete high school. He had no prior criminal charges.

Kawakita's appeal to President Harry Truman stated the following in part:

I have been confined in Alcatraz prison, itself, since October 8, 1948. I believe that executive clemency in my case would help the relationship between the United States and Japan who, from time to time have written on my behalf. I have now served longer than Tokyo Rose, who broadcasted directly to soldiers during the war and longer than any of the prisoners of war who were sentenced, growing out of occurrences at Camp Oeyama, where I was sent as an interpreter during the war.

Mr. President, you as a former military man will clearly understand the situation. I was born in Calexico, California, and went to grammar and high school there. Then my father wanted me to prepare for foreign trade and commerce between the United States and Japan and thought this would also be an opportunity for me to visit his father who was then in his 80's. I went to preparatory school in Japan in preparation of entering Meiji University.

When the war broke out, I was one of the few Japanese who could speak English fluently by reason of grammar and high school training. I was virtually drafted into the service of the government when the company for whom I was working, and its employees were drafted under the Japanese law called the Total Mobilization Act. I was called upon to interpret between the American prisoners of war brought to Japan from the Philippine Islands and the Japanese officers at a prisoner of war camp established at Oeyama. I took orders from Japanese superiors. Often, the American and English prisoners blamed me for the orders that I was merely interpreting from Japanese officers.

The acts for which I was convicted, in retrospect, must indeed look very trivial to Your Excellency, who served as an officer of the United States Navy during the war. Principally, I was charged with trying to make prisoners of war work who were not working. They were, under the Hague Treaty, required to perform sufficient work at least to pay for their meals and upkeep. I was also charged with assisting Japanese officers and guards in the punishment of American soldiers. Unfortunately, the guards only spoke Japanese and since I interpreted their orders, the blame for these demands fell on me rather than on the guards who issued them, and the hatred that apparently these men developed against these guards was transferred to me. This, of course, was wartime and the guards were very strict, but I also suffered the wrath of these guards, all of whom have been released from prison camps in Japan.

It would do no good for me to replay my innocence of the charges for which I stand convicted and have suffered fourteen long years of punishment. All of the acts of which I stand convicted, under careful analysis would amount to no more than assault and battery. It would have been deemed the mildest kind of punishment which the American Army inflicted on prisoners in its own encampments. Assaults by guards towards prisoners are practiced even today in prisons in the United States for disciplinary measures-not charged with treason (giving aid and comfort to the enemy of today's Cold War) or even brought to court on assault charges.

I have now suffered fourteen long years, but for the fact that I was born in the United States, with which I had no choice, I would not have been subjected to this trial and severe punishment in Alcatraz.

Kawakita being led to a Los Angeles court on charges of treason for his brutal treatment of American prisoners in Japanese prisoner of war camps during World War II. He was convicted and sentenced to death in 1948, but his sentence was later commuted to life in prison by President Eisenhower. It was the first case of treason ever tried in Southern California and the coverage was headline news throughout the trial. During Kawakita's indictment hearing, more than 100 veterans came forward willing to testify.

Bulger remembered:

The "Meatball" worked in the hospital as both a dental and medical assistant. They trained him to handle minor procedures. He had good food and drinks like fruit juice and coffee. It was the best job on the Rock. He was even able to shower and sleep in the hospital, not in a 5x9 foot cell like the rest of us. He had a cell on the flats of C-Block with all his belongings, but I don't remember him ever residing in that cell. He was always in the hospital and did easy time. The Alcatraz authorities made life too easy for him considering what he did to our men. I could never understand why he wasn't held in D-Block segregation. Robert Stroud (Birdman of Alcatraz) spent all of his time in isolation during all his years on Alcatraz. In my book, Stroud was an angel compared to Meatball.

When I read the story of Kawakita, I was angry. The next time I was up in the hospital, Kawakita saw me and gave me a friendly greeting. I told him, "You rotten bastard...I'll do anything I can to make your fucking life miserable, you cowardly bastard." The guard and the medic tried to shut me up and Kawakita jumped back.

Guards and cons alike despised him. Lawrence Bartlett, an ex-Army veteran who we all called Sarge, was in charge of the clothing room. Bartlett loathed Kawakita and he would make an audible growl whenever Meatball came down for clean clothes. The cons always gave him a deserving greeting, usually a veiled threat during the rare times you'd see him in the cellhouse or basement. There was a song by a famous comedic musician who was popular on the radio (later identified by Bulger as "You're a Sap Mr. Jap" by Spike Jones). His music was piped in on the Alcatraz radio system often and always got a lot of laughs from the men. I'm guessing he must have written it during World War II, but his band recorded a song which had been written to insult or ridicule the Japanese during the war. Can't describe it exactly, but it had wacky sounds in it like cowbells, and very similar in tone to the men hitting their prison issue tin cups against the bars or striking them with other objects and making those sounds.

Though Meatball lived, showered and ate in the hospital, he still walked through the cellhouse and down into the shower room area in the basement to get his clothes. He always came down to the shower room alone, and sometimes a guard would stand at the top of the stairs to watch over everything. This song is offensive by today's standards, but I remember guys singing it as they'd pass Meatball.

Cons didn't know all the words, so sometimes they'd make up their own lyrics. Once when I was working in the clothing issue, guys made up a chorus line waving towels and singing the song so loud it filled the shower room area and echoed like in a music hall. It looked like

Robert Stroud, the Birdman of Alcatraz. Stroud served 17 years on Alcatraz on two murder charges. He would spend his entire term in isolation status.

something out of a Broadway musical! Meatball looked to the guards for safety, but they just broke a grin and didn't come to his rescue. They allowed the men to burn off steam and have their fun at his expense. They'd pause and then gave a slight wave to signal him to keep moving toward the counter. I always tried to be the one to give him his clothes. I'd toss them in his face and curse at him... He'd just keep his head down without making eye contact and then try to make his way back upstairs into the cellhouse. I couldn't do more than that, but it was a reminder to him that we didn't forget. Years later when I visited Alcatraz as a tourist with my girlfriend, that song played in my head as we walked through the shower room. I can remember it like it was yesterday. I can still hear the voices of the men singing and the echoing of that song throughout the basement. It's hard to describe but standing in that space; a place I spent so many hours, it brought back a flood of memories.

Kawakita finally paid the price when he decided to make a bold move and come onto the yard on a weekend. I remember I was shocked to see him walking along the C-Block corridor when the cons were starting to file through the door. I was a distance behind him, and just as he started to ascend the main stairwell leading to the top of the bleachers, Carl Rosen (1394-AZ), punches him in the head, appearing to knock loose several teeth and then walks up and

Carl Rosen

kicks him in the head. Kawakita had taken a hard beating with heavy blood loss coming from his mouth. The guards descended onto the yard in a storm of force, and both were dragged away. To the men, Rosen was a hero as Kawakita had tortured so many U.S. soldiers and put them through so much pain. We never saw Kawakita much after that.

I don't remember when Meatball finally left the Rock, whether it was before or after me, but one time I was brought into the visitation room where the families sit and visit on opposite sides of thick bulletproof

An Alcatraz report describing injuries Kawakita sustained following a violent assault on the Alcatraz recreation yard by fellow convict Carl Rosen.

Administrative
Form No. 7i

UNITED STATES DEPARTMENT OF JUSTICE,
BUREAU OF PRISONS

U.S. Penitentiary

Alcatraz, California
(Location)

Date 2/27/60 , 19

REPORT OF ACCIDENT, INJURY, EMERGENCY DRESSING OR EMERGENCY TREATMENT
(Of Anything but the Most Trifling Character)

Register No. 1059 Az. Name KAWAKITA Cell Location

Brought to hospital 2 27 60 11:00 a.m./p.m.
Month Day Year Hour

Nature of injury, condition, etc. Contusions and lacerations of upper and lower lip, Fractures of central incisors, Maxilla.

The following history was obtained Inmate states that █████ struck him in the face without provocation, while they were in the recreation area.

Nature of treatment given Wounds cleansed and sutured. U S P H S Hospital was called and Dr. Wayne Dean responded and came to the Island and removed the central incisors from the Maxilla.

Was he admitted to hospital   YES   NO

Was he given quarters   YES   NO   How many days

About how long will he be incapacitated for his usual work two days.

Signature of attending physician

FPI—LK—4-2-54—5,000—779

5USC552(b)(6)

glass. Warden Madigan wanted to meet with me and there was a desk where we could talk in private. When they brought me there to wait, Kawakita was sitting in the same room by himself and then the next thing I know, we were both left in there alone together. A guard was watching us through a control room window and staring at both of us. Meatball was sitting there in a full business suit, and I guess they were getting ready to take him for a court hearing. Somehow, he knew I was from Boston and tried to make small talk. Looking back, maybe it was my accent, but I remember thinking how does he know where I'm from? I told him to turn around and shut the fuck up. That was that... My big regret is to not have risked it all and made him pay the price. Not long before the assassination, President Kennedy commuted Meatball's sentence and forced him out of the United States. I was glad he was off our soil.

Charlie Hopkins, 1186-AZ, remembered:

I think one of the Spike Jones songs that Whitey might have been thinking of was about Hitler and titled "Der Fuehrer's Face." John Duncan (1359-AZ) played old records on the weekends from a cell in A-Block that was amplified loudly over the intercom speaker system in the cellhouse. There was another convict Kenneth Frazier (1077-AZ), a military prisoner who was in for unlawfully killing a Korean sometime during the war. I remember that Frazier liked Hitler and he told Duncan if he didn't stop playing this song, he was going to whip his ass. In regard to Kawakita, I got to know him pretty well. I celled in B-140, Allen West's cell in the 1962 escape. Kawakita was in B-136 and John Dekker in B-138, the same cell that Frank Morris escaped. Nobody messed with Kawakita during the time I knew him because he hung out with Red Lovett. Red was serving time for the murder of an FBI agent and was well respected by the other cons. After Red transferred to Atlanta, Kawakita was left to his own accord, and everything changed.

Kenneth Frazier

CF

BUREAU OF PRISONS GA PLS

TO MR. WILKINSON

FROM WARDEN MADIGAN, USP, MCNEIL ISLAND, WASH

ON SATURDAY EVENING I TALKED TO A MR. CORONAGO, REPRESENTING A JAPANESE NEWSPAPER IN WASHINGTON, D. C. HE HAS KEPT ABREAST OF THE KAWAKITA MATTER AND TOLD ME HE WAS IN TELEPHONIC COMMUNICATION WITH HIS PAPER IN TOKYO. HE ADVANCED THE THOUGHT THAT TOKYO WAS LOOKING FOR SOME OVERTURE ON THE PART OF OUR STATE DEPARTMENT BEFORE MAKING A DECISION TO ACCEPT KAWAKITA. JAPANESE PROTOCOL MAY REQUIRE SOMETHING OF THIS NATURE BUT OUR STATE DEPT MAY NOT FEEL THAT WAY. IT IS PASSED ON FOR WHAT IT IS WORTH. WE ARE STILL KEEPING KAWAKITA IN A CELL EXPECTING RELEASE SOMETIME HOWEVER JOHN BOYD I\\\\ I. 30113 8///// JOHN BOYD I. N. S. DOES NOT FEEL IT IS IMMINENT BY ANY MEANS. KAWAKITA HAS EXECUTED A REQUEST FOR A VISA AND WE HAVE SENT IT TO MR. TAKASUGI, CONSUL GENERAL IN SEATTLE. THAT IS WHERE IT STANDS TODAY.   END OR GA PLS
2833
WILL DELIVER MESSAGE   TU OUT

Sent
9-12-63
2:20
P
Long

Now, therefore, be it known, that I,
John F. Kennedy, President of the United States of America, in consideration of the premises, divers other good and sufficient reasons me thereunto moving, do hereby remit the ten-thousand dollar ($10,000.00) fine and commute the aforesaid life sentence to expire at once on condition that the said Tomoya Kawakita be deported to Japan and that should he ever be found within the territorial limits of the United States that he be committed to serve the remainder of the aforesaid life sentence.

In testimony whereof I have hereunto signed my name and caused the seal of the Department of Justice to be affixed.

Done at the City of Washington this twenty-fourth day of October in the year of our Lord One Thousand Nine Hundred and Sixty-three and of the Independence of the United States the One Hundred and Eighty-eighth.

By the President:

Attorney General

FILE
DEC 5 1963
Bureau of Prisons

President John F. Kennedy commuted Kawakita's life sentence under condition for deportation to Japan and never to be allowed to return to American soil. It would be one of the final acts of Kennedy before his assassination in 1963. Former Warden, Joseph Madigan would also assist in the arrangements and planning with the Attorney General Robert Kennedy for his release from prison.

Kawakita dressed like a doctor in a white lab coat when he worked in the hospital at Alcatraz. Whitey and Lovett were friends at Atlanta before he transferred to Alcatraz. When Whitey came to Alcatraz and figured out who Kawakita was, he cursed him out and didn't hold back what he thought of him.

Bulger:

The men of Alcatraz may have been criminals, but they never lost their sense of country. They were patriots and you had to admire that. There was a special pride in how we handled the Army's laundry. We all shared a deep respect for those men serving our country and that pride showed in their dedication. I remember holding the soldier's uniform shirts and having real sense of appreciation when I would look at their worn patches and sewn insignias. Meatball would have been a trophy kill had he ever found himself alone among any of the cons who were serving a life sentence. You have to keep in mind that it was his crimes against our country that singled him out, not his race. While everything was reasonably segregated on Alcatraz, remember it was the late 1950s–1960s and a lack of segregation would have caused tension, but all of us maintained a sense of respect towards one another. We never singled a person out or started a fight because of their skin. It didn't work like that. A good example was Wayne Fong who celled next to the Anglin brothers on the flats of B-Block. He lived in the last cell and was always the last guy to eat in the mess hall. I didn't know his nationality, only that he came from an Asian ancestry. Lieutenant Severson would call him over using derogatory names like "Fong Fu" and the guys would always come to his defense. Wayne was of short and very thin stature, but he never cowered and always extended his hand to shake if you looked straight at him. Fong kept to himself. I didn't know what he was serving time for, but the word among the guys was he had been involved in a famous murder trial up in Oregon for killing a young woman. Apparently, he was acquitted, but they got him on another rap. The warden was trying to recruit him into a passman role, a servant for the warden. Cons were always leery about the men who worked as passmen. Fong rejected the offer, and this earned respect. He also kept the Morris and Anglin escape to himself. He didn't put his nose into other peoples' business, and no one bothered him. The point here is that we gave respect based on substance, not skin.

Wayne Fong, who was one of the last prisoners ever sent to Alcatraz in April of 1962, resided in B-156, the end cell of B-Block and only a few cells away from John and Clarence Anglin who disappeared in June 1962 during the famed Great Escape from Alcatraz. Wayne was arrested in 1958 as a principal in a heroin drug ring that was described by federal agents as the biggest narcotic operation on the West Coast during that era. He was paroled in 1970 but returned to the criminal drug trade and only three years following his release from prison, he was again convicted on drug related charges. Fong, along with his wife had been central figures in a scandalous 1954 murder trial involving the death of a teenage babysitter in Portland, Oregon. Both were never convicted despite a retrial, but Wayne's own fate was permanently sealed when in 1976, he died at only 47 years of age under suspicious circumstances following an apparent "fall in the shower" at McNeil Island, a federal prison located in Washington State.

I later thanked Joe for pulling my coat to the "Jap." Joe's act of exposing Kawakita was something that I considered patriotic and a good gesture on his part. That was my way of seeing it and I appreciated it. Joe was only in his early 30s, but he was older in his wisdom.

I never made peace with any of the war criminals on Alcatraz, or any other prison where I served time. When I was at Atlanta, Rudolf Abel, the Soviet KGB master spy who was convicted of espionage against the United States, was being held in the upstairs segregation unit alongside Frank Morris, Richard Sunday, Charlie Catalano, John Paul Scott and me. I know he was in general population at some point, but at this time they must have thought Abel would have been targeted by the other cons if he'd been released to the general population. They kept him under close watch and separated from everyone else. He had a job but worked minimal hours. I recall that he and Frank spoke often throughout the day, but quietly amongst themselves and I never asked what they talked about. Morris was quiet and a deep thinker, and his curiosity being celled next to someone convicted of espionage was likely intriguing to him. Morris subscribed to various science periodicals and his conversations probably were around these types of subjects. He had a quick mind and loved to do crossword puzzles out of the newspaper.

Fred Wilkinson, the Atlanta warden who later became the Assistant Director of the Bureau of Prisons had a big role in the spy exchange when Abel was released back to the Soviets. Outside of the escape, Wilkinson was one of the best wardens I ever got to know. He was a tough former marine. He was tough, but always fair. He'd been wounded during the bloody Battle of Iwo Jima where over 6,000 men were killed in action in only a six-week period. The cons called him "Friendly Fred" and he had lots of facial scars and would walk the yard in Atlanta by himself along with his friendly dog. He was well respected by the convicts and being a student of military history, I had great respect for him.

I remember Wilkinson would come into segregation to see Abel and they'd talk so quietly no one could hear the exchange. I think it was Charlie who joked that Abel was teaching him to speak Russian and we'd all laugh. We were all on restricted diets in isolation, but Abel always had a secret stock of hard coffee candy. They were those

Soviet KGB Master Spy, Rudolf Abel.

Name	ABEL, RUDOLPH IVANOVICH					No.	80016-A	
Alias	/FOREIGN AGENT W/O NOTIFYING SEC.OF STATE							
Crime	CONSP.TO.TRANS.INFOR.TO A FOREIGN NATION & ACTING AS/							
District	E-N.Y.				Race	WHITE	Age	57
Sentence:	30 Yrs.	X Mos.	X Days		Fine and Costs: $	3000.00		
Date		11 - 15 - 57			Committed Fine YES Not Committed			
Sentence begins		11 - 15 - 57			Rate per mo. g.t.		10 DAYS	
Committed to Fed. Inst.		5 - 29 - 58			Total g.t. possible		3600 "	
Elig. for parole		*4 - 9 - 68			Extra g.t.		24 "	
Expires w/g.t.		*6 - 1 - 78			G.T. forfeited or withheld Federal Detention			
Expires (extra-part) g.t. XX		*5 - 8 - 78			G.T. restored Headquarters, New York City, N.Y.			
Expires full term		*4 - 9 - 88			Date of release FEB 7 - 1962			
Full term less 180 days		*10 - 12 - 87			Method of release			
Residence	NEW YORK, N.Y.	*147 DAYS INOPERATIVE ON APPEAL						
Name	ABEL, RUDOLPH IVANOVICH					No.	80016 - A	

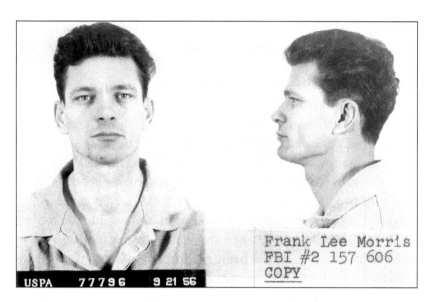

Frank Lee Morris
FBI #2 157 606
COPY

USPA 77796 9 21 56

Frank Lee Morris during his imprisonment at USP Atlanta in 1956. He would be transferred to Alcatraz in 1960.

candies that you can still buy in those bulk bins at the grocery store. How and where did he always get those? He always had a large stock! Somehow, I'd end up with a few when they'd be tossed into my cell and admittedly, I'd savor them. I vividly remember the taste all these years later. Wilkinson was a tough warden, but I liked him.

Another good friend of mine was Red McGraw (1406-AZ). He had also served time at Atlanta, and he knew Rudolph. Red was plotting an escape and Abel tried to insert himself and asked if he could take part. He offered to get them into Mexico, and then from there over to Russia with a new identity, money and freedom. For patriotic reasons Red declined. He told me all about this when we worked together in the clothing room at Alcatraz.

Just before I was released, I remember asking Wilkinson about the exchange, and whether he'd been a part of it. That was important history to our Country. He confirmed what I'd heard, and that he'd accompanied Abel to Berlin to help oversee

Red McGraw

the swap for the American U-2 spy plane pilot, Francis Gary Powers. Francis had been shot down by a missile when he was flying through Soviet airspace and became a prisoner of war after bailing out of his aircraft. There was a bridge that connected East and West Germany and Wilkinson stayed with Abel until he was handed over to the Soviets.

Charlie Hopkins remembered Abel: "In 1961 I transferred back to Atlanta and was celled on the fourth tier of B-Cellhouse. By that time, Rudolph Abel was in the main population and had to pass my cell at least two times each day, so I saw him as he'd leave for work in the industries and for meals. He was a real good artist and he'd look over at me and straight into my eyes, but we never spoke. I was in the hospital and awaiting transfer to Springfield when I heard on the hospital radio that he was at the bridge in Berlin and being swapped. It was the talk of the men back then."

Bulger :

Morton Sobell (996-AZ) was hated by most in the prison population and accepted by the rejects. Frank Hatfield and Harvey Carignan (a.k.a. The Want Ad Killer) saw him as a friend, but these guys were also despised by most. At Atlanta, I can list those who tolerated Sobell—all fellow communists—and every one of them was a cut above "Morty" and it was obvious. Kurt Ponger, Rudolf Abel, Irving Potash and a couple more would meet in the hospital where most of them worked. They all praised Stalin. I'd always mention to them his pact with Hitler which was necessary for the invasion of Poland, Lithuania, Latvia and Estonia. It was Hitler who broke the pact and Stalin almost immediately surrendered territory in the first days of the invasion of Russia. It was only Hitler who wanted it all, so no deal. Also, every one of the above were Jewish and Stalin was ready to purge all of the Jewish doctors in Russia. He died just as it was to become law. Still these guys revered him.

I kind of liked Ponger as a person but despised his views of communism. He was an espionage agent for the KGB. He used to encourage me to write a book after I was released from prison on the LSD study. One thing I did like about him was that he didn't push his views on everyone like some of the others. He worked in the hospital as a dental assistant. In fact, he did dental work on me and once filled a cavity. On weekends when there was no staff working, he'd handle

Atom Spy, Morton Sobell.

many of the urgent procedures for fillings and extractions. He learned the dentistry trade all at Atlanta! He had a medical kit and would travel to the prison farm and do all the dental work there. Ponger was a really bright guy but a dedicated communist, so most avoided him. I remember the day he received the telegram that his wife had died. I felt bad for him. He didn't show any emotion and carried on, so I kept silent. He was a proud guy who had come from Austria. I despised traitors against our Country, but their role in history was interesting

Kurt Ponger being led to court in New York on espionage charges in 1953.

to me. The dental work held up well and the filling he did lasted until I went on the run more than thirty years later.

After prison, I had heard that Morton Sobell, the Soviet spy and codefendant of Julius and Ethel Rosenberg, had been released. I'd heard he lived on the East Coast for a long time and then relocated to San Francisco. Interesting he didn't defect to Moscow and the truth was that once he knew there was a pending warrant for his arrest, he instead fled to Mexico City. The feds finally captured him, and the rest is history. I later read the *New York Times* article where he confessed his guilt. The headline "I'm Guilty—I was an Atom Spy." Had I seen him while I was first on the run—he wouldn't have given that interview. I'll bet he sold the story…

I always felt so many U.S. servicemen died in the Korean War and that spy ring was responsible for many of their deaths. Had they not spied for Russia, it probably would have taken them an additional ten years and billions to develop their own Atom Bomb. Without it, they would have never wanted or allowed the proxy war. Sobell and his partner were lowlifes! David Greenglass made a deal to save his life by testifying against Julius and his own sister Ethel! On Alcatraz, Sobell was hated…Frank Hatfield was his friend and a fellow liberal, and he loved to tell the story of "Morty." In interviews, Morty was always exaggerating the conditions and racist atmosphere of the Rock. He was loud, foul mouthed and loved to put America down.

While on the lam, I always looked for him in the parks where the elderly played chess. I had read that was how he spent a lot of his free time. If I saw him, I planned to execute him. I had come to the conclusion that he played a big part in Stalin giving Mao Zedong the go ahead on the proxy Korean War because they had the A-Bomb. As a veteran and proud American, this was a subject that was always very close to home for me. My family and our neighborhood were profoundly affected by the war. We have a memorial with local guys who died in that war including my sister's husband, West Point Class of 49', Joe Toomey, Lt. 1st Cavalry Division. My close friends Joe Thompson, 187 Reg. Combat Team and Paul Foley, U.S. Marines also gave their lives as the ultimate sacrifice for the pursuit of freedom. Guys I can remember as if I saw them a week ago. I wanted to pay Sobell off when he was serving time in Atlanta, but I hate to admit it, back then I wasn't willing to pay the price. After I went on the run and was a fugitive, it would have been him paying the price. Lucky for him it never happened and as I said, he's lucky we never crossed paths…I saw the photo in your first book (*Alcatraz: A History of the Penitentiary Years*), showing him smiling on the ferry going back to visit Alcatraz. Seeing that photo of him sickens me. Glad I wasn't on that boat with him that day.

The only other convict I remember as being despised to that degree was Dr. Spears (1493-AZ), and no one hated him more than Mickey Cohen. Whenever Spears walked within sight of him, Mickey would get right up in his face, poke his finger into his chest and tell him to count his days. I remember once as we were filing out to the rec yard, just as we walked under the gun gallery, Mickey shoved him so hard he went to the floor. The guards rush over, and Cohen said something like, "I slipped into that piece of shit and I'm going to be carrying his stench on me until I can shower." The guards helped Spears up and told Cohen to move on.

Robert Spears was a terrorist type criminal and Cohen saw him as one of the lowest breeds. Spears admitted that he had planted a bomb on a National Airlines flight killing everyone on board after departing from Tampa, Florida. He was responsible for killing forty or fifty people in what later turned out

Robert Spears

to be a life insurance scam. He'd actually killed his crime partner in the scheme by hiding an explosive device in a carry-on, or other luggage, and it detonated over the Gulf of Mexico killing everyone on board the plane. Apparently, his partner had no idea of the plot and died along with everyone onboard. Doc talked a big game about his life in crime. He told stories about being an aviator during the First World War, a doctor, a hypnotist and bragged to anyone who'd listen that he'd made hundreds of thousands in counterfeiting and other money schemes. The men didn't tolerate the killing of innocent women and children and my memory was that his wife later felt he'd hypnotized his crime partner to board the flight with a bomb. Sounds a bit ridiculous to me.

He was a low life and whenever he tried to make conversation, I'd tell him to take a walk.

Going back to Joe Carnes, he lived on the third tier of C-Block, just down from me. He'd say hello and deliver the library books from cell to cell. We'd talk about episodes of Alcatraz's past—attempted breaks, books, sports, etc.... Joe was a friendly guy, but at that time we didn't know each other all that well. I knew he'd spent years in the hole and D-Block for his part in the '46 escape. I lifted weights all the time in the yard. On Sundays, I'd mostly just walk and talk, or relax on the bleachers looking out at the Golden Gate. Carnes played handball—I seldom talked to him. Just a word here or there.

One Sunday night I was listening to "Groucho Marx" cracking jokes on the radio in my cell (we had earphones and the choice of listening to two stations) and he got me laughing really hard. All of a sudden, I could hear Carnes hollering real loud, I pulled off my earphones and asked the guy in the next cell "What's up with Carnes?" He said he's flipping out and threatening to kill someone in the morning. I asked "who?" and he said "you"—"He thinks you're laughing at him!" Well, I wasn't going to try a long-range explanation. That would look like I was copping out, so I told the guy in the next cell, "Fuck him...I'll be ready..." I was in good physical condition and would fight if it had to be—so come morning I stepped out onto the tier and Joe and I get into to it. A fall from the third tier would have meant certain death, so replayed the fight in my head over and over to be as prepared as I could be.

When the cell doors racked open, I charged towards him and grabbed both his wrists figuring he had a knife. I bashed him hard into the bars of the cell door. But I quickly realized that he didn't have much strength (likely from a sedentary life behind bars) and wasn't too difficult to restrain. This is not a knock on him, only a truthful observation. While holding him down, I told him I wasn't laughing at him, I was laughing at Groucho on the radio and that he needed to cool down. It was all over in a matter of seconds. He just looked up and said "Aw—I was just uptight."

It was also at this point that I knew some of the guards hated Joe. As I was holding him down and during the struggle, my eye caught a guard in the gun gallery watching us. For just a flash, he seemed like he was green lighting me to hurl him over the tier. Joe's cell was on the end and eventually the guys bunched up behind us and blocked the view. It ended quickly and we went off to the mess hall without being stopped or questioned by any of the guards. Considering all he had been through in his life, I harbored no ill will. I always respected him. Joe was a proud guy. Solid. A guy who could be trusted. Most guys felt the same way about him—so a minor scuffle and it was over and a non-issue. At times he was a bit neurotic and bitter against whites, but I never focused on that. I never lost sight of his young years in D-Block, only being in his early twenties and that helped bring him to where he was in life. Those were only flashes of emotion, frustration, regret, and hate filled memories that would surface from time to time.

The guards who disliked Joe held grudges stemming from the '46 escape. Fred Mahan for one, never let it go. He always stared him down and he didn't soften or hide his threats. During the break, Joe had a baton that he'd taken off one of the guards. He carried the club and used it to keep the hostage officers quiet. When Joe would walk by him, Mahan would make comments under his breath such as "I've got your club right here, motherfucker…" I asked Joe why some of the guards taunted him. He told me about Mahan coming to his cell after the officers stormed the cellhouse. He remembered that after Coy, Cretzer and Hubbard were killed, he thought he was going to be shot dead in his cell. He said he was sitting on the toilet, heard a noise and looked up; Mahan had a .45 caliber pistol pointed straight at him through the bars. He thought it was the end of him, but Mahan just stoically gestured with a wave of the pistol and walked him over to A-Block. Mahan just walked casually through the cellhouse with the pistol in his hand for all the convicts to see. Think about that. That was unheard of to have guns in the cellhouse. He felt like Mahan was looking for a reason to take him out. Seems hard to imagine a guard walking through the cellhouse with a pistol, but that was the mindset, and they were looking for any excuse to kill Joe. He thought they were either taking him somewhere to shoot him with no witnesses or take him down in the dungeon and leave him to rot and starve in the darkness. The old timers talked about the '46 break all the time. Joe earned my full trust…He never let it get to him and always went about his own business.

Later when Frankie Morris and the Anglin brothers were working on what became the famous escape, I knew Carnes was in the picture. He was trusted, and considering he was in the plot and alerting guys to the "Jap," caused me to consider him a real good guy. Many years later, I learned that Joe re-offended and that he was back in the federal prison hospital located in Springfield, Missouri. I sent him $500 for

Correctional Officers Fred Mahan (L) and Philip Bergen (R) standing on Broadway in the 1950s.

his commissary account and told him to write or call me anytime. So, Joe called, and I recognized his voice right away. I was really glad to hear from him. He explained he had received a large sum of money that had come from a made-for-TV movie about his life. Sadly, it was all too much. Wanting freedom, he broke parole and went off to San Diego—booze, women and later broke. Finally pinched and sleeping on a park bench, he had little chance to make it straight. Joe told me he had been paid more than $30,000 for his story. For a time, he was a celebrity and thought the stream of money would last forever. Many so-called friends borrowed money and took advantage of him. He ended up drinking heavily and found himself sleeping on a park bench and homeless. He'd felt guilty he'd lost all his money on booze and women. I reassured him that it was his money and it made for some well-deserved happiness and carefree moments after so many years of suffering. I explained that regrets are useless and there were better days ahead when he got out. When we spoke, he told me when he was getting out in a couple of months—I told him I'd meet him in a limo on the front stairs and buy him a Cadillac of his choosing. I wanted to help him get back on his feet. He asked me if I was serious, and I explained I was completely serious and wanted to help.

Julius "Jess" Blankenship

He told me that things were going good for him and that he heard that I was doing well as "Alcatraz's most successful graduate." I had talked with Joe only days before his death and there was no detecting he was that bad off. He talked of the future, and I had him in good spirits. During our call, he told me how Jess (Julius) Blankenship (707-AZ), a close associate, was stabbed to death over a gambling debt in prison. I knew him in Atlanta before shipping off to the Rock along with his close friend and another Alcatraz alumni, John Eklund (775-AZ). Blankenship was a powerfully built guy. He always had a smile and the opposite personality of his friend Eklund. It was an odd friendship, and they would amble around the yard together talking on weekends. I knew them both well. I remember Eklund being a really intelligent, well-spoken convict who had attempted a string of brazen prison escapes. I think he'd come from the Washington D.C. area. He was hated by the colored convicts,

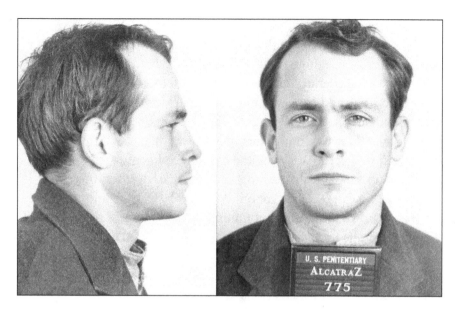

John Eklund

and he'd been convicted of something like five racially motivated murders. Violent and senseless killings...Eklund was hateful towards the colored convicts and was always trying to start a fight for no reason, so I made an effort to keep a good distance. I didn't share that attitude and gave everyone respect unless they gave me a reason otherwise. He reminded me a lot of Jack (Twining). He was thin in statue and looked bookish, but he had a violent temper and thrived on instigating race clashes. Senseless and baseless from my view.

When Bulger learned that prison officials had buried Carnes in a pauper's grave, he located Joe's family and offered to move Joe's body to an Indian cemetery where he could be properly laid to rest with his own family. He purchased Carnes "the most beautiful and expensive copper and bronze top casket," and then had his body exhumed and transferred to the Isaac Billy Cemetery, a traditional Indian burial ground located in Atoka County, Oklahoma. Bulger stopped at no expense and personally made the arrangements for the burial ceremonies. He remembered the undertaker being perplexed by what seemed an extraordinary gesture considering he'd already been buried. He recalled:

The undertaker couldn't understand "why a businessman in Boston would do this for an Indian?" I explained that Joe was a good friend of mine and a good person. He asked about how we got to know each other, and I told him that we were at Alcatraz at the same time and

Joe Carnes visiting Alcatraz as a tourist in 1980.

how we came to know each other. I told him the story of the "Jap"
Kawakita, and he seemed impressed by that... He told me he would
look at Indians a lot differently from that point forward.

The ceremony included a Choctaw preacher, and three Indian women who
sang consoling hymns in their traditional language. Next to the casket was a
large cross made of white and red roses, and a small plant adorning a childhood snapshot of Carnes. By all accounts, it was a sad but beautiful service.
It was likely the kindest gesture anyone had ever paid to Joe Carnes; to make
right a wrong and give Joe his final wish. Bulger later commented:

On the day of the funeral, it was sunny and crisp, and there were
rolling hills around. A cow grazed in the distance with the sounds of

Prison officials—believing that Carnes had no surviving relatives—buried him in a pauper's grave at the Catholic Cemetery of Springfield. Once Bulger read about Joe's death in the newspapers, he intervened to have his body exhumed and transferred to Joe's family plot for a proper service and burial. He was buried in a traditional Choctaw funeral ceremony with storytelling, singing and spiritual rites of passing. This is the gravestone purchased and placed by Bulger for Carnes, and the photo was purportedly taken by Bulger following the ceremony.

the bell around his neck echoing through the pastures. Joe was laid to rest between his sister and brother. It was such a peaceful place. Joe was free at last. While on the run I visited him to make sure the stone and bronze plaque was placed appropriately. I was relieved to find that it was. As it was custom, the last time I visited I left something to drink and some tobacco.

ON ALCATRAZ, guards and convicts spoke very little to one another. It was usually a nod hello or other small gesture, but that was about the extent. I remember the first day I arrived, I think it was in the very first hour, I met the lieutenant everyone called "Double Tough" Ordway. He walked up to my cell on Broadway (C-145), put his hands on his hips, rocked back and forth and introduced himself. "So, you're Bulger?" "You think you're tough?"—"Well, I'm Lieutenant Ordway and they call me 'Double Tough...' so don't forget it..." It was hard to keep a straight face talking to him. God, he was a comical character. He believed he was the real thing and "Double Tough." He reminded me of a penguin and the cons gave him the nickname "Double Puff." About two and half weeks later, he came to my cell and told me I had been assigned to work in the kitchen. I hated to think of that job. Waking up before the rest of the population, working the long hours, living on Broadway with no privacy... So, I said, "OK... Do they have meat cleavers and butcher knives in the kitchen? He reacted, "Why do you ask?" I told him, "That's a place where a lot of my trouble is, and I may need to have access to things." He left—came back in an hour and told me, "You're working in the clothing room and are being assigned to C-314 on the top of C-Block!" I thought, perfect!

Alver (A.G.) Bloomquist was a guard who started his Alcatraz career in the 1940s, and he's the only guard in all my years in prison that I can remember having a civil conversation with. All of the others had a certain air about them that was confrontational. Bloomquist was quiet, slender, never raised his voice, never used profanity and I don't recall him even telling a dirty joke. Guys assigned to the laundry often carried bad reputations, such as being considered hostile, incorrigible and often had trouble during assignments to other jobs on the Rock. The cons referred to him as Bloomie and he treated all of us with respect. It meant a lot to many of us to be treated as human beings. We learned the value of hard work and a good work ethic. I rack my brain and can't come up with one memory of any civil exchanges between any of the convicts and guards. The entrance to the laundry building was close to the water. There was a double fence with barbwire and

gun towers, but every once in a while, a dense fog would come in fast. The towers were high, and the fog would be thick along the water. At that moment I was always concerned for Bloomie. He was alone and had to phone in every fifteen minutes to the control center. I mentioned to other cons that I hoped no one would hurt Bloomie trying to get into the water. Several of these guys were desperate contemplating their bleak future of living out their best and youthful years on the Rock. My friend Hawk felt the same way. The respect for Bloomie rose to such a level among the prison population that there was an unspoken code that in the event of any escape attempt, Bloomie would not be harmed.

On the inside, we had guys from all walks of life. Some men were full of hate and quick to insult a guard with a mix of humor and acid tongue. Many of the guards were unpopular. Some were hated and I saw it firsthand. One-time Bloomie really shocked us all and showed some trust

Maurice "Double Tough" Ordway, captured in photographs taken by Leigh Wiener on the day Alcatraz closed in March of 1963. Wiener was a famed Hollywood based photographer known for his legendary images of presidents, celebrities, musicians, athletes, and other iconic figures. Bulger was permitted a copy of Alcatraz—The Last Day, a book featuring Leigh's incredible photographs of those final hours. Bulger felt that Wiener's images captured Ordway, his gestures and the essence of his character perfectly. Many of Bulger's close friends would also be part of the collection of photographs and he'd later comment he'd spent hours browsing the pages of Wiener's book.

back. Bloomie was the only guard I ever saw who brought his son into the prison. He brought his son Dean and they stood next to the door that leads from the rec yard into the cellblock. Guys were coming in from work and Bloomie stood there, introducing us to his son as each guy passed. Every one of us greeted his son and shook his hand. We all told him, "Your father is really a good man." My good friend Charlie Catalano gave Bloomie and his son a genuine, happy, good-to-meet-you type of gesture and handshake. It really knocked us all off of our balance since we'd never seen such a thing. It's ironic: the Hollywood depictions of the relationships between convicts and officers were often conflicted and full of friction, but Bloomie became an iconic figure to me.

Looking back, Bloomie became a trusted friend even following my release from prison and after he retired. We had dinners together. We were in contact, and I flew out to visit him. One time, when I flew out to meet him for dinner, we showed up at the restaurant and we were both wearing the same Alcatraz belt buckle. We laughed so hard and thought if people only knew. Can you imagine? The Con and the Keeper meeting for a social meal. We both had a good laugh and spent the evening reminiscing.

Later on, I got deeper into organized crime, and we drifted apart and lost touch. He was one of the finest guys I ever met in or out of prison. I wished him a long life, but also part of me always hoped that he didn't hear about me being on the run for such serious crimes.

I had the wrong attitude, figuring that I'd try hard for one year to make it work, and if it didn't, I'd revert back into crime, then you have to play the game more seriously because it's do or die. I applied for several legitimate jobs including the Massachusetts Bay Transit and thought being an engineer on a subway train would be a good job. I thought working independently would be a good fit for me, as well as good benefits and a pension. I interviewed but was told with my prison record it would never be an option for me. Instead, I took a job working in a large print shop making only $52 a week. Then I got a job in construction making about a $150 per week as a laborer. I had trouble fitting in and promoting into better positions, and on a few occasions got into fights. It was a matter of time before it was all a disaster. I couldn't figure out how to make it work or fit in…I didn't drink, do drugs or smoke, and felt as though I was an outsider. I fell back into crime and holding a normal job seemed liked a distant reality for me. It was a bad period in my life as I wanted to find a good

Name: *James J. Bulger* No: *1428*
Work assignment: *Clothing Room* Cell No. *C 314*

Bulger's first work assignment was working in the clothing issue, located below the cellhouse in the basement shower room area. Al Capone once worked in this same location. During Bulger's time on Alcatraz, Mickey Cohen ran the clothing issue beginning in August 1961, until his final departure in February 1963. John Anglin, one of the principals in the 1962 Great Escape from Alcatraz also worked in this location with Cohen in 1961.

BULGER	Record Form No. 36 Rev. Oct., 1940	1428-AZ	ASSOCIATE WARDEN'S RECORD CARD	FP1—LK—6-1-56—55M—8414

Offense Robbery of U.I. Bank	Race White Age 9-3-29
Sentence 20 Years Begins 6-21-56	Married no Deps. none
Date Imp. 6-21-56 At Boston, Mass.	Citizen Yes USA Relig. Cath
Date Rec'd 11-13-59 fr Atlanta	Physical Cond. Regular Duty
Par. Elig. 2-20-63	Mental Cond. High Average Intellig
C. R. 11-24-69 Max. 6-20-76	Education: S. A. T. 10.2
Comm. Fine None G. T. 240 days	G. S.
PREVIOUS RECORD:	PSYCHOLOGICAL & APTITUDE TESTS:
Jails 6 Ref.	IQ 113
Pens: Fed. State	
Detainers: Fed. State	Occupational Skills:
Escapes: Fed. State	
CUSTODY:	Laborer
Crimes Involved: (Enumerate)	Avocational Interests:

History of Occupational Experience

Occupations	No. Yrs.	Verification of Performance	
		Quality	Dependability

Investigation at Atlanta disclosed that subject furnished
a hacksaw blade to 3 men in B Cellhouse. Two of these
men were subsequently transferred here. (Names not given)
On 8-24-59 subject was again returned to Adm Seg when
information received that subject was again plotting with
others to escape.

Number	Residence	Occupations
1428-AZ	Mass.	Laborer

BULGER, JAMES J. JR

job to support myself and someday consider a family, but it all seemed to be a distant dream and far from my reach.

Bloomie was a rare individual. He tried to find the balance of doing his job without losing empathy toward the hard lives these men were living or his own sense of self. I can't think of Bloomie without plunging into a deep depression. I wish him and his family had lived forever. I know if there's a heaven, Bloomie is up there.

On Alcatraz, you had guards like Ordway who brought their egos to work each day. Some of the guards looked for a reason to take down a con. One of the most hated was a guy named Jameson. He had a reputation and one of the stories among the men was that he'd tried to starve a guy in D-Block until he was near death. He would dump most of the content off his tray and give it to other guys. On the regular line, guys could eat as much as they wanted so long that they didn't waste and ate all that they took. In D-Block, they only received a single tray of food and that was it. I believed those stories of Jameson.

I can remember seeing Jameson in the gun gallery when we'd be in the mess hall. He'd kneel down on one knee and show everyone he had his machine gun on the ready. Once when they caught on that we were going to wreck the mess hall over the worsening quality of the food, I could see Jameson leering with hope that we'd give him an excuse to fire into the men. The menus had been getting worse and it got to the point where they were serving fried bologna for both lunch and the

A.G. Bloomquist and his wife Lyla in a 1940s photograph. Bloomquist was the work foreman who watched over the prisoners assigned to the laundry, where Bulger worked from December of 1960, until he left Alcatraz in July of 1962. Bloomquist and Bulger became good friends and stayed in touch following his release. Friendships between officers and convicts were rare, but Bloomquist treated the men with such respect and trust, that many cons looked up to him. Bulger indicated that while they remained friends outside of prison, he kept his lawless life a secret and Bloomquist never knew his elite status in the criminal underworld.

main meal and this brought everything to a boil. Jameson could never walk into the mess hall without the cons booing and cursing him. He'd rarely come in because of that reaction.

The cons bestowed the mess hall with the nickname the "Gas Chamber" since there were mounted tear gas canisters spaced along the ceiling, spanning the entire length of the dining area. Three times a day, all the convicts marched in single file, and you'd have the entire main cellhouse population together in the same space. My memory is that the windows didn't open and there was always a veiled threat of being gassed or shot by a guard patrolling in the gun gallery if anything got out of hand. Everyone was locked together in the same space and the gas canisters looming over the tables was a sobering reality.

Most of the time, the food at Alcatraz was on par with restaurant dining. The food really was that good. Occasionally, they'd get into a rut, and you'd see the same menu items over and over, several times a week. You'd have the same soup for lunch and dinner, or thinly sliced lunch meats as a main meal item. It wasn't often, but when it did occur it would happen for a long stretch of time, and it caused a lot

A letter written by Bloomquist to the Classification Committee in February of 1962, commending his work conduct and endorsement for eventual parole. He closed the letter stating, "I believe he will make every effort to lead a law-abiding life."

of friction. Guys would slam down their trays and yell insults at the culinary staff and guards. I dreaded it, because whenever we went into a lockdown status, the meals would be overly basic and be delivered to your cell in a paper bag. They would be something like a bologna sandwich, with the meat dry on the bread (no spread, no lettuce, and one thin slice of meat). No coffee, iced tea or other drinks. It was a deterrent that kept men from complaining too often.

Outside of those rare occasions, the food was leagues ahead of other prisons. The menus were like a smorgasbord. You had an open selection of the main menu items and could choose your portion sizes with no restrictions. "Eat all that you want, eat all that you take" was the rule. The Alcatraz bakery was something to really boast about. The aroma of fresh bread would not only travel out to the recreation yard when we'd come up for lunch, but occasionally permeate the entire cellhouse. On the weekends when we didn't work and relaxed in our cells, I could sometimes smell the baking of fresh bread coming from the kitchen. During the winter months when the windows were closed, you could smell the meats baking in the ovens or cooking in the fryers. It's odd to me that having read at least ten or so memoirs about Alcatraz, this has never once been mentioned, yet it's one of the most prominent memories I have. At breakfast, you could smell the sausage and eggs and fresh bread baking throughout the day. I didn't smoke or use tobacco, so maybe my senses were heightened, but whenever I see photos of the mess hall, the smell of fresh bread always comes to mind.

There were several favorite menu items that the men all enjoyed. Chili and cornbread were always popular. You'd have chili listed on the menu, but then a couple different styles you could choose from on the steam tables. There'd be a few different options such as ground or chuck meats, green chili, red chili, Mexican or Southern style, etc., the prison chefs took great pride in serving different varieties and the men didn't complain whenever they appeared for both lunch and dinner. You'd have men going back for seconds and thirds and wanting to savor all the varieties. Spaghetti was another favorite and of course, they always looked forward to the holiday cuisines. There were always special meals on holidays. Christmas and Thanksgiving you'd have roast turkey or baked ham; then spareribs or t-bone steak on Veterans Day, Fourth of July, everyone looked forward to seeing what was on the menu. Steak was the most popular with guys. Each holiday, they always gave the option of either steak or turkey. The t-bone made for a good weapon, so after the meal, the guards would make sure the bone was left on the plate when you got up from the table.

I remember one Christmas the steward in charge of the kitchen wanted the upright piano bought up from the basement room where the band would practice. It was really heavy and awkward getting it up the stairwell that ran from the basement entrance area to the dining hall. He asked me and a few other guys who lifted weights to do the job. We agreed, but only if he gave us a t-bone steak once it was in the mess hall—he agreed. I remember the steaks were really thin, but what a treat! I've never forgotten how good it tasted. We ate every ounce and even the fat that was seared to a crisp.

Once every few months, there was a Chef's Menu Special that was a real treat for the men. Whenever the men noticed this written on the chalk board during lunch, they all looked forward to the evening meal! Most often, they were fresh catch from the guards who fished off the shore of the island and included everything from salmon, sturgeon and striped bass, to even leopard shark meat. I even remember once

The Alcatraz Mess Hall (aka the Gas Chamber). Three times each day, the general population convicts all assembled in the mess hall for meals. The food was considered the best in the federal prison system. The dining area also had ten permanently affixed tear gas canisters mounted to ceiling beams that could be activated remotely from the exterior catwalk which had window views into the dining room. Tear gas was an additional security measure paired with the armed officers in the gun gallery and exterior catwalk. Although they were installed when the federal prison opened in 1934, the tear gas units were never activated. It was, however, a constant reminder to the convicts of the ever-present warning of the dangers they might encounter in the event of any violent outbreaks.

The Alcatraz Culinary Department prisoner staff assembled in the dining room on Christmas Day in 1948 with Public Enemy #1 Alvin Karpis seen fourth from right. Holidays were special events and often included live music, extended dining hours with rich menus and movies.

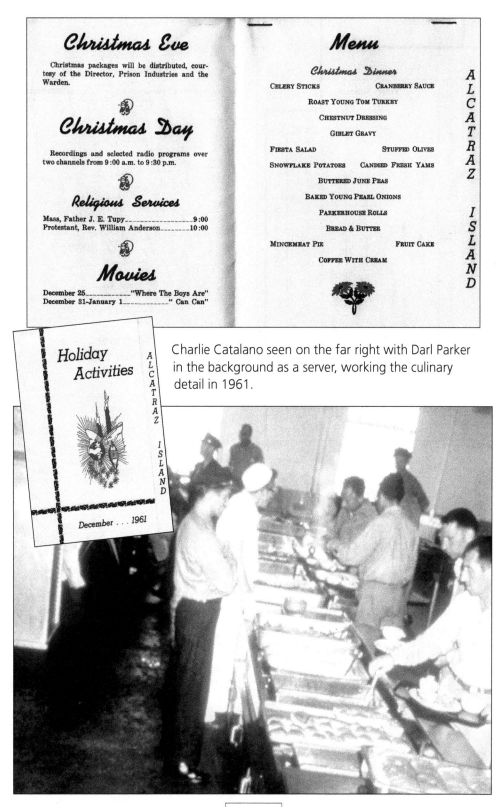

Christmas Eve

Christmas packages will be distributed, courtesy of the Director, Prison Industries and the Warden.

Christmas Day

Recordings and selected radio programs over two channels from 9:00 a.m. to 9:30 p.m.

Religious Services

Mass, Father J. E. Tupy_____9:00
Protestant, Rev. William Anderson_____10:00

Movies

December 25_____"Where The Boys Are"
December 31-January 1_____" Can Can"

Menu

Christmas Dinner

CELERY STICKS   CRANBERRY SAUCE

ROAST YOUNG TOM TURKEY

CHESTNUT DRESSING

GIBLET GRAVY

FIESTA SALAD   STUFFED OLIVES

SNOWFLAKE POTATOES   CANDIED FRESH YAMS

BUTTERED JUNE PEAS

BAKED YOUNG PEARL ONIONS

PARKERHOUSE ROLLS

BREAD & BUTTER

MINCEMEAT PIE   FRUIT CAKE

COFFEE WITH CREAM

ALCATRAZ ISLAND

Holiday Activities

ALCATRAZ ISLAND

December . . . 1961

Charlie Catalano seen on the far right with Darl Parker in the background as a server, working the culinary detail in 1961.

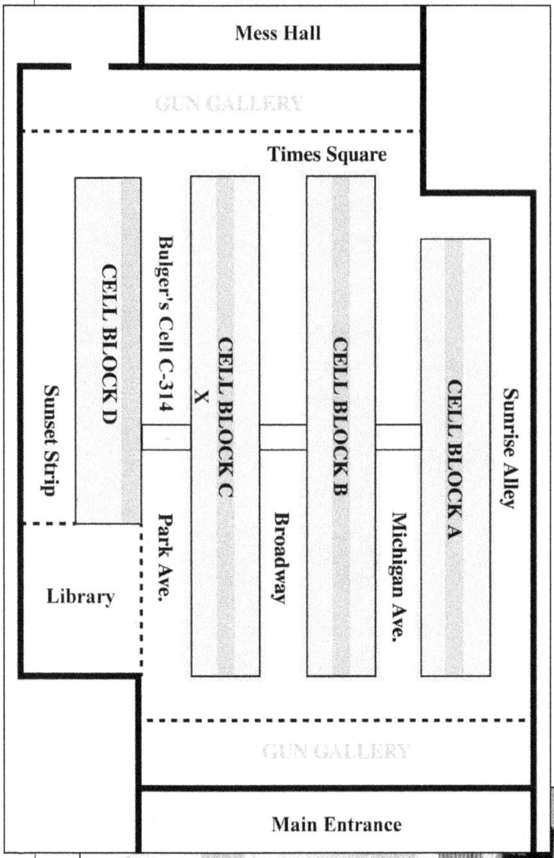
Mess Hall
GUN GALLERY
Times Square
CELL BLOCK D
Bulger's Cell C-314
X
CELL BLOCK C
CELL BLOCK B
CELL BLOCK A
Sunset Strip
Sunrise Alley
Park Ave.
Broadway
Michigan Ave.
Library
GUN GALLERY
Main Entrance

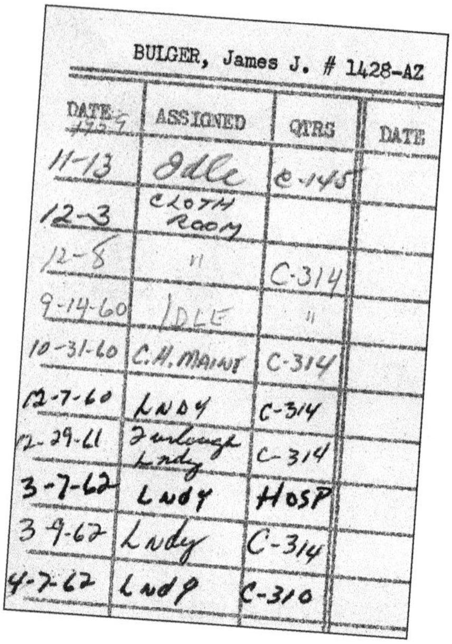

BULGER, James J. # 1428-AZ

DATE 1959	ASSIGNED	QTRS	DATE
11-13	Idle	C-145	
12-3	CLOTH ROOM		
12-8	"	C-314	
9-14-60	IDLE	"	
10-31-60	C.H. MAINT	C-314	
12-7-60	LNDY	C-314	
12-29-61	Furlough Lndy	C-314	
3-7-62	LNDY	HOSP	
3-9-62	Lndy	C-314	
4-7-62	Lndy	C-310	

The ten-man benches were replaced with four-man tables in October of 1961.

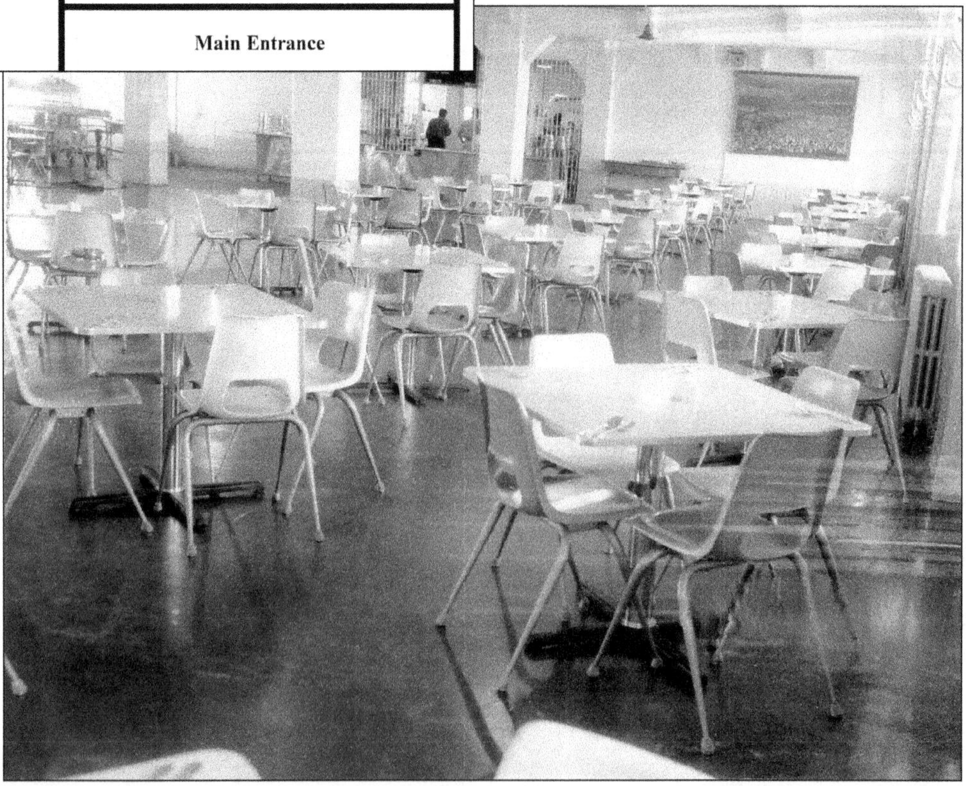

a very small strip of crab meat placed across a salad that we'd heard was from crab traps set by the officers. Sometimes they'd serve fish and chips with vinegar for the fries, and everyone would talk about it for days. Whenever they'd have these special fish fries, they'd extend the mealtime to one or two hours. These were big deals, and you'd never see a happier group of men. This was a good gesture on the guards' part and the men would all thank them, and relations would improve for a period of time. There was a chalk board at the entrance of the mess hall, and you'd see a special menu written out as "A Taste of Mexico" or "A Taste of Italy" or the fish fries "An Evening at Fisherman's Wharf" and a variety of foods that included fresh sourdough bread. The dining is something that is forever imprinted in my mind. I don't remember any other prison where they had a bakery that was so skilled in baking a variety of breads like rye, wheat and sourdough. The breakfasts with fresh cinnamon and pecan rolls, and these special dinner menus were always such a treat for the men that otherwise lived such a grim existence.

As I mentioned previously, there was a protocol the guards followed in terms of how convicts flowed into the mess hall, and it never changed. The seating convention followed the cell assignments, so whoever you celled next to was who you sat next to during meals. This was a major reason you saw men changing cells so frequently. Cell location rather than neighbors was the bigger factor for me. I saw my friends at work and on the yard but wanted to maintain privacy where I could read and listen to the radio without someone pestering me. I kept to myself and aside from small talk, preferred the privacy of living on the top tier of C-Block. Guards rarely walked that section unless they had a reason.

Compared to prison today, I look back at the Alcatraz mess hall as a five-star restaurant. The room filled only with quiet whispers, an atmosphere of respect, and then when finished the guards would give the signal and everyone would march quietly back to their cells. Good food, decent atmosphere, and no loud chatter where you couldn't hear the guy next to you in conversation. If you were caught sneaking food back to your cell you'd be in a serious pinch. No one could eat anything from about 5 PM until the next morning. There was no canteen and no exceptions. The only thing I ever took back to my cell was a small piece of bread to feed birds that came into the cellhouse through open windows.

If the culinary crew knew it was your birthday, they'd sometimes bake a cake and pass you a big slice. Sometimes, they'd even slip a cup of homebrew. In nine years, I only had one cup of homebrew—it was my birthday and we had just switched to the four-man tables. One of the guys working in the kitchen heard it was my birthday and passed me a cup and said, "drink it fast," so I did. When I got back to my cell, I started feeling woozy. I relaxed and stretched out and kind of drifted off. It was a pleasant feeling, but once was enough and I preferred a good book.

I can still remember the sounds of the Alcatraz cellhouse as if it were yesterday. There was a convict I remember who I've never forgotten. Every morning when the buzzer went off to signal the cons to get up, Gene Fuller (1027-AZ), would holler "Stop the world, I want to get off." He would mimic the Road Runner character in the famed cartoon. You could hear Fuller's "Beep-Beep" resonate and echo off the cement walls and floors. Gene was serving a life sentence for the murder of a U.S. Marshal. He didn't fit the persona of that type of criminal. Real quiet; easy going and memorable. He did that most every morning. At night, when the radio shut down at lights out, you would hear all of the headphones hitting the concrete floor. The men would just pull them off their ears and throw them to the floor. It was very distinct sound that you heard every night. I never did it. I always felt that tomorrow is another day and why risk having to lose the use of headphones while they are being repaired. It was the same sound at both Atlanta and Leavenworth. The cells had an old-style light bulb in the center of the ceiling. There was a thin chain about a foot long, then a long string that reached the bunk. You'd hear the headsets drop as the radio was shut off, then you'd hear what seemed like a thousand clicks of the lights all being clicked off. Sometimes after work, "Jeep"

Gene Fuller

Marcum would come in and start boxing at the string. You'd hear the chain hitting the bulb and an annoying ping sound as he'd lunge at the string. Finally, I'd yell down to him to "Knock it off," then all would go quiet. Nights were hard time. On the summer nights with the window open you could hear the sounds of the City. It was hard on everyone. I'd wake up in the middle of the night and just think of everything lost.

When I moved up to my cell on C-Block from Broadway, I was sitting on my bed after coming from chow. It was one of the first moments in my new cell and an older guy is in the doorway and asks me in a really serious tone "Did you see anyone with my *Movie Screen*?" I stood up and felt this nut is looking for trouble. I asked him what movie screen and thought he meant the kind they project a movie image onto. I asked him to describe it. He says, "Elizabeth Taylor and Eddie Fisher are on the cover." The old fool was talking about a magazine! He goes on to say he didn't like Elizabeth Taylor since she ruined Debbie Reynold's marriage! I couldn't believe this fucking fool was serious and I'm thinking this is an Alcatraz bad guy! Next thing I know, all the men on this tier are swapping their *Movie Screen* magazines and everyone is talking celebrity and Hollywood gossip stories! That's the talk on the top tier of C-Block in America's most notorious prison!

C-Block was an ideal location on Alcatraz. The guard in the gun gallery had no view into my cell, and I could see the entrance to the yard and D-Block. I had no cells across from me, so there was a great sense of privacy that was not afforded to many of the other areas of the cellblock.

On the yard, Joe Carnes would be down in the areas where guys played chess, checkers, or dominos. During my years, they sat on folding canvas, wooden style chairs in the far-right corner of the yard, to the right of the baseball diamond. The guys who played bridge, dominos or checkers would spend their whole yard period in that one area. To us, they looked like a bunch of old guys hunched over and concentrating intently on their games. They seldom moved or looked

Bulger spent the majority of his term on Alcatraz in C-314, located on the top tier of C-Block, along a corridor known to convicts as Seedy Street (the corridor between C and D cellblocks). This location was reasonably private with no facing cells and the gun gallery officers had no direct view.

Historical views of correctional officers patrolling the C-Block corridors of Alcatraz during the 1950s and 60s era.

up. They were all really hooked on their games. It's about all that a lot of guys had to look forward to. Chess and bridge were a big turn off for me as some of these guys obsessed over it. I preferred books and exercise. I hated the noise in the cellhouse when guys were playing and yelling moves from cell to cell. It was distracting…It was fine on the yard, but I enjoyed the quiet periods when I could read and not be disrupted.

I saw the pictures in your book [*Alcatraz—A History of the Penitentiary Years*]. This had to be an old "before" picture because they are sitting on stacked cushions, not the folding chairs, which were real light and not sturdy enough to be used as a weapon. When they were not in use they were stacked up and kept in the covered space underneath the yard stairs leading up to the cellhouse.

Looking back at all the pictures of the guys on the yard, the weights, the bench we made in the industries, and the view, brings back great memories. The weights were a big part of the day for me. I'd really get lost in the workouts and it did produce a high. I always looked forward to the next workout. Originally, the weights were kept by the door to go down to the shops and laundry, but pre-closing they were kept behind a chain link fence next to a basketball court that was added later to help divide sections of the yard. This allowed men to play ball and other activities without disruption to the men playing bridge and other board style games. We always stacked them in neat order. When we were lifting, there would usually be a guard right above us on the gun walk. He would be armed with a rifle, a fully automatic .30 caliber carbine, and a handgun attached to a lanyard that he wore around his neck. The wall next to the door that led to the industries was where the convicts played handball, which was to our right where we lifted weights. Close to that was a horseshoe court. There were two stakes and metal horseshoes. When any trouble started brewing, we always pointed to the horseshoes saying, "Use them, and don't mess with the weights." The warden had made the promise that if anyone ever used the weights as a weapon they would be removed. So, we had to make sure not to lose them.

It made me sad to see the weights scattered around like that in some of the pictures. My time on the yard was always spent working out and on weekends, walking and talking with my close friends from Atlanta: Catalano, Arquilla, Twining, etc. I guess people would have a hard time believing it, but those are fond memories.

The Alcatraz Recreation Yard. Bulger reminisced that the top of the bleachers and in the weights area is where he spent most of his time. He enjoyed the scenic views of the San Francisco Bay and the ships passing under the Golden Gate Bridge.

In the movie with Clint Eastwood, *Escape from Alcatraz*, there was a scene with black convicts sitting high up on the bleachers. The film implied it was their territory and no one could approach the leader "Bumpy Johnson" (real good guy by the way) without permission, etc. Great movie, but never did such a thing exist for blacks, whites or any race for that matter. If anyone black or white had carried himself that way, it would have been an insult and challenge that would have led to violence.

I have fond memories of sitting out on the yard bleachers. I used to stand on one high point, a little alcove with room only for one person. I'd stand there and look out at the sailboats on the Bay, and gaze at the Golden Gate Bridge. It was such a wonderful full view of the Bay from Alcatraz. I remember seeing Sterling Hayden's sailboat *The Wanderer*, a full-scale replica of the Bounty, and I watched it sail out of the fog and into Frisco. That was a big deal for all the guys. He was in a couple of crime films all the men were familiar with. One with Marilyn Monroe (*The Asphalt Jungle*) and another that was a racetrack heist (*The Killing*). We all watched *The Wanderer* sail into the Bay from the bleachers. I can also remember seeing the warships and submarines going in and out of the Bay. We all felt a great sense of pride and patriotism. These were all beautiful sights; they remain forever etched into my memory.

At some point, someone on Alcatraz came up with the idea for a cell activity that would promote relaxation—knitting! The next thing you know guys are signing up! I thought it was completely ludicrous and it made us all look ridiculous. The guards would chuckle at some of the guys sitting in their cells knitting scarfs and the like. Bob Luke's crime partner Joe Dellamura (1445-AZ) was one of those guys who signed on. Dellamura was later arrested for another bank heist with a fellow Brooklynite Eddie Pravato (1432-AZ) and wound up on the Rock around May of 1960. Dellamura was given up to the feds by his niece and other relatives after he bought them new cars. Luke was long gone by then. J.D. lived below me on either the second or first tier of C-Block. He always had a permanent five o'clock shadow, looked swarthy and had a gruff voice. It's easy to picture him with a sawed-off shotgun hollering "Get-'em up—this is a stick-up!" not "Knit one, purl two!" I'll never forget seeing him sitting on his cell bunk knitting. Picture him in a nun's outfit assembling a machine gun and needing a shave. Well, some magazine printed a cartoon of Alcatraz cons

Board style games was a coveted pastime for prisoners on the weekends during the recreation period. Bridge remained one of the most popular games on Alcatraz for nearly three decades. Bulger recounted that you'd see prisoners hunched over for hours in serious play. Dominos were used in place of standard playing cards, since cards were coated with cellulose, a flammable substance that could be used as an explosive. Given the almost unrelenting wind that swept across the island, dominos were also better suited for outdoor play.

Armed officers supervised prisoners from perimeter catwalks during weekend recreation periods. General population inmates were permitted two visits per week (Saturday and Sunday) to the recreation yard, weather permitting. A variety of activities were permitted during their recreation period including board games, basketball, baseball, handball, or volleyball — or they could simply walk the yard for exercise.

Hollywood actor Sterling Hayden aboard his sailboat The Wanderer with his children on the San Francisco Bay. Bulger had a fond memory of watching the vessel enter the waters of the San Francisco Bay from the top bleacher steps of the recreation yard.

knitting and we all heard about it. Poor Joe! His tough guy bank robber image was destroyed.

Larry Trumblay (1129-AZ) was another who took up knitting. My recollection is that he became quite obsessed with it. Larry was knitting sweaters, scarfs, gloves, and just about anything you could think of. He was a bank robber based out of Chicago and I later learned that we cased some of the same banks in Indiana. Larry was a solid and tough convict, but his cell looked more like a French clothing boutique. Larry was transferred to Leavenworth a few months before I shipped out to Lewisburg. We got to know each other really well. I enjoyed reading some of the later articles about him and his friendship with Father Bush on Alcatraz. I don't recall any conversations with him about their friendship, but he was the type to get lost in his thoughts and we talked a lot about life on the outside. I knew Father Bush as he'd visit our group from Boston on the yard and he was a nice guy.

Larry Trumblay

Warden Madigan (R) and Associate Warden Blackwell (L) admiring a scarf knitted by bank robber, Darwin Coon. For a short period, knitting became a popular pastime for prisoners.

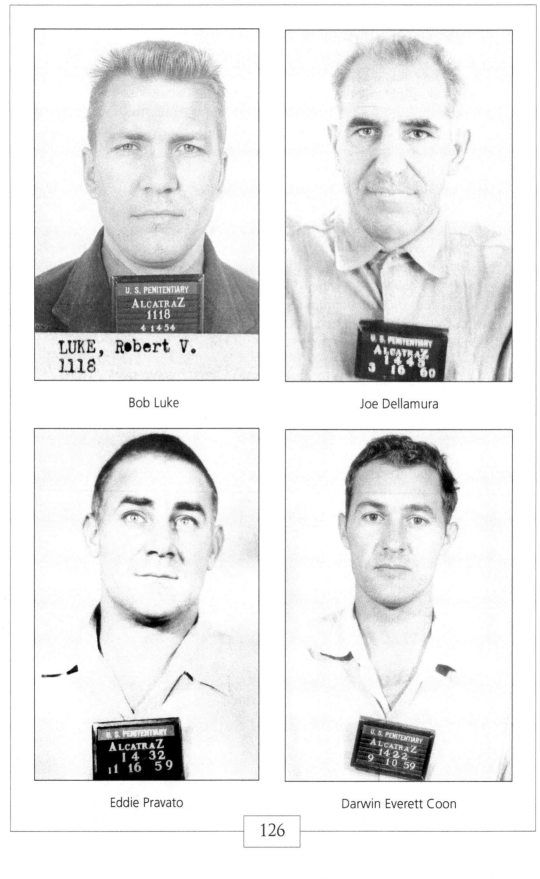

Bob Luke

Joe Dellamura

Eddie Pravato

Darwin Everett Coon

Sometimes my memories blend together, but I vividly remember Larry and I laughed hard about the knitting. Suffice it to say it didn't survive long on the Rock.

Right after my parole in 1965, I heard about Larry being killed in a car accident shortly after his release from prison. Blackwell had passed the message to my parole officer, and he broke the news to me. It caught me off guard. I wasn't especially close to him, but we did share a lot of laughs. I raised a glass for Larry and had many good memories of our conversations. I wish he'd had more time to build a new life. He died too young.

ALVIN KARPIS

Alvin Karpis was one of the more famous convicts on Alcatraz when I did my time there. He ends up serving a longer sentence on the Rock than any other convict. During the 1930s, he was Public Enemy #1 and J. Edgar Hoover's rival. In later years, guys like Leon Thompson writing books about their life at Alcatraz put themselves in the middle of important events and always talk about how they walked the yard with Karpis or were best friends. I knew him well, but only through occasional conversation. He didn't go out of his way to mix with others and mostly walked the yard by himself. He often walked alone and at a steady pace. You could tell he was working to get exercise and he appeared to be in a good state of health.

Alvin Karpis

I never heard anyone call him "Old Creepy." Rumor had it that Blackie Audett (208-AZ, 551-AZ, and 1217-AZ) was the one to make up the name and Karpis hated him. Audett had the sole distinction of serving three separate terms on Alcatraz. I don't ever recall ever seeing Audett in the prison yard, but never looked for him either.

Karpis disembarking an Air Canada flight in Toronto, Canada, following his release from prison in 1969. He was released under the condition that he would be deported back to Canada, his place of birth. Using money he earned from his autobiography, interviews, and movie rights to his story, which had been optioned by Harold Hecht (producer of the Birdman of Alcatraz) for the motion picture The Last Public Enemy (which never made it into production), he moved to the coast in the south of Spain. He spent his final years in quiet solitude and died in August 1979 at the age of 71. He would serve more than a quarter century as a prisoner on Alcatraz.

Guys didn't like him, and most didn't trust the cons who worked in the officer's mess hall or as passmen in the warden's home. The only con I remember him being close friends with was John Machibroda, 1373-AZ, a bank robber who like Karpis, was a Canadian and both men worked in the kitchen. Years later I met up Machibroda after he was released and hiding out in New York City. Tom Devaney and I met with him at his apartment, and he prepared a special chicken cordon bleu dinner for us. While on the run, he worked as a chef at a high-end restaurant in New York City and kept a low profile. He had a big bandage on his hand, and

I asked him what happened? I remember him saying that a couple New York cops had caught up with him and wanted him to ring the bell on another con so that they could capture him without a gunfight. The cops worked him over when he refused and broke his hand to get cooperation. They failed. He moved to a different neighborhood and landed a job in an upper-class restaurant. Karpis was deported back to Canada, and I remember seeing him on television later giving interviews. There was also a made-for-TV movie about his life and we made a big night of it, and I really enjoyed watching his years before Alcatraz being played out in a movie. I just recently read his memoir and I'm glad he made his way to the coast of Spain to live out his final years.

John Machibroda

WILLIAM "HAWK" HAWKINS

The photos of the laundry building today look so different than it did back then. Without the mangle and other equipment, it looks much bigger than I remember it. When I worked in the laundry, there was a guy on the mangle opposite me. He was the only black man working in that area with us. He was a real nice guy from Washington D.C. named Hawkins (1245-AZ). He was also in USP Lewisburg located on the first tier in the first five cells with Catalano, Marcum, Maloney and me. Later on, I looked for him. I was once in D.C. staying in the Hyatt and called every Hawkins listed in the telephone directory. I was real interested in seeing how he was doing and whether I could help him out if things were not so good.

I didn't know his first name, we just called him "Hawk" while on Alcatraz. Well, picture me engaging each voice with "I'm trying to locate a friend of mine, but I don't know his first name—we worked together on Alcatraz—would you happen to know of him?" Needless to say, I never located him, but years later I learned that he got trapped in a bank heist and committed suicide.

William "Hawk" Hawkins

He was one hell of a nice guy—bright, well-spoken, and he came from a nice family. His father worked at the White House as a chauffeur. A couple of times he'd say, "Bulger, read this…" It would be a letter from his sister describing a wedding, for instance. His sister sounded like my own sister, who was a couple of years older than me. Once his sister got upset about the bad behavior of a black public figure and she commented, "God, he sets us back doing that." I was always surprised that the letters Hawk received were allowed, as she'd spray them heavily with perfume and the scent would linger on my hands.

Hawk was on the mangle with me—he was on one end of a sheet (wet or damp), and I was on the other. This was a real mechanical type of job, and we would talk about books, current events, and get lost in our day. There was a lot of racial tension on the Rock and little things could cause rumbling, muttering, bristling and dog-eyeing. However, in

The west side of Alcatraz Island with the Industries building in view.

130

Historical and contemporary photographs of the Alcatraz laundry.

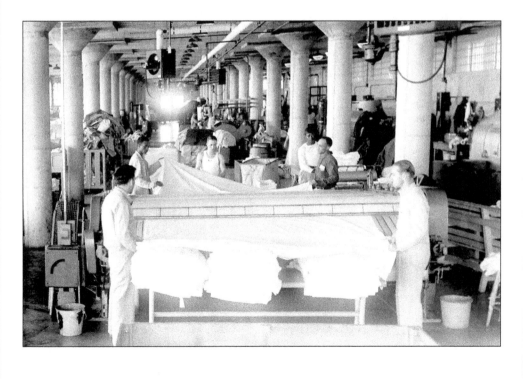

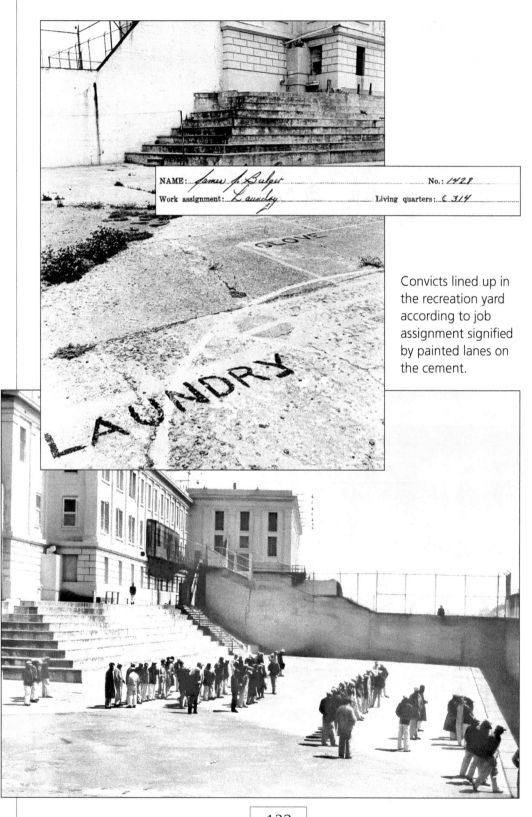

NAME: *James J. Bulger*   No.: *1428*

Work assignment: *Laundry*   Living quarters: *C 314*

Convicts lined up in the recreation yard according to job assignment signified by painted lanes on the cement.

The expansive bayside windows of the Industries building boasted extravagant views of the San Francisco Bay and Golden Gate Bridge. After finishing work, the men would listen to the radio and take in the breathtaking panoramas of life beyond the prison walls.

the laundry, there was no racial tension whatsoever. We all got along well, but it was still on peoples' mind. I remember Hawk one time commenting "I don't think you like my kind of people?" and he smiled. My answer, "Not all of them...Just the same ones you don't like." That really got a good laugh out of him. I always had a lot of respect for Hawk. He always carried himself well and like a gentleman. He was quite a guy. I remember the guards would always comment that he had the cleanest cell in the prison. He always acknowledged that he was fanatical when it came to cleanliness and was always dusting and keeping everything spotless. I hope that he had some good times after prison with family prior to his death. Hawk was on the last chain out of Alcatraz. Both he and Duncan were transferred together to Lewisburg the day the island closed, and it was good to see him before I was released.

FORREST TUCKER AND TEDDY GREEN

A guard here asked me if I knew Forrest Tucker (1047-AZ). The actor Robert Redford is apparently playing him in a new movie (*The Old Man & the Gun*) being advertised on television. Redford was in *The Sting,* a film set in early Chicago that I enjoyed. I knew Forrest well and considered him a friend during my years on Alcatraz, as well as

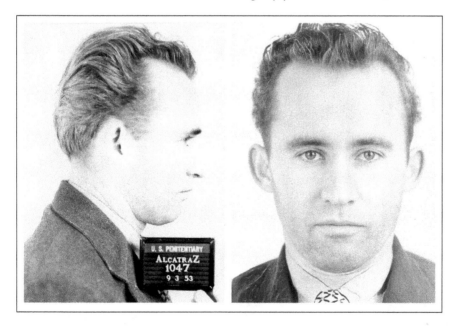

Forrest Tucker

a few of his crime partners. I hope the movie does justice to him and his story. I doubt I'll ever be able to see it. Forrest was the band leader of the "Rock Islanders" on Alcatraz. He was a really talented musician and I remember him playing both piano and guitar!

He was an all-around great guy and had an interesting career— always up for an escape. He was a non-violent bank robber and a real gentleman. When he robbed banks, he always spoke softly using only soft threats. I think when it came down the wire, he would have never used physical violence. Forrest robbed more than 50 banks in his career with a catch of more than $5 million! I don't remember the exact number, but I think he'd made around twenty successful escapes from prison. Tucker was the true definition of an "Escape Artist." He'd seen it all; did hard time in some of the toughest prisons in the U.S., and even worked on a few grueling chain gangs; he had a thousand stories. Newspapers used to call him the Houdini of his era. I've always felt that Teddy Green (1180-AZ) let him down, and the same with his other crime partner Nick Montos (1299-AZ). I wish I had heard about his plight, though it's probably better for Nick & Teddy that I didn't. If the stories I heard had any truth to them, they might have paid the price. Both of them were older than me and have long passed.

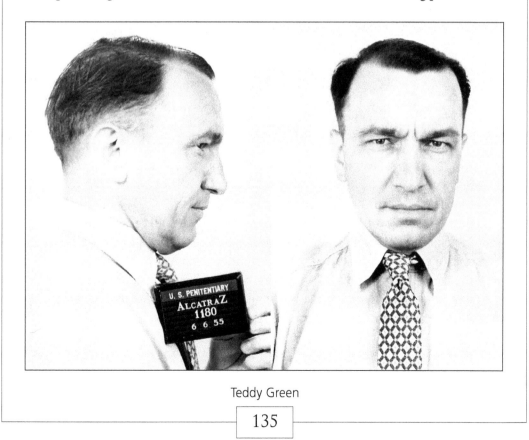

Teddy Green

Nick Montos

I probably would have given Teddy a pass for all the hardship and suffering he endured, but not Nick. I didn't hear these stories until it was all too late to step in and help. I helped several men back then and could have done the same for Forrest.

Teddy and I remained good friends when he was released from prison only a couple of years after me. He'd moved to Dorchester when he made parole. Teddy, Tom Kent (1443-AZ) and me all shared the same parole officer. In the early 1970s, Teddy had taken a job as a car salesman at a nearby dealership and I always saw to it that he had a lot of business! We'd sit in his office and spend long hours reminiscing about our years on Alcatraz. Teddy's life completely spiraled out of control when his daughter, Diane, in her late 20s or early 30s, was murdered by her abusive ex-husband. It all took place in an apartment building less than a mile from where Teddy and his wife were living. His daughter was a beautiful young woman and she'd worked as a waitress at the Playboy Gentlemen's Club in Boston's Park Square. It wasn't a place I frequented often, but I'd met Diane several times and really thought a lot of her. The ex-husband stalked and then murdered her while her children were asleep in the next room. The kids found their mother the next morning. After killing her, he left her apartment, went home, and then committed suicide. Can you imagine the pain and horror poor Teddy had to suffer through? Later in life it was something that was close to home, and I better understood. Teddy didn't stand a chance, he turned to heavy drinking, lost his job and then it was back to a life in crime. He moved to Florida and our paths didn't cross much after that. He was only a shell of his former self after Diane's death. He really suffered…

Forrest was a career criminal who had also spent a lifetime in prison with only a few short intervals of freedom. I'm not making excuses for him as he understood the risks and owned the time, but there's something about the non-violent guys just trying to take enough to survive, that paints a sad picture to me. I remember once he showed me photographs of his family when he lived in San Francisco. You could tell that he held a deep love for his wife and son. He told me that she visited him when he first transferred to Alcatraz and announced she was filing for a divorce. He was crushed but understood and supported her. It weighed heavy on him all those years and he always kept those photos close. He was a gifted musician and used the cover story that he made a living writing commercial jingles and doing studio work. His wife had no idea and he'd married her using an alias. She never knew his real name or identity. When the FBI came to their house with a warrant, she laughed at them believing they had identified the wrong man as it seemed so ridiculous.

Alcatraz was filled with hard luck stories like Forrest's, and all these decades later, I still remember feeling grief for him. Forrest, Teddy and Larry Trumblay were involved in a few escape plots that I believe they were all caught together, and all did a lot of hard time in a dark cell. Teddy bragged that he once dressed as a priest to escape. He'd been involved in a major break attempt at the State Penitentiary in Massachusetts sometime in the late 1950s with Martin Feeney (1548-AZ) and a few other cons. They'd taken hostages and it was a violent affair. My memory is that they captured the warden, associate warden, a priest and several guards. Assault teams were ordered to storm the prison and to kill on sight if they met resistance. Martin and Teddy were lucky to survive it. I remember Teddy asking me when I worked in the clothing

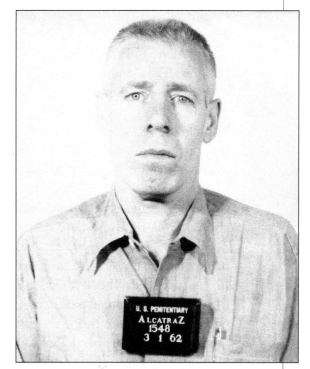

Martin Feeney

room if I had access to anything that would be useful as a disguise if they could make it to the mainland. I'm sure that Teddy and Forrest were plotting something on Alcatraz that never came to fruition.

Forrest was a soft-spoken and a soft-around the edges type of person. His downfall was that he was hooked on bank robberies and easy money. He talked constantly about pulling off the perfect heist in a retirement style take. He drove everyone nuts being so obsessive, and he picked everyone's brain on tactics he could adopt. He was clever and never wasted a minute plotting his next break. Every minute was spent plotting and scheming either a heist or escape, depending on what side of the wall he was on! He made one of the more ingenious Alcatraz escapes after being transferred to a hospital in Los Angeles for an operation. As he was being wheeled in for surgery, they stopped to remove his leg shackles. Since he had an IV and acted rather sedated, they figured he posed no risk. They should have taken heed to his long history of successful escapes! He carefully pulled out his IV from under the blanket, and then like a flash bomb, sprang from the gurney knocking down one of the Federal Marshals guarding him, and then bolted outside to a parking lot while still in his handcuffs and a hospital gown! He stole a car and made it halfway back to San Francisco before being apprehended by highway patrolmen. I always wondered why you don't see Forrest's break listed as one of the official escape attempts. In technical terms he was still under the custody of Alcatraz! It was genius...We heard that story on the yard a thousand times! He loved telling that one over and over!

Years later a friend clipped a newspaper article about a big heist he plotted. Forrest and his crime partner were able to acquire Brinks Armored Guard uniforms from a dry cleaners, entered a bank and were escorted right into the bank vault! They walked out with a half million dollars! I later read about it and knew he'd studied the armored car schedules and arrived in advance of the real guards. Forrest was always clever. He also made a spectacular break from San Quentin. Tucker and a few fellow convicts built a kayak with paddles, then painted prison uniforms to look like they were part of a rowing team from a yacht club. They'd stenciled a logo and lettering on their backs, then purposely paddled past a guard tower! The guard walked out onto the catwalk, and they waved at each other as they headed toward the Marin shore! The kayak looked like it was professionally built! This was long after Alcatraz. Imagine paddling away from San Quentin and also seeing Alcatraz in the faint distance! Forrest wasn't captured for nearly two years! I saw the photos in the newspaper and always enjoyed hearing about his escapades!

I've heard a few different versions of how he was shot and captured in his final round. All versions are troubling. One account is that the FBI was surveilling Teddy at his home in Palm Beach, but I always found it rather suspicious that Teddy didn't have some idea there was an army of agents watching him. I hate to make the accusation as I considered both of them friends, but it's something I've never been able to figure out. Teddy liked publicity and he was the kind of guy you couldn't trust with a secret. I can't say I fully trusted him, whereas Forrest was solid. Teddy returned to Boston years later looking for me. I asked him some hard questions and the answers felt shady. I didn't like his associates. Nick Montos was a crime partner of Teddy and Tucker and another shifty guy who also served time at Alcatraz. Nick was from Chicago, and I considered him a low life. He had a long life in crime. While awaiting trial in March of 1956, I heard his story on the radio program *Gang Busters*. That was a popular program during those years, and I also remember hearing the *Battle of Alcatraz* played out in a similar radio drama. Nick died recently in a Massachusetts State Prison. I could never figure out why Forrest and Teddy would even associate with his kind. He was captured in a robbery attempt of an antique store in Beacon Hill and the owner, an elderly woman who was a Holocaust survivor, hit him over the head with a baseball bat and gave him a good beating. It was all over the papers and word on the street was that Teddy was outside in a getaway car and fled when he realized there was trouble. I disliked Montos and I remember telling him to shut up more than once when he'd be seated at my table in the mess hall. During the days of the long ten-man tables, he'd be close to me and was a big talker and an annoyance. Again, couldn't stand him or his type.

Forrest had arrived on Alcatraz in the early 1950s and I was aware that he was close with Dave Edgerly (1033-AZ) going that far back. I think he was fascinated that Dave in the 1940s had made a lucrative career out of robbing armored cars and saw the promise in the potential. Joe Borecky (1032-AZ) was known as "Joe the Pollack" and was the partner of Edgerly. I knew them both on Alcatraz and Edgerly told me the story of an armored car heist that went south. They attempted to rob a Brinks armored car on a payroll run. Back in the day, banks would take large deliveries of cash on payroll days when people lined up to cash their checks. Brinks guards had dangerous jobs

Dave Edgerly

as they were prime targets. Edgerly held the guards at gunpoint with a Thompson submachine gun. He told me in the heat of the moment when he was pulling a handgun from the guard's holster (who was holding his hands up), Edgerly accidently squeezed the trigger, killing him. The other guard went for his weapon, and he shot him with the machine gun. Brinks posted big rewards for their capture. They placed the money bags into the trunk of their car and then drove into a storage garage. They had another car waiting on the street and waited until things cooled off before going back to get the money. When they rolled up the door, the trunk of the car was open, and the bags of cash were all missing.

The Chicago Police force back in the 1940s was tough and crooked. I knew men in that department and had paid off a few Chicago cops in my past. Buying cops back then was a routine practice and expectation. They tortured Edgerly and forced a confession. They broke bones and beat him to the brink of death. He took a life sentence and later landed on Alcatraz.

Forrest and Teddy had been working several heists and allegedly taken over a million in gems and cash. The FBI trailed the men to a parking garage in West Palm Beach where they had arranged a meeting. As Teddy walked toward Forrest as he started to get out of his car, a gauntlet of FBI agents moved in and drew their weapons. Teddy surrendered, but Forrest dropped back into his car and pulled the door closed; slid down beneath the steering wheel, then hit the gas pedal and blazed through a hailstorm of gunfire. As the bullet-riddled car skidded onto a busy roadway, he quickly realized it was a grim situation as he was bleeding from several gunshot wounds. He finally passed out, wrecked the car and was taken by agents. Forrest was unarmed and an embarrassment to the FBI since they'd shot an unarmed elderly man. He survived, but he didn't escape his fate.

He'd die in prison. Sad ending...Had he touched base with me, I would have helped him out. I made the offer many times to friends in later years. With a little help, he could have hid out forever in my neighborhood. I miss sitting with Forrest on the recreation yard steps and hearing him tell us all about his adventures!

FRANK WATSON

I have many great memories of working in the Alcatraz Laundry and so do many of the men I worked alongside. Frank Watson (1363-AZ) was serving a twenty-year sentence for stealing four cars after he'd escaped from a North Carolina State Prison. Following the escape, he stole a car and crossed the state line, ran out of gas, then stole another and repeated this a total of four times. His fingerprints were left on the cars, leading to his capture and he received a five-year sentence for each car theft and a one-way ticket to the Rock. I met Watson at the federal prison in Atlanta and we later worked together in the laundry on Alcatraz. Frank was on the same chain as Twining and while I don't remember them being close, they often cracked jokes about being shackled to one another on the trip over. Both Frank and Jack were

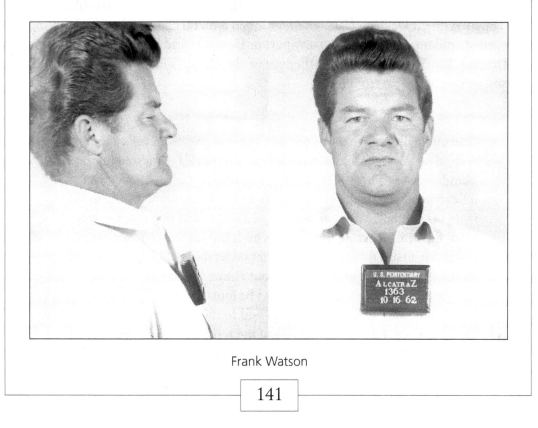

Frank Watson

James Gilliam

from North Carolina, and they spent a lot of time talking about home and wanting to return someday. Frank was a big card player, and one of those guys obsessive over table games and always trying to recruit others to join. There was a black convict named James Gilliam (932-AZ and 1361-AZ as he served two different terms on Alcatraz) who had also been on that same chain as Jack and Frank. He tangled with Twining and the two were threatening to kill each other, but somehow Frank was able to talk Jack down and smooth things over.

Charlie Hopkins (1186-AZ) also remembered James Gilliam commenting: "Gilliam was 6-foot 4-inches and 190 pounds. I watched Gilliam stab another black convict in the back while he was at work in the brush shop. A badass black guy named William Deloach (1089-AZ), grabbed a metal chair and started poking against Gilliam. He didn't want any part of Deloach, and he kept backing up as Deloach kept poking him with the legs of the chair. Gilliam had a reputation and was nothing but trouble."

Bulger:

> Gilliam finally got what was owed to him only a few months after I arrived on Alcatraz, and it was the first violence I'd witnessed on the island. Joe Wagstaff (1072-AZ), a young bank robber with mostly a quiet type of personality, took a knife and fiercely stabbed Gilliam in front of everyone. Wagstaff, the son of a singer and movie actor, was kind of a straight arrow, but at times he could get the younger guys going. My first sighting of Joe was him on a table stabbing at a guy with a fork for saying something about Hitler. He was no tough guy, so in my estimation he just wanted to be looked at as a "Bad Guy," so he raised a lot of hell at times. It's odd to think that later on he carries the reputation of being one of the most dangerous convicts at Leavenworth.

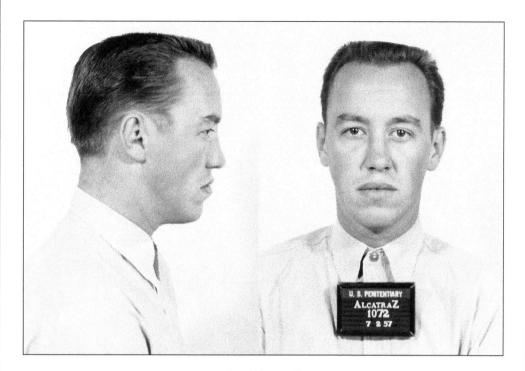

Joe Wagstaff

Gilliam had a reputation for staring men down with hard looks and mouthing foul slurs to white prisoners that created racial tension. He kept stirring things up until the men who had enough of him, and his threats, wanted him dead. I remember he mocked all of us over the work strike and was one of those always searching out trouble. While in D-Block, Gilliam was yelling threats to all the men in lockdown. He yelled "When I get out, I'm breaking into your houses and I'm going to rape all your motherfucking white wives, mothers, sisters, children, etc." The men told him "You won't ever get out of here alive." This alone almost triggered a race riot. This was his second time on the Rock and my recollection is that he was in prison for breaking into a person's home, robbing and assaulting them. A lowlife type of crime and threats not taken lightly by the guys serving long sentences. These guys were not going to gamble on those types of threats.

His behavior wasn't condoned by the black inmates and even Bumpy Johnson didn't associate with him. Most of the black cons on Broadway were from D.C. and real decent men. I remember a black convict named Bill Banks (1135-AZ) who called out another who had been convicted of rape. Banks gave him a fierce beating in the mess hall and none of the officers could pry him off. We later learned it was a young girl he'd raped, and it just went to show they didn't tolerate this type of behavior from anyone. The men put out a contract on Gilliam and drew straws as to who would take him out. Joe Wagstaff pulled the short straw. It was decided that Gilliam would be rubbed out in the mess hall. As Joe entered and stood in the food line, he was slipped a knife and Billy Boggs (1415-AZ) and Jerry Clymore (1339-AZ) staged a fight to divert the attention. The fight was intended to confuse the guards to allow Joe a clean shot. Gilliam was working in

Billy Boggs

Jerry Clymore

the kitchen and had made a few remarks to Joe under his breath. I was standing in line waiting to get my meal and saw the exchange take place. Just a couple days earlier during rec time, I watched Gilliam walking along the bottom bleacher step, hard to explain, but he jumped off and hit Joe's shoulder real hard. It was obvious something big was about to go down. So, while Joe had drawn the short straw, it wasn't as seemingly random as one would think since there was animosity between them.

Joe made his move when Gilliam least expected it and got what he had coming to him. The staged fight turns out to be a complete comedy. They were off on their timing as Wagstaff made a premature move; he'd thought he had a clean shot as Gilliam was carrying an insert to pour food into a container. Joe pulled the kitchen knife and, in a flash, drove it hard into Gilliam. The force knocked him to the ground so hard that he slid across the floor, and he crawled away leaving a small trail of blood. He hid behind a steam table next to the kitchen bars while Bill Long and a few other guards try to disarm Joe. It was a comedy watching Long screaming in a panic as Joe held his grip. No one paid any attention to Boggs and Clymore and everyone was laughing at them. Clymore is hollering at Boggs who's kicking him while he's down yelling "Stop you son of bitch!!! Stop!!!" It was a wasted attempt to confuse the guards. Gilliam did a lot of hollering, but the knife hit a bone and he was lucky the wound was superficial. The weapon was a dull butter knife that was allowed at the tables and wasn't enough to do the job.

An officer in the exterior gun gallery (located on the outside wall of the mess hall) took a mallet and knocked out a windowpane. The muzzle of the rifle popped through the small square opening and took aim at the men. I was waiting for the tear gas canisters to be activated and thought we'd be trapped in the gas chamber with no way out. Long was screaming at the top of his lungs for help and couldn't get the knife away from Joe. Finally, on his own, Joe let up and they carried a bloody Gilliam past all of us and up to the hospital. He is apologizing saying it was just D-Block talk. Joe was dragged to his feet and taken to a dark cell.

Next, it was Stanley Seltenrich's (1440-AZ) turn. Stanley was another bank robber and was on the same chain from Atlanta with Frank Morris (1441-AZ). Joe Carnes walks by his cell on the flats of B-Block, close to Frank Morris's cell, and he places a *Life Magazine* on the pillow. Stanley can see his cell from his job in the barbershop cutting hair, and he's aware that hidden inside the magazine is a knife. Everything halts when a guard walks by his cell, reaches in to take a look at the magazine, and out falls the knife onto the floor of his cell. The guard spins around and says to Stanley, "Let's go Seltenrich...off to D-Block."

Everything was repeated just months later in the shower room with Jerry Clymore making the hit this time. Everything falls together as the clothing room is the main hub for passing contraband

Stanley Seltenrich

and hidden in the shelf frames and clothing are various weapons hidden to drive off Gilliam's people. I worked with Clymore in the clothing room, and we knew each other really well. Jerry was a little guy, quiet and I remember him reading a lot. He praised Mahatma Gandhi and his philosophies of Ahimsa. I was just feet away when Clymore caught Gilliam off guard and this time drove the knife in deep into his back. The original plan was to stab Gilliam, then retreat into the clothing room and shut the door. We would be wired in, armed with metal bars, a shiv, and the guard would be trapped in with us. All the cons felt they would attack to get Jerry and we planned to hold them off. When Gilliam was stabbed, he was leaning over and drying one foot with a towel. He was naked, bent over with one foot on the ground and the other up on the bench when Jerry stabbed him. It was a real good sturdy and sharp knife, and it went in deep into his spine. Gilliam let out a short scream, straightened up, and then collapsed on the floor. The knife was lodged into his spine. Jerry tried to pull it out to finish the job, but the knife was lodged tight, and he couldn't pull it out. He then started kicking him in the head. The guards acted fast and were herding convicts up the stairs and back to their cells. While one guard grabbed Jerry, another younger guard pulled the knife out of Gilliam and the blood flowed. After the stabbing, the lieutenant asks one of the guards to call the Doc...He hands him the phone, starts talking, then yells and curses at the officer! "I said call the Doc, the Doctor, not the fucking Dock."

Gilliam would survive, but never walks again. He was carried off Alcatraz on a stretcher and that was the last we saw of him. Clymore is tried in court for attempted murder, and Bumpy Johnson (1117-AZ) and Robert Lipscomb (1141-AZ), both black, stepped up and testified on Jerry's behalf that it was self-defense and not a racially motivated attack. The jury hears Gilliam had attempted to stab Clymore and that he acted in self-defense. The cons, both black and white, banded together like a band of brothers. It was the same arrangement for Roland Simcox (1131-AZ) when he murdered Edward Gauvin (1134-AZ) in the shower room. He sliced him open, his intestines spilling out everywhere, and the jury was fed a story that resulted in Simcox walking away with a not guilty verdict.

The story of the witnesses is that Gilliam came at Jerry in the shower room, not the other way around. Clymore grabbed Gilliam's wrist; twists his arm behind his back and knocks him to the floor where he falls with all his weight onto the knife, severing his spine. Clymore's attorney argues that he never even touched the knife. The jury handed down a not guilty verdict and Warden Madigan went nuts. He thought it was a major failure of the justice system. He was later quoted in the press criticizing the jury's verdict as saying

The shower room in the cellhouse basement where the clothing issue is also located. Gilliam was stabbed in this location and was also the area where Edward Gauvin was murdered by Roland Simcox in 1957. In the 1930s, Al Capone had been stabbed in this same area, but survived his injuries.

JOHNSON	Record Form No. 8E Rev. Oct. 1940	1117-AZ	ASSOCIATE WARDEN'S RECORD CARD		FPI—LK—5-5-58—47M—5517		
Offense	Violation Narcotic Laws			Race Negro		Age 10-31-08	
Sentence 15 years	Begins 6-12-53			Married Divorced		Deps. 3	
Date Imp. 6-12-53 AtNew York, N.Y.				Citizen USA		Relig. Prot	
Date Rec'd 9-9-59 from Atlanta				Physical Cond. Regular Duty			
Par. Elig. 12-8-58*				Mental Cond. No Report			
C. R. 1-2-64	Max. 12-6-68*			Education: S. A. T.			
Comm. Fine $9000	G. T. 1800 days			G. S. 11.2			
PREVIOUS RECORD:				PSYCHOLOGICAL & APTITUDE TESTS:			
Jails	Ref. 1			IQ 118			
Pens. Fed.	State 3			Occupational Skills:			
Detainers: Fed.	State			Barber			
Escapes: Fed.	State						
CUSTODY:				Avocational Interests:			
Crimes Involved: (Enumerate) Aslt (16) Burg. G.L.							

History of Occupational Experience				
Occupations	No. Yrs.	Verification of Performance		
		Quality	Dependability	
*178 days inoperative on appeal.				
Testified in the case of Clymore 1339-AZ		-1-12-61		
1-14-54 trf to AZ fr Lk				
12-21-58 trf AZ to Atlanta				
9-9-59 trf Atlanta to AZ				

Aliases:
Raymond Holmes, Raymond Johnson, "Bumpy"

	Number	Residence		Occupations	
	1117-AZ	New York, N.Y.	Barber		

JOHNSON, ELLSWORTH

Ellsworth "Bumpy" Johnson

"Clymore's a 140 lb. weakling and Gilliam is 260 lbs. of lean muscle. You're saying Clymore twisted his arm up behind him with Gilliam having the knife, and he takes him to the ground and stabbed him in the spine? This is so fantastic, and it is completely absurd…" Madigan had his number on that one. Probably no coincidence that the name and address of Jack Burnam, Clymore's attorney, were found in the waterproof pouch floating in the bay that belonged to Clarence Anglin after their escape. Burnam was the same attorney who represented Simcox and had him successfully acquitted twice! Clarence likely felt he'd be a good contact if they were captured.

The last time I saw Jerry was at Leavenworth. A black convict got into a violent fight with a Texan cowboy type, and he beat him into a serious and bloody condition. Jerry comes on-scene, pulls a knife and starts stabbing the assailant repeatedly until the blade broke off in his shoulder. I watched it all play it out. Jerry was grabbed on the spot and dragged to the hole. I thought about those conversations in the shower room and him talking about the philosophies of Gandhi and studying faiths of Buddhism. For someone who studied peaceful faiths, he certainly was a violent individual. I never saw him again after the Leavenworth stabbing.

SIMCOX	Record Form No. 16 Rev. Oct. 1946	131-AZ	ASSOCIATE WARDEN'S RECORD CARD		FPI-LK-4-24-59—66M—6640

Offense ASSAULT & MUTINY-DISOBEDIENCE

Sentence 42½ yrs   Begins 2-16-52

Date Imp. 2-16-52   At Korea (Army)

Date Rec'd 5-17-54 fr Leavenworth USDB

Par. Elig. 4-15-66

C. R. 9-4-80   Max 3-15-94

Comm. Fine   G. T. 5100 days

PREVIOUS RECORD:

Jails   Ref. Ohio State Sch

Pens. Fed.   State

Detainers: Fed. 0   State 0

Escapes: Fed.   State

CUSTODY:

Crimes Involved: (Enumerate)
Burglary - assault on superior
officer in Army - Mutiny at Ft. Lv.

Aliases:

Name
   SIMCOX. RONALD E.

Race   White   Aged 25-32

Married   no   Deps. 0

Citizen USA   Relig. Prot

Physical Cond. Regular Duty

Mental Cond. Rather Anti-Soci

Education: S. A. T. not psychot
   G. S. 7th Grade School

PSYCHOLOGICAL & APTITUDE TESTS:
   IQ 106

Occupational Skills:
Landscaping - clothing factory
in Boy's School, Ohio

Avocational Interests:

Occupational Experience

Occupations	No. Yrs.	Verification of Performance	
		Quality	Dependability

6/57 Killed inmate Galvin - one other attempt to MURDER.
Continues to slash and stab his victims.

Testified in the case of Clymore 1339-AZ 1-16-61

| Number 1131-AZ | Residence Columbus, Ohio | Occupations | |

Roland Simcox

Simcox's story is also interesting. Everyone knew the story of him murdering Gauvin in the shower room. I remember reading an article that claimed he and I were friends and that we lifted weights together on the island, but it's not true. I only met Simcox one or two times down in the clothing issue, and rarely saw him at Alcatraz. He was a tough convict who could hold his own, but he was disliked by most. The murder happened just before I'd arrived, but when I worked in the clothing issue, that story was told a hundred times. A couple of the guys I worked with told me they'd witnessed the whole thing happen. Simcox was a former Army prisoner as was Gauvin.

The accounts from the cons who witnessed the killing called it like this: Simcox and Gauvin had disagreed over some issue while in D-Block and Simcox told him "I'm killing you…" He had a knife hidden on the underside of one of the benches in the shower room. Simcox was working in the clothing issue when Gauvin came down for a shower. I heard that when Gauvin came down, Simcox softly apologized saying that it was just D-Block talk and reached out to shake Gauvin's hand. As Simcox clasps Gauvin's hand, he pitches him off balance, reached and came up with a knife and cut him down. It was fiercely violent, and he ripped him apart. Blood was everywhere and the guards froze. No one could blame them. I heard that Gauvin's guts were eviscerated out of his

Edward Gauvin

abdomen, and it was a brutal scene. The guard who claimed to grab Simcox was off on the side throwing rolls of toilet paper at him hollering "STOP-STOP!" All the guys nicknamed him "Shit Paper Slim." The version of the officers printed in so many books is a face-saving story.

As is customary in prison circles, many guys covered for Simcox claiming it was self-defense, even though many of them hated Simcox. They hated the guards and Alcatraz even more. On Alcatraz, Simcox became a marked man among cons. He thought a lot of himself and bullied several of the weaker convicts. He was sent to D-Block and Joe Carnes and a few others told him that once he comes out of D, "You Die." He never came out of D-Block. Had he ever made it back into population, he would have gone out like Julius Caesar.

Getting back to Frank Watson (1363-AZ), he wasn't too bright, a big barrel-chested guy with a deep loud laugh. You could always hear

his laugh over the heavy machinery in the laundry building. His dream was to have a "Buscadero!" What's that I asked? It's a hand tooled leather holster for two pistols "Western Style." At that time there was a popular western song "Big Bad John" by Jimmy Dean. It's a country style song about a guy named "Big Bad

John" who dies in a mine disaster and he's the big hero to the other mineworkers. I used to tell Watson in front of the other guys in the laundry "They were thinking of you when they wrote that song." I'll tell you, it really made his day. He'd give out a big laugh with a big grin. He was one of the guys who would exercise after we finished the laundry work. We did pushups, chin ups, etc., as part of our daily routine, including Bloomie. Those were the good old days…It was the best job I ever worked in my long life of only a few legitimate jobs. I have great memories being in the laundry after we'd finished our work. Sometimes we'd finish two hours early and stand at the window looking out onto the San Francisco Bay. I enjoyed watching the sailboats as they passed the island. It was a million-dollar view, unlike anything you'd ever see in any other prison. Bloomie had a small radio, and you'd have music like "Big Bad John" playing and you'd see Watson strutting by like a square dancer. It's odd what stands out in your memories. I remember standing at the window and just listening to the radio. They'd play some of the same popular songs over and over and we'd just stand and gaze quietly at the San Francisco Bay through the window. When I think back to those years, my thoughts always go back to Alcatraz. Tony Bennett's song "I Left My Heart in San Francisco," always made me think that maybe I did leave my heart out there. Part of the change in me before prison was my interest to just get the money, the gun was just a prop to expedite things, but I could never picture using it on anyone.

It's hard for me today to look back on those years and think about the tough lives all of us led back then, but they were still filled with so many good memories of men trying to make the best of a tough situation. Alcatraz affected everyone differently and you could see the toll it took on some of these guys who'd been there for long stretches. I remember seeing Floyd Wilson (956-AZ), who attempted to escape from Alcatraz a few years before I arrived. I'd see him on the yard and in the mess hall—he always looked like he'd had a rough life and always looked sad. It's

Floyd Wilson

funny, but I do remember feeling sympathy toward him. He seemed like a gentle, decent, non-violent and legit guy who didn't belong in a hardcore prison. He seemed different than most of the cons. I used to feel sorry for him and don't remember him in conversation or anyone's company. All of us knew that he'd once tried to escape from Alcatraz and had evaded officers for several hours.

There was con named Tom Lindsey (1547-AZ), a bank robber and also a really talented ventriloquist. He wasn't on Alcatraz long that I can remember, but one time I was sitting on the rec yard bleachers with Frank Sprenz (1414-AZ) he comes over with a puppet made from a cut shirt sleeve. Hard to explain, but each side has a painted face that resembled an officer. The puppet even had a coat and hair made from yarn. We'd laugh so hard that both Frank and I were in tears. I never laughed so hard in my life. He'd mock "Double Tough" as "Double Puff" Ordway; make the puppet do a little strut, then come back as another officer. He pegged their mannerisms, and it was always welcome when he'd offer comedy to break the dreary isolation. He'd do a little routine and then we'd talk for a bit, and he'd walk away to work the yard and share his bit with others. He also knew a few magic tricks that the men found really entertaining during mealtime.

Tom Lindsey

It was a tough ending for Frank Sprenz—dying in prison. I'm glad he died peacefully in his sleep. The government certainly got their pound of flesh with Sprenz. They were mistaken with him. He was a non-violent person. Daring, yes, but not mean, cruel or at war with society. He'd once been on the FBI's Most Wanted list and a personal adversary of J. Edgar Hoover. Sprenz was a private pilot and flew coast to coast pulling bank jobs and made off with a respectable amount of cash. He was adept at stealing planes and cash. He was hard to trace casing banks in random areas of the country. He'd search for airplanes that looked like they'd been parked

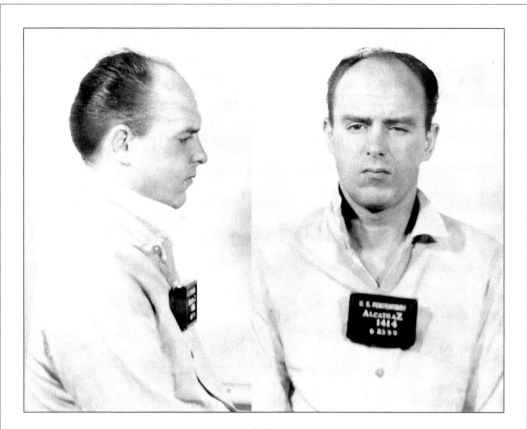

Frank Sprenz

for long stretches and not be noticed missing until they were found somewhere across the country. I think it was Hoover who dubbed him the "Flying Bandit." He fled in a small plane to Mexico and had planned to refuel, then continue his journey to Cuba. A cow wandered onto an abandoned strip of runaway, causing him to swerve and hit a tree. The plane was totaled and Sprenz was captured and deported back to the US. Later Hoover used his influence to send him to Alcatraz. We were good friends and kept in touch for a while after prison. When he was released, he remained free for around twenty-five years, a good stretch.

He was a bright guy but got into a sleazy racket. I liked Frank and would have never insulted him, but I stayed clear of his business and didn't want any part of it. It's something I would have run from... Sex trade massage parlors were the lowest. I always felt sorry for the working girls, and I never wanted anything from them. I didn't allow these "sludge" parlors in my neighborhood. The girls led sad lives, yet the government never moves on the pimps that use them for sex slavery. They never place bugs on the men who lead this trade or try

to help the young women. There were two brothers who moved into my neighborhood that ran this type of ring. I was told they'd get these girls hooked on heroin and then put them on the streets to work. I knocked on their door after they moved in and told them to pack up and get out in ten hours. They wanted to talk it over and cut a deal. I told them in so many words to get out or they'd be used for target practice. After they move out and one day when I'm in the garage at Winter Hill, I'm approached by an associate asking if we can make a deal with them. I told him no and it was final. No heroin and no pimps. In the Mafia this was a firm line we held, and the businesses could not put kids at risk. I also said no to baseball gambling machines you'd find in liquor stores. Kids can play them as they were always hidden in the back area, but they'd seldom win any money. I figured the mothers would hate me if their kids were dropping their lunch money into these machines.

After I went on the run, there was an epidemic of heroin deaths in the town and people reportedly said this wouldn't have happened if Whitey were here. I'm pretty sure even the *Boston Globe* printed a story with a similar statement. It's true and I personally knew some of the victims. I've read stories accusing me of having a hand in heroin rackets. That is the biggest lie. These stories are completely false, and

I never would have been a part of any of it. During my reign, we chased people out of town who ran crack houses and once a friend asked me to help. An ex-con lived next to a vacant house. The drug dealers took over this residence that was really nice, and they were stealing electricity from one of the outside outlets of my friend's home. People were coming and going buying hard drugs and he was worried about his children but didn't want to create a problem since he was on parole and trying to stay clean. Kevin Weeks and I knocked on the door and told them that they're out by 10 AM the next morning. It was late in the evening and raining hard. We told them we'd give them time to pack. They wanted to come to an agreement and talk things over. We drew a hard line and said you're out by 10 AM or we kill you. The next morning, Kevin and a few associates show up with sheets of plywood and started nailing them over the windows and they fled like cockroaches, and we made sure they never returned. We painted 'Drug Free Zone—Keep Out' and made clear they'd pay a price if anyone returned. The claims I was involved in drug rackets is simply not true. I worked to keep angel dust and heroin out of South Boston. We did the same with whorehouses in South Boston. We'd kick in the door and make clear you're out of here now. We didn't tolerate anything that resulted in harm to children.

I tried to keep the goodwill of the people. I liked and wanted to protect our neighborhood. When I was released from prison I was drawn into organized crime. Lots of money, violence, murder and notoriety which I tried to avoid. Sprenz was later indicted for the deaths of two women who perished in a deliberate fire. He fired a couple of girls who worked in the parlor, and they threatened to expose the operation. He didn't set the fire and was never at the crime scene, but it was claimed that he'd hired someone to apparently scare them, not kill them. Either way, real tragic... Easy for others to point the finger in desperation to try and take some of the heat off themselves. I knew Frank well and couldn't see him involved in such a crime. It wasn't in his character to kill. I knew killers, but Frank wasn't made of that cloth. At least when I knew him.

RICHARD BARCHARD, CARL SMITH AND LOUIS ARQUILLA

As a preface to Bulger's memories of Louis "Louie" Arquilla, during our interviews he openly reminisced about their close friendship but hesitated to provide much on Louie's girlfriend Dorothy "Dottie" Barchard, who had admitted to authorities being in a relationship with Louis while still legally married to Bulger's crime partner, Richard Barchard. As chronicled earlier, Barchard, his wife Dottie, and Whitey's former girlfriend had conspired in the Hoosier bank heist for which he was later convicted. Bulger encouraged me to talk directly with Richard to ask about Dottie, but what he did offer was that he thought a lot of her. In one letter he wrote her nickname was "Kiss of Death," as she

Richard Barchard

had a lot of men in her life that wound up dead in gang wars. In one example he wrote: "Louie was with Dottie and later shot dead…Ronnie Dermody went with Dottie and was shot dead…Joe Barboza's attorney went with Dottie, blown up by a bomb and lost his leg…Henry Reddington helped Dottie and was murdered by her boyfriend Jimmy O'Toole, who in turn was murdered—I was convicted of the murder—and so on…When she suggested her and me team up, I graciously declined."

Despite these comments, he thought she was intelligent, attractive and pleasant to be around. Additionally, he offered that Dorothy's relationships with Richard and Louis created tension, and that he and Barchard rarely spoke to one another while at Alcatraz, but it was mostly by Richard's own doing. He stated that Richard worked in the kitchen and kept to himself, and only rarely came out to the yard on weekends, and when he did, he kept a clear distance from the Boston crew.

Richard declined to engage in a formal interview, and we only spoke once, but he did offer some points of clarification on a few subjects. He remarked "It was a real bad situation" and he was trying to do his time without putting himself in a position where he'd end up in a fight that would result in an even longer prison sentence. When I asked him about Dorothy, he denied that the tension arose from her and Louis's relationship. He said that he had left Dorothy a short time before she hooked up with Louie, and that he had been running with another woman, which was the basis for a lot of hard feelings (this is also confirmed in Dorothy's case file). Richard made that clear he and Dottie had already separated and it wasn't a factor in keeping a distance from the others while serving time on the Rock. He also stated that there was a lot of mistrust between him, Bulger, Arquilla and even Carl Smith whom he acknowledged as being a good friend of his during those years. Barchard and Smith had struck up a friendship while serving time at Charlestown State Prison. Barchard had served two sentences for armed robberies to which he'd pled guilty in January of 1951. Smith also had an impressive resume of convictions related to various break-ins and robberies. The two had remained close until Alcatraz; but later, Barchard made a decision that he was going to focus on getting his life turned in a positive direction, not on fighting or getting involved again in more criminal endeavors. He said firmly, "I was done. I made my mind up that I was going to get my life back on track. There were no hard feelings, I was just moving on with my life. After a year in solitary confinement, I realized that I didn't want to rot away in prison. A couple months after arriving at Alcatraz, Carl and I had to settle a score on the yard. This guy (James McKinney, 1233-AZ) and few of his friends threw a coat over me, knocked me to the ground and worked me over. The guard who watched the whole thing go down didn't

Carl Smith

step in to help, and I didn't give him a pass. Carl grabbed a baseball bat and we made sure he wasn't able to walk off the yard on his own. Both of us end up in solitary and I'm locked in my cell 24-hours a day for a whole year. What's left out of the story is that Carl and I were locked down in D-Block for an entire year before Jimmy came on scene at Alcatraz. I doubt Jimmy and Carl ever saw each other because I don't think he ever came out of some kind of lockdown status after the fight on the yard."

Though Bulger never fully revealed the details, Barchard admitted that it was Carl Smith who had devised the story he used to implicate Bulger in a murder. The allegation was wholly fictional, but he'd told officials and allegedly confessed to a "Salvation Army Preacher" that following the bank heist in Indiana, Bulger had committed a murder and dumped the victim's body into a lake. One theorized angle was that he wanted to get them both released from solitary with a reduced sentence as Barchard might have believed that either Bulger or his girlfriend had cooperated with officials to reveal his involvement in the planning of the bank heists. Bulger was imprisoned at Atlanta during this period, and the fabricated story resulted in an immense amount of stress for his family and the ruthless interrogation of his then girlfriend, Jacquie McAuliffe Martin. Bulger later confronted Barchard, and his version was that he'd felt the confession would get the three of them back at the County Jail for questioning and provide the perfect opportunity for escape. Bulger commented, "I was painted as the bad guy. Later he was apologetic and took responsibility. Wrong move, but I liked Richard and let it slide." On November 3, 1960, Barchard wrote a four-page letter admitting to officials that he had fabricated the story and apologized profusely, writing in part "In retrospect I can see the seriousness of it and the immaturity of myself... this is an honest attempt on my part to right a wrong and under no coercion in any form, clear James Bulger."

When Bulger arrived at Alcatraz, he addressed it head on, but both declined to offer much detail. Barchard stated, "Jimmy and me settled everything...I think I was already working the kitchen detail when Jimmy arrived; I found that I liked the assignment and kept to myself. I was on Broadway, in a cell right across from Bumpy Johnson, and the work was seven days a week. I went from being locked in my cell 24-hours a day, one hour the yard and one shower once each week for more than a year; to working outside my cell, visiting the yard and being allowed to take a shower every single day. Everything went from night to day and it woke me up...Madigan gave me his word that if I kept my head down; minded my own business; kept out of trouble; he said I could be out of prison in five years. I had a twenty-year sentence, and this was enough motivation for me. I made the decision I was going to get out and

James McKinney

stay out. Jimmy and I were still friends and we squared things up..." As my interviews with Bulger continued, I called and wrote more letters to Richard, but he never again responded back. He died in 2016.

Carl Smith, however, had more and more difficulty coping with the isolation. On the morning of March 13, 1957, prisoner Jack Hall (1214-AZ), who was only serving a five-year sentence on assault and stolen vehicle charges, committed suicide by hanging himself using a makeshift noose from twisted clothing and wrapped around the bars inside D-12, a closed front solitary confinement cell on the flats of D-Block. Barchard remembered everyone watching Hall's lifeless body being carried out and laid on the cement cellhouse floor. Many of the prisoners stood on their bunk to get a clear view and they watched intently as he was pronounced dead, and a white sheet draped over his body. This weighed heavy on Smith's mental health as he was convinced Hall had been secretly murdered by officers. After 346 days in isolation, Smith was removed from D-Block and brought to the prison hospital for evaluation. He had been progressively

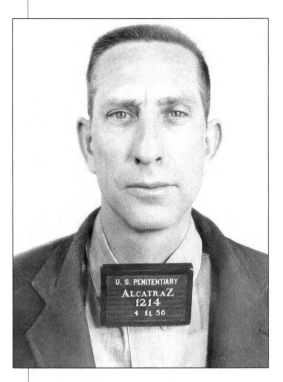

Jack Hall

showing pronounced paranoid trends and became insistent that the associate warden was attempting to have him murdered. He had written letters that he needed psychiatric help and the prison psychiatrist noted that that he "frequently expressed the delusion that his food is being poisoned as part of a plot to kill him." He began making death threats towards the associate warden and felt that it was his "duty" to kill him before the Alcatraz guards got to him. The paranoia had become so extreme that large quantities of food had been found in a pillowcase that he insisted had been poisoned by officers. A memo written by the Chief Medical Officer on December 3, 1957, he had to be placed into a ceramic strip cell inside the Alcatraz hospital, as he had become "extremely hostile, violent and obscene in his actions," and another report stated, "his attitude has continued to be suspicious, belligerent and menacing."

D-Block

An inside view of D-12 where Jack Hall took his own life.

The solitary confinement closed front cells of D-Block.

Only months before being confined in the prison hospital, Smith started a campaign of writing letters to public officials expressing his suspicion that the staff at Alcatraz was plotting his murder. In October of 1957, he wrote letters to then-Vice President Richard Nixon and the Director of the Bureau of Prisons James V. Bennett. In his letter to Bennett, he stated in part:

> "I am at Alcatraz and the officials here are trying to murder me like they did Hall and Gauvin, and because I know about them and their system, they come to my cell and laugh at me, and tell me I'm wrong so that they can get me in the right place to kill me...Will you send someone to investigate these murderers before they kill me?"

In January of 1958, Smith was transferred to the Medical Center for Federal Prisoners in Springfield Missouri, and less than three years later, he helped plot an elaborate escape. Accompanied by four other convicts, including Walter Splitt (1408-AZ), a friend and cohort of Charles "Jeep" Marcum (1407-AZ) (who also happened to be Smith's brother- in-law and early crime partner),

Letters written by Carl Smith to then Vice President Richard Nixon and the Director of the Bureau of Prisons, James V. Bennett. Smith was convinced he was being targeted for murder by the prison administration. In a sad case of irony, he would be murdered a decade later in prison by a fellow convict.

162

they escaped from the kitchen using a cutting torch to remove window bars and a cast iron manhole cover to gain access to a large sewer tunnel under the prison. They had made it underground about sixty yards outside the perimeter fence by the time they were discovered missing. Without any weapons, the men surrendered without a fight when they were surrounded by guards yielding high powered rifles. Smith would later be transferred back to Leavenworth and then onto Terre Haute, Indiana in 1965.

Finally in 1974, as if fulfilling a self-prophecy, Carl Smith was brutally murdered by fellow prisoner Howard Lane. A case file report read

Walter Splitt

Smith was one of the rare cases where it was documented he had been held in one of the ceramic isolation cells inside the Alcatraz hospital. These cells were rarely used and reserved for only the most extreme cases.

in part, "Mr. Smith ran down the steps and fell at the bottom of the stairwell. He was bleeding heavily from multiple open wounds in the chest and back, apparently made from a sharp instrument. There was a great amount of blood spattered over his entire body. The inmate was pronounced dead at approximately 10:25 PM. An autopsy was performed at St. Anthony's Hospital and the provisional anatomical diagnoses were: (1) Stab wounds, left and mid chest; Multiple (front, side, and back) with penetration of the heart (left ventricle and lungs)." It was another sad ending to a troubled life. Bulger would also highlight that Walter Splitt was later shot to death during a robbery in Florida with crime partner Charles "Jeep" Marcum, who was also wounded. Bulger stated he attempted to locate him in 1995 and learned he was serving time in a Florida prison, but never made contact again. Brutal endings to violent lives...

LOUIS R. ARQUILLA

Louis Ronald Arquilla was a close friend of Bulger from Massachusetts. Well liked, well spoken, good humored, and one who kept to himself. Bulger felt a close bond to Arquilla and commented that even decades later, he felt sorrowful whenever he thought back to Alcatraz and his time with "Louie" and the tragic death that followed. His inmate case file provided the following:

Louis R. Arquilla

Louis Ronald Arquilla was born in Barrington, Rhode Island; he was reared largely in Massachusetts, where his father operated a manufacturing business. His mother was Irish and his father of Spanish origin. However, he came from a broken home, afflicted by domestic violence. In his youth, the father shot and killed the mother and then committed suicide. The subject was taken into the home of a maternal aunt in Somerville, Massachusetts. He joined the Army in 1947, receiving a minority discharge on April 20, 1947. He re-enlisted February 3, 1948, and was discharged on February 15, 1949, under Honorable conditions, but on account of lack of adaptability.

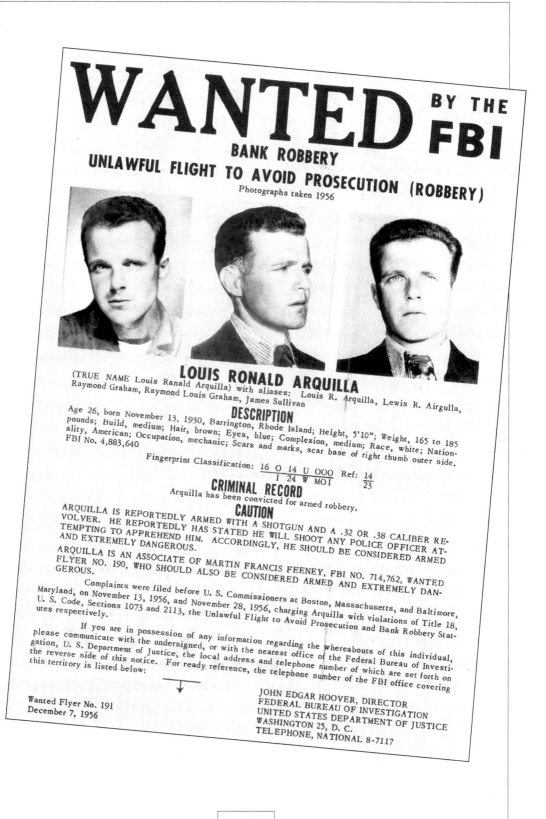

WANTED BY THE FBI

BANK ROBBERY
UNLAWFUL FLIGHT TO AVOID PROSECUTION (ROBBERY)

Photographs taken 1956

LOUIS RONALD ARQUILLA

(TRUE NAME Louis Ranald Arquilla) with aliases: Louis R. Arquilla, Lewis R. Airgulla, Raymond Graham, Raymond Louis Graham, James Sullivan

DESCRIPTION

Age 26, born November 13, 1930, Barrington, Rhode Island; Height, 5'10"; Weight, 165 to 185 pounds; Build, medium; Hair, brown; Eyes, blue; Complexion, medium; Race, white; Nationality, American; Occupation, mechanic; Scars and marks, scar base of right thumb outer side. FBI No. 4,883,640

Fingerprint Classification: $\frac{16 \ O \ 14 \ U \ OOO}{I \ 24 \ W \ MOI}$ Ref: $\frac{14}{23}$

CRIMINAL RECORD

Arquilla has been convicted for armed robbery.

CAUTION

ARQUILLA IS REPORTEDLY ARMED WITH A SHOTGUN AND A .32 OR .38 CALIBER REVOLVER. HE REPORTEDLY HAS STATED HE WILL SHOOT ANY POLICE OFFICER ATTEMPTING TO APPREHEND HIM. ACCORDINGLY, HE SHOULD BE CONSIDERED ARMED AND EXTREMELY DANGEROUS.

ARQUILLA IS AN ASSOCIATE OF MARTIN FRANCIS FEENEY, FBI NO. 714,762, WANTED FLYER NO. 190, WHO SHOULD ALSO BE CONSIDERED ARMED AND EXTREMELY DANGEROUS.

Complaints were filed before U. S. Commissioners at Boston, Massachusetts, and Baltimore, Maryland, on November 13, 1956, and November 28, 1956, charging Arquilla with violations of Title 18, U. S. Code, Sections 1073 and 2113, the Unlawful Flight to Avoid Prosecution and Bank Robbery Statutes respectively.

If you are in possession of any information regarding the whereabouts of this individual, please communicate with the undersigned, or with the nearest office of the Federal Bureau of Investigation, U. S. Department of Justice, the local address and telephone number of which are set forth on the reverse side of this notice. For ready reference, the telephone number of the FBI office covering this territory is listed below:

Wanted Flyer No. 191
December 7, 1956

JOHN EDGAR HOOVER, DIRECTOR
FEDERAL BUREAU OF INVESTIGATION
UNITED STATES DEPARTMENT OF JUSTICE
WASHINGTON 25, D. C.
TELEPHONE, NATIONAL 8-7117

Martin Feeney and Louie Arquilla following their arrest in 1957.

This man was sentenced April 11, 1957, at Baltimore, Maryland to serve twenty-five years for conspiracy, robbery of a FDIC bank, and aiding and abetting. On November 21, 1956, the subject carrying a .45 caliber revolver, and accomplice by co-defendant Martin Francis Feeney, who was carrying a sawed-off shotgun, robbed the Fidelity-Baltimore National Bank. Arquilla and Feeney entered the bank together and scooped up the money from the teller's drawer while Feeney stayed in the customer's area near the front door. Later they picked-up Arquilla's girlfriend who later was acquitted of a conspiracy act, but on November 7, 1957, was sentenced to a one-year and one-day for misprision of a felony. His earlier history dates back to January 1950, when he was sentenced to a twelve-to-fifteen-year term in the Charleston, Massachusetts State Penitentiary for armed robbery and was paroled July 10, 1956. During the service of this sentence, he was reported for vile language, refusing to work, and being insolent to an officer. He was also reported on November 29, 1950, for being involved in an escape plot. He also acquired other violations including

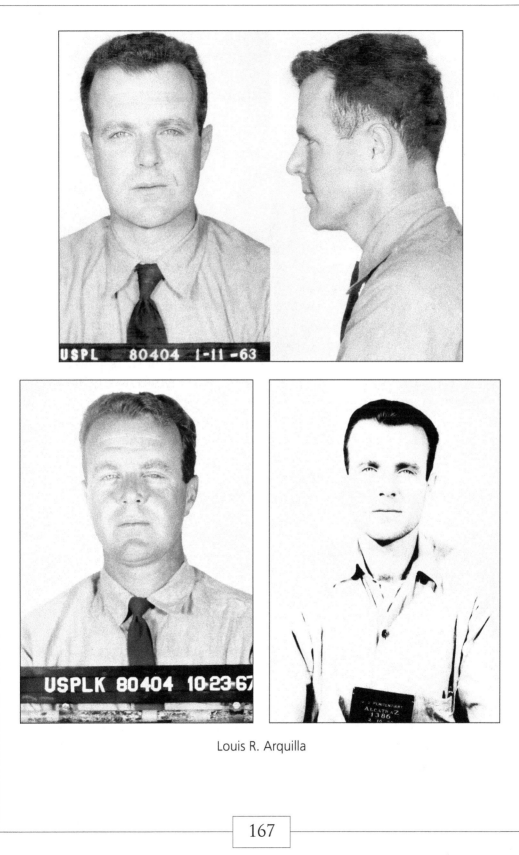

Louis R. Arquilla

suspicion of stealing, participating in a riot, fighting, and being out of bounds. Committed to Atlanta April 25, 1957, Arquilla was transferred to Alcatraz, February 9, 1959, after he forfeited good time for attempting to escape with John Paul Scott, Charles Catalano and Stephen Kritsky over a roof.

Bulger wrote about Arquilla:

"Louie" was one of my closest associates. He was also involved in the escape plot at Atlanta that helped earn our ticket to Alcatraz. A few of his crime partners were Tom Kent (1443-AZ) and Martin Feeney (1548-AZ) who were both Boston natives and both served time on Alcatraz. Kent and Louie had cells next to each other. Poor Louie endured a long life of pain and suffering. When he was a child, his brothers Richard and Jack were sitting with their mother in their beautiful home, wearing suits, eating breakfast and getting ready to drive to church. Louie's mother was full Irish and his father full Italian. This is a bad combination. The parents fought all the time and always were insulting each other. Louie's mother was yelling insults at the father and telling him to hurry up. He rushes down the stairs, pulls a gun and shoots the mother in the head while sitting at the table. He then sits down, puts the gun in his mouth and blows his brains all over the kitchen. Louie and his brothers are traumatized, and their lives are changed forever. They all suffered. I knew all three and one of them later became a preacher. That's something he carried with him his entire life. I liked Louie and miss him.

Louie, along with Tom Kent, robbed a little bank in Turners Falls, Massachusetts. They netted only $5,000 and it turned out that it was Kent's girlfriend who had tipped off authorities and landed them both in prison. Tom and Louie met in the Charlestown State Prison in Massachusetts, which opened in 1804 with no plumbing, only buckets to relieve themselves, and they ate while locked in their cells. They served time alongside Walter Perry, an old convict who made the papers for nearly escaping from the same place in a *Shawshank* style break. At one point the guys there had cats and canaries for pets. They had an electric chair and used it often. The very last guy they executed was on death row for murdering a store clerk during a botched robbery. As he was being led into the execution chamber, he passed a con on a work detail listening to a baseball game on the radio. He hollered over to him, "Who's winning?" He wanted the score of a ball game that was being broadcasted! Imagine that!

While there, Tom Kent was part of an escape plot using wooden guns that looked authentic and used them to hold up guards. As I remember, Tom had forcefully pushed a guard with the barrel. He used so much force that the fake gun broke. When the guard realized he'd been tricked, a fight erupted. Tom at some point during the mayhem, grabbed a hammer and hit the guard over the head. The guard survived the attack but became disabled and was forced to retire. Tom was young then and I remember his mother and father were real Irish Catholics. Tom was the only person I knew who deliberately bought a ticket to Alcatraz. He wanted to add that to his resume. I know that sounds bizarre, but that was the real Tom Kent. He was a bizarre individual. I still laugh whenever I see him in documentaries talking about the Alcatraz escape. Most of these were made up stories that he contrived.

Louie, Martin and Dorothy [Barchard] had been captured in Minnesota and were being transferred back to Baltimore to stand trial for bank robbery. When Louie was being flown and accompanied by U.S. Marshals, he tried to make an escape and hijack the plane. Louie, a very mild guy on the surface asked, "Can you please free one of my hands so that I can eat?" Louie catches them off guard and erupts as he slams the Marshal with the food tray and rushes the cockpit. The pilot, co-pilot and flight attendant slam the cabin door closed. The

flight attendant is brave, and she puts herself in harm's way while the Marshals beat him unconscious as passengers scream in panic. The media had a field day with complaints of flying prisoners and the flight attendant is hailed as a hero. I later ask Louie why he tried such a risky move. He said he read that planes that carry U.S. Mail have a rule that they must carry a gun in the cockpit. I asked him, what if there wasn't? He said he'd crash the plane. He wanted to be free or dead, and he had a powerful death wish.

On Alcatraz, Louie somehow convinced Warden Madigan that the "Christian Science Monitor" was an objective reporter of international and domestic news. Long story short, "Promising Paul" [nickname given to Warden Madigan by the convicts] allowed it in. It was published and printed in Boston, and I really enjoyed reading it.

At Alcatraz we had no commissary or canteen rights. We were issued a toothbrush and tooth powder in a can. The only thing we could purchase which was later on, was a box of chocolates at Christmas time, and only if you had not been written up for any violation. A friend, Don Iannelli (1375-AZ) wasn't eligible to purchase any, so Louie made three equal shares out of our two boxes for "Big I," himself and me—common practice on the Rock. Years later when on the run, I tried to reach Iannelli in a suburb of Chicago and was told that he had died a painful death.

DEPARTMENT OF JUSTICE
UNITED STATES PENITENTIARY
LEWISBURG, PENNSYLVANIA

22217 NE

5-28-55   DONALD R. IANNELLI

Don Iannelli

Louie spent a lot more years behind bars before getting free. We became good friends on the street well before he was shot and killed. The two of us started into a thing, with a big score, etc.

Poor Louie, he had a problem and for some reason he didn't tell me about it. If he had, I could have saved his life. In his last years, Louie came to me and said "I'm packing it up... I've got a lot of money and no more banks or armored trucks..." He mentioned that he'd like to get some money on the street and wanted my advice. I encouraged him. I explained the traps from the law, and I told him that he could tell the Mafia he was with me, and no one would try to take you over. This was important because independents get taken over and are forced to pay "rent" to stay in business. I told him if ever he has a problem, get in touch and if anyone tries to shake you down, tell them you're with me and I will have a talk with them—end of problem. I was in a good position to handle these types of issues back then. I remember Louie thanked me and gave me a duffle bag with his "equipment" that he hoped he'd never need again. Later on, he was gunned down as he walked out of an apartment. He was struck down in the legs with a shotgun, and then took two slugs in the head by a .38 revolver. I'm sure he never had an idea of what was coming…He met a violent end. I wish he would have come to me for help. I could have solved his problem.

ARQUILLA, Louis R.

Louis R. Arquilla

Arquilla's death was cited in the February 23, 1977, issue of the *Boston Globe*, reading in part:

State and Braintree police are looking for a motive in the shotgun murder of a Plymouth man last night outside a Braintree apartment building. Police said Louis R. Arquilla, 46, was shot four times from close range as he left a friend's apartment. Investigators said Arquilla left the apartment about 7:30 PM and as he was walking up to a sidewalk leading to a parking lot, someone jumped from behind the building and fired four shots. Neighbors in the adjoining three-story buildings said they heard four shots coming from the building. One neighbor said he heard a man shout "Oh no!" seconds before the shots rang out. When police arrived, they found Arquilla lying about 50 feet from the front door on the snow-covered ground. His new Cadillac was parked about 80 feet away in a parking lot. Police learned that the murderer walked to the side of the victim after firing the shotgun, pulled a handgun and fired two shots into his head. Police said they have no motive for the murder.

Bulger commented:

The Mafia thought I'd killed him. Larry Zannino (aka Larry Baione), the consigliere of the Patriarca crime family approached me about Louie's death. I knew early on that Louie had connections to the Mafia and occasionally handled business for Vito Genovese. It wasn't any secret as they were photographed and in the news together back in the

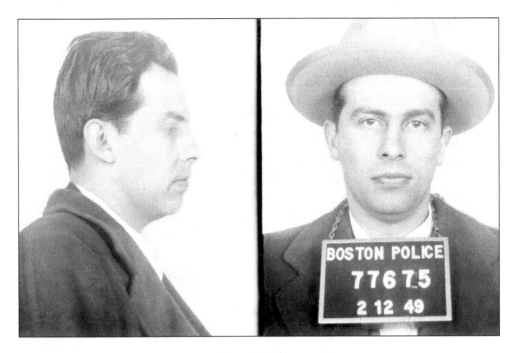

Larry Zannino

1950s. Only a couple of years after leaving Alcatraz, Louie and Vito end up serving time together at Leavenworth. When Louie's back on the street, he handles a favor for Genovese. Vito sends word to Boston to do something nice for Louie, but instead he winds up dead. Louie was half Irish and half Italian, he kept relations on both sides, a risky play. Things get complicated when suspicions surface. I'm not saying that made him a target, but the lines of trust get blurred when loyalty falls to question.

So, Larry asks me "Why did you kill Louie?" I didn't like the question and I told him, "Louie was my friend. I walked the yard with him for years in prison—Atlanta, Alcatraz and Leavenworth. I would have protected him." I knew all about the killing of Louie. I'm accused of taking revenge on strangers who killed friends of mine while in prison and I am a believer in revenge but found the question insulting. I could have saved him if he had come and told me the truth about his problem. Sadly, he didn't. I made it my mission to search out who pulled the trigger and hold them responsible. Turned out it was a friend of mine. I got him to admit to it and he told me all the details. He wore a ski mask but pulled it up when Louie asked him to at least show who was finishing him off. I'll never name him, and though he was a friend, it put me in a tough spot because I had to deal with it. I can tell you with 100% confidence that the name everyone ties to his murder is not accurate. I know who pulled the trigger and the details behind it. Every word is true. This isn't a second or third hand story. This is what happened.

Poor Louie, he had finally gone straight, had made some money and packed it in. When he said he was finished with crime, I was happy for him. I was not in the same position to just walk away. During my trial, they showed an early photograph of weapons spread out on a table.

Vito Genovese

Louie Arquilla with Vito Genovese, the crown figure of the Italian Mafia. Genovese was an enforcer for the Mafia during the Prohibition era and a childhood friend and longtime associate of Lucky Luciano. He would later become the patriarch of Luciano's crime family, which was renamed the Genovese crime family in his honor. Bulger considered Louie a close and trusted friend but suggested that ties on both sides of the Mafia eroded trust and it may have been the basis of his murder.

Sub-machine guns with silencers—a very dramatic display by the prosecutor in an attempt to influence jurors. He referred to them as 'Bulger's Murder Kit' that I kept on hand in case I decided to kill someone. Several of these guns, including the submachine gun seen on the far end, belonged to Louie and were part of his gift package to me. Louie's forgotten, but he had lots of nerve, robbing banks and armored trucks after prison. His life was finally good, plenty of money to buy a house, furnishings and cars with plentiful cash to start a normal life, but his past had finally caught up to him.

I ran into his crime partner Martin Feeney years later. It was on Broadway in South Boston, and he was coming out of a bar at about 2:00 PM in the afternoon. He said hello, but I could see he was really nervous. He made some excuse to start walking and get away from me. I could read him like a book. Louie has just been gunned down and Feeney was taking no chances. Martin lost his taste for crime and kept his head down after that. I'll give him credit that he had a long trail of escape attempts from prison and never stopped trying to make his way out. I remember in one attempt, while going over the wall, he fell and broke his back. He was dragged a long distance and finally captured. He was put in the hole, and everyone could hear him screaming in pain, but he never gave up names. I'd heard that when he was captured with Louie and Dottie, Louie put a gun to his head and Feeney pulled it away, talking him down. He was already thinking suicide. If he would have made it in the cockpit of that airplane when they were being transferred together, Louie might have killed everyone. He was at a point of being utterly desperate. I'll never forget him...

THOMAS KENT

I've seen Tom's name come up in books and documentaries claiming he was in the know on the Alcatraz escape of '62. I saw him many times on TV as the voice of authority. I would always get a good laugh seeing his talking head flash on the screen. He was insane, to put it mildly. He would always talk real excitedly, taking quick short breaths. When he got out of prison, he took the shoes they gave him on release, cut them open and brought them to the parole officer and threw them down on the counter. He told him, "I know what the game is. These wires are for tracking me and sending messages." We had the same parole officer, and he described this crazy scene to me. He also said

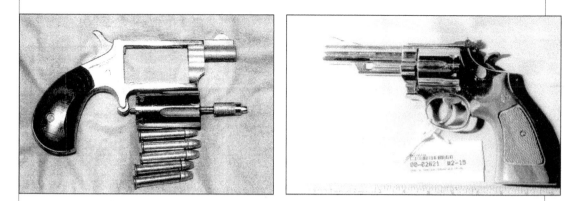

A series of evidence photographs shown during Bulger's trial and referred to as tools from his "Murder Kit." Several of these firearms were gifts from Louie Arquilla.

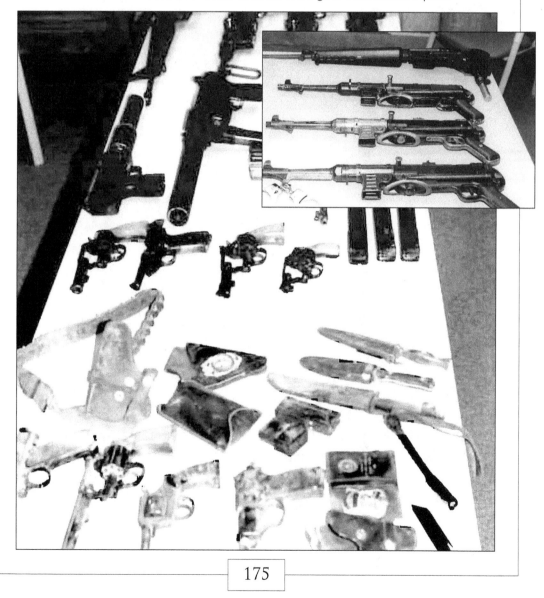

Thomas Kent

Thomas Kent (below center) and fellow convicts being led from court in March of 1946 while on trial for their roles in a violent escape attempt at Charlestown State Penitentiary in Massachusetts. The escape resulted in grave injuries to a correctional officer following a brutal assault.

that he'd later learned that he repeated this same performance at the FBI office. Not long after, Tom knocks on my door when I was still living in the projects. I didn't like that he knew where I lived. I had an ice pick ready just in case. I had a beef with him over his accusing Arquilla of ratting him out. Well, that evening he shows up at my house, ranting like a mad man that the Feds were out to get him. He bought a bike and then recorded in a journal all his moves throughout the day. What time he got up, when he leaves his home, where he goes, times, mileage, and everyone he talks to. The guy is nuts. He took a job in the harbor working on a barge. He offered me use of it if I wanted to dispose of bodies, etc. I didn't answer him, and he wouldn't stop talking. I didn't invite him in, but I remember thinking that if I catch him lurking around, he's gone! Later he went to San Diego and I lost track of him. I had also saved him from being killed by Jack Twining. Jack had approached me at one point telling me of a problem that was driving him crazy and the only way he was going to be able to stop the guy was to kill him. I remember him saying, "If I told you his name you would never believe me." I told him I figured it out. I named Kent and he almost fell over. I had his number back then.

Every Sunday, all of us guys from Boston would stand against the wall in the yard and talk. Louie, Kent, Red Holiday (422-AZ), Martin Feeney, etc…So, one day we're standing against the wall in the Alcatraz rec yard, this is all during the early days of spaceflight. We're all on Alcatraz when Russia was first to put a man in space and this dominated the news and our conversations. It was the talk of Alcatraz that Russia was forging ahead of America, and everyone was glued to their headsets at night listening to the news broadcasts. So right after the Russian flight, America launches a man into space, and there's a lot of talk on the radio about the NASA astronauts, etc. Kent starts talking about how he's going to pitch his theories to NASA and that he's figured out how to put man into space. He tells us that he has invented a technology where you cut a man's head off, hook it up to an oxygen circulator, then mount it next to a thick window and launch it into space. The guy sees everything, and then when he's returned to Earth, NASA can join his head back with his body and he can recount his experience. Well…That did it for me…I told him he was fucking crazy. I turned to the guys and said I'm not yacking out here with this fucking nut and told Kent to take a walk. Louie is a real loyal guy and tells me, "I know he's nuts, but I can't abandon him. I'll walk with him on Sundays." I was done. I told him to go ahead, but I couldn't listen to that fucking nut and his rants anymore.

One last word on Kent. One night as the Rock is closing and they're slowly shipping guys out in small groups, Kent was in the cell next to Louie Arquilla and he pens this insane letter that plots how to break Louie out. Kent writes that when he gets out, he will come back with a boat and scuba gear to help Louie make a break. There was a popular television series called *Sea Hunt* that followed the adventures of a scuba diver and had a crime-solver type theme. About a year before we ended up on the Rock, an episode aired where guys using scuba gear break a prisoner out of Alcatraz. Kent's obsessed with the idea and plots it all out on paper. Louie reads it and then goes back to his business reading a *Newsweek* magazine and slips the letter inside. Later that same day, a guard walks up and tells Louie he's being rolled out. He grabs a few personal items, steps out onto the tier and says goodbye to Kent. He's transferred to Atlanta. Several months later, he's transferred to Leavenworth (same place they send me after Alcatraz) and I'm glad to see him, but he's really skinny; his nails are bitten down, and he looks real bad. He then goes on to tell me the story as to when he gets to Atlanta, he's locked in isolation for this escape plot they found scribed in   his cell. He then hears that Tom Kent

is spreading that Louie ratted him out by pointing to the guard to check the magazine and all this is killing Louie. He's furious. I assured him that I'd shut Kent up when I got to Lewisburg. By this time, I knew I would be transferred soon, and we both knew this was where Kent was sent. When I get to Lewisburg, I grab Kent in the

In January of 1959, the popular television series Sea Hunt starring Lloyd Bridges aired the episode The Alcatraz Story. It gave Tom Kent the idea to break out Louis Arquilla using a similar scheme. Kent wrote down his plot and delivered it to Arquilla who was allegedly caught with the notes in his Alcatraz cell but was dismissed as an implausible scheme.

yard and address it. Kent is ranting that he saw Louie tip off the guard, but I finally convinced him to shut up or else, not to mention how ridiculous this is! Over the years, my opinion of Kent never changed. Whenever I see his face on television as the Alcatraz expert, I get a laugh. He was nothing more than a lunatic.

It was sometimes hard to discern who had mental issues until you interacted with them. I remember one was with a guy everyone called "Chino," Daniel Contreras (1444-AZ), a Mexican convict, muscular and he fancied himself as "bad." He was a loner with no friends, and he couldn't seem to get along with anyone. He was known to stare

Daniel Contreras

men down. One day I was working out on the yard, and he came over and just started glaring at me from about 12 feet away. I glared back and started hating this guy...I felt like he was forcing me to lose good time and if that was the story, I intended to inflict serious damage if I was backed into a corner. I never looked for trouble and was trying to do my own time. I walked over and got in his face and asked him, "What's your fucking problem?" "You want something?" "You want to leave here alive?" He right away started backtracking and saying, "You've got it all wrong...I'm not looking for any trouble..." That was the end of it...Finally, one of the Mexican convicts came over and said Contreras was a mental case and to stay clear. Turned out everyone knew the guy had problems, even the Mexican prisoners didn't associate with him.

Later in the kitchen, Chino was beaten over the head with a brass pipe then stuffed under a sink and covered with cloths. He messed with the wrong guy. He ended up having surgery with skull fragments having to be removed from his brain and he was left a vegetable. I just feel sorry for his family, as they are the ones left to care for him and take on that burden. Good riddance. He deserved it. Most guys are just trying to do their own time and he's walking around casting threats at everyone he sees. Some of the Alcatraz books say guys referred to him as Wolf. Never saw him called that or heard of him as being a sexual predator. Never liked the guy, but I'm not going to give him a bum rap on something I never witnessed or heard about.

JACK WRIGHT TWINING

Jack Twining was a trusted and close friend to Bulger during his early prison years. Despite his violent past of bank robbery and murder, Twining was well liked by the correctional staff at Alcatraz and was known to always have a smile and be cordial in conversation. During an interview in August of 1994, Alcatraz Correctional Officer Irving Levinson remembered Twining as being a close associate of Frank Morris, one of the principals of the legendary 1962 break from Alcatraz. He commented, "One I remember well was an inmate named Jack Twining. He'd killed a prisoner on Alcatraz. As I remember, we figured the con he killed backed Jack into a corner with no way out. You know, the con he killed preyed on the weaker ones. Twining was quiet, always kept his head down, always polite, and very likeable. He had the looks of being a whole-some kid. He didn't seem to belong in a place like Alcatraz. You would never have known just by the looks of him. Years later, I read the papers about him killing the patrolmen. Seeing his picture and the young men he killed shook me. I didn't sleep all night after seeing it on the news and Jack taking his own life. I had such high hopes for him. I thought he was going to do well once he made parole. He was respectful and courteous; at least towards me. That's my memory of him and one puzzle I've never been able to put together…"

Twining's Alcatraz case file chronicled his turbulent youth and criminal life:

> This white man, age twenty-four, single, is serving a total sentence of twenty years. He was sentenced at New Orleans, Louisiana to serve thirty years for robbery of an FDIC Bank. Alone he entered and robbed by use of a gun, removing $11,897 from the tellers' cages. A few minutes later he was stopped by police for questioning and returned to the bank where he was identified, and the money was recovered. On August 18, 1959, his sentence was reduced to twenty years by court order. Committed to the penitentiary in Atlanta on December 11, 1956, he was transferred to Alcatraz July 11, 1958, after he forfeited good time for possession of security keys and also in view of his escape record. A detainer has also been filed by Raiford, the State Prison in Florida for escape.

Jack Wright Twining

Born in Louisiana, the identity of his parents is unknown. At age three he was placed with foster parents and reared in Danville, Virginia. The subject became delinquent at an early age and placed on probation at age fourteen for breaking, entering and theft. A year later he was arrested for burglary and at age fifteen he was committed to the Industrial School for Boys, Beaumont, Indiana, but was released two years later in April of 1952. In August of 1952, he was arrested in Little Rock, Arkansas, for an investigation in connection with a violation of the Dyer Act (federal law that makes it a crime to transport stolen motor vehicles across state borders in interstate or foreign commerce). He escaped detention, being committed to El Reno in November 1952, and was paroled in January 1955 from Chillicothe after transfer. He violated his parole and was returned after he had escaped from the State Prison in Raiford, Florida, in July of 1955 while serving one year for attempted armed robbery. He remains wanted for that escape. He does not receive any visits, does not have any correspondents, and has no known family. He subscribes to the magazine *Motor Boating* and has no funds in his commissary account. At Alcatraz he has been reported for misconduct and possession of contraband (a homemade explosive device), fighting with #1333 Mollett, and killing person of the same in the dry-cleaning plant. The case was investigated by the FBI, but while he was not prosecuted, he forfeited fifty-five days of good time credits. He is very quiet at his current work assignment and is very pleasant while being interviewed.

In February 1959, Twining stabbed to death fellow Alcatraz inmate Walter Mollett, a known sexual predator while incarcerated at Alcatraz and other institutions. Twining was cleared of all charges since the stabbing was considered an act of self-defense. Mollett was portrayed by fellow convicts as an aggressive sexual predator and hated by most of the population. A former military inmate, he was transferred from Leavenworth to Alcatraz in June of 1958. Mollett was serving time for robbery and assault with intent to murder, and interstate car theft. Mollett's Alcatraz inmate case file included multiple conduct infractions and represented that he was aggressive towards fellow convicts. One case file entry dated on July 20, 1958, read, "He forfeited good time for an assault on another inmate with a knife, and was known at Leavenworth Federal Penitentiary as a highly aggressive homosexual who used strong-arm tactics in achieving his objectives." An early case file entry read, "Mollett was placed in isolation after an investigation revealed that he had threatened another inmate with death if he did not submit to an act of sodomy. This man has a lengthy record of strong-arming and assaultiveness [sic]. He is known to be a very dangerous man who would stop at nothing to enforce his demands. He has previously been held in our segregation unit because of his persistent aggressive activities until it was decided to give him another chance to adjust in the population. He has failed to change his tactics, and it was considered imperative to return him to segregation in order to protect other inmates from his threats and intimidations."

While at Alcatraz, Mollett set his sights on Twining and began sending threatening notes and unwelcome advances. Just a month prior, both Twining and Mollett were reprimanded for fighting in the rec yard, a result from what Twining

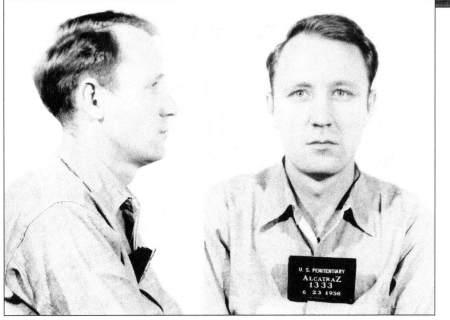

Walter Mollett

described as continual harassment by Mollett. On the morning of February 12, 1959, Mollett, who was assigned to work in the laundry, approached Ernie Lopez (697-AZ) in the brush shop and asked him for a shank (knife). When Lopez inquired what he wanted the shank for, he stated he was going into the dry-cleaning plant to kill Jack Twining. After laughing it off and telling Mollett he couldn't offer him a weapon, Lopez said Mollett walked off stating he was going to "get that son of a bitch." Mollett was able to get past an officer and enter the dry-cleaning plant where Twining was working. Lopez would later see the two fighting, but quietly went back to his work bench until about five minutes later when he saw Twining emerge with blood on his hands. Fellow con Benny Rayborn (1028-AZ), also remembered Twining complaining that he was being stalked by Mollett. Twining had quit his job in the brush shop because of the constant advancements and harassment he'd received from Mollett. Benny remembered, "It seemed the more he'd [Twining] reject Mollett, the more pissed he got." After endless advances and unrelenting harassment, Twining put an end to the stalking. Twining described the incident events leading up to the assault during interviews with the FBI and separately with the associate warden at Alcatraz that were documented in a Bureau of Prisons investigative summary:

Ernie Lopez   Benny Rayborn

DESCRIPTION OF CRIME SCENE

This crime took place in the Renovation Plant (dry cleaning shop) of the Industries building, located within the prison confines of the U.S. Penitentiary, Alcatraz Island, California. The Industries building is a two-story structure, housing work facilities for inmates. This building is rectangular in shape and is approximately 310 feet and runs in an east to westerly direction.

The renovating or dry-cleaning shop is 19'6" by 34'6", located on the second floor in the western portion and on the south side of the Industries building. The south, west and east side of the dry-cleaning shop is bounded by solid partitions whereas the north side is bounded by one central door and glass window type partitions beginning approximately three feet from the bottom of the floor and continuing to the ceiling. Located on the same floor and just north of the dry-cleaning shop is the brush shop. The western portion of the Industries building on the second floor also houses the shoe and print shop, the tool shop and the two offices which are also located on the south side in the western part of this building. The mechanics shop and the brush shop are located on the north side of this building. The eastern portion of the Industries Building on the second floor encompasses the prison laundry where the victim was assigned. The subject in this case, Jack Wright Twining, is assigned in the dry-cleaning shop.

Twining provided the following account of the events:

> Mollett #1333 had been sending me threatening letters and making advances towards me. It was merely to aggravate and threaten that he was going to get me, and for me to meet him on the yard with a knife. He couldn't understand why I wouldn't want to go with him. I just didn't go for it, and I didn't like it, and that's why I fought him in the yard. Neither of us had knives and we had agreed to let it drop. Without warning, he hit me twice before I was able to fight back with my fists. You know the rest of the deal. He got a cut over his eye, and I got my nose bloody and a cut over my ear. I went to the Treatment Unit (Isolation) and when I came out, he asked me, "Is everything the same or did you change your mind?" I told him, "No," everything was more or less the same. He didn't stop.
>
> On Wednesday morning, this was the 11th I guess, it was the first time I saw him and knew he was in the laundry. He came up and gave me a tap on the back of the heel with his shoes. I thought he wanted to pick a fight with me right there. I had my back turned. I asked him what he was doing, and he said that he came down to the laundry

to work. First, he starts asking me how I liked the job. He wandered around looking at different stuff to put clothing in and all that. Then he says, "You still feel that way?" I said, "That is right." I told him before that I did not want to change. What I want is to stay out of trouble, then he goes out.

The next day in the morning I came in and looked at the clock. It was 8:35 AM, I had put clothing in the washer the day before, as the turn-over was big, I had left them in there. I turned on the washer and then left them in there for a half-hour. When 9 o'clock came around, Mollett came through the door. He had both his hands in his pockets and was just looking at me. I thought something was up. He says, "What's up?" He was standing more or less between the table with a glass top, and I am standing near the draining boards. When I saw him come in, I took my rubber gloves which were dripping and placed them on the bleach barrel. I asked him, "What's up?" He said, "You had your last free chance yesterday, you turned me down again and it is going to cost you your life." I said, "Is that the way it is?" And he said something like, "You don't leave me much choice, you got me pretty up tight now."

I thought he had a knife in his pocket, people later said he didn't, I didn't know. His main reputation is being a knife man. He talked to me so many times about carrying a hatchet or a club in Leavenworth. So, I stood there and mentioned something about what's going to happen? He started to walk over, and I was getting ready to kick him. He didn't know yet what I was going to do, and I just took it easy. He then took both hands out of his pockets and started to unbutton his pants, grabbed me, and started to squeeze me. I then hit him forcefully with my elbow and fists. I hit him a couple more times and then he held my arm and told me to stop, and was pleading, "I won't do it, I promise I won't." I remember he asked me for a towel, he said, "I can't see, get me a towel." I started looking for a towel and was scared to turn around farther, but he said that he can't see, as he had his eyes full of blood from a cut over his eyebrow and the blood was flowing into his eyes.

It looked like there was a bruise on his nose. Wiping his face, then he asked me, "Do you think we can get out without getting caught?" When I leaned over to work, he hit me in the stomach with his fist, this was the first blow and it was with such great force, it knocked the wind out of me. Then, when I had my hands up telling him to stop, he threw the towel in my face. I tried to get him out of there as I didn't want no more trouble. I asked him why he hit me? It was either before or while wiping his face that he punched me, and we were on each other again. We were both going at it with blows and were messing it up, we got over to the window one time and then got back to where the table with the red barrel that had chalk in it. Before we got out, I tried to pull his legs out from under him. I had my right hand against his stomach, and I was trying to push him down. He grabbed me around the neck and he was putting pressure on me and then he says "I am killing you now…." When I got loose from his hold on my neck, I was trying to reach around his head and with my fingers. I started gouging his eyes with my left hand and I got my right hand against the left side of his face. He let go of me by the window and we got down by the chalk barrel with his head up against my stomach. I pushed my hand against his chin and got my finger in his mouth while he was biting it. I made him let go by pushing my thumb in his eye…I hit him several times with my left hand and he got turned around with his back towards the corner in the little place where we were fighting. I hit him again. He got ahold of my shirt and pulled me to my knees. I started forcefully gouging his eyes with my fingers and he was screaming "Oh my eyes…." I got my hand around his throat and he had me around the head. He rolled over on his right side, and he gets both my hands. He pulled me over right below next to his left and let go. I didn't even have a hold of him. I finally got a hold of his throat and I guess I was strangling him, beating his head up and down on the floor. I don't know how long I did it. He was kicking, I could hear a little sound like a little chalk from the barrel falling down. His arms became still, and everything went quiet, so I quit. I got up and walked out. When they came in, they asked me what was wrong, I couldn't talk and was still out of breath. When they went over there, Mr. Long was asking me, "What's wrong?" Then I sat in the chair at the desk. Somebody then came in, Mr. Christopherson came in and Lieutenant Severson and somebody gave him artificial respiration. With my hands raised up I got up and watched the officer. Everyone said, "He's dead."

Lieutenant Alden Severson provided the following on the killing of Mollett:

I entered the east end of the Laundry at about 09:05 AM on this date, going to the desk at the east end. I checked the laundry roster and noticed a new man on the crew, #1333 Mollett. I walked towards

Alcatraz Lieutenant Alden Severson.

the west end desk looking for him. Arriving at the west end desk I looked over the brush shop crew and then towards the east end. I was still unable to find #1333. It started at about 9:15 AM when Messmore, 868-AZ, came to the office of the industries and said to Davis, "You have a dead man down here if you are interested. At least I think he is dead…" At this time, Twining #1362 staggered out of the dry-cleaning plant towards Mr. Long's desk. He sat on the edge and appeared short of breath. Mr. Long asked him what the trouble was, and he rose and went into the dry-cleaning plant, followed by Mr. Long and myself. Sitting on the edge of the table he pointed towards the right-hand corner of the room. Mr. Long looked over there and said, "Good God." Going over, I saw #1333 Mollett lying in the corner between a tank and the wall. He appeared to be dead but after checking his pulse I found a heartbeat and it was a weak flutter. I called the control room at 09:15 AM and asked for medical assistance.

BM
BU PRISONS GA

U S PENITENTIARY ALCATRAZ
WARDEN MADIGAN TO DIRECTOR
AT APPPROXIMATELY 915 AM THIS MORNING WALTER D MOLLETT 1333-AZ ASSI
GNED TO THE LAUNDRY WAS FOUND IN A BLOODY BATTERED CONDITION IN THE
DRY CLEANING PLANT   AS LT SEVERSON APPROACHED THE DRY CLEANING
PLANT JAC K W TWINING 1362-.-AZ STAGGERED OUT THE DOOR EXHAUSTED
AND FANINT   HE LED LT SEVERSON TO A CORNER WHERE MOLLET WAS LYING
A FAINT HEART BEAT WAS DETECTED BUT HE DIED A FEW MINUTES BEFORE HE
COULD EBE BROUGHT TO THE HOSPITA L   MOLLETT HAS A CRUSHED SKULL
AND NUMEROUS BRUISES AN D ABRASIONS   F B I WILL ARRIVE ON EXT
BOAT   WE ARE HOLDING TWINING IN A BLOCK AWAY FROM OTHER INMATES
MOLLETT LEFT HIS DETAIL IN THE LAUNDRY AND STEPPED INTO THE DRY
CLEANING PLANT WHERE TWINING WAS ASSIGNED ALONE   WE ARE
NOTIFYING OMOLLETTS MOTHER IN ST JOSEPH MISSOURI AND WE WILL
ISSUE STATEMENT TO THE PRESS   END GA FEB 12 1959

THANK YOU ALL AT LUNCH JUST NOW GA END
OK WE WILL KEEP YOU ADVISED END WJB
TU END

FILED
FEB 2 1979
BUREAU OF PRISONS

Going back into the dry-cleaning plant, Mr. Christopherson and I moved him out on the floor. I knelt over Mollett and started artificial respiration.

Twining was asked what he hit Mollett with to which he held out both his blood covered hands and replied, "With these…" [showing only his bare hands]. "I'd like to say that before the attack, I never made any aggressive action towards this man…I didn't start it."

Bulger remembered:

Jack Twining was a very close friend of mine. It's saddening to look at pictures of him. I wish his life outside was different and didn't end the way that it did, and the four young officers didn't have to lose their lives in a wake of such violence and hate. I admit though, after getting to know him, I knew his life would end in a hail of gunfire, and so did he. No one could slow him down. He was on a suicide mission.

It seems like yesterday that I met him. Young guy, always with a smile; he worked in the hospital as an x-ray tech at Atlanta with Scottie (John Paul Scott) and me. It's still hard for me to picture Jack killing anyone back then. I didn't know anything about his life; he just made small talk. He seemed to be a really easy-going guy, but he never talked about his past. John Duncan (1359-AZ) was also an interesting guy. The State of Maine paid the Feds to incarcerate him as he was too incorrigible and violent. He caused a riot during an escape attempt and using Molotov cocktails, tossed them at a guard tower in an attempt to burn it down. He had also been involved in an escape plot with Twining and Scottie, where they tunneled through a deep shaft in the basement of the hospital building and was nearly completed. They were close and would have been a mass escape like Sutton at Eastern State and made history.

I knew that he was in for bank robbery and think that he pled guilty so that they would release his girlfriend, who was arrested down in the New Orleans area. He was sentenced to thirty years. Courtney

DEPARTMENT OF JUSTICE
United States Penitentiary
Lewisburg Pennsylvania

29778 NE

3-27-63   JOHN D. DUNCAN

John Duncan

Taylor, the prolific jailhouse lawyer at Alcatraz, did some legal work for Jack, and had him file an appeal in New Orleans, which got his sentenced reduced to twenty years. Courtney was as good as any lawyer in free society and responsible for many successful appeals. That was sometime after he had killed Mollett, because when he was in the Parish Jail on appeal, he was put in a cell with a big chain as double security on his cell door and a sign that read:

CAUTION—DO NOT APPROACH THIS CELL BY YOURSELF.
THIS PERSON HAS ALREADY STRANGLED A MAN TO DEATH

From birth, Jack always traveled under a black cloud of bad luck. During the Christmas holiday he would always give me his Christmas cards. We lived on the same tier, and he would always make sure he passed his over to me. This was a big deal back then, since it was the only time we were allowed to send a note to anyone we wanted, even if they were not on the mailing list. I felt guilty accepting them. I always asked him, "Don't you know anybody out there?" He would just respond that he didn't get any mail and didn't have anyone on the outside. I always felt sorry thinking of his life with no family. He was never wanted, never a mother's touch, no family meals...Only reform schools, chain gangs, prison, and then finally Alcatraz. Everything molding him into a killing machine.

I feel I knew him better than anyone. John Duncan, Frankie Morris and I were the only people who really ever got close to him. It took me years to get Jack to talk about his life. He was really guarded about his past. By degrees, he told me his story. It was very sad for me to hear. He always had a smile but was never really happy. We never had much when I was young, but we were really close as a family and somehow always had a good meal on Thanksgiving and Christmas. Jack never had either, and never sat down with a family; he grew up as an orphan. He was adopted by a young couple, and while picking up a ball that landed in some bushes by a window, he heard the guy say to his wife, "Why did we bring that bastard home?" Jack heard that and ran away.

He was caught and sent back to the orphanage, a runaway juvenile place. And then he was sent to various jails, the chain gang, the state prison for bank robbery, and then, finally, Alcatraz. Poor Jack, I don't think he had many happy memories or moments. He had rage and hated like no one I ever knew. At least two times while we were in prison, I feel I prevented him from killing other convicts. Jack sought revenge, and as usual, innocent people suffered.

When Jack took hostages during the Newhall Incident, it was fortunate that he spared them. And I'm glad that he did because if the cops had stormed the house, it may have been fatal for the hostages. I suppose I'm glad that Jack killed himself; he finally found peace. It saved him and everyone else the pain of years of trials, appeals, isolation, death row, and execution. I guarantee you that his last moments in that house, he was calm and at peace with his fate. The gun battle had undoubtedly left him spent, and he was approaching the end he sought.

Years later, I read a feature article in a detective magazine and saw the pictures of the four California Highway Patrolmen. They were young guys and looked like all-American boys; married; real healthy looking; real tragic. No picture of Jack…I also read that he had killed (or was suspected of killing) a federal agent and two other men when he was coming south from Washington state. The guy who was with Jack in Newhall was shot and he survived, but he later killed himself in prison. Sad story all the way around.

I first met Jack back in Atlanta, before Alcatraz, and considered him a friend. He was also close with Louie Arquilla. On the Rock, I prevented him from killing a black inmate named Mitchell. I did so for Jack's sake. Mitchell was real lucky after Jack killed Mollett. As far as I was concerned, Mollett committed suicide. He underestimated Twining. On Alcatraz, Mollett was relentless in his threats toward Jack, and he spawned a hurricane of hatred. Jack didn't look imposing, intimidating or very muscular. If you didn't know him, he'd seem a bit timid. Mollett went one threat too far and when he approached Jack, Twining exploded with a fierce karate chop to the neck. He dropped him; knelt on his chest; strangled him into unconsciousness, then let him come to and said "Now you die…" He strangled him; tried to rip his eyes out and then beat his head against a capped-off pipe. Mollett's head cracked wide open, and his brains spilled out. From that moment on, Jack lived to kill, and his rage continued to brew. He was put in isolation for doing the world a favor…Jack had a violent explosive temper combined with hate; he wanted revenge and his own death. He spelled it all out for me and said, "I know, but can't help it and I know you're right." I told him how it would end if he kept going on this way. On a couple of down moments he'd say, "I don't care about anything or trust anyone. I don't have any friends and I don't need them!" It shook him up when I told him that I was a good friend, as well as Louie and Duncan. He didn't answer, so I let it go. I can think back to all those conversations.

Jack was transferred to Leavenworth several months after me, and we remained good friends after Alcatraz. We spent a lot of time on the yard and talking about life. I can remember once we were

George Whitacre

with an older former Alcatraz convict named George Whitacre (1161-AZ). He, I and Jack were walking on the flats at Leavenworth, and we could see a black & white television with a Budweiser commercial playing during a broadcast. So, I said to Whitacre and Jack, "Looks good! I'd like one of them!" Twining says "Yeah, me too!" Whitacre was much older than us. He was a kind, gray haired and soft-spoken old con. He just stayed quiet, and I asked him "What's up?" He told me the last time he'd had a drink like that was in Alaska. He said, "All I remember was waking up in a cell and they told me, 'You killed the room clerk in your hotel.' I don't remember anything about that and that's why I was in Alcatraz." Fortunately, I remember he was freed to live with his sister either in Minnesota or Wisconsin. He was a really nice old guy. I still get flashes of those conversations every so often. It weighs on me to think back and I can still remember Jack's soft voice.

The Newhall Incident referenced by Bulger endures as the worst tragedy in the history of the California Highway Patrol. Following his release from prison, Twining and crime partner Bobby Davis (a fellow convict he met while serving time at Leavenworth), went on a violent crime spree that would end in the deaths of four police officers. After killing the officers and following a nine-hour standoff, Twining turned the gun on himself and took his own life.

The official summary report chronicled the incident through witness statements and first-person accounts:

SHOOTING INCIDENT—NEWHALL

The following is a report of the events which began on the night of April 5, 1970, in the Newhall area and resulted in the death of four California highway patrol officers:

SUNDAY 11:20 PM

A serviceman stationed at Port Hueneme, accompanied by his wife, was driving south from Gorman on US-99. As they approached the area known as Pyramid Rock, a northbound vehicle made a "U" turn across the center divider into their path. He managed to avoid a collision and when the other vehicle slowed, he pulled alongside, and his wife rolled her window down. The serviceman told the other driver (Davis) that he didn't like the way he was driving and that he would like to "kick his ass." When both vehicles came to a stop, the other driver pointed a revolver at him and called him a "smart punk." The serviceman told him a California Highway Patrol vehicle was approaching from their rear (this was a ruse on the serviceman's part). The other driver looked back, then motioned with the gun for them to leave. The serviceman accelerated away and began looking for a telephone. During this confrontation, the serviceman and his wife noticed only one occupant in the other vehicle.

SUNDAY 11:36 PM

At Violin Canyon Road, approximately eight miles south of where the incident occurred, the serviceman's wife telephoned the Newhall Office of the California Highway Patrol. Radio Dispatcher Jo Ann Tidey took the call and was given the license number of the suspect vehicle along with information which described it as a red, late model General Motors product. A registration check was made which disclosed that the vehicle was a 1964 Pontiac two door registered in Orange, California, with no warrants.

SUNDAY 11:37 PM

Newhall Dispatch contacted Unit 78-8, Traffic Officers Gore and Frago, and informed them of the incident. Information to identify the vehicle was given to them along with details concerning the time element of the incident and direction of travel as last observed.

SUNDAY 11:50 PM

Unit 78-8 inquired if the name of the complainant had been obtained and if he would sign a statement. The unit was informed that the complainant was due back at Port Hueneme and was traveling back to that location.

SUNDAY 11:52 PM

Unit 78-8 requested the registration information previously obtained by Newhall on the suspect vehicle and was informed there were no warrants. The officers then staked out at Castaic Junction to watch for the suspect. It is important to note that up to this time Officers Gore and Frago were presented with information indicating that only a misdemeanor had been committed. This type of report is fairly common in the area because of its rural geography and because it is open to hunting and shooting. It is not unusual to receive complaints of persons brandishing weapons.

SUNDAY 11:54 PM

Unit 78-8 notified Newhall Dispatch they were behind the red Pontiac, south-bound at the Castaic Commercial Vehicle Inspection Facility, and requested back-up. Unit 78-12, Traffic Officers Pence and Alleyn, stopped on the south-bound on-ramp at Valencia, two miles south of the Inspection Facility, to await the arrival of the vehicles. Considerable car-to-car traffic followed between the two units as the suspect vehicle approached Henry Mayo Drive. When the suspect exited the freeway at Henry Mayo, 78-12 turned around and headed north toward that location. Unit 78-8 then stated the suspect vehicle had turned right on Henry Mayo and north on "Old" 99 and was pulling into the Standard Service Station adjacent to J's Coffee Shop. This area is well lighted and the vehicles, suspects and officers were clearly visible to witnesses.

Unit 78-16 Officers Holmes and Robinson, were approximately three miles away in Saugus when they monitored the call for back-up. They started toward Henry Mayo Drive but when 78-12 indicated they were almost there, Unit 78-16 abandoned their response and returned to patrol.

SUNDAY 11:56 PM

An excited voice, identified as Officer Pence's (Unit 78-12) radioed for an "11-99, shots fired, at J's Standard." Newhall Dispatch rebroadcasted the 11-99 and Units 78-16, 19, 54, S6, 15, and two officers responded. The call was also relayed to the Los Angeles County Sheriff's Station at Newhall and several sheriffs' units also responded.

The following represents a reconstruction of the events after the suspect vehicle entered the driveway at standard station at Henry Mayo Drive and Old Highway 99. While no exact reconstruction can be made, over thirty witnesses and considerable physical evidence provides a relatively clear picture of the sequence of events:

As the suspect vehicle pulled into the driveway Officer Gore (the driver) turned on the red spotlight, and Officer Frago (the passenger) the white spotlight. Both Officers exited and advanced to the front of the patrol vehicle. Officer Frago was armed with a shotgun and Officer Gore with a .357 Magnum revolver.

Although witnesses' statements vary as to the officers' actions at this point, it appears certain that Officer Frago remained near the right front headlamp and slightly to the rear. Officer Gore leaned over the left front fender of the patrol

Gunmen Kill Four Patrolmen; One Captured, 2nd Kills Self

Jack W. Twinning
Takes Life

NEWHALL, Calif. (UPI)— Two rampaging killers gunned four young highway patrolmen to death Monday and one of them took his own life as furious deputies stormed a secluded canyon home where the owner had been held hostage almost five hours.

The second gunman, wounded in the chest by the driver of a camper truck which he commandeered in a wild escape attempt, was captured on a freeway as he sought to speed off in the stolen vehicle.

The killers were first identified as Jack Wright Twinning, 35, and Russell Lowell Talbert, 28, both of Winston-Salem, N.C. The Los Angeles sheriff's office revealed, however, that it

had been notified by North Carolina authorities that the second man may not have been Talbert but someone who had stolen his identity papers. The FBI was running a fingerprint check in Washington.

TEN HOURS

Ten frantic hours elapsed from the time the four California Highway Patrol officers, all married and with young children, were slain until Twinning shot himself to death with a shotgun after releasing his hostage.

Twinning talked with newsmen by telephone from the home of truck driver Glen Hoag, which was ringed by a small army of more than 250 CHP officers and sheriff's

deputies with three helicopters circling overhead.

"I don't blame the police," Twinning said. "They have a job to do and so do I. After what happened, they can't offer me anything. I don't want to spend the rest of my life in death row."

The CHP said the quadruple deaths at the same time in the line of duty was unprecedented. The slain officers were Walter C. Frago, 23; Roger D. Gore, 23; James E. Pence Jr., 24; and George M. Alleyn, 24. All lived in small towns near this suburban community 27 miles north of Los Angeles.

The tragic chain of events began around midnight when motorists on the Golden State Freeway leading from Bakers-

car with his revolver extended toward the suspect's vehicle. One of the officers, probably Gore, ordered the suspects out of their car. His voice was clearly audible some distance away, and the command was repeated three times "Get out with your hands up!" and "We told you to get your hands up!" The driver, Bobby Davis, got out of the suspect vehicle and was ordered to lean against the car in a search position. He complied, and Officer Gore moved forward about five paces and slightly to the left rear of the suspect vehicle to begin a search.

At the same time, Officer Frago approached the passenger side of the vehicle, holding the shotgun in a "port arms position" (it is not known whether be had chambered a round). As he reached the passenger door it was suddenly opened and Officer Frago was heard to yell "Hold it!" The passenger suspect, Jack Wright Twining, turned in the seat and fired two shots from a .357 Magnum revolver, striking Officer Frago in the chest. The officer died almost instantly. Officer Gore, attracted by the sound of the shots, turned to his right and was himself fired upon by the passenger suspect who had stepped out of the car. Officer Gore fired one round at the passenger suspect which struck a parked vehicle in the restaurant parking lot. With the officer's attention diverted, the driver suspect drew a .38 caliber revolver and also began firing at Officer Gore, two of his shots striking the officer in the chest. The bullets entered the left front and lodged in the right back area. Officer Gore collapsed and also died instantly.

SUNDAY 11:56 PM

Unit 78-12, Officer Pence (the driver) and Officer Alleyn (the passenger), arrived and were immediately under fire from both suspects. (Radio message from this Unit mentioned previously). The passenger suspect, his revolver empty, removed a .45 caliber automatic from the vehicle and fired one shot at the officers as they came to a stop. This weapon jammed and the suspect entered the vehicle again and obtained a second .45 caliber automatic, exiting the vehicle on the driver's side. In the meantime, the driver suspect had obtained a 12-gauge, sawed-off shotgun from the vehicle and began firing at the officers.

Officer Pence returned the fire from his position behind the left front door of his vehicle. Officer Alleyn exited with the shotgun, chambered a round, and moved around the rear of the first patrol vehicle (Unit 78-8). He took up a position behind the open right front door and fired three rounds. One blast from the officer's shotgun penetrated the rear window of the suspect vehicle, just as the passenger suspect was entering the vehicle. This shot caused a minor wound to the suspect's forehead (One live and three spent shells were found next to the right front door of the first patrol unit, indicating that in the excitement, Officer Alleyn apparently forgot he had chambered a round and ejected a live round out of the gun). With the shotgun empty, Officer Alleyn moved to the rear of the patrol car and took up a position near the left rear and began to fire with his service revolver. As he moved around the rear of the vehicle, the driver suspect moved down in front of and between the patrol cars and using the sawed-off shotgun, mortally wounded Officer Alleyn.

While this was happening, Officer Pence was exchanging shots with the passenger suspect who was near the left front of the suspect vehicle using the car for cover. When he ran out of ammunition, Officer Pence ejected the spent cartridges from his revolver and retreated to the left rear of his vehicle (Unit 78-12) to reload. The passenger suspect (Twining) moved out from behind his vehicle to where he had a clear view of the officer and again began firing. Officer Pence was struck with four .45 caliber bullets, two in the legs and two in the chest, with one of the leg wounds resulting in a compound fracture. An examination of Officer Pence's revolver revealed that although mortally wounded, he was successful in reloading the weapon but had no opportunity to fire additional shots. It is apparent that just as the officer completed reloading, he was fatally wounded by the passenger suspect who had crawled along the left side of the patrol vehicle, raised up over the fender, and fired from close range.

While Officers Pence and Alleyn were exchanging shots with the suspects, a witness arrived at the scene and observed the officers in their respective position behind the patrol vehicles. He stopped his vehicle approximately 200 feet south of their position and turned off the vehicle's headlamps. As he watched, he saw Officer Alleyn fall to his right and away from the protective shield of the patrol vehicle (Officer Alleyn had been hit by a total of 10 Double 00 shotgun pellets in the face and chest). Leaving his vehicle, the witness ran to assist the fallen officer. He got behind the patrol vehicle and tried to drag Officer Alleyn out of the line of fire from the driver suspect (The suspect had abandoned the sawed-off shotgun and taken Officer Frago's revolver from the fallen Officer's holster and was using it against Officer Alleyn even though the officer was down and mortally wounded).

When he was unable to move the downed officer, the witness picked up the CHP shotgun and attempted to fire at the suspect (Davis), but the weapon was empty. Seeing the driver suspect advancing toward him along the right side of the Pontiac, he dropped the shotgun and picked up Officer Alleyn's revolver lying at his feet. Holding the weapon in both hands, he fired one shot, single action. The bullet probably struck the suspect vehicle and splintered with portions striking the suspect in the chest (two copper-jacketed fragments were found embedded in the suspect's chest after his capture). When he tried to fire again, the witness found the revolver was also now empty. The witness heard a loud voice behind him and turned to see the passenger suspect (Twining) approach Officer Pence who was down, yell something to the effect, "I got you now..." He fired one round from a .45 at close range. This shot struck the officer in the back of the head, killing him instantly. When he saw Pence go down, the witness abandoned further attempts to help officers and took cover in a ditch situated along the east edge of the road.

SUNDAY 11:59 PM

Unit 78-16, Officers Holmes and Robinson, arrived just as the witness took cover. They were immediately fired upon. Officer Holmes fired two shots with his service revolver as the suspects jumped into their car and accelerated through the Service Station.

All of the above action took place within the span of approximately four-and-one-half minutes from the initial stop at 11:54 PM until the arrival of unit 78-16 at 11:59 PM. During this period more than forty shots were fired, fifteen by the officers and the remainder by the suspects. Included in the suspects' arsenal were a .38 special caliber; a .357 magnum revolver, two .45 caliber automatics; a sawed-off 12-gauge shotgun; a .44 magnum Ruger automatic rifle (not used), and an 18-inch machete. In the course of the shooting, the suspects took the service revolvers carried by Officers Gore and Frago and the CHP shotgun carried by Officer Frago.

The suspects drove their vehicle approximately 150 yards where they abandoned it at the end of a dead-end road. Both fled on foot north along the freeway fence. The driver suspect turned east and the passenger suspect west.

The driver suspect (Davis), worked his way north to San Francisquito Canyon where he came upon a parked pickup camper. The camper was occupied by a male subject who was awakened by the suspect with the demand that he get out of his vehicle. The subject ordered him away and the suspect fired one round through the rear door of the camper with Officer Frago's revolver. The subject returned fire with a .38 caliber revolver carried in his camper. The suspect retreated and threatened to set fire to the camper unless the subject came out. Fearing for his life, the subject left the camper and was immediately advanced upon by the suspect and beaten with the now empty revolver. The suspect took the camper and headed north on San Francisquito Road toward Antelope Valley. The subject, severely beaten about the head, walked to a nearby power station and reported the theft of his truck.

MONDAY 4:17 AM

A radio broadcast was made informing all units of the camper theft. A Los Angeles County Sheriff's unit responded from Lancaster and staked out on San Francisquito Road. Approximately two or three miles south of the end of the paved road the Sheriff's unit encountered the stolen vehicle. Blocking the road, the deputies stopped the vehicle and ordered the suspect out. The suspect exited the vehicle with his hands up and meekly surrendered.

The intensely tragic and heartbreaking aftermath following the violent killing of four CHP officers (all four men were in their early 20s). Following his release from prison, Jack Twining and crime partner Bobby Davis went on a violent spree that would end in tragedy on April 5, 1970. After being pulled over for brandishing a weapon and erratic driving in Newhall, California, and not willing to go back to prison or be taken alive, Twining and Davis shot and killed two California Highway Patrol officers. When two other officers arrived on the scene, Twining and Davis ambushed them. Davis killed one officer with a shotgun and Twining killed the other officer using a .45 automatic handgun. A witness, who happened to be a former marine, grabbed one of the slain officers' weapons and shot Davis in the chest, but he survived his injuries.

When the suspects split up, the passenger went west across Old Highway 99, doubled back southbound parallel to the freeway, and walked three-and-one-half miles to Lyons Avenue, coming out only a few hundred yards north of the Newhall Area office of the California Highway Patrol.

MONDAY 4:45 AM

Shots were heard coming from a residence behind Denny's Coffee Shop at Lyons Avenue, and all available units responded to the location. It was determined

Twining fled the scene and sought refuge by making a violent entry into the home of a married couple and taking them hostage. Exhausted and in despair after a six-hour standoff with police, Twining turned the gun on himself and committed suicide. Despite a violent past, Twining was well liked by fellow cons and officers at Alcatraz. He was known to always have a smile and be cordial in conversation. The Newhall tragedy continues to be one of the most studied and analyzed officer involved shootings by law enforcement agencies nationwide. It has been credited as having helped saved the lives of numerous other officers through strategic and tactical training scenarios based on those tragic events.

that the suspect (Twining) had entered a home situated on top of a hill and was holding one of its occupants hostage. The area was closed off and a cordon of officers placed around the house.

MONDAY 8:00 AM to 10:30 AM

Los Angeles County Sheriff's Deputies were able to engage the suspect in conversation over the telephone (in the course of this conversation, the suspect said of Frago "As the officer approached the vehicle on the passenger side, he got careless, so I wasted him..."). During the next several hours, numerous attempts were made to get the suspect to release his hostage. A reporter from the *San Francisco Chronicle* had somehow located the phone number to the Hoag residence and made contact with Twining. In a cool and calm voice to the reporter, he stated that he had killed all four officers. He understood he would be executed for the murders and expressed to the reporter that he didn't plan to make it out alive.

In a desperate plea for Twining's surrender, a communications line was established between the Hoag residence and USC Medical Center where Bobby Davis was being treated following his capture. Davis had agreed to help law enforcement plead with Jack to give himself up. Despite Davis's plea, Twining expressed that he was going to kill himself rather than go back to prison. He agreed to release the hostage unharmed, and the police gave him until 10:00 AM to surrender or he would be taken by force. At 10:02 AM, with no communication by Twining, the police fired rounds of tear gas that permeated the residence. An assault team composed of three Los Angeles County Sheriff's Deputies entered the house under cover of a tear gas barrage. After firing several gunshots, they reappeared outside after commenting they were unable to see anything due to the heavy concentration of gas. Twenty minutes later, they reentered the house and worked their way toward an interior hallway. As they approached, a shotgun blast was heard and the deputies returned the fire, believing the suspect had shot at them. When they were able to approach the suspect, they found he had committed suicide by placing the muzzle of Officer Frago's CHP shotgun under his chin and discharging the weapon.

Twining's death certificate showed a cause of death as "Gunshot wound to the head with destruction of the skull and brain." Thomas Noguchi, the famed medical examiner known as the "Coroner to the Stars," who oversaw many high-profile death cases in Hollywood such as Marilyn Monroe, Robert Kennedy, Sharon Tate, Janis Joplin and Natalie Wood, took custody of Jack's body. He was held in wait for fifty-three days at the Los Angeles Medical Examiner's office. With no family or friends to claim his body, he was finally

Officer George Alleyn

Officer Walter Frago

Officer Roger Gore

Officer James Pence

cremated, and his ashes were interred anonymously into a community grave marked only by the year at the Los Angeles County Crematorium Cemetery. Ironically, his final resting place would be in Boyle Heights, the very same neighborhood where Mickey Cohen grew up. It was a tragic ending to a tragic story...

Bulger noted:

> Seeing the pictures of him and talking about this makes it all seem like yesterday. I feel he's at peace, but that he left a lot of people suffering in his wake, including mothers, fathers, siblings, children and friends. The police officers made the ultimate sacrifice for doing their jobs to protect the public and were robbed of their futures. It takes a certain type of bravery to engage with a killer and none of them backed down. They'll not be forgotten, and Jack faded into obscurity. I have never seen any further mention of him relating to the Newhall Incident. Looking back, not many people knew him. I remember driving past that stretch of highway and seeing a section of the California Highway named after the four officers he killed. I know it gives meaning to the families. It's tragic that all the case workers didn't help him during his youth, and the result was innocent people dying. Society still hasn't figured that out. These prisons graduate people like Jack and myself, and then the people who get in our way suffer. Man learns the hard way. Some never learn. When the volcano erupts, it's innocent people who die, not the tormentors he met along the way. In most cases like this, the names are forgotten by society at large—but not by the families of the victims. Those young officers who died were innocent victims. I'm sure all were really good men. To Jack, their uniforms were a symbol and target of his hatred. Man can't stop hurricanes or volcanos from erupting, but in Jack's case, I feel society failed him way back in his childhood. Myself, I had chances but never took advantage of those given to me. But Jack never had any of those things. I've always wondered if only someone, a social worker, etc., could have taken interest in him at a young age if that would have saved lots of lives and pain for their families. Instead, he was left boiling with hate and living for revenge...

Following Bobby Davis's capture, he was convicted of capital murder and sentenced to die in San Quentin's gas chamber. They searched Davis's Long Beach apartment after the incident and found extensive lists of banks and their managers' names with his intent to target them in robberies. In 1972, his sentence was commuted to four consecutive life sentences, and he'd spend more than three decades in Folsom and Pelican Bay State Prisons. He was last transferred to Kern Valley Prison in August 2008, where a year later he was found hanging dead in his cell. Davis refused interview requests and never offered any insight to the Newhall murders or Jack Twining.

The Newhall Incident marked the CHP forever. The incident continues as a reminder of the potential dangers law enforcement personnel face in the course of normal duty. It also continues to be used as a training scenario for police officers to help improve safety during high-risk traffic stops.

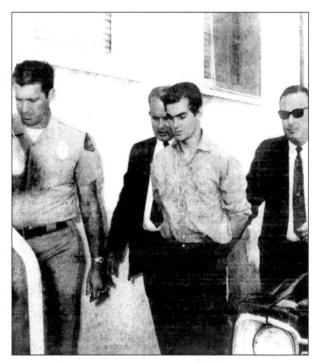

A news clipping showing Twining's partner Bobby Davis being led to court on capital murder charges. He was convicted and sentenced to death in California's gas chamber. His sentence was later commuted to life in prison without the possibility of parole. After nearly four decades in prison, Davis took his own life in August 2009 while an inmate at the Kern Valley state prison.

LEON BEARDEN

Leon Bearden (1564-AZ) attempted to hijack a plane to Cuba. I remember him on his first day and he ended up sitting at the end of the table in the mess hall where I was sitting. He was a little guy and seemed confused as to why he was sent to Alcatraz. Carlos Santiago (1544-AZ) asked him, "Why are you here?" (not a question I would have asked) and Bearden said, "I don't know" and he seemed like he was in a state of shock. The next meal, Santiago gives him a clipping from *Time Magazine* telling the story of the event and tells Bearden "Here's why you're here..." He seemed out of place on Alcatraz. He

Leon Bearden

obviously knew why he was in prison but couldn't reason why he'd been sent to the Rock. You could see his despair and I could understand with his young son in prison (sixteen-years-old) why he was suffering. On the Rock, he mostly kept to himself and was quiet.

In June of 1962, only days following the escape of Frank Morris and the Anglin brothers, Bearden's case was heard before the United States Court of Appeals. Bearden's lawyers felt he didn't receive a fair trial because of the intense publicity the case garnered in the media. The appeal transcript provided details of the hijacking:

The facts of the case are bizarre. On August 3, 1961, Bearden and his son boarded a Continental Airlines Boeing 707 aircraft in Phoenix, Arizona. Each had purchased a ticket to El Paso, Texas, under an assumed name. The flight had originated in Los Angeles, California and was scheduled to proceed to Houston, Texas, with intermediate stops in Phoenix, El Paso, and San Antonio, Texas. While the airplane was in flight over the state of New Mexico, en route to El Paso, Bearden and son, with pistols brandished, announced to the pilot and crew that they were taking command of the aircraft, ordered the pilot to make a forty-five degree right turn (which would have placed the plane across the immediately adjacent Mexican border), and declared it to be their intention to take the aircraft and its passengers to Mexico, and from there to Cuba. There is evidence in the record indicating that a slight turn was perhaps made, but in any event the normal course was almost immediately resumed. The crew was able to convince Bearden that the amount of fuel aboard was insufficient to permit a safe flight to Monterrey, Mexico, so he permitted the flight to proceed to El Paso, with the intention of refueling there and then proceeding to Cuba. While the aircraft was still in flight, ground authorities were made aware of the situation by radio. After a landing at El Paso was accomplished, refueling operations were purposely delayed at the direction of law enforcement

Scenes from Bearden's hijacking in El Paso, Texas. Police shot-out the tires to the aircraft and negotiated the release of hostages after a nine-hour standoff.

Bearden had also involved his teenage son Cody in the hijacking plot. Leon would share his deep regret with Bulger that his son, only a teenager, would suffer having to serve time in prison. Leon was sentenced to life in prison, while his son Cody accepted a plea bargain and was eligible for release on his 21st birthday.

authorities; during the period of delay, the crew members were held aboard the plane at pistol point, as hostages, although Bearden allowed most of the passengers to deplane. Climactically, Bearden demanded a takeoff, notwithstanding the incomplete fueling operations, only to have his escape aborted when a fusillade of bullets, fired by police officers who were pursuing the departing aircraft down the runway in automobiles, pierced its tires and engines. Subsequently, several officers boarded the plane to negotiate with Bearden for his surrender, the crew escaped, and Bearden was subdued by force. All of the events above described were given widespread local and national television, radio, and newspaper coverage. Television and radio broadcasts covering the events subsequent to landing emanated directly from the airport, upon which many local residents, attracted by the television and radio reports, converged to witness the events in person.

Bulger commenting on Bearden:

When I was looking through the book and noticed his name in the list of prisoners, it made me pause. Convicts called him "Lee" and he was in one of the very last groups of prisoners sent to Alcatraz before its closing. I don't think he was there that long, but I recall him telling me he was given a life sentence for the hijacking. He kept mostly to himself, but when he'd see me out in the yard, he'd come over and talk. He seemed young, maybe in his mid to late thirties. Lee was an idealist with an idyllic vision of society. There was a part of me that admired that. Ideals like my brother Bill. My brother is the same in that way. Bill didn't enter politics out of ego; it was a genuine desire to make a difference. He was always optimistic about the future of our country. Lee would come over and sit and we'd just watch the boats sailing on the Bay. He wouldn't say too much, but occasionally he'd tell me all about the hijacking and how he never intended to hurt anyone. He regretted pulling his young son into it and spoke of how bad he felt. He'd wished he could have taken it all back. I think he had a past (bank robbery), and my take was that he was having a tough go at making ends meet for his family. It was more out of desperation and a skewed set of unrealistic ideals that he decided to hijack a plane to Cuba and brought along his sixteen-year-old son. In his mind, he thought he can make a better life in Cuba and was sick over the fading values of American society. I was on Alcatraz when the hijacking took place and remember it well, listening to the news on the radio. The plane sat on the tarmac for several long hours and Lee said he had this moment where he stood in the cockpit and saw the despair of one of the flight attendants and he chose to release nearly all of the hostages. He didn't want anyone to get hurt and said he could see the pain in her eyes and even his son. That really shook him and when he demanded the pilot take off and head to Havana, he was looking through the cockpit windows when the plane started to move and then the police and FBI shot out the tires. He remembered seeing the deflated tires as he was removed from the plane and thought it resembled his own life. A sad story. Just one of a thousand hard luck stories on Alcatraz. I liked Lee. I felt bad for him, and I enjoyed our talks. I was in Santa Monica when I'd read he died. It was just a couple of years before my arrest. It was sad to see his photo. The article showed the photo of him and his son being arrested and the heaviness hit me. I remembered the two of us sitting together looking out at the Golden Gate Bridge. The newspaper said he moved to a rural part of Arizona and lived a quiet life there until his death. I hope he was able to rebuild and enjoy the time he had left.

FREDDIE "CURLEY" THOMAS

Freddie Thomas (893-AZ) went by "Curley" while on the Rock. He killed Joseph Barsock while cutting his hair in the Alcatraz Barbershop with a pair of shears. The murder happened several years before I arrived there, but everyone knew the story. It always stayed in the back of your mind whenever getting a haircut. Following the murder, Curley was confined to D-Block and caused a big ripple of talk when guards found a large meat bone in his cell that could have been used as a weapon.

THOMAS, Freddie Lee
893

Freddie "Curley" Thomas

Correctional Officer George DeVincenzi served on Alcatraz from 1950 until 1957. He remembered the day of Barsock's murder perhaps better than anyone. Ironically, it would be George's first day of independent duty where he was assigned to the Alcatraz Barbershop. George remembered:

It was my very first day; first assignment; first hour! It was eight o'clock and I had been assigned to the barbershop located at the end of A-Block. This was my first independent assignment. I was alone, standing watch with about seven or eight black inmates. Freddie "Curley" Thomas was the inmate barber and Barsock was the first to come up for his haircut. The other inmates sat along a bench against the wall. The area wasn't that big, and I was standing between the inmates sitting along the bench and the barber chair where Barsock was sitting awaiting his haircut. The only thing I had on me was a whistle. That was it. Thomas and Barsock were whispering to each other in very low tones, and I thought that was rather suspicious. As the haircut proceeded, the tempo and tone of the conversation got higher and higher, and at that point I realized something was going on. Barsock suddenly sprung out of the barber chair and Freddie charged at him with the scissors. Freddie viciously stabbed him in the neck, throat and chest. All of this right in front

Correctional Officer George DeVincenzi looking down Broadway in 2003. He worked on Alcatraz Island from 1950 to 1957.

The Alcatraz Barber Shop.

of me. And me, like a damn fool, I started blowing the whistle and I got between them to try to get them separated. We spun around so violently that we knocked over the second barber chair, which was reserved for white inmates, and then all of us ended up on the floor while Curley kept stabbing him. While we were all down on the floor, I managed to get the scissors out of Curley's hands. I had suffered a serious cut on my own leg, and we were all on the floor in a large pool of blood. Then as Barsock was dying, Curley leans over, kisses him and whispers, "I love you…" Just then two officers came rushing in to see what had happened…In a cell located directly across from the barbershop was an inmate by the name of Michael Romano (907-AZ). A day or two later he says to me "Mr. DeVincenzi,

Michael Romano

you blew that whistle so loud it almost blew it up!" The attack by Curley was so violent, I ended up with about a 10-inch laceration that not only cut my lower leg open, but also nearly cut off my shoe. He wasn't trying to get me, but still, I was really lucky I didn't end up with more serious injuries. I ended up in the warden's office being interviewed by two FBI agents, and they had me go back into the barbershop to explain what had happened and walk them through the crime scene. I remember as I was giving them a full rundown as to how the attack transpired, the FBI agents and asked me what was in the large cabinet that was in the barber area. I had to explain that I had no idea as I had never worked in there before and that it was my first day! The cabinet was filled with towels and hidden beneath them was a large shard of glass that was about 11 to 12-inches long. Wrapped carefully around the base, was a couple of socks that had been made into a makeshift handle. It was a really dangerous weapon. Obviously, Curley was going to get this guy one way or another. If not with the scissors, then with the glass.

Bulger remembered:

So, I have a really funny memory of Curley. After the Rock closed, I was in the Leavenworth Barbershop and saw him giving another con a haircut. We all knew the story of the Alcatraz barbershop murder. The guys talked about it and I can remember getting a haircut and overhearing one of the cons telling the barber in a joking voice that he didn't want a famous "Curley Cut." The barbershop at Leavenworth had a long row of regular style barber chairs, all sitting in line and facing a long mirror that ran the entire length of the shop. I remember seeing Curley there back in his old job as a barber. He was there with another guy, who I hope I'm not confusing the two, had been reputed to have chopped a con's head off with a hatchet and then kicked it down the stairs. Anyway, Curley's got a guy leaning back with his neck stretched far back and he's shaving him with a straight razor. So, I call over to him by name and said, "The Vocational Classification Board did a great job here!" I told him the cons had named a haircut after him, but it wasn't too popular! He got a really big laugh out of that!

RAFAEL MIRANDA

Rafael Cancel Miranda (1163-AZ) was sent to Alcatraz in 1954 after making international headlines for a violent shooting spree inside the United States Capitol Building where he, along with three accomplices, shot five congressmen. Miranda was a political activist and member of the Puerto Rican Nationalist Party who advocated for the independence of Puerto Rico. Armed with automatic weapons, they made the assault as a political statement. One later testified she "came to die for the liberty of her homeland." All five victims survived their injuries and Miranda, who was identified as the primary conspirator, received a prison sentence of eighty years, and was sent to Alcatraz. He would serve a total of six years on the Rock before being transferred to Leavenworth in 1960.

Despite the fierce patriotism of the Alcatraz prison population, Miranda was accepted and respected by fellow convicts. In one such example, Robert Schibline, 1355-AZ, a bank robber who arrived on Alcatraz in 1958, commented "He was the

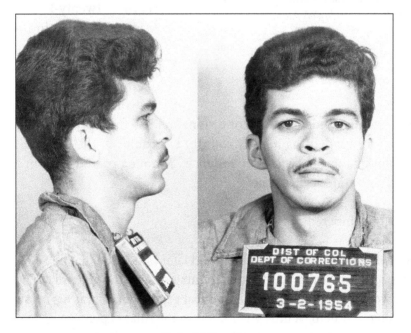

Rafael Miranda

213

Miranda boarding the Warden Johnston launch during his transfer to Alcatraz with Officer Emil Rychner guarding him. Miranda would later complain that the rules of Alcatraz were too rigid. He was not allowed to see his children while imprisoned on the island or speak in Spanish to his wife during her visits.

Puerto Rican who shot up the House of Representatives in 1954, fired thirty shots, wounded five reps and killed none. I used to tease him on Alcatraz. I told him, 'When you get out of prison look me up and I'll teach you how to shoot.' He would scold me for making fun of such a serious tragedy and would counter with his regret for causing harm, but not for his cause."

Miranda did his time quietly. He had served as an altar boy at Catholic services on the island and was often seen on the recreation yard playing board games with men like the King of Harlem, Ellsworth "Bumpy" Johnson and the convicted spy, Morton Sobell. In 1979, after serving twenty-five years in prison, President Jimmy Carter pardoned Miranda and his accomplices. Miranda wrote in a letter just prior to his release: "I won't accept no conditions on my freedom. We demand unconditional release from prison. We believe in that which we are fighting for. My country is a colony of the United States and we are fighting for our own independence." Miranda passed away in March of 2020 at eighty-nine years of age.

Bulger remembered:

Rafael Miranda shot up Congress and later said to me that he "expected to die that day for our country—it was the only way to get the world to listen." Miranda was a real gentleman, as was his fellow shooter "Cordero," a little guy I knew in the Atlanta pen. I used to eat next to him. He started to teach me some Spanish, but the lessons were

Political activist and member of the Puerto Rican Nationalist Party, Rafael Miranda (seen center during his trial with fellow conspirators) served six years on Alcatraz, arriving in late 1954. Miranda, along with fellow Nationalists Lolita Lebron, Andres Cordero, and Irving Flores, entered the United States Capitol building with automatic weapons and opened fire resulting in serious injuries to five congressmen, in the name of independence for Puerto Rico. Miranda was just 23 when he fired 30 bullets into the House chamber as 243 members where on the floor in session. All five congressmen survived, but Miranda and his co-conspirators were immediately captured and sentenced to federal prison terms. On Alcatraz he worked in the brush factory alongside Frank Morris as well as serving as an altar boy during Catholic mass services in the upstairs prison chapel. Bulger later commented that Miranda was well liked and respected by fellow convicts on Alcatraz. The respect was not a result of his crimes, but rather for his pride and being "morally strong." In 1979, Miranda was issued a pardon by President Jimmy Carter after serving 25 years in federal prison. Bulger also served time with Cordero at USP Atlanta.

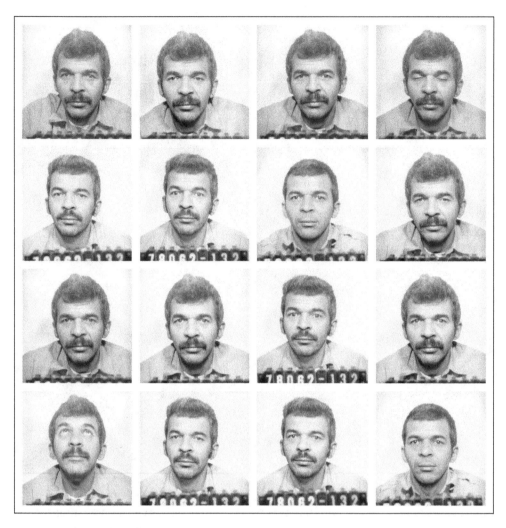

A collage of photographs taken of Miranda at USP Marion in the 1970s. He would serve 25 years in federal prison. In 1979, his sentence was commuted by United States President Jimmy Carter. He died in San Juan, the capital of Puerto Rico on March 2, 2020.

cut short after I was sent to the hole for the escape plot. After my time in the hole, I was placed into administrative segregation. Sadly, he died at a young age.

Both of these guys were "Political Prisoners" and were a credit to Puerto Rico. They were respected by their fellow convicts, and let's be crystal clear, not for shooting up Congress, but for how they conducted their lives in prison—proudly and morally strong. You have to remember that at Alcatraz, all of those men were fiercely patriotic.

216

They respected those who held to their own morals and ideals, but not to any violence against our country.

Years later I flew to San Juan, Puerto Rico just for a change of pace. It was an illegal trip since I was still on parole. It was crowded, and there was a lot of crime, stray dogs, and extreme poverty. In Old San Juan it was much more orderly, and people look to be middle-class. I went into a restaurant that the locals frequented. I was by myself and caught the chill from all of the customers at the bar. I ordered local goat meat, rice, beans and a beer, and enjoyed the meal.

I stopped at the bar for a beer, and a local in a friendly-but-suspicious way started to quiz me. They suspected I was a cop, but I was actually there while I was on parole when I wasn't supposed to leave Massachusetts. I found out that I was in a place where Puerto Rican nationalists frequent, and that they are wary of strangers, especially Americans. I assured them that if anything, I was for them having the right of self-determination. I mentioned that I knew Cordero, Miranda, and had met Oscar Callazo. I told them how the three were given their status in prison.

One of the customers was a writer for their paper and asked me if I would go on record with a photo. I had to explain that I was on parole and if it was known that I was in Puerto Rico, I'd be back in prison. They understood and to their credit they never revealed my identity or took my picture. This is a far cry from media liars in America. Years later I read about Miranda being free and working in his family's store in Mayaguez, Puerto Rico. I called there and had a pleasant conversation with Miranda. He was the Catholic altar boy in church services on Alcatraz and a true believer.

SAM TIBLOW

There is a story about Sam Tiblow (1265-AZ) and his pet lizard being snatched up from a rock and being eaten by a seagull. It happened down where Tiblow worked at the incinerator. There are stories of Tiblow getting revenge and killing lots of seagulls. Killing even one seagull would have never been tolerated by the prison administration. If that had been the case, Tiblow would have been off the incinerator detail and sent to D-Block. This story also didn't line up with Sam's character. On Alcatraz, he had a pet mouse that he trained and brought with him everywhere. In the movie *Escape from Alcatraz*,

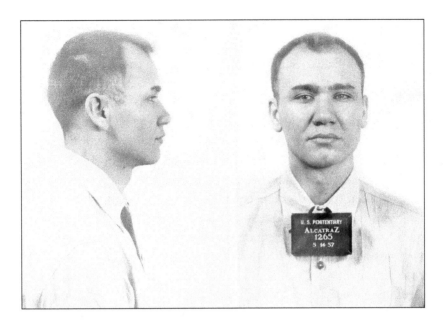

Sam Tiblow

one of the convicts had a mouse as a pet and I always wondered if this is where that story came from? Sam loved that mouse and taught it tricks. Our shirts had a single breast pocket, and the mouse would pop his head out and Sam would always be feeding him snacks and getting him to do small tricks to entertain the men. Courtney Taylor, a prolific and top-notch jailhouse lawyer also had a pet mouse that he kept in his pocket. It was well trained and well fed! Taylor loved and protected that mouse. It would eat, roam free on the table in the dining hall and after being fed, he'd go right back into Courtney's pocket, and poke his head out.

Now, I do recall that Tiblow would sometimes capture the seagulls, paint them using colors like blue and red, and then release them. We would spot them out the mess hall window. Often, we'd throw out slices of bread and the seagulls would catch them on the fly. Once in a while, a kitchen worker would tie a kitchen spatula or other shiny utensil to a large bread roll, and the birds would often be seen flying by with it. Guys would roar with laughter. That is a fact that was seen by many of us.

COURTNEY TAYLOR

Courtney Taylor (1038-AZ) was called "King of the Check Passers" and was sent to Alcatraz for helping cons with their legal work. He was the best prison lawyer in the system and the feds considered him a nuisance. He helped a lot of guys get sentence reductions for technical things like trial errors, etc. He helped Jack Twining get ten years shaved from his sentence, and I remember he was returned to New Orleans to have his case reviewed and won. He helped Mickey Cohen, whose case went back to court. He'd do the research and all the groundwork, then type the appeal and hand it off to the attorney to file. Frank Morris was in the company of Courtney often, and I'm sure he benefited. He had the ability to make fantastic ID papers. I saw his work.

Courtney Taylor

Taylor was an old con and real close friends with Charles Russell (1286-AZ). He was a mastermind when it came to check passing and forging IDs. I wasn't much of a student, but he was talented. Courtney was a center of attention on Alcatraz. Very popular among the prison population since he helped men with their legal cases and was very successful in helping guys with sentence reductions or vacating their entire sentence on appeal. The feds hated men like Courtney (jailhouse lawyers). They would flood the courts with frivolous writs, but Courtney was that of a different breed altogether. He was sharp and freed many guys including Russell. Charlie's case was about possession of a sawed-off shotgun and Courtney helped him prove that he had been forced to incriminate himself. Courtney saw the flaws in the investigation/interrogation process and won Russell his freedom. On Alcatraz, Russell hardly ever spoke to anyone and when he did, he was very quiet. He was timid and struggled to survive in a harsh prison environment. When he was released, it was all over the news and all a result of Courtney's legal maneuvering.

Charles Russell at Fort Mason being released from Alcatraz following a victorious appeal filed on his behalf by Courtney Taylor. He was able to successfully prove that Russell had been forced to incriminate himself and his charges were immediately vacated. Courtney was considered one of the best jailhouse lawyers and was successful in several appeals he prepared for fellow convicts.

A 1950s era photograph of Warden Edwin Swope and Officer Emil Rychner on Seedy Street, the same cellblock where Bulger lived out most of his tenure on Alcatraz.

EUGENE WILSON

Where you celled was very important; friendships were formed by proximity to cells. And that meant standing in line, filing into the mess hall, where and who you ate with. When I lived in C-314, my neighbor was Eugene Wilson (1290-AZ) who celled in C-316 who we simply called "Willie." To my right in C-312 was John Doyle (1435-AZ). Frank Hatfield was also on the third tier at one time; he may have also been in C-312 before Doyle. A lot of guys would stay awake after lights out and read. There were also a lot of guys who didn't read that much, but who were hooked on the sports programs that played on the radio. They listened to all of the games, and some of them would study the sports almanacs for stats.

Eugene Wilson

Once in a while, little field mice would be on the flats getting some of the breadcrumbs that guys used to feed the sparrows. Guys would catch the mice and then tame them down. They'd keep the mouse on a little leash (in their

Homer Clinton

221

shirt, jacket, or their hat). Guys really liked them. Wilson had one of those trained mice that he kept as a pet. At times, if I was real quiet, he would put the mouse on the flat bar and he would come over into my cell. I'd put him on my bed and play with him a little and he'd snap me straight out of my depression.

Some years later, I heard that Wilson had married a woman with two or three kids and was living in Texas and he had opened his own shoe repair shop. Willie worked in the Alcatraz cobbler shop and was a really neat guy. He was real quiet, but you also knew that he was tough. I never knew what he did to get to the Rock; I never asked, and he never brought it up. I only knew that he was an Army prisoner. That was how many of the Army prisoners were. Truth is I never cared why or what they did, I only judged them by how they carried themselves in prison. I wasn't surprised to later learn he was serving a long sentence for murder. John Doyle was also serving a life sentence for murder, and I lived between the two of them.

Bulger would later state that this was his favorite Alcatraz photo; it was taken by a member of the press on closing day. Looking back, he offered that it was a treasured memory watching the small birds fly into the cellhouse along C-D Street. He remembered "Many of the windows were broken or would be left open. The story goes that the warden didn't want to fix them because guys kept tossing objects and breaking them. I liked the windows being open as it allowed little sparrows to fly into the cellblock and we could feed them breadcrumbs."

HOMER CLINTON, "THE GREEN LIZARD"

Homer Clinton (1294-AZ) was a convicted kidnapper who at some point earned himself the nickname "The Green Lizard." I worked with a friend of Lizard's in the clothing issue named Gene Johnson (1347-AZ). Johnson, and a guy named Doc Riley (1353-AZ), all became close friends. Doc lived in a cell below me on C-Block and I remember Gene telling me how Lizard landed himself in prison and also how he got his nickname. All these books and stories give accounts of him swallowing a lizard whole and this is not at all true. Clinton later confirmed the story with me. He explained that he'd had a problem with alcohol, was down on his luck and he would drink anything to

John Doyle

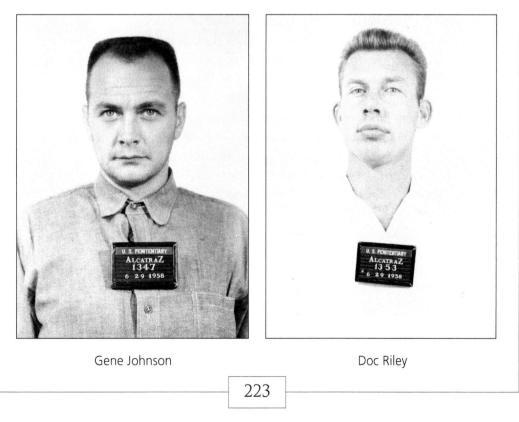

Gene Johnson

Doc Riley

curb his addiction. Apparently, one time when Lizard was drunk, he took a cab from Kansas City, Kansas, to Kansas City, Missouri. This is a short trip, a bit less than ten miles. Drunk and desperate, he held up the cab driver and then on top of the robbery when captured, he was prosecuted for kidnapping and buried in prison with a long sentence. He was an alcoholic and would drink anything with alcohol content including aftershave lotion if he had no other options. There was a green razor and aftershave product back in the 1950s and Lizard apparently consumed the entire bottle to get drunk. Don't recall if it was the brand name or the slimy green nature of the lotion that landed him his name. It was something odd like "Lizard Lavender" and a bright green fluid, and there were other similar products.

I remember Lizard well back then. I'd only been on Alcatraz about a month to experience my first Christmas on the island. There was a large Christmas tree in the mess hall, and I think it made the isolation of Alcatraz even harder for a lot of men. The smell of the tree and decorations set a somber mood rather than joyful. It was one of the tough reminders of all we'd lost. As the convicts were filing in toward the steam trays, Clinton runs full force at the tree and tackles it to the ground. He grabs it and starts running from the guards as they chase him around the tables. Bill Long tries to tackle him and then tear the tree away from his grip. Lizard is violently shaking the tree and bulbs and ornaments are flying everywhere! He's yelling and cursing the hypocrisy of the tree. One by one, the guards converge on Clinton as

A Christmas tree decorated by convicts in the mess hall, circa 1958.

cons cheer. Bill Long twists his arm behind his back as Lizard curses him. Pine needles and decorations are everywhere. The guards, with the tree in tow, drag Clinton into the main cellhouse and out of view. We all knew he was off to D-Block.

Bill Long was always looked at as being a bully towards convicts. The cons took revenge and in the clothing room they cut off one of his sleeves and placed a dead mouse in his hat. When he picked up his hat to put it on, the mouse fell onto the top of his head, and he went into a rage. Bill Johnson, an older guy and crime partner of old Doc Riley, calmly explains to Long that the cut sleeve and dead mouse was revenge for trying to break the Green Lizard's arm in the mess hall over the Christmas tree.

From that point on, I only saw Lizard occasionally. He was always in and out of D-Block. He served a lot of time in isolation because he had refused to quit feeding the small sparrows that would fly into the cellhouse from the open windows. He'd throw breadcrumbs from his food tray and the birds would fly over and pick them up in front of his cell. He refused to stop, exclaiming he was going to die in prison anyway. I don't know for certain, but I think he was kept in D-Block until Alcatraz closed, or at least close to.

MICKEY COHEN

Meyer "Mickey" Cohen (1518-AZ), was a Los Angeles-based crime mogul and a principal figure of America's Jewish Mafia. He served time alongside Bulger, arriving at Alcatraz in July of 1961. He is an important part of Bulger's time on Alcatraz, since he later acknowledged that he watched how Cohen conducted himself among his associates. Mickey Cohen is one of the most famous Alcatraz prisoners from the 1960s era. He was an associate of Al Capone during his early years in crime and would eventually land on Alcatraz serving time for an identical crime of tax evasion. He lived just a few cells down from where Capone served the majority of his years on the island two decades earlier.

When Mickey arrived, he was the talk of Alcatraz. He was a real character and had a hell of a life. He was well liked by all the guys. Tough break that he got struck down with a pipe over the head and left impaired. Mickey was a proud little guy and a survivor. The Mafia tried to kill him more than once, the Dragna Crime Family in Los Angeles, a principal of the Italian Mafia, once placed a large bomb under his house and detonated it. There was lots of damage but out of the rubble comes Mickey. He was later ambushed when coming out of a nightclub, and an associate was killed, but Cohen survived. Mickey was a close friend of Bugsy Siegel, and he would never have been part of his murder. Frankie Carbo was the one who whacked him. He shot him in his Beverly Hills home through the window. I've seen the crime scene photos many times of Siegel sprawled out on his sofa shot in the head (weapon was a .30 caliber carbine like the one carried by the guards on the yard wall—an accurate weapon). On Sundays, you didn't see him come out on the yard that often, so it was always something that caught peoples' attention. I'd be with Catalano, Louie and a few others from Boston and occasionally, Mickey would come over and visit. Catalano and Cohen lived just a few cells down from each other on the second tier of C-Block for a few weeks, and they used to eat at the same table during meals and got to know each other real well. Mickey would often make his way over to say hello to Charlie and then make small talk with the rest of the guys.

Cohen bonded out for about six months during an appeal. I'm certain he was the only convict who was ever able to bond directly out from the Rock. When he told us he was making bond, we urged him to flee to Brazil since there were no extradition laws. He had a hundred stories, and we enjoyed his company. Mickey was a rogue and

Mickey Cohen

loved the spotlight. He told all of us about a clothing store he owned on the Sunset Strip in Hollywood and all about his ice cream parlor. And he told us all about the "Battle of Sunset Strip," a war waged by Jack Dragna who tried to assassinate him and killed a few of his associates. I think they may have tried to blow up his car, but he had a car with stainless steel panels, and they ultimately ambushed him on the street to take him down, but instead they whacked one of his associates. He was at Alcatraz on a tax evasion conviction, but like Al Capone, he had too much power in prison. They sent him to Alcatraz to isolate him, with no ability to acquire special privileges. He had all these connections in Hollywood, a beautiful girlfriend with lots of money, influence and was infamous.

Cohen being led to the prison launch to begin his 15-year sentence for tax evasion on July 28, 1961.

Sometimes he would walk the yard with Frankie Carbo, and they looked rather serious. It was only casual talk, but still not real friendly. Everyone had heard that Carbo ordered the hit on Bugsy and there was always a lot of speculation as to what they were negotiating. Carbo had once been a prominent boxing promoter and was a powerful figure in that industry. Carbo was credited as killing Bugsy Siegel, firing into the living room of his Hollywood mansion.

I recall that Carbo often complained of having bad stomach problems and he appealed to Promising Paul Madigan to be placed on a special diet. Madigan said "OK—You have my permission to be on a special diet. Just select items from the food line you want. You're now in charge of your diet!" He smiled and made a fast exit!

Cohen celled next to Iannelli, a friend of mine from outside Chicago. Mickey was a heavy, loud snorer, and it drove Iannelli nuts during the night. "Big I" would bang on the wall with a magazine and scream "Wake up you fucking Meyer. Roll over!" Iannelli's rant would resonate throughout the cellhouse. Ianelli's nickname was "Big I." He was a powerful and violent guy. He did his full sentence and was freed directly from Alcatraz. The guards were afraid of him and when he was released, he was escorted by the police and placed on a train to Chicago. They wanted to make sure he left San Francisco. He made threats to Lieutenant Severson and others before he left. He said something to the effect "You motherfuckers, I'll be on the dock in X amount of days waiting for you." He was big and though he didn't look tough, he was a scary guy. Very powerful and a bit crazy. At the end of the food and work strike, he banged up the table in the mess hall. He pounded the table and looked straight at Severson and screamed at him, "You motherfuckers, I did every day of my sentence and I'll be free soon…I'll be over on that dock waiting for you…" He was physically powerful and dangerous, and I bet they lost sleep on the threat. Years later I looked him up and located his family in Crystal Lake, just north of Chicago. It was tragic to learn that he'd died. I told them I was sorry to hear of his passing. He was a good friend and well-liked by all of us who knew him. His family said he'd died a painful death. Sad ending.

One thing you find out is that all your friends in prison change when they're released. No more restrictions, regimentation, rules, access to alcohol, women, drugs and food; temptations of their old lifestyle. The pressure becomes finding a good job to live a decent lifestyle (car, house, recreation), a difficult prospect when you're an ex-con and stained. If and when you can't find a decent job, it's back to crime, but now you're even more desperate and dangerous, not wanting to risk going back to prison, having suffered through everything lost, especially time.

A few weeks before I transferred out to Leavenworth, I was on the yard and sitting at the top of the bleachers. It was a real warm day, and I was enjoying the sunshine, ocean

Frankie Carbo arrived at Alcatraz in 1962 and served alongside Mickey Cohen. A known enforcer and New York City Mafia soldier for outfits like Murder, Inc. and the infamous Lucchese Family, Carbo was rumored to have planned the 1947 murder of Bugsy Siegel in Hollywood, California, on the alleged order of Meyer Lansky. He was later to become one of the most powerful promoters in professional boxing.

229

breeze and watching the ships sailing past the Golden Gate. Cohen's appeal had been denied and he was brought back to Alcatraz. I noticed him come through the cellhouse door, down the steps and then he walked straight across the top of the cement bleachers, and sat down next to me and at first, he didn't say anything. It really caught me off guard. About a month before that, I had an encounter with Cohen and thought maybe this was the reason he was approaching me. It was just a misunderstanding, but I wasn't going to be surprised if Mickey wanted to call me out. I was dreading this as I didn't want any trouble with Cohen and respected him.

There was a guard desk near the visitor area, and once when I approached the desk to ask the officer a question, I noticed Mickey sitting at the visitor's window talking with his girlfriend. I could see her clearly through the bulletproof glass of the visitor port. She looked much younger than Mickey; blond, beautiful; a rare sight in those bleak surroundings. This was the first woman I'd seen in a couple of years, and I caught myself unconsciously staring a little when Mickey then turned his head and looked straight at me with a hard look. I wasn't trying to be disrespectful, and it wasn't anything I did consciously, so I nodded and turned away. During my years on Alcatraz, I never once saw a child or wife of a guard and only once heard their voices through an open window. Occasionally, while working in the laundry, we could see a tour boat pass and you could faintly make out the figures of women on the deck, but it was always at such a long distance away. When we finished our work, we'd sometimes go to the windows and stare out onto the San Francisco Bay, looking at boats and the Golden Gate Bridge. I do remember once

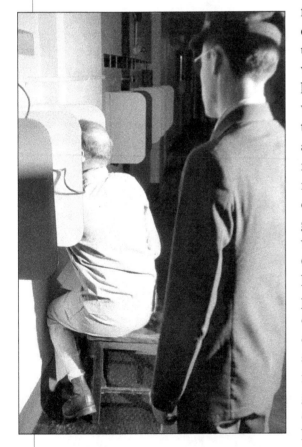

The prisoner visitation area at Alcatraz.

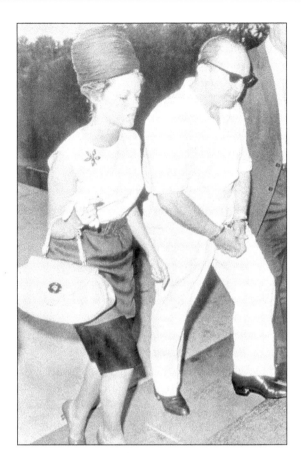

Sandy Hagen

Cohen and his girlfriend Sandy Hagen during his appeal hearing in 1961.

being in the hospital when I had the flu and on a really quiet night, I heard strange distant sounds through a cracked window, and it took me a couple of minutes to figure it all out. I got up and moved closer to the window and it was then I realized that it was a baby crying. I hadn't seen a woman or any children in years and it really shook me up.

Aside from a brief hello, Cohen and I never really spoke one on one, so I figured he was coming down to have a talk with me about glancing over in the visitation area. It was the only reason I could think of. As it turned out, nothing could have been further from the truth. Mickey reached out and gave me a real firm handshake. We sat together for about an hour and had a friendly conversation. He told me the story of how he met Al Capone during his youth, boxing, girlfriends, and a little about his businesses. I've read a lot of books that mischaracterize him, especially during his time on Alcatraz. As an example, cleanliness was important to him, but I discount some of the stories that claim he was overly obsessive. When he worked down in the clothing room, he was able to take showers daily, but not any strange behaviors like what some of the guards later

231

wrote about him. It wasn't anything I personally witnessed. I also enjoyed reading the Bureau of Prisons report written when he returned to Alcatraz. I read through it a few times. We faced similar challenges with authorities, consideration, although he obeys the rules and regulations when faced with them. The cellhouse officer states, "This man is apt at getting what he wants by any means open to him." Cohen is a member of the Jewish faith and attends such services regularly.

OFFICIAL ALCATRAZ REPORT

COMMITTED NAME: COHEN, Meyer Harris
REGISTER NUMBER: 1518-AZ
DATE: December 13, 1962

SENTENCE DATA:

This forty-nine-year-old resident of Los Angeles, California was sentenced July 1, 1961 at Los Angeles to serve fifteen years for an attempt to evade and defeat income tax. He was committed directly to Alcatraz on July 28, 1961, but released on an appeal bond on October 17, 1961. He was returned to Alcatraz on May 14, 1962. He is eligible for parole on January 18, 1967.

He has a clear conduct record. After his return to this institution, he was assigned to the clothing room on May 24, 1962, and has remained there to date. His work supervisor reports that he is a very good worker. This is because he is concerned about doing his share of the work for fear that someone will think he isn't carrying his share of the load and is riding on his name. In the cellhouse he is very cooperative and polite towards officers. He keeps one of the neatest cells in the cellhouse, goes to the yard whenever he can, and seems to be well adjusted to his present situation. He has a great tendency to be a packrat.

In the cellhouse Cohen is reported as having made a good adjustment and spending his time in many things, with card playing heading the list. He is not observed to be of any trouble to the inmates and has an attitude that he deserves special consideration, although he obeys the rules and regulations when faced with them. The cellhouse officer states, "This man is apt at getting what he wants by any means open to him." Cohen is a member of the Jewish faith and attends such services regularly.

He reads a great amount, according to his book loans from the institution library, and reads such a wide range of material, such as general works, history, detective stories, sports, science (math), poetry, better speech and English, philosophy, travel, character, biographies, and biology books. It is noted that his loans of the books are strictly non-fictional in nature.

Aside from a brief hello, Cohen and I never really spoke one on one, so I figured he was coming down to have a talk with me about glancing over in the visitation area. It was the only reason I could think of. As it turned out, nothing could have been further from the truth. Mickey reached out and gave me a real firm handshake. We sat together for about an hour and had a friendly conversation. He told me the story of how he met Al Capone during his youth, boxing, girlfriends, and a little about his businesses. I've read a lot of books that mischaracterize him, especially during his time on Alcatraz. As an example, cleanliness was important to him, but I discount some of the stories that claim he was overly obsessive. When he worked down in the clothing room, he was able to take showers daily, but not any strange behaviors like what some of the guards later wrote about him. It wasn't anything I personally witnessed. I also enjoyed reading the Bureau of Prisons report written when he returned to Alcatraz. I read through it a few times. We faced similar challenges with authorities, receiving special treatment resulting from our notoriety. Looking back, that conversation on the yard was a big deal to me. I really like the picture of Mickey and Mike Wallace. He looked sharp and was confident in his prime. I had a lot of respect for how he carried himself.

BACKGROUND AND HISTORY:

Meyer Harris Cohen, known as Mickey Cohen, was born in New York City, New York, September 4, 1913 to Max and Fanny Cohen, Russian-Jewish immigrants. They were natives of Kiev, Russia, and came to New York, according to Cohen, sometime around the turn of the century. He states that his father had another name other than the Americanized version, but he is unable to recall it. He is also uncertain about whether or not his parents ever took out citizenship papers. According to family members, his father operated a fish market in New York until his death from tuberculosis in 1914.

The family has related that his parents were very happy in their marital relationship, very hard-working, and industrious. Cohen has remarked that although he never knew his father, his mother always worked very hard until her recent years, when her age and infirmities would not permit. The parental home was characterized by his sister as being very religious with both parents keeping the Hebrew Sabbath strictly to the letter.

Mickey was not yet two years old when his father passed away. His sister recalls that the funeral took place at home, and that many friends came to the ceremonies as was the custom of the church. The five children, with Mickey, the youngest, were present. According to the wife [Mickey's mother] and his sister, Mickey did not speak much about the loss of his father but has always been sympathetic towards his mother. His only knowledge of him being what he has been told.

Cohen, in relating to his childhood, states he has been told that his mother had to borrow money to come to Los Angeles following his father's death because of her health. Both his mother and his older brothers and sister are understood to have suffered severe hardship during this time. He remembers that the older children were better educated than himself, through his father providing them an education. He, however, was denied this privilege, suggesting a feeling of being underprivileged in this respect in comparison with the other siblings.

In his recollection, he relates closest to his sister Lillian, believing that this was circumstanced by her having to take care of him as a small child. His mother tried to work after her arrival in Los Angeles, to alleviate the dire financial circumstances. He stated that at a very early age—five or six years—he started to hustle papers for the now extinct "Record," "Express," and "Examiner" newspapers.

According to the family, during this period of Mickey's early life, the mother came to Los Angeles because of her health. It is reported she suffered from mental health issues and is thought that she received some clinical treatment in Los Angeles after her arrival. His sister was nine years of age when little Mickey was made her responsibility. She remembers him as an easy child to manage. The home was kept immaculately clean with the example set by the mother. His sister states that he is also now fanatically clean, and was probably impressed by this early training.

Cohen, at this time, relates that his next brother in age is about eleven years his senior. He remembers that he did not play or associate with any of his brothers during childhood, that he had to "fight his own way" particularly with the other young newsboys in the Boyle Heights district. Explaining these years, he recalls, "If you came from Los Angeles, you know Boyle Heights." Through these years, by savings in being held by the older boys, Mrs. Cohen bought a small grocery and later a restaurant, working fourteen and fifteen hours a day.

At about the time he quit school the other children had left the home, and he continued to sell newspapers on the corner of Soto and Brooklyn

Avenues. From that time until about the age of fourteen he made a name for himself in boxing as part of the Newsboys Association in Los Angeles. He recalled with pride that he often made as much as twenty dollars a fight, often being placed on cards held at bootlegging clubs.

Cohen states that he went to Cleveland through the Newsboys Association, where he continued in boxing. His sister-in-law, Mrs. Harry Cohen, relates that she and her husband started him out when he first came to Cleveland and tried hard to help him. Harry was a fight promoter at the time in that city. While Cohen did not relate this situation, he has mentioned that he worked in Harry's drugstore as a soda jerk and points out that he first boxed as an amateur and later turned professional.

Much of his time was spent hanging around the gymnasiums, which were habituated by workout pugs, gamblers, and hangers-on. While at first financially successful, the advent of the Depression soon placed him at his wits end and struggling to make a decent living. At that time, and possessing no education and lacking any skills other than boxing, the activities he relates became more directed

Cohen trained in the 1930s as professional featherweight boxer, but eventually made his way into the underworld of organized crime. He made his way to Chicago where he ran a gambling operation for Al Capone's Chicago criminal syndicate. He would return to Southern California in 1939 to later become the "King of Los Angeles" as a principal in the Jewish Mafia.

235

towards gambling, a field he states nearly every "pug" takes up when he's with boxing. He relates that he became identified with the group of other similarly circumstanced boxers who did not know where their next meal was coming from. While boxing, it is reported that he became adept for newspaper publicity whether good or bad. This trait of personality seems to remain with him.

Cohen relates that his first difficulty with the law occurred in the company of some other unemployed boxers with whom he associated. Going to Chicago, Cohen relates that he continued his gambling activities and became further identified with the underworld. His appearance on the Los Angeles scene took place in 1939. The prosecuting agency—in reporting his activities and their development from this time—reports that he has been the focal point of numerous police investigations. The most recurrent offenses appear to be brutal assaults on persons who did not agree with the business methods he outlined. Public expenditures of funds in investigating and prosecuting Cohen (and his subordinates) over a period of thirteen years would total several hundred thousand dollars.

Cohen's record in the Los Angeles area from November, 1939—according to the prosecuting agency—shows that he was arrested by the Los Angeles Police at a bookmaking place that he was operating and was charged with robbery. He was released on November 15, 1939. In May of 1940, he was arrested by the police for assault with a deadly weapon and for vagrancy and was released with the charges being dismissed on June 24, 1940. He was again arrested in September 1941 and held for questioning in connection with the attempted murder of Benny Gamson. In July 1942, he was arrested by the Los Angeles Police for cutting the telephone wires of a horse racing gambling operation, after beating the owner of the services.

In May 1945, he was arrested in Los Angeles for shooting and killing Maxie Shaman, a competitive bookie, in a bookie joint owned by Cohen. He admitted the shooting and though there were no direct witnesses, he alleged that he acted in self-defense. A complaint was refused by the Los Angeles County District Attorney's Office, his gun was returned to him, and he was released. He has since bragged that it cost him $40,000 to escape this charge of murder.

In November of the same year, he was arrested by the Los Angeles Police Department on a charge of robbery at a gambling place owned by him. The complaint was refused by the Los Angeles County District Attorney, and he was released on November 19. He was again arrested by the Los Angeles Police in January 1946 on a bookmaking charge; the case was dismissed on February 6. Cohen, in May 1946, was one of the suspects questioned and released in the unsolved homicide of Paul Gibbons, a bookie competitor and hoodlum. The investigation made by the Beverly Hills Police Department notes that it was rumored at the time that Gibbons was the person who had broken into Cohen's home on June 16, 1944. At the time it was the underworld conversation that Cohen had obtained the services of Benny "Meatball" Gamson and George Levinson, two known police characters, to do away with Gibbons. Gamson's car was placed at the scene of the crime and he was arrested in a complaint filed by the District Attorney's Office, which was refused, and he was released.

Levinson, also taken in custody, obtained an attorney to represent him but the police were unable to interview him for two days after the killing and then only in the presence of his attorney. Cohen was interrogated and he volunteered information that Gibbons was a stool pigeon for law enforcement officers and had double-crossed several members of the underworld. Cohen states that Gibbons was an employee of the Shannon brothers, also known as a Shaman, who Cohen had killed the preceding year.

With Gibbons' elimination, Gamson and Levinson acquired a reputation amongst the underworld as killers, and it was reported that they had been given the assignment to eliminate Cohen by rival gamblers. Cohen found out that they had an apartment at a Los Angeles address. On October 3, 1946, both Gamson and Levinson were killed there. It was the general conversation amongst the underworld that Cohen had these gunmen eliminated. The Beverly Hills Police kept him under surveillance constantly, questioning him and his guests at frequent intervals, as he returned home early in the mornings until he finally moved to West Los Angeles.

In June 1947, Cohen was one of the suspects questioned and released in the unsolved homicide of Benjamin "Bugsy" Siegel and afterwards took over part of Siegel's interests. He was again questioned in August 1948 as one of the suspects, and was released in the unsolved homicide of his bodyguard Harry "Hookey" Rothman, and the wounding of two members of Cohen's gang, Albert Snyder, and James Risk in Cohen's place of business. Rothman had been on the downgrade through the use of drugs for several years prior to the shooting and Cohen had come to distrust him. He had a severe beating administered to Rothman for

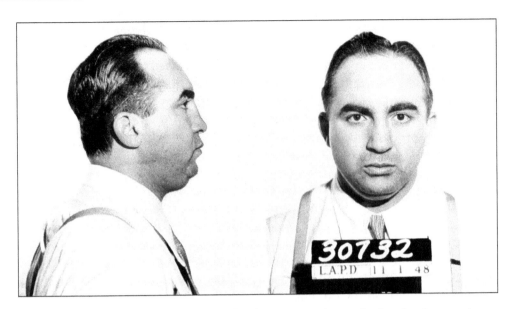

Cohen in a 1948 LAPD booking photo for the arrest and questioning for the murder of bodyguard Harry "Hookey" Rothman. He had also been a suspect and questioned a year earlier in the unsolved homicide of Benjamin "Bugsy" Siegel. He would later takeover part of Siegel's interests.

throwing his weight around at the Del Mar Track. After the shooting, Snyder left town and was last reported in Pittsburgh.

On July 20, 1949, Edward "Neddie" Herbert, a close associate of Bugsy Siegel, was shot in front of Sherry's, a restaurant located at 9039 Sunset Boulevard on the Sunset Strip, and he died six days later. Cohen was wounded in the shoulder and in all probability was the prime target. Harry Cooper, an investigator for the attorney general's office and Dee David, a call girl, were also wounded. Herbert had taken over "Hookey" Rothman's job with Cohen after Rothman's killing. A prior attempt had been made on his life at his home on June 22.

The common opinion was that Cohen was behind the shooting in an endeavor to teach Herbert a lesson. Early in August 1949, David Ogul and Frank Niccoli, two of Cohen's henchmen, disappeared. They were under indictment with Cohen and five of his hoodlums for assaulting a local businessman who had bookmaking connections. Ogul and Niccoli's testimony probably would have made the case against Cohen and the other defendants. Cohen was acquitted after the disappearance. At the time of this incident, he was trying to smear the police department in a political maneuver by involving them in the case, the attempt being unsuccessful.

Cohen's Attorney, Samuel Rummel, was killed with a shotgun in front of his home in Los Angeles on December 11, 1950. He had been Cohen's attorney for years, but it was known that they had been in disagreement for several months prior to the killing. Cohen's home at 513 Morino Drive, Los Angeles was bombed on February 6, 1950, which was indicative of the violence surrounding his activities. Residents in the vicinity have petitioned the City Council to have Cohen evicted for public safety reasons.

The Los Angeles Police reports that Cohen's life story was run in serial form by the *Los Angeles Daily News* in 1949, which is indicative of the great amount of public interest in his case. His connection with organized crime has been apparent for many years. His contacts and quite possibly his superiors in the underworld include Frank Costello in New York, Anthony Milano in Akron, a member of the Mafia, Jack Dragna of Los Angeles,

Cohen in 1959 when he was named in connection along with four others in the 1959 slaying of Jack (the Enforcer) Whalen. Cohen would amass a lengthy rap sheet of arrests and warrants during the 1940s and 50s.

Mafia Chief of the West Coast, and many others of similar background. The list of his gang members, at least some of the members, has been furnished to the institution by the prosecuting agency.

According to the prosecuting agency, he has handled betting transactions with many of the biggest betting commissioners in all parts of the states. His haberdashery, located at 8804 Sunset Boulevard in West Hollywood, operated as a blind for his activities; featured a bulletproof steel door, a bulletproof sedan listed as a company vehicle, and a nominal amount of actual sales. Despite his record of professional gangsterism and his intimate association with repeated acts of violence, Cohen has a reputation for aiding needy persons and causes, and for generosity for his friends and relatives.

He is obsessed with a craving for publicity and fine living, indicative by his announcing immediately after he was sentenced for income tax evasion that he planned to write a story of his life as the subject of a motion picture.

Mickey Cohen appeared on Mike Wallace's evening television show Night Beat in May of 1957. He criticized the Los Angeles Police Department for their conduct and harassment, claiming he had taken the road to reform. Cohen would be quoted in the program as stating: "I have killed no men…who in the first place didn't deserve killing."

Cohen served his time quietly at Alcatraz and was considered a model prisoner. He worked in the clothing room located in the downstairs basement section of the prison, the same area where Al Capone and Whitey Bulger had held similar job assignments. Cohen would later write in his 1975 memoir *In My Own Words*:

> This Alcatraz is unbelievable in the United States of America. You couldn't believe the treachery in this place. It was a crumbling dungeon. Like you see in the motion pictures with water dripping down from the ceiling. In Alcatraz, you were sitting in the middle of the ocean. At no time did you ever get away from the clamminess. I don't remember ever being warm there. I was in charge of the clothing room, which gave me access to take a shower twice or three times a day, or at least once a day for sure—which was the thing that saved my life.
>
> When I had to eat the joint's food, it wasn't too bad. See, Tony Marcello—String Bean was his nickname—had charge of the kitchen. He was a good cook; all Italian guys are. So, every day I ate there, he'd

say to me, 'What do you feel like eating?' 'What should I cook today?' And then he had a menu thing done with chalk put up so you could see it when you walked into the cafeteria. So, like after Frank Carbo comes in, String Bean put on the menu: Frank Carbo Day—Spaghetti. Then when he'd make corned beef, he'd put Mickey Cohen Day—Kosher Corned Beef. He was a character. He died in my arms later at the Springfield joint."

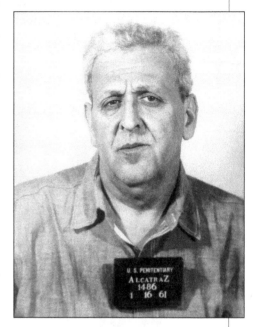

Tony Marcello

Cohen was transferred to USP Atlanta in January 1963, only a couple of months prior to the closure of Alcatraz. On August 14, 1963, fellow Atlanta inmate Berl McDonald (1542-AZ)—who had served time on Alcatraz with Cohen—escaped a secure prison compound, entered an electronics repair training facility, and wielding a 3-foot iron pipe, snuck up from behind Cohen. He bludgeoned the unsuspecting Mickey into unconsciousness. Cohen recounted the attack:

"I was in the television room watching the noon news program with my back towards the corridor. I don't know if the fucking building fell on me or what happened, and the next thing I know, I came out of the coma I had been in for two weeks."

Bulger recalled:

Later when he transferred out to Atlanta, Berl McDonald, who served time with us on Alcatraz, came up behind him and struck him down. McDonald was a fucking low life. A real zero and had to be jealous of Mickey. There were only two occasions I can remember talking to McDonald. Both times I told him what I thought of him. I don't recall ever seeing him in Leavenworth or Lewisburg. A real punk. I pictured him heavier back then, much heavier than he looks in his Alcatraz photo. Never saw him on the yard much. I remember the first time was over an incident involving Carlos Santiago (1544-AZ). McDonald had related to Santiago that there was a young, skinny, nerdy and bookish guy (apparently had a kind of Irish name) and was supposedly causing all kinds of trouble with other cons in the cellhouse. So, one day, Santiago walks by my cell and says in a serious tone "Jimmy, I'm going to D-Block and won't be seeing you for a while" I asked him why? He told me about the guy McDonald was upset about. This was all news to me. I remember thinking, how could this be? I'd never heard anything about this before. Santiago had a small knife and was going to cut him up in the shower room and put all this to rest. I asked him if I could see the knife. He handed it to me, and I threw it over the tier and it fell to the flats catching the attention of a guard who recovered it. I told Santiago,

Berl McDonald escaped a secure compound at USP Atlanta, scaled a perimeter wall and entered the television repair shop where he attacked the unsuspecting Cohen while he was seated watching a newscast. Cohen and McDonald had served time together on Alcatraz.

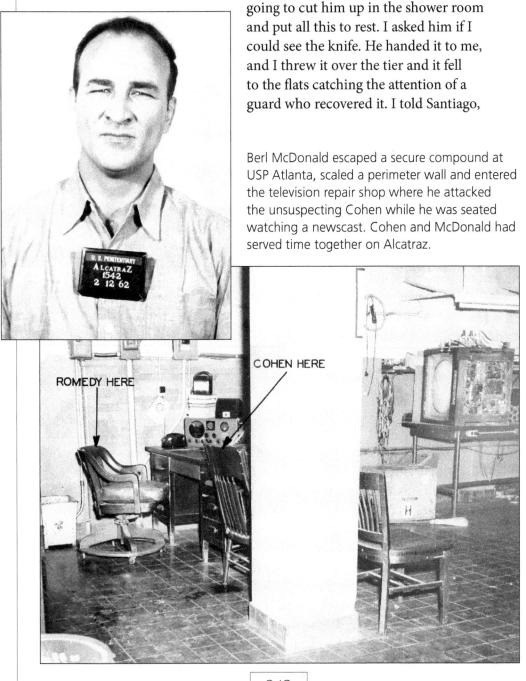

"You fucking nut. Don't you ever want to go home to Puerto Rico? Are you crazy? Go shower and I'll handle McDonald." I went to McDonald and told him to handle his own business matters, and not use Santiago ever again. I explained that Santiago was a friend of mine and called him a few choice names. That was it. Never had problems or dealings with him again. McDonald was a really strange guy. I remember Santiago was an ex-Army prisoner who was sent to federal prison like Sunday and Simcox, but I never knew exactly why he was in prison. He had no real friends and didn't really stand out from what I remember… On the street, McDonald wouldn't have been nothing more than a bum. On

Carlos Santiago

the Rock he was a nobody. Santiago was very superstitious and told me that in the dark he'd always see the "red head." I asked him who the "red head" is and he replied, "The guy I killed!" He regretted it. His victim was a fellow soldier and he suffered in guilt. I never asked why. Santiago was easily led and could be talked into violence easily. Richard Sunday hated him. Never understood his reasoning, but it was easy to keep the peace between them. All of us worked in the laundry together alongside Frank Watson. Quite a collection.

Mickey was a clever guy and I always wondered if maybe he had staged the attack in Atlanta? Maybe McDonald took it too far and he had thought he could secure a medical parole. Not sure, but it was always a thought in

Mickey Cohen's original request to work in the clothing room.

UNITED STATES DEPARTMENT OF JUSTICE
BUREAU OF PRISONS
INMATE REQUEST TO STAFF MEMBER

To: *Associate Warden*   Date *Aug - 2nd - 1961*
    (Name and title of officer)

SUBJECT: State completely but briefly the problem on which you desire assistance. (Give details.)
If I may, I would like to go to work in the shower and clothing room, I have a problem with my right arm, which was hit in a shotgun blast with a 30-0-6- shell, I was told that I would lose all use of it at the time, but I still do have limited use of the arm,— although it does go out on me occasionally.

ACTION REQUESTED: (State exactly how you believe your request may be handled; that is, exactly what you think should be done, and how.)

NAME: *Meyer Harris Cohen*
Work assignment: *NONE*   No.: *1518*
                              Living quarters:

243

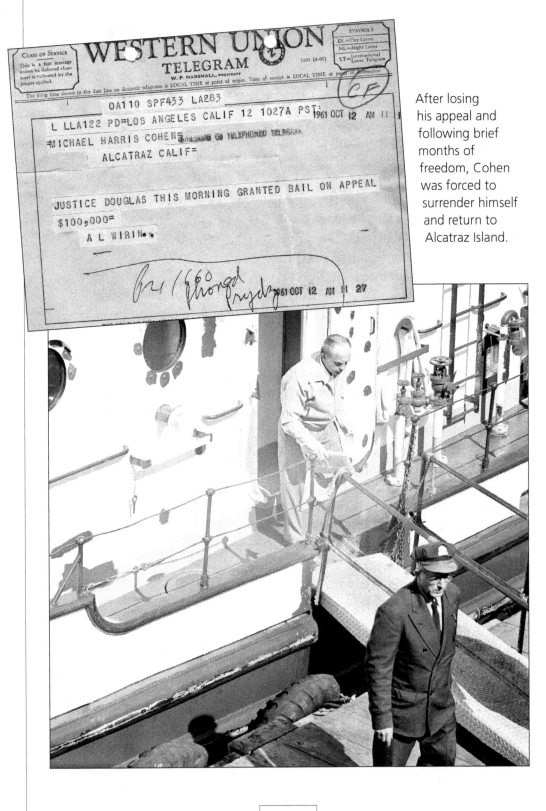

After losing his appeal and following brief months of freedom, Cohen was forced to surrender himself and return to Alcatraz Island.

Cohen covered his face as officers led him back to the launch for his return back to the Rock. The prison launch can be seen through the car window as it approaches the Fort Mason dock area from Alcatraz Island.

the back of my mind. Not sure about that though. Tom Kent later told me that he along with Cohen, Santiago and McDonald, all transferred off the Rock the same day. About a month before Alcatraz closed, Kent was shipped up to Lewisburg, and Cohen, Santiago and McDonald to Atlanta by train. They were all together in the same prison rail car. My guess is that it all started on that train; friendship or fight, I heard stories that the railcars were like pressure cookers.

McDonald worked in the kitchen at Atlanta and most of them had strange hours. They hung around the mess hall talking over food and coffee which was their payoff for their work. Mickey was old by the time he was finishing out his sentence at Atlanta and I doubt he ever saw it coming.

Cohen sustained a critical head injury that resulted from the shards of skull fragments that had to be removed from his brain tissue. He underwent extensive neurosurgery and following a two-week coma, doctors inserted a steel plate to replace the mangled bone fragments in the rear region of his skull.

On January 6, 1972, Cohen was released from Atlanta and returned to a quiet life in Hollywood, California. He had been misdiagnosed with an ulcer, which turned out to be stomach cancer. Though he survived the brutal attack without any known mental deficits, he would be completely disabled for the remainder of his life. He spent his final years in solitude. Mickey died peacefully in his sleep in 1976 at the age of 62. He is interred at the Hillside Memorial Park and Cemetery in Culver City, California.

ELLSWORTH "BUMPY" JOHNSON

Known as the "Al Capone of Harlem," Ellsworth "Bumpy" Johnson (1117-AZ) was serving his second stint on Alcatraz when he and Bulger first met in 1959. In the 1950s and 60s era, prison officials maintained racial segregation within the cellhouse, and persons of color were all confined on Broadway, the main prison corridor. It was considered the least popular area in the cellblock as it lacked privacy and faced highly populated sections of the opposite cellblock.

Bumpy Johnson

Broadway also had the highest volume of foot traffic, with officers walking back and forth at various times both during the day and night. The convicts assigned to the kitchen detail were celled nearest the dining room gate in the area known as Times Square and they typically started their workday a couple of hours earlier than the rest of the population. The racking of their cell doors at early dawn was considered a major nuisance and disruptive to those residing in this section.

Bumpy Johnson lived in cell B-111 along the flats of Broadway, along with numerous other prisoners of color. There have been many unsubstantiated rumors relating to Johnson's role (if any) in the 1962 escape plot with Frank Morris and the Anglin Brothers. The rumors were numerous and ranged from him helping secure cash for the escapees from a civil liberties group (who frequently had attorneys visiting the island to investigate claims of abuse and institutional crimes violating human rights, and who allegedly wanted Alcatraz closed), to rumors that Johnson, leveraging his contacts on the outside through a corrupt officer, arranged for a boat to wait for the convicts. None of these theories have ever been proven, but there is evidence in his case file revealing that he likely had some influence with at least one officer. Culled from official prison records and a memo dated February 9, 1962, from Warden Blackwell to the Director of the Bureau of Prisons, they indicated that Johnson had been sent to solitary confinement for possessing contraband items that had likely been secretly passed to him by an officer. The reports read in part:

> It has been brought to the attention of the officials that there was every
> reason to believe, beyond any reasonable doubt, that this man had
> been for some time, getting contraband brought into the institution
> and distributing it to other inmates, such as chewing gum and cigars.
> These items were acquired as a result of his known dealings with an
> officer, although we could not prove it.

A reasonable theory of Bumpy's role was that he helped negotiate the silence of the convicts living in the cells behind the escapees, all prisoners of color. A convict would have had a lot to gain by tipping off prison officials of the escape plot. They could have negotiated a transfer off Alcatraz or other subtle benefits. The rumors that Johnson had arranged contacts with the outside, or any evidence to substantiate the civil liberties group, have never been directly sourced or validated. Regardless, there were some who adamantly believed that a civil liberties group had interest in aiding in the escape. It was rumored that an underground force and "possibly members of a human rights organization helped fund the escape in an effort to close Alcatraz."

What is known about Johnson is that he was a leader among this population of inmates and a respected figure in organized crime. His early classification reports illustrate his early life growing up and his stature on Alcatraz, reading in part:

> As a child, Johnson's father was gainfully employed and the subject attended private schools up through eighth grade then took to the streets, entering criminal enterprises. In later life, he was considered the crime boss in the Harlem area, controlling numerous rackets in a large section of that part of town, ran numerous gambling establishments and handled the distribution of narcotics to wholesalers in that area. It is also alleged that Johnson used this reputation to sell protection to smaller number operators or others engaged in criminal activity and would charge them for the privilege of using his name or would accept a fee to "straighten out" someone who had gotten a little out of line. This "straightening out" process could involve anything from arbitration to a beating or shooting. In view of his mode of living and apparent wealth, subject was certainly having a rather large income from someplace. There is no question that he was engaged in illicit narcotic traffic for monetary gain and is considered one of the most vicious individuals to come to the attention of the law enforcement agencies for many years. Although he has been arrested on numerous occasions, Johnson has always been able to "beat the rap" due to his "connections" and reluctance of various witnesses to appear against him. He was the arbitrator in disputes between colored criminals in Harlem and Italian East Harlem criminals. He was an impeccable dresser, talked with a smooth well-modulated voice and gave the impression of being a substantial businessman in his community. However, he was one of the most dangerous and vicious criminals in Harlem.
>
> Under confinement he has been an extremely difficult individual to control, bitterly resenting the fact that he has to be confined and has refused to conform to institutional regulations. He has had a stormy career in and out of prison and the reports show that he has been shot several times and has frequently boasted that bullets can't harm him.
>
> He was originally transferred to Alcatraz in April of 1954, and after exhibiting a favorable adjustment, he was approved for transfer back to the federal prison in Atlanta in 1958. His negative social influence

amongst the prison population created enough concern for officials that he was transferred back to Alcatraz in September of 1959, for closer custody and Johnson having had a reputation of being assaultive and dangerous.

The cellhouse officer states he is known to everyone as a sort of "jail house lawyer" but that he is very shrewd and has a very good influence upon other colored inmates. He seems to have been a leader of the colored population. He has used his influence on one or two occasions in keeping down the trouble. He was reported as being a stabilizing influence during a period of racial tension. A stable individual who is highly respected and looked upon as an advisor by our colored population. He is on good terms with all inmates and is courteous and respectful to personnel at all times.

Former Alcatraz con Charlie Hopkins, who corresponded with Bulger in his final years of life, later wrote about Johnson: "One thing was certain: everybody—and I mean inmates and guards alike—respected the man. He was somehow above race…he showed so much class to me, that to this day, I think so much of him that I have his mug shot on my hallway wall. A day doesn't go by I don't think of him." Bulger later wrote that he studied how Bumpy carried himself among the other convicts:

Bumpy Johnson had a New York accent and was a real fast talker and was fairly outspoken. He didn't have what I would consider a mild manner. If you were next to him, he'd keep a conversation going… That's the kind of guy he was. I watched him and Mickey Cohen closely during those years…Both had such integrity among other convicts, that no one ever raised an eyebrow if they shared a laugh with a guard. Others couldn't get away with that, but Bumpy and Cohen were solid, so I guess you can say that I learned from both of them. I can still remember how they'd greet each other in the mess hall. Cohen greeted him by calling out, "Hey Bumps" and he replied back to Cohen "Hey Mike" which I seem to remember was his real name, but it always really stood out that he always called him out as Mike. I learned that giving respect to everyone earns an even higher respect, so you can say that I took a lot away from watching how they communicated with everyone."

THE ALCATRAZ STRIKE

In September of 1960, there was a major strike protesting the food, work conditions, and other general protest issues on the island. The complaints ranged from food quality and menu options to issues like compensation for kitchen staff. Prisoners also wanted a commissary to purchase food and other items like at other federal prisons. The biggest ask was allowing prisoners to assemble in the mess hall or open the cellblock for two to four hours on weekends during rainy weather. Madigan allowed it once, and the prisoners enjoyed playing board games and conversing, but the guards complained it was too dangerous and hard to manage and it was never allowed again. Eddie Pravato (1432-AZ) started the strike and recruited everyone. I hated to go along as I didn't agree with what they wanted to fight for, but I felt I had no choice. In my mind, the food was always better than the other prisons, and a quiet weekend in my cell with reading and radio during the rainy season was a welcome break. The food issues were generally temporary. It seemed they'd run low on funding and the menu would wear down to soup and rice style meals for a week or so,

Alcatraz Warden Paul Joseph Madigan. He was given the nickname "Promising Paul" by convicts for making promises, but never honoring them.

then get back to normal. I wanted no part of it because I had a good routine. Half day working in the laundry and the afternoons working out in the yard. Working under Bloomie seemed like a privilege and you couldn't ask for a better job. It was the best job I ever had in my life, but I'm in prison and if the convicts decide to go on strike, I have to go along, even though at some point we know it will end badly for us.

I tried to reason with some of the guys since I felt we had it good considering the circumstances. I even passed a message to Morris to see if he could talk them into reason since the stories he told us about Angola made Alcatraz seem like a Four Seasons resort. In prisons like Angola, you had men working chain gangs, wearing a ball and chain, suffering in heavy prison clothes, working in the blazing sun and high humidity. They would suffer in the heat and the food was not kept in an ice cooler and the meat would spoil. Morris told me that when things got especially tough, convicts would purposely have another con break their leg with a sledgehammer to get to the hospital, out of the heat and away from the rotting food.

Despite these efforts, Pravato got everyone's buy-in to go along. They originally try to get Karpis to be the spokesman, but he declines. He speaks up that he isn't favorable of the decision to strike. He tells the men, "I know how it will end and it will be a waste of time, but I'll go along with it…I won't be the first to quit and the last to come back…That's the way it is…" John Duncan (1359-AZ) steps up to be the spokesman. Every morning, the cells rack open, and the guy's heads would pop out looking back and forth down the tier, but no one would dare leave. A minute later, they'd rack closed and then a few hours later, guards would drop off two small lunch bags with a sandwich and apple and say here's your breakfast and lunch. Later on in the day, they'd come by again with another small brown paper bag, same meal, but this one was dinner. Towards the end, guys would go to the mess hall to eat and then refuse to work. I didn't do either. I stayed in my cell.

During the strike, the radio never came on, and whatever books you had in your cell was all you had. Madigan told the local press that guys were doing all this because they wanted to be able to read newspapers and buy chocolate. This was not true, but clever play to influence public opinion. Some people bought it. Not the real reason. Madigan had years of unrest and knows the routine. Madigan was a fair guy and I know he helped a number of cons, but loses a lot of respect for how he handles this.

Madigan finally calls Duncan forward and says they want to make changes and asks him what the problems are. He promises no retaliation for speaking up. John Duncan steps out and asks for a few

Alcatraz reports of conduct identifying Bulger and his role in the 1961 work and food strike.

U. S. Penitentiary
Alcatraz, California

Report of Misconduct

Inmates Name: Bulger   No. 1428   Work Assignment Cloth. Room   Quarters 314

Date. Sept. 14, 1960

Nature of charge:
Refusal to work, and participating in a Strike.

On Friday Sept. 2, 1960 Bulger refused to go to work. He was ordered to work on Tuesday Sept. 6, 1960 at which time he refused. He was ordered to work again on the morning of Sept. 12, 1960, and twice on the morning of Sept. 14, 1960, each time he refused. Wednesday, September 14th all but 8 inmates in the cellhouse went back to work and Bulger was one who did not go back to work.

Reported by: L. Meushaw

Date:

Comments of investigating Lt.

Investigated by:

Inmates statement to board: After the report was read to Bulger he was asked, "Is that True?" He answered, "I guess so." He admitted he refused to go to work and was given the opportunity to do so. He said the reason he refused to go to work was that he felt sorry for the guys in S.T.U.

Date September 28, 1960

Disciplinary board action:
Continue idle in cellhouse - Remove from job - Recommend Good Time Trial

L. I. Miller, Lieutenant   E.E. Rychner, Actg. Associate Warden   T. A. Renneberg, Actg.
Member   Chairman   Member   Captain

Record Form No. 8
(July, 1936)

UNITED STATES DEPARTMENT OF JUSTICE
BUREAU OF PRISONS

CONDUCT RECORD

U.S. Penitentiary   Alcatraz, California
(Institution)   (Location)

Record of   BULGER, James J. Jr.   No. 1428-AZ
FPI-LK-5-18-56-24M-3396

DATE	PRISON VIOLATIONS	DAYS LOST
9-14-60	REFUSAL TO WORK AND PARTICIPATING IN A STRIKE: On Friday September 2, 1960 Bulger refused to go to work. He was ordered to work on Tuesday September 6, 1960 at which time he again refused. He was ordered to work again on the morning of September 12 and twice on the morning of September 14 1960, each time he refused. On Wednesday September 14th., all but eight inmates in the cellhouse went back to work and Bulger was one of the eight that refused to return. L. Meushaw, C.O.	
5	INMATE'S STATEMENT: After the report was read to Bulger he was asked, "Is that True?" He answered, "I guess so." He said the reason he refused to go to work was that he felt sorry for the guys in S.T.U.	10-18-60 200 SGT
	BOARD'S ACTION: Continue idle in cellhouse - Remove from job Good time trial recommended. E.E. Rychner, Acting Assoc. Warden	

minor improvements, all reasonable, and Madigan answers, "Put him in the hole!" Guys had written down their long lists of demands and Madigan was in the cellhouse having men pulled from their cells and reading out loud their list of demands. He turns over the lists to the press, but the public isn't sympathetic because they think it's all over being able to buy chocolate. Public opinion falls on the side of Madigan, and we remain in lockdown.

The real trouble starts when the men all run out of cigarettes and tobacco. Everything escalated to violence. With no cigarettes or tobacco, men start burning property in their cells. Blankets, mattresses and paper burn in several cells throughout the cellhouse. Smoke fills the corridors and when guards start to open cells wherever they see smoldering smoke or fire, the prisoners come out fighting. My neighbor, John Doyle (1435-AZ), serving a life sentence for murder, was hated by the guards and always fought back whenever cornered. When a guard walked by to hand him his bagged lunch and whispered some kind of slur under his breath, Doyle grabbed his sleeve and started slamming him into the bars of the cell. The guard pulls free, but minutes later I hear the guards calling out Doyle's name. The goon squad assembles and marches up the tier to drag Doyle to D-Block. I had a good bearing back then and warned him to go quietly and not resist. He couldn't win and I told him not to give them an excuse to work him over. He calmed down and walked quietly to the door of D-Block. They opened it and he hesitated to enter. He kind of leaned in, looked left to right, and then started pulling away from their grip. "Double Tough" Ordway was behind him and shoved him hard between the shoulder blades. We were at the front of our cells watching through the bars and in a flash, Doyle spun around and hit Ordway with a hard punch that took him off his feet and sent him sliding on his back. The goon squad clubbed Doyle violently until he went down. The entire cellblock erupted into cursing, threats, and everyone started throwing bars of soap at the officers. It spread into nearly a riot. In moments like that, lambs turn into lions. I remember Frank Hatfield being one of the loudest voices challenging the guards, "Come up here you motherfuckers…" We could hear D-Block start up and it made for a loud, and very long night…We also heard about Clymore and Boggs fighting guards as they were pulled from their cells and dragged by guards into D-Block.

We then start hearing stories of self-mutilation and several men in D-Block cut their Achilles tendons. Heel cutting was just another means to break the strict conditions. Madigan played it down in the press, but several had to have surgery to repair injuries. Ianelli later told me that he felt his tendon snap. Several others, including Duncan, Chebetnoy, and Clymore suffered serious injuries, though all self-inflicted. The strike is all over the news, but nothing changes. Madigan and Blackwell are both walking the tiers attempting to have civil conversations with the men. When Madigan came to my cell, he pleaded with me to go back to work, and also made the promise they'd improve on the food and try to include a special Chef's Menu at least once a month. It was a nice gesture, but it never happened.

In a very public display of force, the "Goon Squad" congregate outside of Eddie Pravato's cell which was near the door to the yard.

He was a little round guy, well fed, from Brooklyn, New York, and he idolized the Baseball Hall of Famer Mickey Mantle. He was a bank robber and crime partner of Joe Dellamure (Bob Luke's old partner). They opened up all the cells on the flats and the Goon Squad said, "All right Pravato; Come on out and get to work right now or you're off to D-Block…" I could hear his voice clear as day for miles. It was a physical threat as they wore padding and carried clubs. Out pops Pravato and over his shoulder in his Brooklyn accent he says, "Come on guys, it's all over…" Little creep started all this and guys are doing time in the hole with casts on their legs after cutting their tendons and he says it's over? It was like a green light for all the traffic. Then Tier II and Tier III. I said the hell with this, I'm putting my photographs of my family together, got my cell in order and sat on my bed ready.

For the first time in weeks, the cellhouse is calm and quiet… I hear a distant voice yell out, "Bulger…It's Lou…I knew you would hold out…Fuck them…I'll be here waiting…" When everyone went back to work, there were only two holdouts. That was Lou Hess (1344-AZ) and me. Hess is in B-Block down toward the end near the main entrance. There were six guys still in D-Block in isolation who were hold-outs and wouldn't give in. Hess and I were ready to join

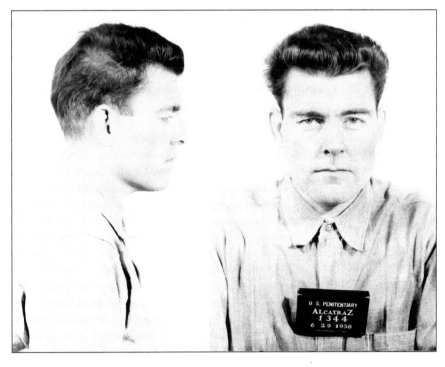

Louis Hess

them as a matter of principle. Neither of us were for the strike but went along when masses of cons quit and went back to work.

About a year before I arrived on Alcatraz, there was a young rookie guard who had been taken captive at knife point; blindfolded, bound and gagged, then tied to a tree during an escape by Clyde Johnson (864-AZ). His partner drowned in the attempt and Johnson was placed in lockdown. Clyde was a friend of mine and had some spectacular stories of bank robberies and all his other adventures. All this took place about a year before I arrived. The guard's name was Miller, and the cons gave him the nickname M&M, short for "Missing Miller" since after the convicts were discovered missing, they couldn't locate Miller until they found

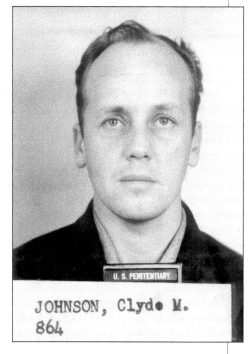

Clyde Johnson

him tied to a tree in a remote part of the island. We had nicknames for nearly all the guards, and they were used in general conversation amongst ourselves. Ordway called himself "Double Tough" and we referred to him as "Double Puff," and then there were others like "Herman the German," "Bloody Bill," "Missing Miller," "Promising Paul," "Gypsy," "Loser Long" and so on. Miller hated the hazing by prisoners and always walked around with a grim and threatening look.

On the morning the strike ended, Lou and I were left on deadlock until the next day. In the morning for the breakfast bell, the cell doors started racking open and I figured I'd go eat and then come back to my cell. The cells opened for everyone except me. I yelled out that my cell didn't open and a guard yells back "You're not having breakfast, Bulger." After the guys file off the tier, Miller walks in front of my cell and says "Bulger, you're fucked...We're making room for you in D-Block. They're clearing out a few cells and you'll be doing time in the hole." An hour later Rychner shows up in front of my cell with other guards and they escort me to D-Block. It was the first time I'd seen that part of the prison. They place me in a dark cell but allow me to keep my clothes on...It's pitch black and not a sliver of light even leaks from around the door seal. I sit on the steel floor in complete darkness for about an hour, then a light in the cell switches on. Rychner opens the cell door and states I have a board hearing and I'll also be meeting with Warden Madigan. They pull me from the dark cell and then lead me to the end of the cellblock for a shower and a fresh set of clothes. It'd been almost a month since I'd had a shower and you can imagine the feeling of standing in that stall under a hot stream of water. Years later when I visited the island as a tourist, I stood at that very shower cell and remembered back to the best shower of my lifetime. I've never forgotten that shower... They brought me upstairs to the theatre area and sat me down at a large conference table.

The following is the actual transcript of the hearing:

Report of Good Time Forfeiture Hearing in the case of BULGER, James J. Jr., Reg. No. 1428-AZ held on September 28, 1960 at 9:00 AM:

MEMBERS PRESENT

E. E. Rychner, Capt., Acting Associate Warden, Chairman
T. A. Renneberg, Lt., Acting Captain, Member
L. I. Miller, Lieutenant, Member
A. M. Dollison, Superintendent of Industries,
J. W. Casey, Chief, M.T.A., Consultant

MR. RYCHNER: Your name is Bulger?
BULGER: Yes sir.
MR. RYCHNER: What is your number?
BULGER: 1428.
MR. RYCHNER: Bulger, this is a Good Time Trial Board appointed to consider possible forfeiture of good time in connection with charges against you which I will read: "Refusal to Work and Participating in a Strike—On Friday September 2, 1960 Bulger refused to go to work. He was ordered to work on Tuesday September 6, 1960 at which time he refused. He was ordered to work again on the morning of September 12th, 1960 and twice on the morning of September 14, 1960. Each time he refused. Wednesday, September 14th all but eight inmates in the cellhouse went back to work: Signed: L. Meushaw.
MR. RYCHNER: Is that true?

BULGER: I guess so.

MR. RYCHNER: Where are you working?

BULGER: Down in the clothing room.

MR. RYCHNER: Did you refuse to go back to work? The last morning you didn't come out. Fifteen or twenty minutes later we sent them down and we let everybody out to go to work. You did have the opportunity?

BULGER: Yes, I did.

Mr. Renneberg: On which side are you living on. We opened the cell doors twice and then checked. Was there any reason for refusing to go out?

BULGER: I wasn't in sympathy. I felt bad about the guys in the hole I worked with. How could I face them? I have to live with them and I can't let them down, that is the reason I stayed in.

Mr. Renneberg: It will be long enough in doing your own time for yourself?

Correctional Officer Harold Miller, seen with Warden Paul Madigan during a press conference on September 30, 1958. The 27-year-old correctional officer was bound and tied to a tree during the attempted escape of Clyde Johnson and Aaron Burgett. Miller was unharmed but would receive ridiculing from the prisoners and was given the nickname M&M, short for Missing Miller. He was later to become the warden of USP Marion in Illinois, the prison specifically designated to replace Alcatraz when it opened in 1963. Burgett would drown in the fated attempt and Johnson, who decided not to test his fate in the swift currents of the bay, would later die in prison from cancer in 1995 following a lifetime spent in crime.

BULGER: I understand that. Maybe I have been foolish and blind, as I have never gone through anything like this in my life before.

Mr. Renneberg: How do you feel about this strike and the demands of the strikers?

BULGER: I never heard of any demands or complaints. There has been five months of rumbling in the mess hall and I can't say that prior to this time I ever heard any grumbling in the mess hall. This thing snowballed out in the yard, they decided no work and that was it. If they felt like this, how the hell can I go out? I felt that I didn't have any choice.

MR. RYCHNER: Mr. Dollison?

Mr. Dollison: How about when the other men went back to work? If from 250 inmates here, 200 went back to work, how is it going to hurt them to be ostracized?

BULGER: I don't know about 250 inmates, Hayes and Sunday never agitated, however, some guys did agitate. When I saw those guys that agitated go out the door to go to work I was disillusioned. I could not understand it. I figured probably someone would be around to talk to me. I didn't feel that I could go back to work as I figured they would think I was letting them down.

Mr. Dollison: Hayes and Sunday are still in there; you still feel the same?

BULGER: I know it is a lost cause; sometimes you learn by experience.

MR. RYCHNER: Mr. Miller, do you have anything to say?

MR. MILLER: You should have learned a good lesson from that strike? Remember one thing, your sentence is yours alone. Any time you fool with a thing like this you are fooling with your own time.

BULGER: I knew I had to lose. I did feel obligated and I didn't know silence was consent.

MR. MILLER: At the time it started you were probably doing a good job? When they started back to work you should have gone instead of continuing to lay in your cell?

BULGER: I know it now; I made a mistake.

MR. MILLER: Do you have a personal beef on the chow?

BULGER: Only when I first came here the food was better than it is now. It is still better than Atlanta, and at Atlanta I had no complaints. When I first came here I heard no one complaining about the food. It has only been in the last four or five months that I heard somebody saying anything about the food.

Mr. Miller: When a new Steward comes to the institution there are always complaints about the food, whether it's good or bad.

Mr. Rychner: Mr. Casey, is there something you want to say?

Mr. Casey: What is your personal reaction? Did you have any complaints about the food?

Bulger: No, I had no complaints.

Mr. Casey: Was there anything heard in respect to the work strike?

Bulger: I wasn't even involved. It seems it started about a penny. I didn't even ask anybody. It seems to me someone talked about a penny.

Mr. Casey: You have had no physical or mental trouble since you been here?

Bulger: No sir.

Mr. Dollison: Do you feel that these people who agitated and went back to work feel or think they let you down? Or did they just have a change of heart?

Bulger: I feel that they are just a bunch of neurotics, probably unhappy unless they are starting something. They start things going and then quit, I can't figure them out. It takes a psychiatrist to figure them out. All I know is, that if I go to the yard and see some of those guys, I know they wouldn't even look me in the eye. This kind of puts me in the middle.

Mr. Rychner: How do you feel about the inmates going back to work?

Bulger: My friends stayed. I told the guys to go to work by all means when they opened the cell doors the second time.

Mr. Rychner: After you leave the room, Bulger, the Committee will discuss your case and if we do recommend forfeiture of your good time you will be notified, after it is approved by the warden and we will let you know how much good time is forfeited. That is all, Bulger.

Mr. Miller: Are you ready to go back to work now?

Bulger: Yes sir. When you send me back to work I will be glad to go back.

After the inmate left the room, the Committee discussed the case and all agreed the inmate was guilty of the charges and we are unanimously recommending to the warden that he forfeit 200 days good time and it will only be official when approved by the warden, at which time the inmate will be notified how much good time will be forfeited.

W. E. Prydz, Reporter
9-28-60

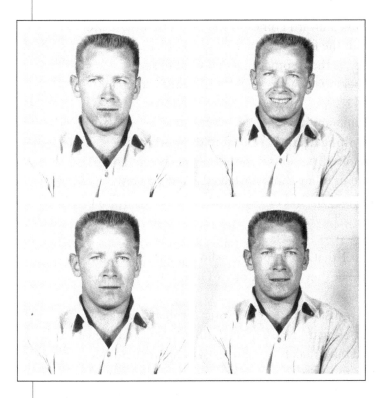

Prison portraits of Bulger taken for family while at Alcatraz.

After the hearing, they take me back to the closed front cell in D-Block and I sit there all day. Finally, I get called back up and Madigan comes in and sits down right next to me and goes on to give me a firm lecture. He explains he doesn't see much value in placing me in segregation and I was taken back to my cell and placed into a deadlock status. None of this was too upsetting since I enjoyed reading and Joe brought me some great titles.

Some of the guys on the dock crew didn't honor the strike and all kept working. We all took great offense to this... Jim Leather (1348-AZ), Glen Lowe (1350-AZ), Gino Scusselle (1356-AZ) and Jim Long continued to work. It was not a popular decision on their part and all of them became outcasts and most didn't associate with them afterward as they were no longer trusted. They were all awarded transfers for not participating.

THE GREAT ESCAPE
FROM ALCATRAZ

"The morning of the escape was one of the happiest moments of my life. I can still remember it as if it were yesterday. When the frantic guards realized that Morris and the brothers had escaped, the cheers were so loud that it could be heard for miles! It was a brilliant move on their part. As far as I'm concerned, it was the greatest escape in the history of the United States, and achieved under the most extreme security measures... It was a moment of freedom for all of us..."

THE FAMED 1962 ALCATRAZ ESCAPE of Frank Morris, along with brothers John & Clarence Anglin, sustains as one of the greatest prison breaks in American history. Over a half century later, it continues to be a central topic of debate among both investigators and historians. It was Bulger's close friendship with Jack Twining that brought him deep into the planning circle. As a trusted associate of Frank Morris, Twining leveraged expert knowledge from other trusted cons to help form a plot that was methodical in its redundancies to balance any potential failures. Over the course of more than a year in planning, the convicts who aided the principals deliberated over a variety of elements which included everything from water survival techniques to disappearing and evading capture. These discussions were also later to become the foundation of Bulger's own evasion of capture while on the run.

A correctional officer looks toward the dock tower from the residential building. On the night of the escape on June 11, 1962, the dock tower was the only tower staffed of the original six when the prison opened as a federal penitentiary in 1934.

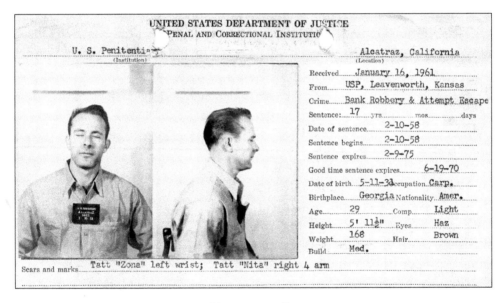

John William Anglin

Clarence Anglin

On June 14, 1962, a senior ranking special agent from the FBI drafted a confidential report to Bureau Director J. Edgar Hoover. The report included an admission statement from Allen West, the fourth conspirator and one of the primary architects of the escape plot. The confidential report provided a detailed overview of the escape plot based on the interrogation of West the day following the escape. The report read:

Department of Justice
VERY SERIOUS ESCAPE RISK PENAL AND CORRECTIONAL INSTITUTIONS
U. S. PENITENTIARY   ALCATRAZ, CALIF.
(Institution)   (Location)

Received 1-18-60
From Trans. fr. Atlanta
Crime Burglary of FDIC Bank
Sentence: 14 yrs. mos. days
Date of sentence 9-19-56
Sentence begins 9-19-56
Sentence expires 9-18-70
Good time sentence expires 2-11-66
Date of birth 9-1-26 Occupation Mech.Draft.
Birthplace D. C. Nationality U.S.
Age 33 Comp. Med.
Height 5' 7¼" Eyes Hazel
Weight 135 Hair Black
Mental Cond. Superior intelligence
Scars and marks Tat: Devil's Head upper R. arm; Star on each knee; star on L knee with 7 above
11 below; Star base L thumb; 13 base L index finger

Frank Lee Morris

Allen West, an inmate of United States Penitentiary, Alcatraz Island, California, was interviewed in the presence of Arthur M. Dollison, Associate Warden at that institution. He was initially advised that he need not furnish any information and if he did, the same could be used against him in a court of law. He was advised as to his rights to consult an attorney. No threats or promises were made to him.

West advised that on May 5, 1961, he was released from the Treatment Unit at Alcatraz and returned to the main cell area. At that time, he began to think about looking for ways to break out of Alcatraz. It was general knowledge among the inmates that above the cellblocks were eight ventilator holes leading to the roof which had not been used in several years.

These holes had been covered up; however, it appeared that the one above cellblock "B" had not been according to information among the inmates. When painting in that area about nine to ten

Allen Clayton West

months ago, he was able to verify that the lid covering this ventilator hole to the roof was not cemented like the others. He believed then that it was possible to break out that way. Around this time plumbers were working in the utility corridor which separates the cells in "B" cellblock. This corridor contains all of the plumbing facilities which lead to the back of all cells in that block.

After the plumbers had finished working, West was instructed to clean the refuse from the utility corridor. This corridor is approximately 3 feet wide and extends to the roof of the building. While cleaning the floor, West was scraping up some material while on his hands and knees. Underneath a cement support, he noticed something wrapped in an oil paper. When he opened it, he found that it contained some rusty saw blades and little pieces of files, all makeshift and which had evidently, from their condition, been secreted there for some ten to twenty years. He left this material where he had located it. He mentioned to John Anglin, an inmate having cell #150 in Block "B." He had become acquainted with John Anglin previously when they were both in the Florida Penitentiary in Raiford, about 1952. When discussing this with John Anglin, it was apparent that he was already aware of the possibility of escaping through the ventilation area in the roof. They discussed the possibility of breaking out of Alcatraz and swimming to the mainland. West said that swimming to the mainland was impossible. They considered cutting a couple of the front cell bars and possibly going up the left front part of the cell area to behind the steel cage door and working on this as a means of exit, then they decided that this could not be accomplished.

West said that he had told them that he had cut out of cement before at other institutions and it could be done so long as they had plenty of time. West said that they could go out through the roof through the ventilator hole as he felt that he could get the lid off. It was then apparent that they had to get out of the back part of their cell into the utility corridor to get to the roof. The only possible escape area at the back of the cell was through a 6-inch by 9-inch iron ventilator grate. It was decided that this hole could be enlarged by taking out the cement to approximately a 10 inch by 13-inch hole. West volunteered that he had previously checked through library books while at various institutions and had ascertained that cement would start disintegrating at from 500 to 900 degrees. West obtained some element wires similar to those in a toaster. He does not recall the source of these wires; however, he recalls that this occurred in October of about 1961. West

On Alcatraz, oil painting was a popular pastime and prisoners often worked on several works at any given time. John and Clarence Anglin were skilled portrait artists and used painting as a cover. The flesh tone paints would be used on the dummy heads to create lifelike decoys.

plugged this wire into the electrical outlet in his cell, but he could not get enough heat through it to deteriorate the cement. He had discussed this, as well as the escape, with John Anglin and Clarence Anglin, brother of John, who resides in cell #152 in "B" Block.

John Anglin said that he had a spoon which he had sharpened, and which somewhat resembled a screwdriver. John Anglin started poking around the side of the ventilator in his cell and he made a little bit of headway into the cement. This was around December of 1961 and by this time West had discussed the plan with Frank Morris 1441-AZ who was in #138 in "B" Block and who was to work with them. Clarence Anglin obtained a spoon and made a few dents in the cement next to his ventilator. The four of them got several spoons, the source of these spoons being not recalled, and by bending them similar to a screwdriver, started making holes in the cement. It was decided to start drilling the first hole a short distance from the top left-hand corner of the ventilator grill. They started to work shortly after the 5:15 or 5:30 PM count in the evening and would work until 9:30 PM, which is lights out.

The cells of the two Anglin brothers were adjacent to each other. The cells of West and Morris were also adjacent (West occupied cell #140). One evening, one of the Anglin brothers would watch while the other worked, and the next evening they would change positions. West and Morris used the same method. Finally, after about three days' work, West dug a hole about 3-inches deep, then for a period of about thirty days, West was able to dig about two such holes every other night. During this period of time the other three inmates were making headway in their respective cells. West made approximately fifty such holes around and to the left of this ventilator grill. He made holes directly to the left from the top left-hand corner of the ventilator grill for a distance of approximately 4-inches. He then dug the holes directly towards the floor for a distance of approximately 10-inches. After this, he drilled small holes to the right and under the grilled ventilator for approximately 13 inches. He completed his hole by then taking the lower right-hand corner and drilling small holes up the wall until it hit the lower right-hand corner of the metal grill. As West completed each small hole, he plugged it with toilet paper and soap and then touched the outside of it up with paint so no one would notice it. The other three inmates were doing the same thing.

They found a couple of pieces of metal and stuck them in the holes they had bored, and through this method they were able to make the

The trio used a star drill to bore out holes around the perimeter of the ventilation grills in their cells, and then once completed, the handles of the heavy steel spoons were used to carve away the final segments of cement.

A fake grill cover was used to mislead correctional officers during routine visual counts and cell checks.

holes larger and break one hole into another. Finally, the deep slab of cement adjacent to the screen came out. Just prior to taking the slab of cement out, they made false cardboard fronts which would fit in the area to be removed. They put paint and shellac on the cardboard so it would appear the same as the rest of the wall and they used a small amount of cement to put the cardboard in while they were not working. They then hid their few drilling tools behind this false front. They then made a false ventilator grill front of cardboard and painted and varnished it so it would appear to be identical with the grill work of the ventilator plate presently there.

They loosened the frame and the reinforcement rod of the ventilator grill and broke out the crisscross pieces of metal. This took several weeks to accomplish. The little bits of residue metal were either flushed down the toilet in their respective cells or hidden behind the false cardboard area which they had inserted in the wall.

After taking out the ventilator grill, West then had an area to the left and below the grill to knock out. This was also approximately 3-inches in depth; however, with the ventilator grill out, West could place his arm through the 6-inch by 9-inch opening and get better leverage. West as of April 25, 1962, had practically completed knocking out the small remaining portion of cement. He decided not to disturb the side of the cement adjacent to the utility corridor any further since, if anyone checked the plumbing, they might notice the same. John Anglin had knocked his completely out about this time and one evening had crawled into the utility corridor. Anglin made a false cement back to cover the area he had knocked out of the wall leading into the corridor so it would not be noticed. John then did work from the corridor side and assisted Clarence Anglin in completing his hole.

John and Clarence Anglin then made a small dummy face out of cement and gave it a flesh color. They put hair and eyebrows on it with glue and they named it "Oink." After Clarence broke through his hole in the wall, they made a dummy back for the hole which can be removed. This was made out of cardboard and painted. One evening Clarence Anglin went up the utility corridor toward the roof, using the network of plumbing in the corridor as a ladder. He crawled on top of the cellblock. He used a screwdriver and tried to take the screws out of the 18 1/2" diameter metal coupling, which was between the roof ventilator and the roof. He couldn't accomplish this by himself and needed help. About this time, West, in connection with his work detail, had to paint one day in the utility corridor and above the cellblock area in the vicinity of this roof ventilator. While painting in that area that day, West took the screws out of the ventilator coupling. He had taken clasps from his bed and bolted them together, then used them as a clamp, thus succeeding in loosening the screws of the coupling. The coupling, although unscrewed, was still in place so no one would notice anything amiss.

About this time, Clarence Anglin made a second dummy head of cement which was stored on top of the cellblock next to the roof. This one was called "Oscar" and was to be given to Frank Morris. Then Clarence Anglin and Frank Morris went up to the utility corridor next

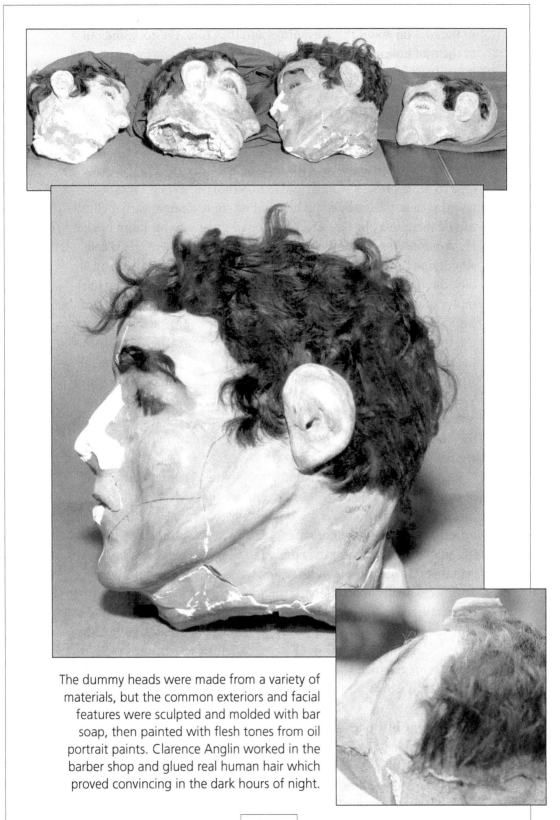

The dummy heads were made from a variety of materials, but the common exteriors and facial features were sculpted and molded with bar soap, then painted with flesh tones from oil portrait paints. Clarence Anglin worked in the barber shop and glued real human hair which proved convincing in the dark hours of night.

to the roof on about three evenings and they took the coupling out of the roof hole and from the ventilator. They put grease around it so it would slide out easily and replaced it so that no one would notice anything amiss.

While working around the cellblock area painting, West noticed that bolts in certain instances were screwed in with a tap pin and were not braided. He thus believed that this type of bolt could be loosened and therefore, since this was the type on the lid, covering the ventilator hole to the roof, they would be able to remove it. When West was painting near the barbershop he grabbed some electric barber clips, placed them in a plastic bag and dropped them into his paint bucket. He removed them later the same day and secreted them in his cell. About that time, one of them was able to obtain about a dozen drill bits, the source of which was unknown to West. He then set up the motor of the barber clippers so that it could be used with the aid of the drill bits as a drill. Morris and one of the Anglin brothers tried to use this as a drill to remove the bolts of the lid covering the ventilator to the roof. They said the motor was too small and wouldn't do the job. About that time the vacuum cleaner in the cell area broke down and West had a chance to examine it to see if it could be repaired. West noted that it had two motors in it. He took one of the motors out and then he wired the other motor up so that it would run the vacuum cleaner.

On the day he obtained the motor from the vacuum cleaner, one of the inmates was lethally assaulted by another inmate in the kitchen area and during the confusion he was able to smuggle the motor to his cell without anyone noticing. This motor was given to Morris and the Anglin brothers, and they took it to the roof to use as a drill. They said that it made too much noise and they could not use it much. They were finally able to loosen the screws to the lid that secured the ventilator to the roof. After loosening and removing them, they replaced them so they could easily be removed without significant effort. Sometime before this, Clarence Anglin made a dummy head out of cement which was to be used by West, when and before he left his cell, and which was to be stored on top of the cellblock near the roof.

About the first part of May 1962, West obtained a raincoat made of an olive drab rubberized material from one of the inmates who was transferred from this institution and over the next few days obtained a couple more of such raincoats. Over the next few days, he would pick up another raincoat when it was placed down by another inmate and when this individual was not looking. In the evening he would take these raincoats and cut them up and paste them together with some glue which had possibly been obtained from the glove factory at the institution. He would also sew some of the material together. He made a yoke life preserver out of this. He made valves out of pieces of tubing which he could pick up at various times. At night the raincoats and the residue were hidden on top of the cellblock near the roof and the ventilator pipe. West made all four yoke life preservers. John Anglin was using the same type of raincoat for making the raft they proposed to use. Upon occasions, bits of this material were handed into the back of West's cell so he could splice and glue the pieces together.

A raft was made which was approximately 6' x 14' and which had 15-inch pontoons around the edge into the underneath section of the raft. Originally, John Anglin had said that he had made a wooden type valve arrangement for one of the sections of the pontoon, but he discarded it in the ventilator pipe near the roof in favor of making the pontoon with a rubberized valve type.

About a month and a half ago, Frank Morris bought a concertina, which is a type of instrument inmates were allowed to purchase at Alcatraz. The keys to the concertina were taken out, and a valve type arrangement was made with it so that you could put your foot in one of the straps and with your hand push the other portion of the strap down so that the concertina would act as bellows.

Monday night, June 11, 1962, Morris had told me that we still had to complete taking the top off the ventilator to the roof and separate the bars. In addition, he indicated that there was little work left to complete the raft. Frank Morris said that the Anglins were talking about completing the work and breaking out that night. Clarence Anglin and Frank Morris left their cells and went up the utility corridor to the roof about 7:00 PM on June 11, 1962. Morris came down at about 8:45 PM that evening and said the bars were out of the hole on the roof and I gave him some water as he was thirsty. My vent to the utility corridor was not quite completed since my job as to making the life preservers and assisting with the raft did not call for me to leave my cell. Also, if I had completed mine, it would have been necessary to make the false rear to it to possibly prevent detection. John Anglin had cemented up a portion of mine to the rear where I had cracked the side of the cement to the utility corridor so no one would notice it. In addition, while working in my cell, I helped make the paddles we intended to use. I made four paddles, they were plywood, 12" x 8" and with a wooden handle. I put about two or three bolts through the paddle and handle to hold them together. These paddles were stored up on top of the cellblock and inside the ventilator pipe.

Morris indicated that we could go that evening if we got the lid off of the top of the ventilator. He said that the bars below it were out of the way and he felt they would get that off by 9:30 PM. He left the back of my cell and returned to the roof. Shortly thereafter, I heard some loud sounds and I started making noise to cover it up so that no one would notice. At 9:22 PM that date, Clarence Anglin tapped on my ventilator and said that they could see the moon. I tried to kick the rest of the cement out of the hole at the back of my cell. I could not do it. He tried to help for a minute or so but couldn't do anything. He then went up and got Morris. Morris came down and put the dummy in his bed. The lights were out at 9:30 PM and Morris went up to the roof and got a 2-inch piece of pipe and handed it to me. I tried to push it out but couldn't do it without making too much noise. Morris left to go get Clarence Anglin to help clear out my hole. This happened at 9:37 PM that evening. This is the last I heard or saw of them. As there was no dummy head that had been left to place on my bed, I was afraid at that time to break through and leave my cell until after the 3:00 AM count.

At about 1:45 AM of June 12, 1962, after waiting for some time for them to come back I became anxious, I broke through my hole and went to the roof by way of the utility corridor. Initially, I didn't have a dummy head to leave on my bed, but when I got into the utility corridor, I noticed that they had left "Oink" lying there and I used this dummy head in my bed. I took my blue dungarees, undershirt and blue serge pea coat to the roof with me. I could see that they had already left since a lot of the items we had fabricated were gone. In addition, there had been a 100-foot-long heavy electrical cord which had been lying on the floor of the utility corridor and I had noticed upon leaving my cell that it had disappeared. This cord was to be used in lowering our material down from the roof of the cellhouse and possibly in assisting in lowering one of us down.

I put my life preserver on and my and pants and started to go through the hole in the roof. I had to remove my clothing before I could get through the hole. When I got on the roof, I put my clothing on again and went to the edge of the roof near the cage where the large black pipe leads to the ground. We had contemplated going down this pipe. I looked around and could not see them and figured it was too late for me to go. Also, they had taken the raft which was to be our means of escape. The last time I saw Morris was at 9:37 PM on June 11, 1962, and it is my belief that they would have been able to leave the island by 10:30 PM that night or possibly no later than 11:00 PM that evening.

We had talked about going to Angel Island. It was believed that there would be less chance of detection if we proceeded in that direction. Upon getting to the mainland, we had decided that we would commit a burglary so we can obtain guns and clothes, and then steal a car. It was our desire to go as far from this area as we could, although we had no plan as to where we would go. Just the four of us were involved in the escape. To assist in this effort, I had made a periscope out of paper and mirrors which we could stick out of the hole on the roof to see if there were any guards in that area prior to leaving the hole. I had given this periscope to Morris for one of the Anglins and it was stored next to the roof. The only weapons which they would possibly have is a kitchen knife or some similar type objects which they might have sharpened.

When we were working attempting to get out of our cells, we would work from between 5:30 PM and 9:30 PM at night. Generally, Morris was with one of the Anglins when they went to the roof. I didn't desire that the two Anglins go there together as I didn't trust them. If we were successful in escaping, Morris and I had planned that sooner or later we would go in one direction and let the Anglin brothers go in another.

This concluded Allen West's interview, but the same FBI report summary continued:

West stated that this is all of the information he had to furnish concerning this matter. The search of escapees cells uncovered hacksaw blades, spoon handles with sharpened edges, four flesh-colored dummy faces, "Popular Mechanics" and "Sports Illustrated" magazines containing photographs and descriptions as to how to make rubberized rafts and lifesaving type vests; paint, paste, tape, and twine between cells, evidently used as a signal device. On the roof of the cellblock, one of the life-preservers fabricated from the raincoats was found as well as a partially completed raft of similar material, electric drills fashioned through use of a motor from barber clippers, liquid plastic, a homemade periscope, and other miscellaneous items located there.

A homemade wooden paddle and about 100-feet of heavy black extension cord was located on the cellhouse roof, and a similar cord was located on the beach. On 6/12/1962, a wooden paddle was picked up near Angel Island in the San Francisco Bay, and on 06/15/1962, a homemade life preserver was observed to wash ashore on Fort Cronkite Beach, which is on the Sausalito side of the Golden Gate Bridge. On June 22, 1962, another homemade life-preserver was picked up in the San Francisco Bay some fifty yards east of Alcatraz Island. All items are similar to those recovered at the prison. On June 14, 1962, a waterproof package, apparently made of raincoat material containing names, addresses, photographs and personal property identifiable with the Anglin brothers, was picked up in the San Francisco Bay. West stated earlier that they planned to escape to Angel Island, and then to the mainland where they planned to commit a burglary to obtain guns and clothing, steal a car and then leave the area.

He said that he did not believe in signed statements and would not furnish one. West advised that the other three individuals, as far as he knew, had the same type of clothing to take, namely, his regular denim garb and a pea jacket. He said he knew of no other clothing which would protect them from the cold water, and he had none.

Bulger would reminisce about the escape and the year of intensive and covert planning. He considered the escape one of the most memorable experiences of his lifetime, and also credited much of the experience of planning and discussion as a means to his own success while on the run from the FBI over three decades later.

I knew Frankie Morris at Atlanta. I had arrived at the federal prison in Atlanta in July of 1956 as USPA #77607, and Frankie got there in September of 1956 as USPA #77796. Even though we were all at Atlanta together at one point, I didn't come to know the Anglins until Alcatraz, and met John when he'd first arrived. We called Frankie "Paco," short in Spanish for "Little Frank." Frankie, Richard Sunday and I served time across from each other in the segregation unit at Atlanta, just before shipping out to the Rock. We were housed in separate open front cells and got to know each other well. I was

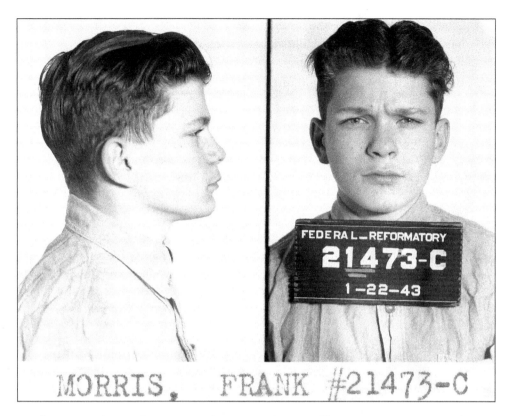

MORRIS, FRANK #21473-C

Frank Lee Morris at only 17 years of age. Morris's case file represents a tragic and troubled childhood. His criminal history dated back to grammar school. His early crimes were primarily centered on burglary and theft.

serving time in segregation for my role in helping friends in an escape plot.

I remember Morris recounting a lot of stories about serving time in the Louisiana State Prison at Angola. Frank told me stories where they welded the front of cells shut and men would be trapped inside for months and fed through a small slot in the door. He feared being sent back. Morris had already escaped from Angola once. Not easy by any means. He had several escapes in his past. Freedom was so important that he risked his life each time, and each time he got better at it. I remember him saying "If I go back to Angola, I'm escaping… I'm dead if they send me back." He felt that because he had already made a successful break that they would kill him. He told us lots of stories of how violent and corrupt the place was. Back in the 1950s in the Southern prisons, they used armed convict trusties as guards, and in Texas they used "Barn Bosses." Some of them were real tough,

275

armed with blackjacks and straight razors to keep law and order in the barracks. These guys were allowed weapons since they were in prison for non-violent crimes and usually had pending release dates. If they thwarted an escape, it would often earn them their own release.

Frankie had escaped from so many prisons, he confided to me that he knew they'd make an example of him. At Angola, he worked in a sugar mill and hard labor camps. The scenes were straight out of the Paul Newman movie, *Cool Hand Luke*, but even tougher. Guards rode on horseback with high powered rifles and anyone who tried to escape was chased down by bloodhounds and shot. Both Angola and Kilby had reputations of killing prisoners who tried to escape. Frank told me the story where during one of his escapes, the bloodhounds chased him and his partners through the swamps and down to the Mississippi River. One of them got into trouble crossing the river and then a guard shot him as he begged for help, and they let him drown. Frank didn't see it happen, but he said that he could hear full throated screams for help in the distance, then a gunshot rang out and everything went silent. Later one of the guards was laughing and showed off notches he'd etched into the butt of his rifle, noting how many prisoners he'd shot trying to escape. Frank said he was once dragged by his hair and the guards tried to run a horse over him. He felt they tried to kill him and then locked him in a filthy and poorly ventilated cell in the sweltering Louisiana heat.

A photograph from a news clipping of Morris in 1952 while incarcerated at Angola, the state penitentiary in Louisiana. Morris recounted to Bulger that he did tough time while at Angola.

As I said, these prisons were rough places and I've never forgot those stories Frankie told me about guys being placed in a cell where the door was actually welded shut for months. They put titles on cons such as "Texas Bad Boy," etc., and then set them up to be shot down. In Kilby, convict guards would get a pardon if they killed a

Four Fleeing Convicts Recaptured

One Of Five Angola Escapees Believed Swallowed By Mud

prisoner trying to escape. We used to hear a lot of these stories in Atlanta. I read some of the documents written in his youth. Kind of shakes me up reading the things he wrote at such a young age. He had a hard life...

I never considered Morris or the brothers as dangerous people. Frankie and the Anglins were all exceptional guys. They never hurt anyone but paid a hefty price with years of slow time in prison. Their plan of escape was not that of a "Do or Die" plot like Coy and Cretzer in '46. Also, Paco robbed banks, not with a gun, but by burglary and a cutting torch. He didn't use violence. Looking back, I remember Paco sizing everyone up and not saying or revealing much. He was always suspicious of others around him. I expect he must have been burnt by so many of those he trusted in his younger years. In regard to the brothers, they were a credit to their families. Clean living and adventurous. That's how I remember them. They were quiet and fixated on one thing—to escape Alcatraz. Their actions helped close the Rock, not to mention helping many of the old timers get their freedom. I believe that if Alcatraz were to have remained open, they would have been forced to live out the rest of their lives there. As a general rule, men were rarely paroled directly from Alcatraz, and a life sentence meant just that. Many fellow convicts who were serving hard time benefited from the trio.

Allen West was a different story altogether. All of us gave him the nickname "Eagle Eye Fleegle," a cartoon character out of that era. West played a crucial role in the escape. He had figured out how to do some cleaning and also paint the top of B-Block and the cellhouse ceiling. He was permitted to put up old blankets to prevent dirt and paint from getting on the tiers and people below. More importantly, it blocked the view of the guard in the gun gallery. It was "Double Tough" Ordway that told West to put blankets up after West on purpose splashed a little paint and dirt over the tiers. The blanket completely blocked the

Allen West had been given the nickname 'Eagle Eye Fleegle' by fellow convicts, based on a cartoon character in the popular syndicated Lil' Abner comic strip.

view from the east gun gallery and was the only reason they were able to pull it off! I don't know the particulars, but I remember that Morris was upset with West. The rumor was that West was bragging to someone about the escape plot. Morris and the Anglins told him from now on when you're out of your cell, you're on watch with one of us. This might be why West dragged his feet stalling on the night of the escape, because he was nervous about the other guys having plans for him. I was aware that Paco and the Anglins had a knife with them. Morris had procured the knife from someone working in the kitchen. If anything went wrong that night, then West would be stabbed, figuring he'd set them up. I'm not saying that it was the plan to take West out, but had he proven to be a liability, you know. If he'd laid a trap for the trio and it had been sprung, right then West would go down. If they'd been caught and taken alive, they would never get out of D-Block, and like I told you, Morris feared Angola. He always thought they'd send him back there eventually.

When it came down to the mechanics of the break, the trio planned it well and dealt with all of the points. When Morris first arrived on Alcatraz, he worked in the prison library and lived in C-Block on the second tier right below me for a short period. We passed each other every day…In the library, he became friends with Joe Carnes, who had been on Alcatraz since 1945. Joe knew the layout and workings of the prison better than anyone. He was eager to help a fellow convict beat the system. Carnes's job assignment was to distribute books to all the cells. Convicts would order books from the library using a catalog that was issued to each cell, and then when finished reading, cons

Frank Morris lived in C-256, the last cell on the second tier (visible in this photograph), and then to C-220 which was located right below Bulger's in C-Block prior to moving to B-Block where he would escape along with the Anglin Brothers.

would place the book on a cart located at the entrance of the mess hall at breakfast. Joe knew all of the guards and their personalities. He knew who was most alert and who was lazy. He knew their individual habits better than anyone. Joe had heard all of the escape stories from those involved. So many things could have gone wrong. In any other prison they would have been betrayed. The bottom line is that they worked hard and risked it all for freedom.

They were disciplined. They exercised, they were young, strong, and in excellent physical shape. By degrees, they dealt with the issues of acclimating to the shock of cold water. They trained hard knowing full well the challenges they faced ahead. Morris was a natural athlete. I remember him playing handball, and he also had a good arm when playing baseball and basketball on the Alcatraz rec yard. They exercised to build strength by running in place without socks on the cold cement floor of their cell. They draped cold wet towels across their neck and shoulders, and inside their clothing to adapt while doing strenuous activity in cold conditions. The water temperature in the showers was always kept real warm, so I had suggested that they get in and get out fast to allow more exposure while standing wet on the cold cement. During the same period as the escape and just before Alcatraz closed (in typical government fashion and waste of taxpayer dollars), the Bureau of Prisons installed a second faucet for hot water in each cell. We had hot water for the first time! This construction work was in progress, and it also helped cover the sounds of the escape efforts.

These guys were resourceful and wanted every advantage. I used to do skin diving with aqua lungs (double tanks) back in the 1950s and used both wet and dry suits. Jack Twining and Frankie were close friends and I offered to help. I, as well as many others, were all on Alcatraz because of our involvement with escape attempts or plots. I never approached the trio directly and everything I discussed was relayed through Twining. Paco had initiated the discussion of tides and equipment that I was familiar with by the way of Twining. So, when Frankie was plotting the escape, I mentioned when using a wetsuit how buoyant it was and it had to be overcome by use of a weight belt and how the suit helped ward off the cold. These were all important details, and they were very interested in attempting to understand every detail, especially the suit design. I had explained how when I came out of the water and into the cold air, I'd pull the wristlet away from my wrist, and the trapped layer of water would hit my freezing cold hand and the water was very warm.

The fitting of the suit was tight, and the tight seal around my wrists, neck and ankles was essential. There was discussion of available resources and how to recreate this. The trio had access to all kinds of glue, garments and other materials that could be made to be form fitting. I had also suggested that they fabricate caps that would be tight on their head but would help maintain body heat. I knew the head was a prime area of body for heat loss, and a lot of effort was given to address these types of issues in the planning. They tried to duplicate wet suits. They used a tight garment, then used a glue to spread lightly over the entire surface to create a seal. Later when Frankie was working in the brush shop, he had ready access to bulk quantities of glue and filled a small bottle each day for use on the garments. He would let the glue dry each night and reapply in layers. He then created seals at the wrist and ankles. This provided additional buoyancy by trapping air and a layer of water to maintain body heat. They also fabricated a sealed rubber style bag with the raincoats to keep their shoes and other clothing dry. I remember discussing the idea of using long sleeve wool shirts in two layers, then applying a thin layer of glue to both sides and then let harden. They also used raincoat material in the same fashion to duplicate a wetsuit—the result was to trap air bubbles for buoyancy and warmth. It had to be a tight fit and the layer surface durable to withstand extended exposure to water.

The tide tables were also very important and a concern of Paco's. I remember discussing this matter with Jack Twining and explaining that you would need access to a newspaper that published the tables for the fishermen. They would need to acquire the tide table to help ensure their success, but that was a challenge considering cons were not allowed to read any newspapers on the Rock, only the *Christian Science Monitor* towards the end. I had discussed my experience in diving and if they were taken by the tide, not to fight by going hard left or right. I explained that it was better to use the tide to your benefit and let it carry you without exerting too much energy and move gradually towards land. Most important was not to panic...Distance looks greater when you're in the water. We even discussed swimming and flotation techniques. They had planned to jettison heavy footwear and create cloth type bags for dry clothing and using rubber gloves inside clothing material, similar to what was used in Scottie's (John Paul Scott) escape in December of that same year.

I think the idea for the dummy head decoys came from Willie Sutton's escape at Eastern State Penitentiary. Sutton was an unorthodox bank robber, and I studied his crimes going back to the early days. I always had a copy of his book in my personal library and read it several times. It was still on my bookshelf when I was captured in Santa Monica, and a lot of men at Alcatraz knew that the use of dummy heads as a decoy held promise as a means to successfully escape. Willie escaped several prisons over a span of several years, and he enjoyed long bouts of freedom. The suggestion to use decoys in the '62 escape didn't come from me, but Sutton came up in several of those conversations on the yard. I can tell you that everyone knew the stories about Sutton. The movie *Shawshank Redemption* used Willie's escape tunnel idea from Eastern State in the climax scenes at the end. I liked the ending where the main character is on a desolate beach somewhere deep in Mexico or South America working on his wooden

Many convicts during the 40s, 50s, and 60s era studied the elaborate escape plots of Willie Sutton. In 1945, Sutton used a dummy head to escape from Eastern State Penitentiary. Convicts obsessively studied the strengths and weaknesses of various escape plots to determine best practices, and to leverage the best chance for a successful prison break.

boat. When I saw the movie and that scene, I thought of the trio living their final years in the same style and on the same type of soil.

One time during my early crime days, I was reading Sutton's book when two detectives came into my hotel room in East St. Louis, a wide-open town that had a notorious reputation for corruption. I used one of the names in his book as an alias to evade capture and it worked! One story of Sutton's I remember was when he was captured in New York. A guy by the name of Arnold Schuster recognized him on the street and collected the reward money. He later went on television bragging about how proud he was that he turned him in to authorities and what a low life Sutton was. Albert Anastasia, Mafia head of the Gambino crime family ordered the hit on Schuster. Freddy "The Angel" Tenuto, who was close with Sutton and took part in the escape at Eastern State, shot him down on the streets of New York in front of his home. It wasn't that Anastasia had an issue with Schuster turning him in as a law-abiding citizen, it was strictly because he continued to openly insult Sutton in the press having never known him personally. Long story, but Freddy made it onto the FBI's Most

A bar spreader was found in the brush shop on Alcatraz on March 6, 1961, the same location where Morris was assigned for work. It's possible he had been crafting tools for the break during this period. There is evidence the plot was already in play based on a memorandum written by Lieutenant Lloyd Miller on March 9, 1961, only days after the bar spreader was discovered. The memo indicated he was suspicious about a covert meeting he witnessed take place with Clarence Anglin, Joe Carnes and June Stephens. Both Carnes and Stephens were later confirmed to have had a role in the plotting of the escape.

Alcatraz
March - 6 - 61

Bar-Spreader found in Ind. Brush Shop
Made from parts of "C"-clamp & ¾" pipe

Wanted list and was hit by the Mafia before the authorities ever got any skin. Albert was also murdered around the same time period. There is a famous photo of Albert's murder. He was shot to death while sitting in a barber's chair waiting for a shave.

Though the head decoy idea didn't come from me, I was part of those talks on the yard and shared my ideas. Walter Perry, an old con from Boston, attempted to escape from a prison in Charlestown using a dummy head a few years after Sutton. He dug a tunnel that went completely under his cell and past a wall before his plan was discovered by guards. The escape closely resembled Sutton's and he came real close to breaking out. He used the dummy head as a decoy while he worked quietly after lights out mining through soil and concrete under the cellhouse. A guard discovered a pick handle in his cell during a routine search and foiled the break. Newspapers ran photos of Perry and the tunnel. I never forgot about Perry and years later I remember thinking if there was a way out of Alcatraz, this was it.

On Alcatraz, there was always talk about the ingredients of a perfect crime and what it would take to successfully disappear following an escape. We debated everything, and some of the old timers weighed in about the strengths of different plots. For example, there was a lot of talk of former Alcatraz convict Floyd Hill (451-AZ). He was on the FBI's Most Wanted list back in the 1950s. There were stories of him hiding more than $100,000 in a couple steel thermoses, then burying them for later retrieval. It's one of a thousand examples, but we tore apart the strengths and weaknesses of techniques that held promise. This was a good method to conceal money while on the run, so we learned from each-other and Alcatraz had been home to some of the best in the business. The mechanics of the escape was only one of the many complexities to consider as part of the bigger picture. The Rock was a deep well of ideas.

I believe they acted alone and I'm certain that no guards were involved in the plot. If that were true, they would have been able to move much faster in the escape process. They would have had easier access to equipment and not have to improvise as much. That would have never happened and would have raised suspicions by the other convicts. Why chance involving a guard? What guard would risk everything for money? Plus, guys barely spoke to guards, and never formed a friendship so strong that they would chance this. There was too much mistrust on both sides. Each would think they might be getting set up. The plans rested with the trio alone and no one arranged for a boat. I'm certain of it. I also don't believe they split up. I believe they had a safe house to hide and then later moved to an intended place for the long term. I won't speculate where, but that's my belief. I also don't believe the escape was common knowledge among the convicts. I was only aware because Frank Morris and I shared Jack Twining as a trusted friend. Otherwise, I would not have been in the mix. Many of the guards were perceptive and quick to pick up on behaviors that were out of the ordinary. As an example, the guards on the yard wall could pick up on the interactions of the cons as some would go into conspiratorial mode, lean against the yard wall and talk real low amongst each other. They would dumb up if anyone got close, but the older guards would watch for such behaviors and then start monitoring their individual activities even closer.

Seeing these "expert" theories that Bill Long had a role in the escape is beyond ridiculous. I knew Bill Long. He was in the clothing room with us for months and I got to know him really well. Of all the guards there, he would have never entered into anything like this. It would have taken nerve and greed to pull something like that off—Long had neither. You have to consider that he lived on the island with his wife who was also the postal mistress. They had two paychecks for income, cheap rent courtesy of the Bureau of Prisons, and bargains in the commissary for guards and their families, not to mention all the other perks afforded to them. It would have taken a long time to build confidence from the cons. This would have been difficult at best. There was so much hatred and frustration, not to mention that convicts would have caught on and it wouldn't have been kept a secret. There's no way officers had any role.

Bill Long was like a big kid. He was very emotional, high strung and he had no criminal tendencies. I have had a lot of experience with corruption—too much—and I have experience paying off law going back into my pre-bank robbing times. I was around it for years. I did it and got real good at it… You have to remember that I was sent to the Rock for my role in the escape with Scottie, Charlie and Louie, and bribing an Atlanta guard to bring in two hacksaw blades. What I was able to acquire was superior to the inventory in the prison industries.

There was an inmate named Darby who told the warden "Give me a parole and I'll tell you who owns the blades that were used to cut through the bars in the hospital." It was an escape attempt gone wrong. I spent a long, long stretch in the hole, and back then they raised hell with me to tell them where the blades came from. Warden Wilkinson told me "You will tell me the name of the guard who brought these blades into the prison. Next thing you know he will be bringing in guns." I was the only person who knew the name and I NEVER gave him up to anyone. I made a promise, and I've kept it to this day. I'm sure the guard is long gone by now, but it's no one's business. It's still a secret.

I mention this only to point out that it's hard for some people to recognize the potential traits of those more prone to corruption. No convict would have ever trusted someone like Bill Long. Plus, he was not liked and looked at as a bully. I didn't like him and would have never engaged in any small talk with a guy like him. The bottom line here is that I'd bet my life that no officer, especially someone like Bill Long, had any role in the escape of Frankie, Johnny and Clarence.

The night of the escape was exciting, but it was also unusually quiet at times. There were the typical counts at 5:00, 8:00 and 9:30 PM at lights out. Many of us knew what was in the works. There wasn't much talking between the cells of those of us in the know. We were straining to listen for every pin drop that night. Once we were locked in at 4:50 for the 5:00 PM count, the place would always change. You would not

Prisoners in good standing were allowed to use money earned in their work assignment to purchase quality musical instruments. Guitars and other stringed instruments were allowed to be played in the cellhouse between the hours of 5:30 PM and 7:00 PM. Frank Morris and the Anglin Brothers used the noise in the cellhouse to their advantage. Under this cover, they worked on the roof of the cellblock to cut away the exterior exhaust vent, build their raft and other items to be used in the break during that period each night.

hear cell doors open or shut, only the gates when guards were entering the cellhouse. If you heard a cell door racked open, the whole place would be buzzing concerned that someone was sick, being locked up in segregation, or even dead! It would have had to have been real serious if a cell door was opened after the 5:00 PM count. Any noise out of the usual would cause a reaction if you were reading, listening to the radio with the earphones or writing a letter. It would grab you like a physical thing, and you couldn't ignore it. On B-Block, during music hour when guys were allowed to play their musical instruments, once in a while someone with a trumpet would sound "CHARGE!", and guys would bang the bed frames hollering and laugh like mad. It would distract the guards—but they heard such things often and would write it off as nuisance behavior. Many would be white guys joking with the Hispanics, because there was much of that at times. It was always good natured, and it would go back and forth. It provided lots of background noise for months of escape work. I want to point out again that not many knew what was in the works. Later comes

A view of the area where the convicts worked to build their raft on the top of the cellblock from the east gun gallery. The east gallery was not staffed on the night of the escape and blankets had been approved to be draped over the bars to prevent debris and dust from dropping below on the walkways and into the cells below. West had sought formal approval as part of a cleaning and painting project he'd been assigned to. The blankets were draped over the bars and concealed their makeshift workshop for nearly six weeks.

all these "after the fact" experts who claim they were in the know, but my memory is the trio kept it reasonably discreet. There might have been some details when acquiring the raincoats, but I seriously doubt anyone knew any details or even who was involved. All these guys, decades later, trying to share some of the spotlight. If everyone in the cellhouse would have known about the escape, it would have never succeeded. For example, I doubt anyone on the Broadway side of B-Block knew except those directly opposite the escape cells. That section of Broadway was occupied by all colored convicts, and they never ratted out the trio. I believe if Bumpy Johnson had any role that night that was it. More than likely, he asked them to mind their own business. That was Alcatraz back then; they'd never sell out a fellow convict. A lot of credit goes to those men, but still, you couldn't trust everyone. Did Mickey Cohen have a role and help plan the escape while out on bond? Doubtful.

Shortly after 9:30 PM—Lights Out—it was quiet and then we heard a loud thud on the roof, followed by a loud chorus of squawking from the seagulls who lived on the cellhouse roof. They were startled by the sudden loud noise of the ventilator cover falling over and crashing down as the trio emerged. The noise was real loud and all of us acted out; guys hollering and creating a deafening noise that had to rattle the guards and fortunately proved to distract them. There was a real short interval between the "thump" and the seagulls' reaction, and it worried me that guards would react to it, because never in the history of the Rock had there been such a thing heard, or ever again. Also, year after year of routine counts while walking the flats and tiers, the guards never dreamed of anyone being out of their cells and probably didn't process a noise coming from outside the building. If they lived on the island, the noise of the seagulls may have been routine to them. There were gull nests all over the island (the grounds, sides of the cliffs, building roofs, etc.). "Herman the German" was doing the rounds, and this also played in the favor of the trio. He was a little overweight, always walked slowly and you could describe him as being sluggish. He was also inexperienced and as I've mentioned, most of these guards figured once cons were locked in their cells there was little risk of them escaping. Looking back, had some of the older guards been working the rounds, they would have been more suspect of the strange sounds coming from the roof. So, after we heard the loud thud, we made lots of noise to help divert attention, the sounds just fizzled out and the cellhouse came to a normal quiet. Then a long night of visualizing what it was like for the guys and sweating it out. No alarms and the "quiet" meant hope. I was so excited I couldn't sleep the entire night. Every minute undetected meant one more minute ahead of the authorities.

At night, guards making their rounds were very quiet. They would put felt covers on their shoes—sort of like slippers—to mask the noise of the rubber soles of their shoes. They always wore their hats.

You never saw them without them. Whenever they patrolled the cellblocks, industries or even the gun galleries, they always wore them. I could smell the guards when they started to count on the flats. As an example, Lewis always smelled of pipe tobacco. Others smelled of powder or aftershave or cigarettes. My sense of smell was powerful back then. The absence of motor vehicles and the fresh ocean air seemed to remove the smoke from inside the cellhouse. The prison environment today is recycled air in the pod cells and one of the reasons it makes me look back at Alcatraz with a sense of nostalgia. The sea air in the cellblock at Alcatraz was clean and pure. I love the ocean's salt air and the water was calming. That's why I ended up settling in Santa Monica. When the cellhouse windows were closed though, the thick haze of the smoke would stagnate like fog through the corridors. Most of the guys on Alcatraz were heavy smokers. Near the stairwells at the end of each cellblock, there were large dispensers that held packs of loose Bull Durham tobacco and the cons had to roll their own. I remember the tobacco was cheap and described as being the "sweepings from the floors of the tobacco factories." The tobacco was all dried out, powdery and tied to the bag were cigarette rolling papers that came in a little thin cotton cloth pouch with a draw string. The seal on the dispenser read "Bull Durham—FREE TO MEN."

Bull Durham tobacco pouches and rolling papers were made freely available to men with no imposed limits. Convicts also received three packs of filtered Wings cigarettes three days each week for a total of six packs.

Three days a week we received three filtered packs of Wings cigarettes. I didn't smoke, so I always passed them to friends...I'm describing this to offer some idea of what the environment was like inside the cellhouse when all the cons were locked up during the evening hours. I can remember those nights so vividly where I'd lay there listening to the foghorns, and the seagulls screaming over the cellhouse.

The night of the escape seemed to linger on forever. It felt like a year until sunrise and count time. Anxiety would rise as the guards' soft steps could be heard walking towards the B-Block corridor. This was the big moment, and my heart was racing with excitement. A guard we all called "Sarge," who had retired from the Army, got to Morris's cell and because he wasn't standing up for the count yelled "Morris, GET UP!" Sarge then reached into his cell and forcefully jabbed his head. Imagine his shock when it rolled off the bed and onto the floor. Sarge leaped backwards in horror. He was speechless and pointing into the cell as he tried to get words out. A guard in the gun gallery tried to get an answer as to who was missing and Sarge yells out at the top of his lungs, "MORRIS...MORRIS IS GONE!" Well, the cellhouse exploded into cheers and all hell broke loose. The men were cheering, banging their beds, racking their cups back and forth across the steel bars of their cells.

One by one, they find the others missing. There were cheers of pure elation, joy, laughter and jokes as the guards scrambled frantically. It was a moment of freedom for all of us. I think I can speak for everyone in the cellhouse that morning, it remains one of the greatest moments of my life...

All day we were put on "Dead Lock" as the guards searched the island, cursing at the seagulls as they raced around hills, cliffs and nesting areas, and the gulls were flying up squawking and messing down on the officers during their search. You could hear the distant sounds of the commotion happening outside. The story we heard was that "Double Tough" Ordway was swinging his blackjack at the gulls. Easy for us to picture and to believe. We heard they threw grenades into the caves at water level as the FBI, United States Marshals, San Francisco Police and Coast Guard all searched in vain for the trio. A short time later, we heard about the footprints on Angel Island and talk of an inflatable life jacket being found. Things were tense between the guards and convicts for a period after the break. The trio made history and the guards and warden felt it a personal affront—like they did this to us!

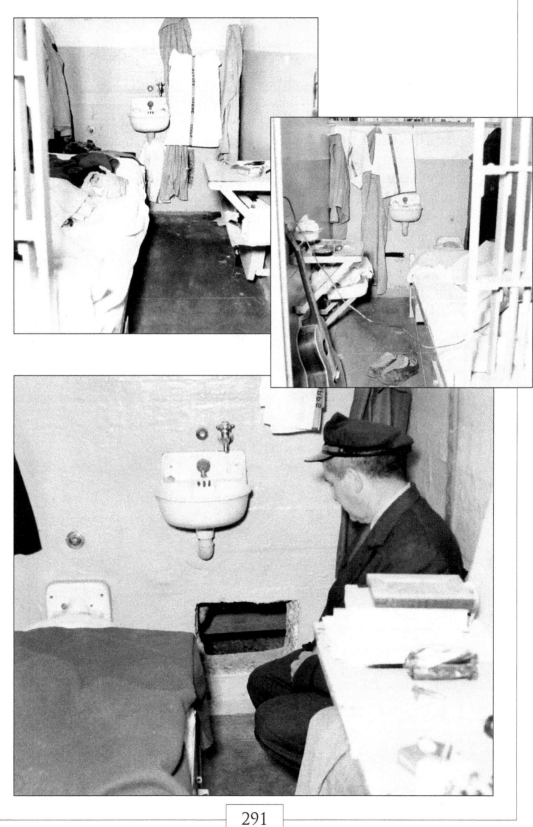

Robert Schibline, 1355-AZ, was residing in cell B-110 and also remembered the morning when his fellow cons were discovered missing:

> There were only ten cells occupied on the first tier of B-Block on the night of the escape. I was in one of them, B-110. I was watching the next morning count with my mirror, in order to witness the guard's reaction to a short count. I was not alone, as I saw two other mirrors also watching. There was supposed to be six of us left to count that morning instead of ten, but Allen West, 1335-AZ, didn't make it out. The last count at lights out the night before was 234 total, the next morning it was only 231. On my tier the final count was seven, three short.

An officer examining the false grill behind Allen West's cell.

The rooftop ventilator through which the inmates made their final exit from the cellhouse.

Bulger remembered the aftermath and the reveal of how the escape went unnoticed:

> Later on, when things started to turn back to normal, Charles
> Herman, the young guard we called "Herman the German" came
> over to the corner on the rec yard where we were lifting weights.
> Sick and miserable, he said "They're blaming me…" Herman was a
> little overweight, always nervous and the scapegoat for the escape.
> I jokingly said "Well, you will never make Acting Lieutenant!" This
> was a common joke among the cons. Every so often they would
> make a regular guard "Acting Lieutenant," but there was no change of
> uniform, no raise in pay, and the title would only be for a short period
> of time. Certain guards would get real serious, walk more erect and
> with more of a purpose. They would exercise their new-found power
> over the guys they worked with. They'd shout loud orders of things
> such as "Hey so and so, check out the library areas," or "Go inspect the
> cut off by the barber chair." The older guards would roll their eyes and
> try to keep a straight face in front of the convicts. And Herman would
> have made a typical Acting Lieutenant. I remember Herman and this
> talk real well. It was one of the rare occasions where a guard mingled
> among the convicts in conversation. Our jaws drop when he all but
> confessed that he didn't do any counts after lights out and knows he's
> going to be fired. People are fascinated by the dummy heads fooling
> the guards, but he didn't do a count that night. He didn't count

OPTIONAL FORM NO. 10
5010-103

UNITED STATES GOVERNMENT

Memorandum

TO : Captain

DATE: 22 June 1962

FROM : L. Miller

SUBJECT: Officer Herman and escape.

I understand the above Officer has made the statement that he didnot count any dummies the night of the escape as he counted at 9:30 P.M. and those inmates were there, and that he <u>didn't</u> count after that, only made out a count slip which he signed.
His job analysis specifically informs him to make a count at 11:30 P.M.

A key letter written to the Alcatraz Captain by Lieutenant Lloyd Miller that supported Bulger's memory and admission by Herman that he had failed to conduct any counts on the night of the escape. It provides crucial insight as to how they were able to go undetected until the morning count. Herman was later suspended for one month without pay. He resigned and never returned to the prison system.

dummies or anyone else. Herman was distressed and confided to us he was going down as the guard responsible for the men escaping...

The hope of the warden was "They Drowned!" The convicts, "They Made It!" I think they could have made it fairly easily. They likely stole a car and had many miles behind them before making a move to get money. They were smart and they had different phases and several contingencies in their plan. They put a lot of distance between them and Alcatraz in quick time. They also knew how to avoid suspicion. One guy fronts and the other two stay completely off scene. They stay completely isolated just watching TV and reading. Like President Lyndon Johnson once said about the smart Texas mule: "A big storm comes and the mule hunkers down and lies there still, quietly waiting for it to just blow over." The saying went something like that, but I thought of it often during my own time on the lam.

The guards monitored the radio and whenever there was mention of the escape, the guards would scurry to cut it off. The guys would cheer and raise hell. Sonny James wrote a song that came out only weeks after the break. It was titled *A Mile and a Quarter*. It was a hillbilly western song. You'd hear the opening lyrics " ♫ A mile and a quarter of treacherous water keeps men in Alcatraz... ♫ " and then click! OFF!

After scaling the fence outside the kitchen basement area, the convicts entering the officer recreation yard catwalk, cut the barbed wire and dropped to a grassy area below. An evidence photograph of the damaged fencing where the escapees made their way over. The large pipe from the bakery is visible and was used to descend from the roof area.

The shoreline where the escapees inflated their flotation devices and entered the water, never to be seen or heard from again.

It would illicit the usual response of cons slamming the bed frames on the floor and loud cursing. The cons went wild every time it came on. It really was one of the happiest moments of my life. I can remember it all so well as I now lay here as the oldest prisoner in my cold dark cell over fifty years later. Those were happy days. The guys were heroes to all of us back then.

I believe they all made it to freedom and followed through with their plan to cut all ties. My opinion is that it was a case of strict discipline on their part to completely cut ties with everyone in their past. This is why no one ever heard from them. Not merely to just disappear, but to also protect their families. Prior to the escape, we discussed in detail the tactics that the Feds would employ in trying to capture fugitives. One of their tactics was to use extreme pressure on the families. I know this firsthand. One of their most commonly

Allen West's life vest, shown here fully inflated. It was also submerged and tested in water. It was proven that the home fashioned life preservers could remain reasonably inflated for more than 40 minutes.

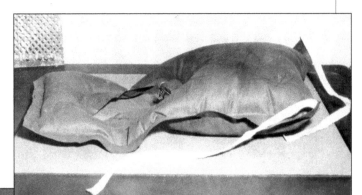

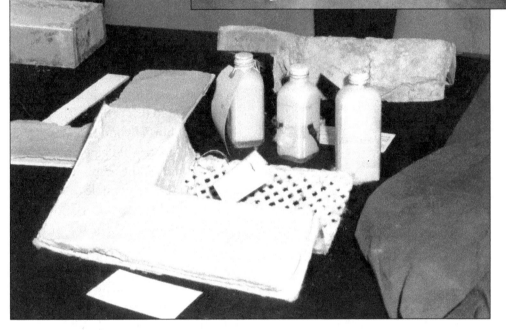

Paint used in the cells for their fake ventilation grills and area of the cutaway.

employed tactics was to pressure the family using harassment, monitoring their phones, watching their mail, following them, and making things uncomfortable to the point that the family will grow tired and give them information to make them stop. If they can catch a family member in a lie, then it gives them a means to prosecute them. Essentially, cooperate or go to prison. This is why no one ever heard from them. This is typically how most all fugitives are eventually caught. They trip up by contacting a family member or close associate, and the Feds intercept their calls and then trace their location. The family's phones are constantly being monitored and their movements traced whenever they travel, etc. The Feds have unlimited resources,

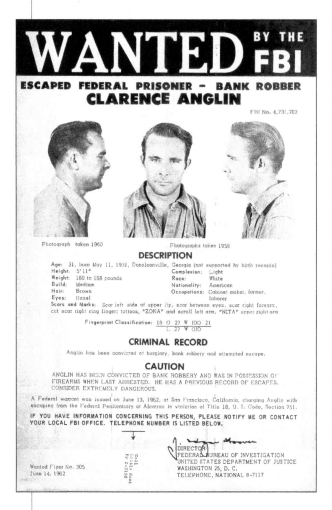

money, equipment, manpower, etc. The trio was also well acquainted with cars and knew how to hotwire the ignition. Following the escape, we heard of the report of the stolen blue Chevy and the motorist who claimed he was forced off the road and that the car was occupied by three men. They were young, healthy, disciplined and learned from their prior mistakes. All those lessons applied to this project. They didn't hurt anybody and made history. It helped put Alcatraz on the map.

I know it's possible to effectively disappear. I know this firsthand. The trio didn't pull off the greatest escape ever in United States history and not have a solid plan on how to survive once they were free. I know that as fact. As much thought goes into that as it does the escape. It's a painful dilemma, but for everyone's sake, they had no choice. The Feds place rewards on their heads and the families become the targets. Morris would have insisted on this also. Complete severance of all ties. It was easier for Morris since he didn't have any close family, but it had to be this way for the security of everyone. The love of family is what drove that painful decision. This is how the trio survived. This is what we discussed and debated prior to the escape. Morris read instructional language books on Alcatraz and had become fluent in Spanish. He could read and write in the language, and this was a major asset. His body features (tan, height and build) could have easily helped him pass as a Mexican and not raise any suspicion. I believe that they were together for a long time, and they helped each other through some of the tougher times.

Morris is a thirty (30) year old, single man, possessing a long criminal record, beginning when he was approximately thirteen years of age. He has been incarcerated or in some type of delinquent difficulty throughout the last seventeen years. At the time of his involvement in present offense he was concerned with getting enough money to escape into Mexico and thence into South America. There are four detainers outstanding against him and he also has a long record of escapes, having escaped last in April 1955, from the State Prison, Angola, Louisiana.

An excerpt from Frank Morris's prison case file. In a previous failed escape attempt, Morris admitted that he had planned to make his way to Mexico and then to South America.

I was a fugitive for sixteen years and was hunted aggressively by the FBI. I was on the FBI's Ten Most Wanted List with a two-million-dollar reward for my capture, along with a hundred-thousand-dollar reward for Catherine. I was on TV's "Most Wanted" programs countless times, not to mention the movies and documentaries. The Feds and the media were ruthless in the harassment of my family. They sent my brother Jack to jail for six months and then another term of house arrest—took his pension just as he had retired. Catherine's sister was subjected to a similar punishment. My other brother suffered greatly also. He lost his career in politics, was forced out of being the head of the University of Massachusetts. All this because no one would cooperate, and all this in spite of my not being in contact with any of them. The families become the targets and are subjected to terrible pressure. If they're caught in a lie, then they are prosecuted for perjury for lying to a Federal Officer. Isn't it a bit ironic that they can lie as part of their tactics and it's just part of their job? The press was relentless in their attacks on my brother Bill. One reporter was always attacking his character and mocking his height, calling him a "Corrupt Midget," and twisting the knife at every opportunity. Bill was a good man and didn't deserve the horrible treatment he received. His only crime was being related to me. When my brother lost his pension, he was forced to take a job in a labor trade and reporters went to his workplace and made it so unbearable, he was forced to resign. A brave man kills with a sword and a coward with a pen. These men and women in the media were all cowards.

In order to survive, I understood the importance of breaking all contact with loved ones and holding to that level of discipline. It was tough to break those ties with those you love, but necessary for my own survival and their protection. We all knew the penalty that would fall on the innocents we cared for. You have to factor that into as to why they were never seen or heard from again. Freedom came at such a big price, but it was still better than the long and lonely years spent in prison. I spent a lot of time looking at the picture of the Anglin brothers in Brazil. I'm convinced it's them. The photo shows them standing next to an ant hill. They had this look like they were saying, "This is really risky, but for a worthy cause." I expect they only posed for the picture to set their family at ease. I believe the escape aided in closing Alcatraz and freeing men like Alvin Karpis. He went to McNeil Island and Madigan helped free him. He was eventually paroled to his sister in Canada. Joe Carnes also later made parole and none of these men would have seen the streets had the Rock stayed open. This was a fringe benefit of the escape, and who knows how many others may have benefited. A non-violent, successful escape, against the greatest of odds.

Whenever I think back to my years on Alcatraz, and that morning of June 12, 1962, it always raises my spirits and I give a silent cheer to Frankie, John and Clarence. I remember Twining telling me about Blackwell the night after the escape, saying to Jack "I bet you're happy," and Jack replied, "You bet your ass I am..." It kind of rocked Blackwell as he must have expected a softer answer. Twining was never the politician and always told it like it was...God bless the trio...My money is still on them. They helped shut down Alcatraz and made history. We were the same age and they were in the prime of their lives. I hope they lived a long and happy life after Alcatraz...Vaya con Dios Paco!

THE HOLLYWOOD ESCAPE

Movies were shown a few times a month in the prison theatre, which was also used as the chapel for holding religious services. Admittedly, I rarely went to the theatre to watch movies, but for a lot of these guys, it was their only means to escape an endless routine. Through the lens of Hollywood, they saw other worlds up close: war, adventure, romance and much needed comedy. The theatre was upstairs above the visitation area, in the front section of the prison. They had a raised theatre style floor and used cheap folding chairs. They rotated cellblocks through so that everyone in general population had a chance to watch whatever movie was being featured. The theatre had a full-size projector that you'd find in a regular movie theatre. My

The last warden of Alcatraz, Olin Blackwell.

memory is that we didn't have the whole population in that room at the same time. Our side of C-Block watched movies on Saturday nights after the dinner meal, but most of the time I stayed behind and either listened to the radio or read books...I enjoyed the quiet. What is still vivid in my memory were the views of the San Francisco skyline through the theatre windows. You had a perfect view and the guards lowered thick sunshades over the windows when they started the movie. During the winter months, you had the scenic nighttime view of the entire San Francisco cityscape. The view was stunning on a clear night.

My recollection is that most of the titles selected by Warden Madigan were old, outdated films from the 20s and 30s. Blackwell was more liberal in this regard, but Madigan always showed the classic style films. The cons all called Blackwell "Gypsy," a nickname that Richard Sunday gave him that stuck. He wore a lot of turquoise jewelry; rings, silver bracelet and belt with a stone set, and it always seemed excessive for someone in the role of a warden. Blackwell

Warden Paul J. Madigan. Prior to his appointment, Madigan had navigated his way through a variety of positions at Alcatraz, which gave him a perspective that was different from those of his predecessors. He had originally transferred from USP Leavenworth to Alcatraz as a correctional officer, and then served as captain, lieutenant, and associate warden, and was well liked by most of the correctional staff at Alcatraz. Madigan had the skills of a soft-spoken mediator and often took a diplomatic approach but was not afraid to issue unpopular directives to both the staff and the inmate population. As a correctional officer, Madigan was taken prisoner and threatened during the 1941 escape attempt by Joe Cretzer, Sam Shockley, Arnold Kyle, and Lloyd Barkdoll. In spite of being tied up, he negotiated their surrender.

always appeared very calm and soft spoken with a quiet demeanor. He never leaned hard on any of the guards or cons. He later went to Lewisburg and was basically the same pleasant guy. I don't feel that his reputation was tarnished by the trio's escape. It wasn't his or Madigan's fault for that matter. Neither of them prowled the tiers or made the counts. Blackwell was a real heavy smoker, so you'd also see a cloud of smoke trailing behind him as he walked the cellblock corridors.

Blackwell was much more liberal when it came to radio and movie selections. I don't recall much censoring or restrictive selections with him. With Madigan, there would be months where they only showed Laurel & Hardy and Charlie Chaplin movies. Regardless, the guys appreciated them and the theatre would be filled with loud laughter. The officer in the gun gallery would open the barred port and you could hear the laughs echo out into the cellhouse. The films would be the talk of the yard on Sundays and during work. It's not entirely true that they never allowed movies with guns or violence. They occasionally had detective style thrillers and I can't remember the name, but there's a Laurel & Hardy film where they're in prison and they dug a tunnel similar to Sutton's break. This was one of the first movies I watched there. I remember thinking it was a risky choice, even for a comedy. In the movie, they're involved in a big escape and then it flashes to a scene where they're fighting with the guards and a gun battle ensues. The sounds alone made me nervous. At this point, the film doesn't feel like a comedy and now the cons look like they're on edge. The guards perk up as the men are all looking serious, and everyone's eyes are roving the room rather than watching the screen. The gallery officer is now peering at us through the large viewing port and he's holding his machine gun at the ready. The atmosphere of the room is getting increasingly tense.

On this night, Warden Madigan is sitting in the theatre watching the movie with the men. As he always did, he's sitting in a chair by himself and off to the side, near a gate used by the guards. His arms are crossed as he's intently watching the movie and smiling. He always carried himself with confidence and spoke in a calm, even toned voice. He doesn't break his glance away from the screen and doesn't't look at all concerned. It's obvious the movie is a comedy, but as the prisoners in the film are fighting the guards, I'm thinking to myself,

Madigan favored playing the early Charlie Chaplin and Laurel & Hardy comedic films for the prisoners. Bulger recounted a story where Catalano and some of the others were so mesmerized by the actress, Paulette Goddard, who starred alongside Chaplin in Modern Times, that he spoke about her for weeks. Bulger commented: "It was a sad reality of becoming so isolated in prison… The movie was made decades before that night, yet they were all living in moments from the past…"

you've got to be kidding me! Any minute the movie is going to get cut and the lights are going to come up...Now I'm nervous thinking the guys are going to let off steam if a guard stops the film. The guards are all standing and look like they're on the ready if anything flares.

One guard I remember well was Emil Rychner, a World War I veteran. Rychner was a fair guy who was sure of himself, never postured or threw around his weight or tried to prove himself to anyone else. He had a very powerful and distinctive voice. He always made his presence very clear. Fair but firm, that's how I remember him. He'd been at Alcatraz since the 1930s and knew Al Capone, Machine Gun Kelly and many of the early crowd. He wasn't one to tell long winded stories or mingle. We didn't know much about his past other than he was from New York and played professional baseball before becoming a guard. Rychner is on the opposite side of the theatre, and he walks straight across to Madigan and leans over whispering something in his ear. We see Madigan shake his head side-to-side giving a 'no' gesture and Rychner then walks a few steps over and stands next to the gate looking as if he's waiting for something to happen. Another guard now stands on the opposite side of the gate. Rychner and the gallery officer seem to watch each other waiting for a cue, and now with another guard on the other side of the gate, they are ready to rush out Madigan if a riot breaks. Slowly, the tension eases, the guard in the gallery takes the machine gun out of view and then the grim faces of the convicts slowly transition to smiles, with laughter again filling the theatre. Aside from that episode, Laurel & Hardy films were popular and gave men at Alcatraz a lot of laughs. When I was living in Santa Monica, I read an article in the local newspaper about Laurel living his final years in an apartment building facing the park where Catherine and I took daily walks. He'd long passed before we moved there, but I felt some connection to him

Alcatraz Captain of the Guards, Emil E. Rychner.

and wished he'd known the laughs he gave the cons on the Rock. I enjoyed knowing we lived on the same soil in the later years of life.

In 1960, when my brother was elected to the House of Representatives, Madigan received a telegram message from him about the election. "Promising Paul" was a frustrated Irish-Polish at heart, and he brought me the telegram and quizzed me a little about my brother. This was uncomfortable since Madigan made a special visit to my cell. It was also unheard of as I never saw Madigan walk the upper tiers, let alone to personally deliver a piece of mail to a convict. During our conversation he asked me why he rarely sees me on movie nights. I explained that the movie selection always seemed to be older films and I enjoyed the quiet time in my cell reading. Madigan wouldn't let up, so I told him I'd give it a try again.

Whenever bad weather would hit San Francisco on weekends and men couldn't go into the yard, Madigan would allow the cons to watch a popular movie a second time. The men begged to have rec time in the mess hall to play bridge and other games when it rained, but my memory is we did it only once or twice and usually had to remain in our cell when bad weather struck. We didn't have many options to break the monotony and Madigan's solution was to give some of the movies a second run. So, one weekend when the storms hit hard, Madigan came over to me and said "Jim, I think you'd enjoy this classic Chaplin film. We're showing it a second time. Do me a favor and come up and watch it." I agreed and I end-up sitting in the middle of Twining and Catalano, who were always squabbling over the pettiest shit. Chaplin played a guy who was down on his luck and falls in love with a beautiful brunette woman who becomes the spotlight of the movie.

I'll never forget that evening in the theatre. The men lost themselves in that moment and everyone laughed the hardest I'd ever seen. They left their troubled lives at the door that night. Catalano was completely mesmerized by the actress in the movie. He was in a trance and he just stared expressionless at the screen. Jack was the same and thought a woman who looked like that would be enough to keep him straight, at home and out of trouble. They were overwhelmed by her beauty and it was a sad reality of becoming so isolated in prison. A week later, the actress was all Catalano was still talking about. He was so taken by her. Another week or so passes and Madigan makes his way up to my cell again. I can't understand why he's so interested in my opinion, but he wants to know if I enjoyed the movie. I told him I enjoyed it, but still wished they could get some newer movies. I

The Alcatraz theater.

explained that it might even help men as they write their wives to talk about recent pictures they've seen, and it would help keep them better connected with modern society. I'm paraphrasing, but Madigan in his firm tone said something to the effect "Jim, I try to steer away from complicated subjects and stay with wholesome and simple laughs. It's easier on the men. You complain about these movies being outdated, but remember, a lot of the men you sat in the theatre with were already in prison when that movie was released. That's the world they remember." That sure made me think.

On holiday nights, guys would talk from cell to cell and lights would stay on for an extra two or three hours. The main topic was books and movies—Crime and Westerns. It's easy to see the influence that movies had on all of us. Alcatraz had several copies of Audie Murphy's book *To Hell and Back*. Murphy was the most decorated war veteran of World War II; he played himself in the movie version, and he looked like a teenager. He was in several Westerns and was a real hero. His book was one of the most popular, and Madigan ran the film for weeks, with special matinees on the weekends during bad weather when the men couldn't spend time in the yard, and the theatre was full every time this movie played. The men loved the

movie and the ending. Murphy is shown receiving the Congressional Medal of Honor. Every time, the men cheered as if Murphy was standing right in front of them. That movie is a special memory of the camaraderie and genuine patriotism shared by all the men.

Jeep Marcum loved movies and after we watched *To Hell and Back*, Marcum asked Madigan if it would be possible for us to see any Alfred Hitchcock movies and whether some of his films could be added to the list? Madigan answered, "Absolutely not…too violent!" We'd just watched a war movie and we all got a laugh out of that. At least for once, "Promising Paul" didn't promise! Decades later, I bought a copy of Audie's book for my personal library as I wanted to show that someone still cares. My old partner Steve Flemmi and I were in Washington D.C. to attend his military reunion. Steve was a decorated veteran, serving two tours in the Korean War. We took time to visit Murphy's final resting place at the Arlington Cemetery along with Catherine and Steve's girlfriend. It was such a pleasant memory. He was laid to rest in a simple plot and only a small American flag to decorate it. He had been popular with the men on Alcatraz, and they watched all his films.

In 1961, Byron "Whizzer" White, the Deputy Attorney General under Robert Kennedy, visited Alcatraz to evaluate the conditions and also discuss integration. I was on the yard the day he visited, and I was the first person he asked to see. John McCormack of South Boston (a friend of my brother Bill) had spoken to him, and he asked for me by name. This really caused a stir with Madigan and the guards. They all became nervous and asked endless questions about what he wanted, why he wanted to talk, etc. It was really a big surprise to me. We sat in the mess hall and talked over coffee and baked goods made by the culinary staff. I remember he had piercing blue eyes and at the time I was caught off guard since he was intrigued with the bank robberies I committed. He also seemed interested in my thoughts on integration in the prison system. I was honest and told him I didn't think it would really work. He pressed me as to why and I finally told him there would be bloodshed without a doubt. I told him we all respected one another, but we were divided and that was the culture. That was the way it was back then and how it worked throughout the prison system. After this we talked lighter subjects. Madigan sat with us and White talked about his years playing football in the NFL, attending law school at Yale, my family, and about Bobby Kennedy's keen interest in Alcatraz.

LEAVING ALCATRAZ

"For better or for worse, Alcatraz was their world…"

RIGHT AFTER THE JUNE '62 ESCAPE, there was an increased amount of tension between the convicts and guards. I kept mostly to myself during this time, but you could cut the tension with a knife. Blackwell told me months before that I had been approved for a transfer and that the plan was to start moving me closer to home. Blackwell told me that if I kept a low profile, he'd advocate for an early release. First, I was to be transferred to Leavenworth in Kansas and then finally to Lewisburg from where I'd eventually be paroled.

Prison life is tough, but at Alcatraz I forged several friendships that stayed with me over my lifetime. Being on the ocean was also something I treasured. At other prisons, they're remote with no views or any sense of what's beyond the walls. At Alcatraz, you had million-dollar views of San Francisco with an ocean breeze. In the distance you could hear the sounds of the city and it gave you purpose

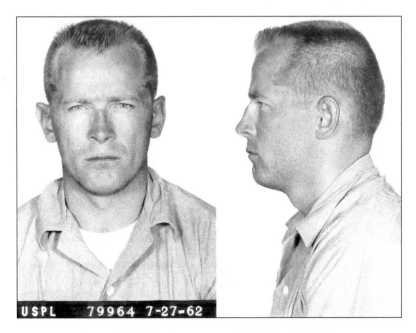

James Bulger at Leavenworth in July of 1962.

to want to leave and be a part of it. I can remember Mickey Cohen mentioning that he looked forward to having dinner at Fisherman's Wharf with a view of Alcatraz in the distance. I doubt a lot of people would understand, but I still feel a deep connection to the place. It's a place I remember back to and many close friendships. It's like visiting an old house where you once lived. It's a place full of memories. A lot of the men were going through profound redemptions reflecting on their pasts, and you become close with those you share these types of experiences with.

When I was leaving Alcatraz, we knew the Rock would be closing. Gene Fuller, who lived in B-Block, seemed rattled by the talk and forced to think of his future and what was ahead. I never saw him serious until the day I left. When I went to say goodbye, I put my hand out to shake, and, in that moment, he looked like he was shocked into reality. When he shook my hand, he had a strange look that I had never seen on him. He had tears in his eyes and I could see that he didn't want his world to change. I really felt bad for him. For some of these guys, this is all they had. For better or for worse, Alcatraz was their world...

In July of 1962, Bulger was transferred to USP Leavenworth, and then roughly a year later to Lewisburg. He was released in 1965, after serving a total of nine years in prison.

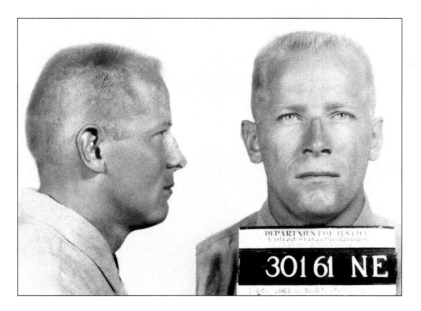

Bulger at Lewisburg in September of 1962.

When I arrived at Leavenworth all the cons were intrigued with everyone who'd done time on the Rock and asked a lot of questions. It was harder time, having to share a cell, and going from a few hundred men on Alcatraz to a few thousand at Leavenworth was daunting. There were no views or any real sense of what was beyond the prison walls. You couldn't hear any sounds of a city or have any connection to the outside world. At Alcatraz, the free world was always in view. Everyone at Leavenworth felt isolated from the rest of the world. There were guards you'd recognize who'd worked at Alcatraz and they'd always stop to say hello. They would be friendly to us guys from the Rock, at least up until the point that John Chebetnoy (1002-AZ) and some others attempted to escape. I knew Chebetnoy from Alcatraz and he was serving a long sentence for murder in Alaska. I didn't like him and once nearly got into a fight on the stairs that led from the recreation yard down to the industries. There were seagull nests all along the hillside and several were visible as we'd go up and down the stairwell twice a day during the week. I watched him kill a young seagull with a rock he pulled from his pocket and threw it hard into the nest. I saw the whole thing happen and I shoved him down hard to make a point. The other cons blocked the view to the officers and then Charlie grabbed me and pulled me back saying it's not worth losing time and being sent to the hole. That crossed a hard line for me, and I never liked him after witnessing that.

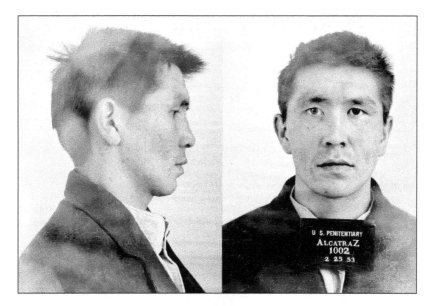

John Chebetnoy

The last group of convicts being led down Broadway on closing day, March 21, 1963.

When John was later transferred to Leavenworth, he and a few other Alcatraz cons attempted to escape, and it really shook up the place. The guards reacted violently, and my memory was that it changed everything, bringing a deep hate between them and the convicts. The escape involved fighting their way over a perimeter wall using a makeshift ladder. Their plan was to make their way onto the wall, overpower a tower guard and take weapons, then use their ladder to climb down the other side and steal a couple of cars. One of the escapees was shot by a tower guard with a .30 caliber rifle, bleeding and clinging for life at the top of the wall and blocking the others trying to ascend the ladder. The guys trying to make their way over ordered Chebetnoy to throw him off and clear the ladder so that they could get over the wall. Chebetnoy refused, as it would have meant certain death since it was a 40 foot drop down to the ground. My memory is that Chebetnoy was also shot, but only a minor or superficial injury. A young guard named Fox was hurt badly and another was knocked unconscious, and the cons took their uniforms as part of the attempt. The guards were seriously beaten and dragged into A-Block. I remember that they had been dragged bleeding and unconscious down the long corridor and it left a blood trail on the cement flooring. It was a terrible incident, and the cons paid a hard

John Duncan (seen at the head of the line), William "Hawk" Hawkins, Red McGraw and many other close friends were among the final group of prisoners transferred off Alcatraz to other federal prisons.

The final menu on closing day, March 21, 1963.

price after. Several cons were worked over during the nights and beaten bad several times for their roles in the escape and injuries to the officers. None of this ever made it into the official files. I heard from Chebetnoy that the doctors didn't file records on the incident and warned me that some of the guards were taking revenge on convicts. I tried to keep out of their business and did my own time.

I've heard Lewisburg being described as a retirement facility, but it was a much tougher prison than any other I'd served time at. On my birthday in 1963, I departed Leavenworth and for the first time since my arrest, I felt optimistic that a release was at least somewhere on the horizon. The Marshals provided me a special birthday meal during the transfer, and on the flight to Pennsylvania, the flight attendant brought me all kinds of snack foods that I savored after a year of terrible food served at Leavenworth.

There were a lot of famous names who served at Lewisburg after me. Jimmy Hoffa, Paul Vario, John Gotti and Henry Hill. I'd lost a decade of my life in prison, but it still wasn't enough to inspire change... After Alcatraz closed, Blackwell became warden at Lewisburg and he held his

Eleven prisoners from the last group of 27 arrive on the front steps of USP Leavenworth in the late night after a long day of travel. It marked the end of an era when Alcatraz closed after 29-years as a federal prison. They were flown to Kansas City and then transferred by prison bus to their final destination. The men are seen carrying their personal belongings up the stairs as they enter the prison.

promise to get me an early release. A large group of guys from the island transferred in and a few of my friends were part of the group. "Jeep" Marcum, Duncan, Pravato (who was also a good friend of Richard Sunday, as they were on the same chain to Alcatraz), and even Hawk. They were all part of the last group to leave Alcatraz and made famous in all the closing day photographs. It was great getting caught up on the prison shutting down and the big talk was Scottie's (John Paul Scott) escape. Scottie ended up back at Atlanta and went back to work in the prison hospital again. I remember at Christmas, we passed around the news clips and they included several photos of Scottie. The story was that he'd made it to shore but was spotted and arrested. Reading the reports of the escape brings back all these memories of him.

John Paul Scott, 1403-AZ (left) another trusted friend of Bulger, is seen here with Darl Parker (right) at the Fort Mason dock as they are led to court for trial resulting from their failed escape attempt from Alcatraz in 1962. Scott, a close associate of Bulger, had a long history of attempted escapes, which continued even after his release from Alcatraz.

I also knew Darl Parker (1413-AZ) and he shared with me that he had almost a half million dollars from his bank heists, stashed in Cuba. He didn't offer much on this, but it didn't strike me as being a big fish kind of tale. I believed him . . . A lot of guys talked big outlandish stories, but had they made it off undetected, they'd have disappeared like the trio and lived out the rest of their lives in Cuba, with books and movies retelling that story . . . The reports from Blackwell read to me like a thriller!

In December of 1962, when Scott and Parker had made their daring Alcatraz escape, plans had already been set in motion to close the prison due to crippling costs and structural deterioration of the main cellhouse. Decades of exposure to the harsh environment of the damp salt ocean air had taken its toll on the prison. Only months after the famed escape of Morris and the Anglin brothers, Scott demonstrated that with properly constructed floats and under the right conditions, it was technically possible to enter the icy Bay waters and swim to the mainland. The reports referenced by Bulger were included in a memorandum written by Warden Blackwell to the Director of the Bureau of Prisons on December 20, 1962, and the summary by the FBI illustrated those prisoners with experience of safe cracking and the use of torches should be watched more closely:

> On Sunday, December 16, 1962, the two above inmates were missed from their detail in the culinary unit, at 5:47 PM. We have definitely established that both of those individuals were accounted for on the official 5:20 PM count and again counted by the lieutenant on duty, Mr. Harold Robbins, at 5:30 PM. The alarm was sounded, immediate search of the area was instituted, and the entire escape procedure was placed into effect. At 6:10 PM our boat officer spotted Parker clinging to a rock some 100 yards off the northwest end of the island, known as "Little Alcatraz." At approximately 7:20 PM inmate Scott was spotted clinging to a rock off Fort Point, which is located almost directly under the south end of the Golden Gate Bridge. Scott was spotted by two teenagers who reported it to the Presidio military police. They reported to the scene and called for a fire department rescue team, who responded and rescued Scott and took him immediately to the Letterman Hospital for emergency treatment. For the first thirty minutes several doctors worked with Scott and stated that they were very much uncertain as to whether he would live or die. He was suffering from numerous cuts and bruises and from severe shock as a result of extreme hypothermia, caused by the icy water of the Bay, which normally runs from 52 to 54 degrees year-round. Parker, of course, was returned to the institution, examined by the medical staff and locked up immediately after he was found. Scott was returned to the institution following his release from the emergency unit of the hospital.

During the investigation it became obvious that the two sets of bars that were removed had been worked on over a long period of time and obviously by more people than just Scott. We are not quite sure of all instruments used to sever these bars; however, we are rather positive that a spatula (with serrated edges); a grease scraper (used by fry-cooks in scraping down grills); a coarse string (impregnated with floor wax) and institution scouring powder, were at least three items that were used to cut through these bars. One set of these bars, incidentally, is commonly referred to as "tool-proof-steel."

As we see the picture, and as admitted now by Scott and Parker, Scott almost completed severing the bars, alerted Parker that he expected to try to escape, and invited him to go along. On the evening of the sixteenth, immediately after the 5:30 PM count, under the guise of taking the garbage to the basement, Scott got on the elevator, took the elevator half-way down, jumped off and completed severing the bars, which he states took approximately five minutes. He then dashed to the elevator shaft and signaled for Parker, who jumped down the shaft, landing on the elevator halfway down, then jumped off to the floor and they both went out through the window.

This window is the last window on the south side of the kitchen basement and is partially hidden by two butane tanks that service burner units in the hospital. They eluded the officer who was patrolling the back of the kitchen by seeing that he had checked that side of the building and started in the other direction. They then hurriedly climbed two pipes at the corner of the building, gaining access to the roof. They crossed the roof and lowered themselves to the ground directly behind the library on a length of extension cord that they had tied knots in, approximately 3 feet apart. This cord was removed from the buffing machine that is used to polish the basement floor. They then slid and fell down the steep hill directly behind Apartment Building A. During this fall, Parker apparently broke his foot and received several cuts and bruises. They then went down the rather high bluff to the water's edge by sliding down a sewer pipe. At this point they inflated rubber gloves that they had inserted in shirt sleeves, and pieces of shirt that had been crudely stitched together, making a set of so called "water wings" to be used as flotation devices.

It was dark and rainy. Visibility was extremely poor. Parker stated that Scott moved out first and he followed after checking his flotation equipment and immediately lost Scott, but thought he saw him. As it turned out, it was a bucket floating in the Bay. He fought the tides as hard as he could but could make no headway and it washed him back into the rock known as "Little Alcatraz," and he hung on to this rock until he was found by our boat. He received further cuts and bruises

Rubber surgical gloves were inflated and sewn into cutoff shirt sleeves that was successfully used as a flotation device.

attempting to stay on the rock.

Scott claimed at first with the poor visibility and fog he couldn't determine the direction to the mainland, but eventually spotted lights; attempted to swim towards them, but the tide carried him past; he then selected another light and repeated the performance, and this continued until he was washed onto a rock out near the Golden Gate Bridge. The tide was so swift and waves so high that at this point he claims to have almost drowned and could

Under the cover of night, rain, and heavy fog, John Paul Scott washed up at Fort Point near the base of the Golden Gate Bridge, exhausted and lethargic resulting from severe hypothermia.

319

not maneuver around on the rock to keep the waves from sweeping over him and causing him to nearly suffocate. It was at this point that he was rescued by members of the Fire Department at the Presidio of San Francisco and taken into custody by the Military Police at the Presidio. He was taken to the emergency hospital for treatment but claims he does not recall the associate warden entering the room and fails to remember several other things for a short period of time.

In searching the basement area several times, we found items which included the impregnated string, and a 12-inch crescent wrench that had been missing for over two years from the old Furniture Factory and apparently had been secreted in the kitchen basement behind one of the huge refrigerators. The rubber gloves obviously had been stolen from the hospital unit and Scott claims they had been there for a long time. The crescent wrench was used to twist out the last section of the outside detention sash, which was extremely eroded from the elements, and of course was never designed to be first-rate security material.

As attached reports will indicate, searches of the basement area had been ordered and apparently completed. The bars had been tapped by officers on both Saturday and Sunday, the day of the escape. At first glance, it seemed strongly indicated that disciplinary action should be instituted against those who were ordered to knock the bars in this unit. However, after careful examination of all of the facts it became highly conceivable, from a technical or mechanical standpoint, that the officers hammering these bars with rubber hammers could very well have struck them a heavy blow (and they insist they did) without noticing any particular difference from any other bar. It is obvious, of course, that their visual inspection was not effective. However, since the cuts were on the back side of the main bar, and the duty of hammering bars is rather monotonous, it is highly possible that they could have overlooked the carefully concealed cut, thinking that they were doing a good job. With all of this in mind, and after careful consideration of all of the facts by the captain, associate warden, Mr. Aldredge, and myself, at this point we do not feel that disciplinary action against the officers is indicated.

Scott appears to have been the prime suspect in this plot. It should be noted that he also has experience using cutting torches, and these techniques should be considered when housing inmates with this type of knowledge and background. Scott should be watched closely in the future. The use of a torch and techniques of safe cracking can

Following treatment for hypothermia, Scott was transported back to the island launch by ambulance and returned to Alcatraz. He later admitted during his interview with officials that he became seriously disoriented in the water and was unable to identify the mainland. His hands and legs became numb from the freezing water, and he acknowledged that he thought he might drown.,.

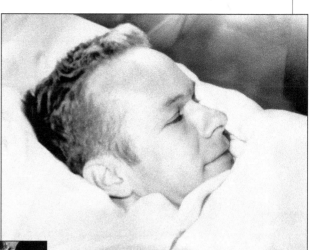

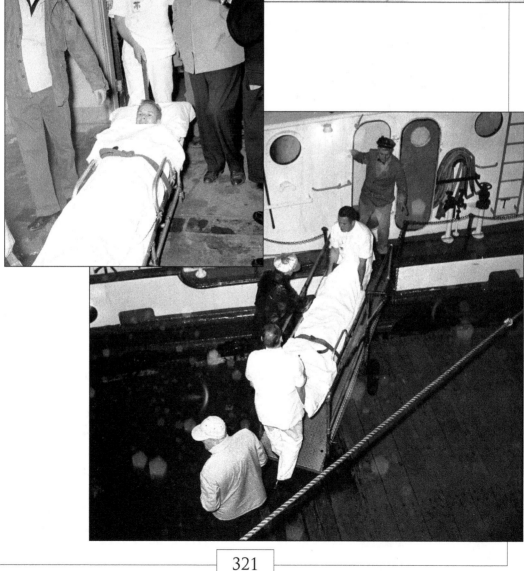

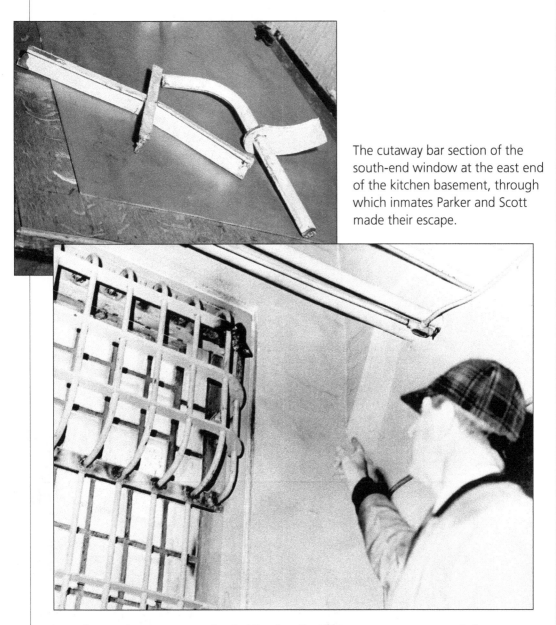

The cutaway bar section of the south-end window at the east end of the kitchen basement, through which inmates Parker and Scott made their escape.

be used in escape methods. The details of his experience is noted that on the weekend of December 15, 1956, J. Paul Scott, accompanied by his brother, Don R. Scott, and Earl Morris forcibly entered the National Guard Armory at Danville, Kentucky, and stole two .45 caliber sub machine guns and three .30 caliber rifles, together with a significant quantity of ammunition. On January 6, 1957, J. Paul Scott, accompanied by the same two men as mentioned above, entered the Farmers and Traders Bank of Campton, Kentucky, armed and carrying cutting torches. While in the bank, Scott was struck on the mouth and

Assistant Director of the Federal Bureau of Prisons, Fred Wilkinson and Warden Olin Blackwell holding a later press conference discussing both the escape of Morris and the Anglin Brothers, and the escape of Scott and Parker.

the arm by two bullets fired by a bank guard. At the time, Morris was on the outside of a window and Don Scott was on the roof of the bank standing guard. They fled from the bank engaging local officers in a gun battle, which resulted in the wounding of a Wolfe County Sheriff.

From Bulger:

As I mentioned before, Scottie was one of the guys involved in the escape in Atlanta that played a part in my being sent to the Rock. Scottie and I were good friends and we worked together in the hospital at Atlanta. He had a high-pitched voice with a southern accent, but no speech impediment, as some of these people who didn't know him talk about. He told me the whole story of being shot by the sheriff in a small town. He had a small flashlight in his mouth to free up his hands

323

while he was busy working on a safe (bank burglary) and the sheriff fired shots through a window at Scotty and his brother. A bullet struck the flashlight and the spring that held the batteries in place lodged into his tongue. It was painful and Scotty fired a burst of bullets with a submachine gun (called a grease gun) and crippled him.

We all knew that Scottie's escape was the ending of Alcatraz. It was to be the closing chapter. I read about Scottie's parole, getting remarried and owning something like four or five houses, but it wasn't enough for him. He ended up doing another bank heist and landed back in prison. He made another spectacular break when he cut through the bars on a prison bus and jumped out. The guards stopped the bus and it all ended in a hail of gunfire... He survived but spent his final years in prison. There's some that have that thirst and Scottie was one who lived by the motto "If you want to win big, then you have to be prepared to lose big..." Everyone is ultimately a loser in this game.

One of the hardest parts of prison life was when I had been notified by the prison priest that my brother Bill called him to let him know my father had passed. He died in the hospital and my family were all there by his side. That weighed heavy on me... It was a hard fact to come to terms with that I couldn't be there in his final hours or with my family. I can remember this as if it were yesterday. It was about a year before my release at Lewisburg, but I felt like this was a turning point.

BULGER WAS RELEASED from federal prison in 1965. He attempted to work in a variety of legitimate occupations before becoming a bookmaker and loan shark with ties to Donald Killeen, the leader of the dominant Irish Mafia in South Boston. He'd quickly found himself back in crime during a turbulent and violent period when rival gang factions were at war. By 1972, Bulger had made a name for himself as part of one the most powerful Irish American gangs in Boston. In 1978, when Howie Winter, the crown of the Winter Hill Gang, was arrested on racketeering and fixing horse races, Bulger stepped in to take over the leadership. It was during this era that Bulger cemented his reputation to build one of the most powerful organized crime syndicates, eventually rising to the highest echelon in organized crime.

By the late 1980s, state law enforcement investigators suspected corruption within the FBI and shifted their focus to Bulger. They'd

Bulger's certificate of parole and release order for March 1, 1965.

FBI TEN MOST WANTED FUGITIVE

RACKETEERING INFLUENCED AND CORRUPT ORGANIZATIONS (RICO) - MURDER (19 COUNTS), CONSPIRACY TO COMMIT MURDER, CONSPIRACY TO COMMIT EXTORTION, NARCOTICS DISTRIBUTION, CONSPIRACY TO COMMIT MONEY LAUNDERING; EXTORTION; MONEY LAUNDERING

JAMES J. BULGER

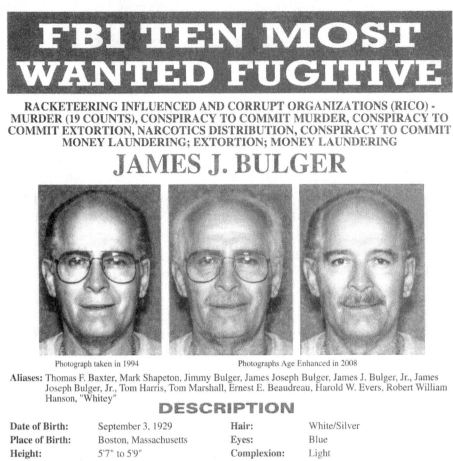

Photograph taken in 1994   Photographs Age Enhanced in 2008

Aliases: Thomas F. Baxter, Mark Shapeton, Jimmy Bulger, James Joseph Bulger, James J. Bulger, Jr., James Joseph Bulger, Jr., Tom Harris, Tom Marshall, Ernest E. Beaudreau, Harold W. Evers, Robert William Hanson, "Whitey"

DESCRIPTION

Date of Birth:	September 3, 1929	**Hair:**	White/Silver
Place of Birth:	Boston, Massachusetts	**Eyes:**	Blue
Height:	5'7" to 5'9"	**Complexion:**	Light
Weight:	150 to 160 pounds	**Sex:**	Male
Build:	Medium	**Race:**	White
Occupation:	Unknown	**Nationality:**	American

Scars and Marks: None known

Remarks: Bulger is an avid reader with an interest in history. He is known to frequent libraries and historic sites. Bulger may be taking heart medication. He maintains his physical fitness by walking on beaches and in parks with his female companion, Catherine Elizabeth Greig. Bulger and Greig love animals. Bulger has been known to alter his appearance through the use of disguises. He has traveled extensively throughout the United States, Europe, Canada, and Mexico.

CAUTION

JAMES J. BULGER IS BEING SOUGHT FOR HIS ROLE IN NUMEROUS MURDERS COMMITTED FROM THE EARLY 1970s THROUGH THE MID-1980s IN CONNECTION WITH HIS LEADERSHIP OF AN ORGANIZED CRIME GROUP THAT ALLEGEDLY CONTROLLED EXTORTION, DRUG DEALS, AND OTHER ILLEGAL ACTIVITIES IN THE BOSTON, MASSACHUSETTS, AREA. HE HAS A VIOLENT TEMPER AND IS KNOWN TO CARRY A KNIFE AT ALL TIMES.

CONSIDERED ARMED AND EXTREMELY DANGEROUS

IF YOU HAVE ANY INFORMATION CONCERNING THIS PERSON, PLEASE CONTACT YOUR LOCAL FBI OFFICE OR THE NEAREST U.S. EMBASSY OR CONSULATE.

REWARD

The FBI is offering a $2,000,000 reward for information leading directly to the arrest of James J. Bulger.

August 1999
Poster Revised September 2008

www.fbi.gov

become convinced that Bulger had exerted leverage with lead officials and was responsible for a variety of high-stakes crimes and scores of murders as part of an organized criminal enterprise. In 1994, the Drug Enforcement Administration, the Massachusetts State Police and the Boston Police Department launched an independent investigation that ultimately resulted in arrest warrants for Bulger and his criminal associates. Whitey would be tipped off by his main contact at the FBI, and then set in motion plans to flee Boston...

According to Kevin Weeks, in 1993 and 1994, before the pinches came down, Bulger and crime partner Stephen "The Rifleman" Flemmi were traveling on the French and Italian Riviera. The pair traveled all over Europe, sometimes separating for a while. It was more preparation than anything, getting ready for another life. Weeks commented, "They didn't ask me to go, not that I would have wanted to. Jimmy had prepared for the run for years...Bulger had established a completely different identity: Thomas Baxter. He had a complete ID and credit cards in that name. He had even joined associations in Baxter's name and was building an entire portfolio

Whitey Bulger's crime partner Kevin Weeks on Castle Island.

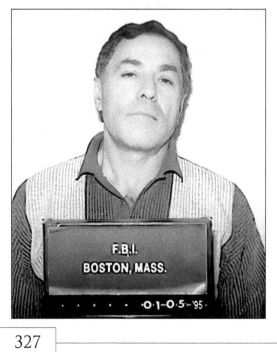

Stephen "The Rifleman" Flemmi

A surveillance photograph of Stephen "The Rifleman" Flemmi, Whitey Bulger and Kevin Weeks walking on Castle Island where he later commented this is where they conducted most of their business.

for the guy. He had always said that you had to be ready to take off on short notice. And he was..."

Bulger had also set up safe deposit boxes containing cash, jewelry, and passports, in locations across North America and Europe. In December 1994, Bulger was informed by FBI Agent John Connolly that sealed indictments had come down from the Department of Justice and that the FBI were due to make arrests during the Christmas season. In response, Bulger fled Boston on December 23, 1994, accompanied by his then girlfriend, Teresa Stanley.

A surveillance photo released by the
U.S. Attorney's Office and presented
as evidence during the first day of trial for James "Whitey" Bulger. Bulger can be seen
wearing his Alcatraz belt buckle which became a trademark.

After fleeing Boston, Bulger and Stanley initially spent four days over Christmas in Selden, New York. They spent New Year's Day in a hotel in the French Quarter in New Orleans. On January 5, 1995, Bulger prepared to return to Boston, believing that it had all been a false alarm. That night, however, Stephen Flemmi was arrested outside a Boston restaurant by the DEA. Boston Police Detective Michael Flemmi, Stephen's brother, allegedly informed Weeks about the arrest. Weeks immediately passed the information on to Bulger, who altered his plans. Bulger and Stanley then spent the next three weeks traveling between New York, Los Angeles, and San Francisco before Stanley decided that she wanted to return to her children. They then traveled to Clearwater, Florida, where Bulger retrieved his Tom Baxter identification from a safe deposit box. Bulger allegedly drove to Boston and dropped off Stanley in a parking lot. Then he met with Weeks at Malibu Beach in Dorchester. Weeks brought along Bulger's girlfriend Catherine Greig. Bulger and Greig then went on the run together. In his memoir *Brutal: The Untold Story of My Life Inside Whitey Bulger's Irish Mob*, Kevin Weeks describes a clandestine meeting with Bulger and Greig in Chicago, Illinois. Bulger reminisced fondly about his time hiding out with a family in Louisiana. He told Weeks, who had replaced him as head of the Winter Hill Gang, "If anything comes down, put it on me."

Bulger's younger brother William was the subject of extreme criticism for reportedly taking a call from his brother in 1995 while James was on the run. James and William took very different paths in life yet remained closely bonded. William was four years younger than his brother James. Elected to the Massachusetts House of Representatives in 1961, then the State Senate in 1970, he thrived in politics and became one of the most powerful government figures in Massachusetts during his career. In 1978, William was elected President of the State Senate, a position he held until 1996, making him the longest tenured Senate President in state history. In November of 1995, William was elected President of the University of Massachusetts. Eight years later he was forced to resign as a result of the fallout from his testimony before Congress regarding his brother.

James Bulger:

> My brother Bill was in politics for well over forty years. The media was rough on him. He had fought against forced busing and was elected to the House of Representatives while I was on the Rock. In South Boston, he was a hero of the poor and foe of the media, and the rich Yankees who hated the Irish. My poor brother suffered because of

While James Bulger was rising in power in the Boston crime syndicate, his brother William (seen here with Senator Ted Kennedy and other political events) was a prolific politician. William Bulger became President of the Massachusetts Senate and later the president of the University of Massachusetts. He was forced to resign from office after it was revealed that he had communicated with his fugitive brother while he was on the lam. William was considered a brilliant and powerful political force during his career. During the 1960s, he led efforts to write the first child abuse reporting laws in the state. He was supportive of environmental protection legislation and was among the first advocates of charter schools and public school choice. During the 1980s, he

advocated the funding of public libraries, the expansion of childhood nutrition services and fuel assistance programs. As Senate president, Bulger led the debate on welfare reform in the early 1990s, with the resulting legislation becoming the model for a national law. The two brothers remained close throughout their lives.

Senate President William Bulger (L) during the presidential campaign of Michael Dukakis (Center) who had announced his candidacy for the Democratic Party's nomination for President of the United States with his running mate Lloyd Bentsen (R), a United States Senator from Texas.

me. They had him up before Congress years ago to testify about his gangster brother Whitey, a killer, etc.

William "Bill" Bulger on the plight of his brother:

There are reasons why I have maintained a reticence on what is for me is a difficult and painful subject. I recognize that my reluctance to comment has been vexing for some, and I also believe that it is responsible for some significant misunderstandings and misperceptions.

Truth to tell over the years, I was unable to penetrate the secretive life of my older brother. He marched to his own drummer and traveled a path much different than mine. Jim had his own ways that I could not possibly influence. The realities of the situation were such that his activities were in fact shrouded in secrecy. They were never shared with me.

I am particularly sorry to think that he may have been guilty of some of the horrible things of which he is accused. He has heard me often enough speak of society's right to protect itself, and to impose severe penalties on anyone guilty of such deeds. I am mindful of the

The cast of the popular television series Cheers with William Bulger in the House of Representatives during a joint session. In the 1980s and 1990s, Cheers had become part of the fabric of Boston in American culture. Bulger was one of the most well-known political figures associated with Boston and was always in the media.

victims in this matter, and I do not have the words that are adequate to let them know of my own sympathy and anguish. But I am ever mindful of the good shepherd story and its lesson that no one is to be abandoned. I care deeply for my brother, but no one should construe my expression of concern as in any way condoning any illegal acts.

I had, in fact, been concerned about the direction of my brother's life for many years. And in truth, my efforts with Jim span the decades. My attempts to change my brother's life were unsuccessful. I wish that I could have achieved success. But I must tell you that reforming Jim Bulger was not my sole twenty-four hour a day focus during the thirty-year period spanning his release from prison, during the mid-1960s, through his departure in 1995. During that entire period I served in the Massachusetts legislature, I was honored to serve in the Massachusetts House of Representatives for ten years, and subsequently in the Senate for twenty-five years; elected by my Senate colleagues for nine terms as President of the Senate. I made contributions during thirty-five years of legislative service; authoring the first bill requiring the reporting of child abuse; championing the cause of public education and public libraries. So, while I never abandoned hope or abandoned my efforts with respect to my brother, the truth is that other important things were happening in my life.

333

"My favorite picture of my brother Bill with opera singer Luciano Pavarotti. My brother always made things lighter with laughter. In this photo he'd just finished singing an Irish tune for Pavarotti, all in good fun and always the center of laughter in my family. This is a very special photo and I had such great admiration for both my brothers."
— James Bulger.

I never wrote my brother off, or walled him off, but public service and my own immediate family placed very large claims on me.

It is natural to focus our efforts on those matters that we can affect. And while I worried about my brother, I now recognize that I didn't fully grasp the dimensions of his life. Few people probably did…By definition, his was a secretive life. His actions were covert, hidden even from or perhaps especially from those who loved and cared about him. The subject that interests so many; the life and activities of my brother James, is painful and difficult for me. But it is a subject I've lived with for a long time…

I first sought political office in 1960, be assured, the subject of my brother was contentious from the start. On the occasion of my first speech, a politician foe told me that I should "be in jail with my brother," and it has been a refrain for forty years. Among the constituents in my legislative district and in the Massachusetts Senate, there was always an awareness of my brother. It was never a secret. But people understood that we were different people who lived different lives and should be judged separately.

Much has been made of that brief telephone call; a call that been a topic of discussion because my grand jury testimony was released to a Boston newspaper in violation of federal law. Many people, including elected public officials, have offered opinions about what was said or what was not said, but few, if any, have spoken about the illegal leaking that underlies the discussion. This call occurred in 1995, six years before my grand jury appearance. The subject of my brother turning himself in never came up in that conversation. I never recommended that my brother remain at large. In 1995 and in subsequent years, I believed that the FBI wanted him killed.

It has been established that FBI Agent John Morris, in 1988, met with the *Boston Globe* spotlight team editor and told him that my brother was an informant; information that was summarily published in the *Boston Globe*. Morris's leak had one purpose, pure and simple, bringing about the death of my brother James Bulger. This is just not my hunch, this is the finding of U.S. District Court Judge Mark Wolf after extensive hearings…The one thing I knew was this, whether it was true or false, the fact is identifying him as such might result in his murder. It was a chilling thing for me…

FBI Agent John Connolly, who was "Bulger handler," agreed with William that the FBI schemed to have his brother assassinated. Connolly was indicted on charges of alerting Bulger and Flemmi to investigations, falsifying FBI reports to cover their crimes, and accepting bribes in 1999. In 2008, he was convicted of second-degree murder for providing information that led to the death of John Callahan. Connolly went on record in 1998 before his conviction:

FBI Agent, John Connelly

Bulger and Flemmi were two highly placed assets of the Bureau. You have to remember why they became assets of the Bureau. We wanted to bring down the Italian Mafia. The Mafia was the #1 investigative priority of the FBI. As such, Bulger and Flemmi were not on our investigative radar screens. They were, however, at a sufficiently high level of their own organization to be able to laterally influence the Mafia. They were long-term sources, and it's important to recognize why they became sources of the FBI. They were targeted for elimination by the [Italian] Mafia.

In 1988, the *Boston Globe* first reported that Bulger and Flemmi were FBI informants...It's now been reported that the Head of the Organized Crime Task Force, John Morris, was the one who reportedly tipped or leaked this info to the Boston Globe. It was an unconscionable act of treachery....I believe the judge in this case asked the right question:

JUDGE: Did you believe that this could get him murdered?
MORRIS: Yes, I thought it could...

There could be no other reason for leaking that to the news media...I believe he was the most corrupt agent in the history of the FBI. Here's somebody who put bombs under people's cars, took money from gangsters, lied under oath, flunked polygraph exams, tipped them off to investigations, and the prosecutors gave him immunity and denied it to me...

I had an unblemished record in the FBI. I was commended by every FBI director in history, including J. Edgar Hoover, until the time I retired. There's one reason why they don't want to give me immunity; the government is afraid of the truth. They indicted these people for gambling and loan sharking, and they were allowed to do it. It was a policy devised by Jerry O'Sullivan from the Strike Force. It was communicated to them on several occasions, by John Morris.

I don't want immunity for any corrupt act. I don't need it, I wouldn't take it…I only need it for the narrow issue of authorization. Illegal activity was indeed condoned by the FBI. Does anybody believe that Bulger and Flemmi would survive the FBI for more than twenty years unless we intended it?

Bulger agreed:

John Morris was the head of the FBI's Organized Crime Squad in Boston, and he took immunity for his testimony against me and John Connelly. I had Morris on my payroll, and he admitted in court that I gave him $7,000 plus cases of wine worth $300 to $500 per bottle. But to be honest, you would have to add several more zeros to the $7,000 figure! This guy tried to get me killed after I refused to solve a personal problem for him. The fact that needs to be made clear is that I bought information from the FBI. I did not give them any information, or at least anything of substance…I never provided a sliver of information to implicate anyone, including my enemies. I bought the information, and then handled lingering issues on my own. When I was in Santa Monica, I wrote page after page starting with my youngest years up through prison; cops' third degree, interrogations, etc., and then taking on the lies. All of this is in my so- called "manuscript" found by the FBI in my apartment. The FBI told me "We've got your manuscript." I dared them to print it for the world to read. The contents will be explosive, and I doubt it will ever surface. I quit writing it years ago. Writing it meant I had to relive those things and trying to explain things was depressing, sitting up all night, and real hard to turn it all off. It's a long story.

It's hard for me to believe that the killers of fifty people were set free for their testimony against me, along with the framing of John Connelly who they gave a forty-year sentence. During my trial, I think the jurors were really shocked by the testimony of John Morris. It went to show the tactics he used. In Boston, there was an associate named Eddie. He was a target of Morris, who was pressuring him to rat information on the Italian Mafia. The FBI used all kinds of scare and interrogation tactics, but he didn't budge and offer any information. So, Morris plays another card and authorizes an explosive device be placed under the frame of Eddie's car. Instead of Eddie driving as they expected, his wife takes the car and drives away with her kids. The strange thing is, the police immediately pull her over, and trailing behind them is the bomb squad. Eddie's wife and kids are moved to safety and the bomb squad goes under the car to retrieve the bomb. They place it in a huge container to detonate it and they tell the wife she is safe. This came up in my trial when Morris took the stand.

One of my old crime partners, John Martorano, confessed to more than twenty murders, and he admitted to killing Roger Wheeler in Oklahoma and John Callahan in Florida. Some of the murders he confessed to were long before he ever knew me and now, he's a free man—writing his book, and aligned for a movie deal! Lies galore and I can prove it. He basically got away with murder. He kills in haste and young innocent people die in his wake. As part of his deal, they only gave him six months for each murder he confessed to. In addition, they gave him $6,000 to use for spending in the prison commissary and then handed him a $20,000 check when he walked free after only ten years of easy time. He also takes in $70,000 for a book deal and $250,000 for movie rights. These guys enjoy being celebrated and wealthy with all their book and movie deals. I feel like it's all to get

John Martorano

John Callahan

the focus off the deals these "justice salesmen" gave these confessed killers of over fifty people, including women and two teens. In this case of the murdered teenagers, the driver of the car was tricked by Martorano to give him a ride across town. The driver had been targeted to die. It's in the middle of the night and there's light snowfall. He asks the driver to pull over so that he can relieve himself; once stopped, he shoots both the driver and a seventeen-year-old boy passenger in the head; both in front of another teenager sitting in the back seat next to Martorano. The girl in the backseat is nineteen years old, real thin, sitting to his left. He turns and shoots her in the head too. During the trial, my attorney asks "Why?" and Martorano says he thought she was a guy since she was wearing a hooded jacket. My attorney points out that he shot her in the right side of the head and there was no hole in the hood. The prosecutor then starts objecting and it's the only time the judge now seems interested and lets him continue. It's hard to keep all this straight, but another guy gets

Roger Wheeler was a completely innocent victim who had been murdered by Bulger's criminal associate John Martorano. Bulger would go on record denying any involvement in his death or associated crime schemes.

into the car and J.M. stabs him a few times. For good measure he also slits his throat and then dumps him near a closed gas station. Amazing deals these four men got, and then my girlfriend Catherine does more time than the killers. Think hard about that… She never hurt a single person and will serve more time in prison than these murderers.

Morris was given immunity for his testimony and confessed he took money and expensive gifts from me and another racketeer named Sam Berkowitz, who is now deceased. I paid off both Connelly and Morris. I bought information on cases they were working and for the names of anyone giving information to the Feds to either implicate my crew or any of our friends. They benefited by me handling these issues. My tactics were more effective. Morris had no choice but to confess. He

A 1990 era mugshot of James "Whitey" Bulger. Despite this and other arrests, he was never convicted of a single crime before becoming a fugitive of the law in 1995.

was given only a year probation and transferred out of Boston. He was later promoted and became the head of the FBI office in Los Angeles while I was on the run. Even FBI Agent Paul Rico was later convicted and sent to prison.

I later learned that Rico had set up my early crime partner, Ronnie Dermody, to be shot down and murdered. Ronnie served time at a young age at Charlestown State prison with his father and brother Joe. It's hard to picture it...Serving time at Charlestown was hard time. It opened in 1804, and being so old it had no plumbing, no dining room; small yard and had a small building with an electric chair and gallows. One day they see the prisoners crowding and walk over to find their father on the ground dead from a heart attack. His brother Joe is later stabbed to death in prison and his other younger brother is murdered in Chicago and tossed into a river. Ronnie was released from prison a year before me and was recruited into the McLaughlin Gang. He gets in too deep, aligns with the wrong associates and then makes a few more fatal errors. The backstory is when Ronnie was released from prison, he struck up a relationship with Dottie Barchard, who had earlier been involved with Jimmy O'Toole of Winter Hill. Jimmy "Spike" O'Toole was vicious. He and Dottie had kids together, but my

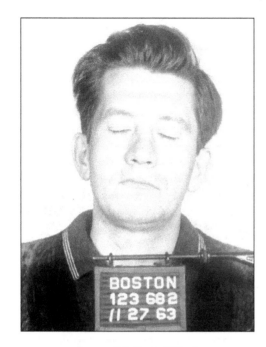

Jimmy "Spike" O'Toole   Buddy McLean

memory is that it wasn't a good relationship. He tortured a friend of mine to death in prison, also killed another friend Tommy Sullivan, an ex-boxer from South Boston. It's complicated. Spike threatens Ronnie, so Ronnie makes a pact to rub out Buddy McLean, the head of Winter Hill, in exchange for the McLaughlin brothers to take out Spike O'Toole. Dermody knows he can't take out Spike on his own, and knows the Winter Hill Gang has marked him, so out of desperation he strikes a deal. His first mistake is that he attempts the hit inside a crowded bar and ends up shooting the wrong guy. Ronnie seeks out FBI Agent Paul Rico for protection. Rico was one of the agents that set a trap and captured me in the 1950s and had arrested Ronnie on a previous charge. Ronnie is without options and confides in Rico that he needs protection. Rico asks him if he's armed, tells him to stay out of sight, gives him a location to park on a dark street in Dorchester and that he's on the way and he'll meet with him to provide help. Rico's dirty, and passes the information to Punchy McLaughlin and Buddy McLean. Rico picks them up in an FBI cruiser and they pull up to Ronnie's car. McLean walks over and plants three bullets in Ronnie's head using a Webley revolver supplied by Punchy. McLean dies a year

The Jai Alai arena in Miami, owned by Roger Wheeler, was a prominent casino style sports venue which included legal wagering and high intensity spectator sports. In addition to sporting events, the arena was also host to top billed music performers including Jackson Browne, Joni Mitchell, Van Halen, Journey and Dan Fogelberg to name only a few. It was a highly popular event venue in the 1970s and 80s.

later while leaving a nightclub. Spike dies in 1973, another murder by Martorano, but I'm the one accused of making the hit.

Paul Rico was a deadly individual and was no stranger to murder. He was also the architect of *World Jai Alai* owner Roger Wheeler's slaying in Oklahoma. In the 1970's, the Jai Alai sport was the most popular large arena sport in all of Miami. It was incredibly lucrative, and the business model centered on casino style betting; somewhat along the lines of what you'd see with horseracing or small arena sports with legal wagering. The auditorium was used not only for the Jai Alai events, but also for musical concerts with top billed performers. After Paul Rico's retirement from the FBI, he became the head of security for *World Jai Alai* in Miami. Wheeler suspected Rico was skimming from the wagering tills and hired a detective agency to investigate. Rico gets wind, and fearing charges of embezzlement if caught, hires Martorano—who happens to be on the run in Florida— to make the hit. Martorano travels to Tulsa with Joe McDonald.

The tragic and brutal crime scene of Roger Wheeler's homicide on an upscale golf course in Oklahoma.

Wearing a disguise and using a silencer, Martorano shoots Wheeler in a country club parking lot after a round of golf.

Later, I'm accused of skimming $10,000 a week off Wheeler, when it was Rico behind everything! Rico was dirty and later proven to have been involved in several earlier crimes as part of his association with Joe Barboza. Rico goes to prison for murder and the truth came out. Rico was the lowest. He helped Barboza frame four completely innocent men and left them to rot behind bars... Two died in prison and the other two served more than thirty years before they were proven innocent and released. The backstory on Joe Barboza is that he was a killer who conspired with Rico, while he was still a special agent for the FBI, along with United States Attorney Ed Harrington. Barboza makes a deal and confesses to a murder charge stating in court, "Yes, I killed Eddie "Teddy" Deegan, but I was ordered to under duress by Louis Greco, Henry Tameleo, Peter Limone and Joseph Salvati to make the hit..." All four were all sentenced to life in prison and no parole. Barboza walks free and robs four innocent men of their lives. The FBI places him in a witness protection program, sends him to culinary school and helps him open his own restaurant. Too little, too late, he kills again and is arrested in San Francisco. He calls Rico in Boston and orders him to fly to San Francisco and get him out of jail. Barboza says, "I'm not asking, I'm telling you..." He threatens that if they are

343

not on the next plane, he'll recant his confession and tell the world how they all conspired and framed innocent men. They're on the next plane to San Francisco and make an appeal to the judge who reduces the charges, and he walks free. Rico leaks to the Mafia that he's a risk and threatened to talk. He's gunned down only days later. The families later sue the government and win more than $100 million in damages for wrongful convictions. Two walked free after serving more than thirty years, and two died in prison for crimes they never committed.

I'm falsely accused of setting up the murder of Roger Wheeler by John Martorano. To be crystal clear, I didn't order a hit on a legitimate businessman with no criminal affiliations. That was against my own principles and the Mafia would not have any involvement in something like this either. I can assure you that I know how these organizations operate and they never would have been associated in anything like this. There's a code in the Mafia and they don't skim and steal from innocent people. They're much more sophisticated than what's being represented, especially as it relates to gambling operations. What a fucking joke to suggest they're skimming and stealing from cash drawers. They're businessmen; not petty thieves. They're running legitimate casino style businesses and not pocketing loose bills and coins. What's implied in the media is disrespectful and not accurate. This is not the work of the Mafia or an elaborate crime syndicate, it's the work of one or two individuals, or possibly a small neighborhood group. This is where Hollywood misrepresents the Mafia. I can assure you the organizations I had exposure to were not walking into businesses and forcing good people to pay rent just to be in business. I would have never been involved or allowed such a thing. I didn't order the hit and I didn't have any part of it.

Everyone was lining up to make a deal at my expense. Martorano indicts his close pal John Callahan, who'd been president of Jai Alai prior to Wheeler in the 1970s... They were friends for decades and he sold him out without a second thought! In true Barboza form, Martorano says "I killed him, but Whitey told me to do it!" Blatant lie! My lawyer on cross asked "How did Bulger tell you? On the phone?" "No...Whitey would never talk on the phone." "Then how?" "Stevie Flemmi told me that Whitey said do it!" Another ridiculous lie. He later admits to putting a bullet in the back of Callahan's head, his close friend, and again points the finger back at me. Not only was I accused (and later convicted) of the murder, but years later I read something accusing me of killing the entire sport because it became too synonymous with organized crime! Unbelievable…In the 1970s it was a featured sport in the Olympics, yet somehow, I influenced its demise? What's fucking next?

Again, Martorano did easy time even after confessing to more than twenty murders in exchange for his cooperation. In prison, they gave him $6,000 in his commissary account inside an easy time prison, a check for $20,000 upon his release, he kept his multi-million-dollar home, a 32-foot sport fishing boat tied at a dock attached to his bay front residence, a motorhome, a BMW, and the list goes on and on. When asked in court how many people he murdered, he said "I can't remember how many." Everything is verifiable. He was part of Barboza's gang and gets his way fingering everyone else in crimes he committed. He was a fugitive for fourteen years with a woman who lied to the grand jury and was still set free. She was never prosecuted. Flemmi's permitted to keep $3 million in assets and easy prison time as part of his deal! I was guilty of a lot of crimes, but I never pinned them on others to do my time.

The Feds never checked to see if these informants were truthful, and they don't want the truth to get in the way of a conviction. They will all be like a chorus, singing me into the electric chair in Florida, or horizontal crucifixion in Oklahoma by needle. Prison life is simple compared to life in organized crime. In organized crime, you're swimming in a pool of sharks, always looking over your shoulder, never knowing who's lurking in the shadows.

MANHUNT

The last confirmed sighting of Bulger before his capture was in London in 2002. However, there were unconfirmed sightings elsewhere. FBI agents were sent to Uruguay to investigate a lead. FBI agents were also sent to stake out the 60th memorial of the Battle of Normandy celebrations, because Bulger was a patriot and avid reader of military history. In 2010, the FBI turned its focus to Victoria, British Columbia, on Vancouver Island. In pursuit of Bulger, a known book lover, the FBI visited bookstores in the area, questioned employees, and distributed wanted posters.

Following his arrest, Bulger revealed that he had in fact traveled frequently. It was clear that he had not been reclusive; witnesses came forward to say that they had seen him on the Santa Monica Pier and elsewhere in Southern California. A report by an off-duty Boston police officer after a San Diego screening of *The Departed* (a film by Martin Scorsese produced in 2006, based loosely on Bulger) also led to a search in Southern California that lasted "a few weeks." Bulger later confirmed that he and Catherine watched the movie at a theatre in Santa Monica, not in San Diego as had been reported, and he was frequently in public.

> I visited Alcatraz a couple of times before I went on the run... The first was back in 1988 when I caught-up with Leon "Whitey" Thompson (1465-AZ). He was another Alcatraz convict who served there a few years before me, but we knew many of the same men. It felt nostalgic to return after more than twenty years. It brought back so many memories. I doubt people could ever understand why I'd feel this way, but as I've mentioned previously, you hold a close bond with people you share such a profound experience with. It was a difficult period for me being in prison, isolated and thousands of miles away from my family, yet still, I feel a deep connection to those memories. What stands out most in my mind was a National Park Ranger asking me if I'd like to visit my old cell. It's strange how it all came back to me, and I was able to walk right to the cell without even looking up at the numbers. I showed him C-314 and I remember he allowed me to take a small memento from my cell, along with a piece of the Rock we picked up in the Industries building where I worked. These were special mementos that I kept with me in the house on Silver Street in South Boston. I admit that there was a profound change in the man who entered that cell and who he was when he left years later.
>
> The media got ahold of the novelty San Francisco tourist photo of my then girlfriend Teresa Stanley and me visiting Alcatraz. They always write this was taken while on the run, but that is completely ridiculous. I would have never taken such risks to place myself where I'd be closely associated. I knew that Alcatraz would be one of the places they'd be looking for me, and I figured the park rangers probably had the FBI wanted posters hanging in their offices. The photo of Teresa and me was taken during a regular vacation and at a time when I didn't have a single warrant. It makes the story so much more exciting and of course, sells more magazines by making the claim I was on the run when the photo was taken. It was nearly eight years after that photo was taken that I fled Boston.
>
> The photo was taken during a second or third trip, after I traveled back to San Francisco to meet up again with Leon Thompson and straighten him out for remarks he made about a few good friends who

Bulger and his then girlfriend Teresa Stanley in an Alcatraz novelty photo taken in San Francisco prior to him going on the run, sometime around the late 1980s to early 90s. Many media outlets claimed this was taken while he was a fugitive, but he later commented he would have never been so reckless to frequent places to which he'd be associated.

I served time together with on Alcatraz. I gave Leon money to help publish his book and then it gets back to me that he's writing tabloid trash. I heard he was running Karpis and Carnes into the ground. I searched for him and even called him at his home. I could never figure out his angle for spreading lies, other than he wanted to sensationalize stories and elevate himself into a persona of being a key figure during his years on Alcatraz. I was an unknown at that time, as was he. It was disrespecting to the men and their memory. This wasn't a case of being hazy about the details. It was a case of writing trash to make it sell. I have no problem with the truth; we all must face it sooner or later, but he wrote these lies at their expense. I looked at it as he gave some

The special edition copy of Leon "Whitey" Thompson's self-published book signed to Bulger. It was one of the books found on his bookshelf in the Santa Monica apartment.

LAST TRAIN TO ALCATRAZ

The Autobiography of
LEON (Whitey) THOMPSON
(Former Alcatraz Inmate)

Leon "Whitey" Thompson during a book signing in San Francisco for the publication of Last Train to Alcatraz.

A photograph of Bulger while vacationing in Acapulco, Mexico, and a recovered passport from the FBI.

of them a legacy they didn't earn or deserve. I lived with many of the same men on the island and I would have heard rumors of so many of the things he was making claim to. Maybe it was to get back at one of them for an old spat, or to sell books giving the public salacious tidbits that you wouldn't believe happened on Alcatraz and were tabloid worthy? He wrote, "Carnes, dumb bastard got $25,000 from his movie and spent it on booze!" I yelled at him for that and said "What do you know about his life and it was his money to spend any way he wanted...Who the fuck are you to judge?" He backtracked and I said I hope you haven't written things knocking guys sucking up to the joint. He says NO! He sends me his draft and he had all the facts wrong and wasn't anywhere to be seen for half the shit he claimed. He mentioned an episode in the mess hall calling a Mexican guy "Soda." I corrected him and told him to give the guy the respect he deserves and get the name right. His real name was Emilio Sosa (1457-AZ), plus I gave him

316/500

To Jim Bulger
Best Wishes &
Your Pal
Leon (Whitey) Thompson
8/10/88

This book is dedicated to my wife Helen, for
without her help and support this book would never
have been written. Also to the men of Alcatraz,
convicts and guards alike, and to Lou Peters, my
old cell partner. To the memory of Johnny House.
Also to the memory of my beloved Wolf Dog Winter.

book may be
except for
a review,
publisher.

An inscription written in Bulger's hand
"The Author has done a disservice to the
guys who were on the Rock by lying about
individuals, conditions, events, etc. This book
is strictly fiction." Inside was Thompson's
business card and news clippings about the
publication.

a whole list of other corrections. He
got very quiet, but I could tell he
was taking notes.

I liked his wife Helen and sent
her money so that she could
travel home to England. I gave
her enough money for a round
trip ticket and spending money
for a full two weeks. I'm on the
phone with her and I can hear
Leon in the background telling her not
to forget to remind me to send $20 for a copy of his book. This was
after I gave him money to help publish it. I laughed and told her to tell
him don't worry, and I'll include money for shipping too. I received
my "Special Edition" book of lies. Leon "Whitey" Thompson should
be remembered as "Leon the Liar." He wrote of things saying he
witnessed, took part in or helped plan, but in many cases, he wasn't
even there at the same time! What a joke. Then, we all see his tearful
garbage all over television. It really turned me off. I'm not surprised
it turned out that his claim to be a notorious bank robber was all a
bunch of lies and he was at Alcatraz on weapons charges.

I've always wondered if he intercepted the large envelope with cash.
That's the truth. I can't remember the sum of money I sent Helen, but
at the time I had so much money from banks, etc., plus had lottery
winnings connected to my store for $2.3 million paid over a twenty-
year period. When I let him and Helen know I'd be in California,
mysteriously he was nowhere to be found. He told me that one of the
main reasons he wanted to publish the book was so that he could send
his wife back home to England. He wanted her to be able to spend
more time with the family she left. At that time, I thought I was in a
position to help a fellow alumnus, so I sent the money and then he
slapped us all in the face. Leon was lucky I didn't bump into him when
I flew out there for that purpose.

LIVING ON THE RUN with Catherine in Santa Monica was like a sixteen-year honeymoon. They were the happiest years of my life. The years were almost stress-free. The other years were gang wars; friends shot down and ambushed, shootings, knife fights, fights, intrigue, murder, extortion traps set for us. A bomber was paid to blow me up with sticks of dynamite with radio-controlled bombs. I tracked him down and captured him and the bomb, which I dismantled. There was car to car shootings, years of violence. I was shot at many times since the age of fifteen, there were police beatings to make you talk (which I never did and never came close).

We never really looked over our shoulders. Our attitude was that we were going to live a normal life. If we were captured, then so be it; until then we were not going to live in a state of anxiety. We went every place we wanted to. Occasionally, I would see or hear the lies and other things on TV and I had a desire to go back for revenge, but I couldn't move without considering Catherine. I owed her that much, and because of her, I never slipped back. We lived a very normal, quiet and peaceful life. We enjoyed one another's company, and I would have been perfectly happy living the rest of our lives together, inside our modest little apartment. It was a good life and I felt infinite love for her...

A few years before I was a fugitive, I stayed just south of Venice Beach on the water. I drove around looking at the areas and passed through the 3rd Street Promenade area and said to myself if ever I need to run, this place is ideal. I also studied the names on various apartment directories and noticed a high percentage of the communities included Polish and Russian Jewish names, so that's why we took Gasko as we felt we'd be able to blend in. Charlie Catalano once told me the meaning of his name was of English origin and it meant "free man," so it felt right to adopt it as a nod to him and freedom being so fragile as a fugitive.

We relished every moment together and enjoyed our daily walks along the Pacific Coast Highway's ocean side trails in Palisades Park. Our favorite spot, the spot that we loved most, was sitting on the bench looking out to the ocean and the rose garden. Peaceful and nice people with children, one block north of Montana and Ocean. We walked the park every day... Got to know the dog people and enjoyed meeting their pets. I can still remember their names and pretty sure some of the owners would still remember who we are. We walked there every day to see the dogs. I can remember so many of them... "Ziggy", a little black bulldog was our favorite. "Bullet" was another that we enjoyed running into.

We tried to be good people and give whenever we could to brighten someone's day. I felt good about doing those kinds of things. Once in a parking lot we saw a young man in an Air Force uniform with his young wife and kids walking into a restaurant. I left a $50 bill and note on the windshield of his car to thank him for his service. We drove through little towns with elderly people sitting on the porch

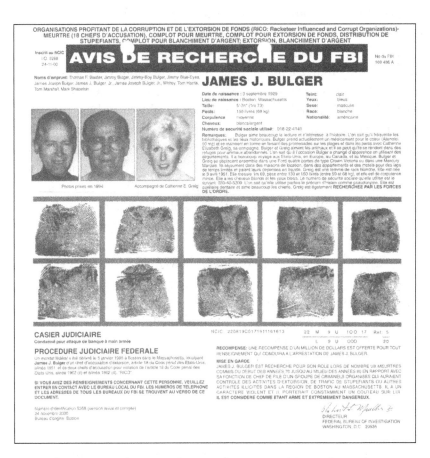

A French FBI Wanted Poster. He was a known world traveler and posters were distributed around the world, including large cities such as Paris, London, Ireland, Berlin and all-over South America.

Wanted posters were part of the fugitive press materials distributed in an effort to locate Bulger and girlfriend Catherine Greig.

Composite photographs and police sketch artist images estimating age progression of Whitey Bulger and Catherine Greig.

with their animals and brought them 50-pound bags of dog food and treats. We'd tell them here's a present for your good looking and loyal pet! This is how we spent our days in the mountains of Appalachia, Cajun Country, deserts of the Southwest and Tombstone. We'd find and rescue lost dogs in the desert and get them to water and food. People would abandon them on highways, and we always tried to help them. Before going on the lam, we vacationed on the Virgin Islands, Barbados, St. Barts, etc., and in the nights, we'd feed the homeless cats that we found on all the islands. We dreamed what it would be like to live there forever with those animals and even talked about owning a shelter. The media was on-target about our love for animals—feeding strays—and that got us caught.

In 2002, I met a guy during our walks in Santa Monica named Jim Lawlor. He had similar facial features, enough that I thought I could pass as him on a driver's license. He was a homeless, alcoholic, Irish New Yorker, bitter, angry, brash and rough around the edges. He had a sleeping bag and slept under a Sears delivery truck in their parking lot off 4th Street. We'd see him sitting on the same park bench and I'd

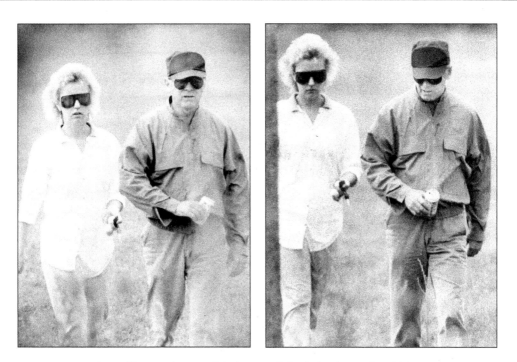

Surveillance photos of Bulger and Greig in the early 1990s.

always stop to talk. I always offered a little money to help him out and over a period of time, we got to know each other well enough that I felt comfortable proposing an arrangement we could both benefit from.

I gave him a story that I was here illegally from Canada and couldn't get a job unless I had a driver's license. I explained that I had some unresolved legal issues and lawful citizenship wasn't an option for me, but I had a solid job prospect if I could somehow get a driver's license or California ID. I offered to pay him $1,000 if he allowed me to use his, and I assured him it was only to be used for general identification, not for any criminal activity. He welcomed the idea, but said it needed to be renewed. I gave him $500 to help get things started. I really felt bad for him after hearing his story of losing everything due to alcoholism. I checked him into the West End Motel off Santa Monica Blvd, the location of his choosing. We rented him a small, single room, upstairs apartment. It was next to an old bookstore and movie theatre, and this deal gave him a better life than what he was living on the street. His room was full of books, he read for hours every day, watched old movies on television and I paid his monthly rent and provided him plenty of money for food and basic necessities. It

"A Picture of Catherine with our two miniature poodles Nikki and Gigi. We loved those dogs and had to leave them with Catherine's twin sister when we had to flee Boston. It was a painful part of my life and the circumstances I put us in." - James Bulger

was a perfect exchange and afforded Catherine and me a considerable level of freedom. If I was ever stopped by the police or in a situation where I needed an ID, no one would ever question me holding a legal driver's license with our appearances being so similar.

The West End Motel was located on Sawtelle Ave, ironically, the same name of a street in Boston next to my old neighborhood, so I took it as a good sign. I frequently brought him wholesome meals and kept out of sight from the other tenants. I always pulled a little fold-up cart, carried two envelopes with cash (one for rent and one for food and living expenses), and carefully watched

The Princess Eugenia Apartments in Santa Monica, California, where Bulger and Greig lived their days on the run in quiet solitude. They lived in Apt # 303, seen on the top right.

Bulger and Catherine Greig took daily walks in Palisades Park and sitting at their favorite bench with views of the Malibu coastline. He reminisced: "What memories of the Rose Garden. Our favorite place and our favorite bench. We always sat there early in the morning - we'd carry a couple paper towels to wipe off the dew. So peaceful..."

for anyone or anything suspicious. Sadly, Jim Lawlor never made his way back from the booze vices that once rendered him homeless. He continued to overindulge in alcohol and chain-smoking. He didn't walk much or get any exercise, complained about politics, and would be nasty at times from excessive drinking. He had a rough life and alcohol would bring back bad memories. We both had the same first name. Over the years as we got to know each other better, I knew that he had an idea of who I was. I gave him my word that I would never hurt him and expressed my gratitude. We never spoke of it again. I accepted it and trusted him. He had served as a Sergeant in the US Army and fought in Korea. I felt sympathy for him and thought of my brother-in-law and his fate in the same war. I understood the things

The California Driver's License of James Lawlor found in the possession of Bulger following his arrest. Bulger paid Lawlor's apartment lease in exchange for the use of his identity.

that haunted him. Through the years, he stashed away about $70,000 in cash from what I gave him and against what he earned in social security. One day he offered to use it to pay his own rent! I told him not to worry, it was a good arrangement and I wanted to hold my end. It would allow him to carry on if one day I never showed up again.

In late July of 2007, I showed up to meet him at our usual spot and he didn't show. We'd been meeting for about five years, so this seemed rather unusual. I waited a week and then showed up again and with still no sign of him. I called his number and he'd never pick up. I grew concerned and finally called the front desk and they told me he'd passed away and had been gone for more than a week before anyone had noticed. Poor Jim died all alone. It really shook me... There was nothing in the papers and it was like he never existed. I felt bad for him, living such a sad existence and all alone. Someone who probably didn't even know him made off with all his cash, and I'd wished I had made arrangements for him. I guess part of the point was that I saw value in helping people and not taking advantage. I'd get a bad feeling if I walked by someone who was homeless and didn't offer anything. I felt it gave me good luck. I've lived a long life, so maybe I did enjoy a bit of good fortune. Then again, I'm here in prison, so there's also justice!

In the Santa Monica days, all of those years were wonderful by degrees, and I started to feel like a human. It was just Catherine and me and we kept to ourselves. I felt love. I guess that after so many years of shutting down my feelings, I felt like ice and capable of anything. It was hard for me to put my feelings into words. I wish I could've let

FORSYTH 11
CHAN 12
SCHLANK 13
GOFF 14
URE 15
16
17
18
MYLES-P 19
ZWEIBACK 21
BURGI 22
MAJORS BRATTSON 23
COLONNO LUKYANETS 24
LEVEL 25
HOLSTAD 26
27
BAINTON LEWIS 28
THOMPSON 29
ROSENZWEIG FEIN 31
32
33
GASKO 33
34
BORSKA 35
SOKOLOW 36
GLUCK 37
HAGOOD MOYNIHAN 38
GOODWIN 39

Bulger and Greig lived under the alias "Charlie and Carol Gasko" while on the run in Santa Monica.

Catherine know how much I loved her, when I can write someday maybe I'll be able to. Once in those years, I saw one of those machines where you put in a penny and two quarters, turn a handle and a penny comes out flattened with words, "I Love You" on it. I remember I didn't say anything and I took the penny out and handed it to her. She looked at it and said "This is so nice, I'll always treasure it..." As I looked over, I could see her eyes had tears...I felt awkward and didn't know what to say, but I felt an overwhelming urge to hold her. I felt so in love. When we would go on walks, she would put her arm in mine, and I felt a real warm calm feeling coming over me. When we went on the lam, she asked me please to not hurt anyone—I promised her I wouldn't, but up to that moment I would have. I meant that promise to her because of fear that if I shot anyone, she could and would be prosecuted and I felt protective of her and would give my life for her.

I always thought of the ideal woman I'd love to meet, and Catherine was all of that, but by the time we met I was already involved deeply in crime and there was no turning back. I was a criminal and quit thinking of working and trying to make a normal living. I accepted this was my life now. I was still on parole, and I couldn't just disappear with her. Plus, there was another woman in my life and I was just living for the moment. When a guy gets out of prison he goes back to the old neighborhood, broke, and feeling real old. You come out of prison sort of rudderless and gravitate into the whiskey bars. The women there all have problems like yourself. When you're angry and bitter like I was, with no confidence that I could make it working in a normal job, the drinking and succession of women, and then when the paths cross with someone in the same boat, that's the hell with it. You're back in the game, but it's more serious, making more money and in the middle of things, then you slowly escalate to extreme things. At that point, there's no turning back and you're all in forever. I'd ask Catherine "How do you do it, sleep right away and all night?" She would smile and say, "clear conscience," my reply "touché.»

If Catherine and I had lived a normal life, not on the run, we could have both worked and had a good life. I felt it after a while as I started to feel human emotions. I was lucky to have those sixteen years. I wish Catherine didn't have to pick up the check for it all.

An evidence photo of Bulger's collection of flattened pennies acquired during his travels. They included a series of novelty pennies from the Santa Monica Pier.

CAPTURE

After sixteen years at large and twelve years on the FBI Ten Most Wanted Fugitives list, Bulger was arrested in Santa Monica, California, on June 22, 2011. Bulger was captured as a result of the work of the Bulger Fugitive Task Force, which consisted of FBI Agents and a Deputy U.S. Marshal. According to retired FBI agent Scott Bakken, "Here you have somebody who is far more sophisticated than some eighteen-year-old who killed someone in a drive-by. To be a successful fugitive you have to cut all contacts from your previous life. He had the means and kept a low profile."

A reward of two million dollars had been offered for information leading to his capture. This amount was second only to Osama Bin Laden's reward on the FBI Ten Most Wanted Fugitives list. Bulger has been featured on the television show *America's Most Wanted* sixteen times, first in 1995, and last on October 2, 2010. According to the authorities, the arrests were a "direct result" of the media campaign launched by the FBI in fourteen markets across the country where Bulger and Greig reportedly had ties.

Deputy U.S. Marshal Neil Sullivan handled the lead that ultimately led to Bulger and Greig's arrest. Authorities received a tip from Anna Bjornsdottir, a former model and actress who had recently returned to her home country of Iceland but had seen the media campaign while watching American television. She claimed that while she was a resident at the Embassy Apartments, located in Santa Monica, California, she came to know Charlie and Carol Gasko, two retirees living at the Princess Eugenia, across the street. She was adamant that they fit the FBI's description perfectly and was certain the Gaskos were the couple the FBI was looking for. She stated the couple took daily walks to Palisades Park along the ocean, and often stopped to pet neighborhood animals, most notably a friendly cat often lounging in the courtyard of the Embassy. "Charlie" always wore a hat and dark glasses, and never seemed to be comfortable engaging or being too friendly with neighbors. What really caught the Marshal's attention was that when they attempted to research the backgrounds of the Gasko couple, they could locate no information that they even existed. No driver's licenses, no tax records, no records of income or properties, only a phone number registered in their name. They had allegedly transplanted from Chicago to Santa Monica. They had also confided with some that they had illegally migrated from Canada and thus, were not able to provide Social Security numbers, but never let on that "Charlie" was on the run.

Located at 1012 Third Street in Santa Monica, the Princess Eugenia Apartments was a nice but modest rent-controlled complex comprised mostly of retirees. The Gasko couple was residing in Apartment #303, a top-floor

The Embassy Hotel Apartments as seen from Bulger's end apartment.

1,100 square foot end unit. It was the perfect hiding place, located in a quiet and unassuming Santa Monica neighborhood that was rich in foliage and only two blocks from the Pacific Ocean. The Gaskos paid $1,145 a month in rent. Similar properties in this area were typically triple this amount, and each month, Carol and Charlie Gasko walked across the street to the main office at the Embassy and made their payment, always in the same fashion. They paid with the exact denomination of crisp new bills. Eleven $100s; two $20s and one $5 bill. On the day of the capture, the manager of the complex, Josh Bond, was napping on his couch and was tired after having been on call during the evenings without a break.

He appeared to be in his early thirties and lived in the next-door apartment to the Gasko couple. In Bond's testimony before a Federal Grand Jury, on July 28, 2011, he described his position as the General Manager for both the Princess Eugenia Apartment building where Bulger and Greig resided, and the Embassy Hotel Apartments, located directly across the street, in plain view of their residence.

On June 22, 2011, at about 2:00 PM, his coworker at the Embassy (the hotel and residential building where Bond had his property management office) called to alert him that the FBI was there and wanted to speak with him about one of the tenants at the Princess Eugenia Apartment complex. When Bond

The Embassy where manager Josh Bond has his business office and the location the "Gasko" couple walked to each month to pay rent and also visit with some of the resident pets in the courtyard.

arrived, two casually dressed men—one of them dressed in a Hawaiian style shirt—entered the office. Scott Garriola, an FBI Special Agent assigned to the Fugitive Squad in the Bureau's Los Angeles office, closed the door and laid out a folder on the desk. In the folder was a collection of photographs that included screen shots from surveillance footage, mugshots and family style prints of two fugitives that he believed might be living in his complex under assumed names. One of the documents was an FBI Wanted poster with the name James "Whitey" Bulger. Garriola asked Bond if the couple resembled the Gasko couple living next door in Apartment #303. At first, Bond didn't immediately recognize Charlie Gasko as Whitey Bulger, but "Carol" was undoubtedly Catherine Greig. The more closely he studied the photographs, the more he saw Charlie's likeness to the Irish Mafia mogul Whitey Bulger. He had trouble taking it all in as he soon realized that his neighbor was one of the most powerful crime figures in America. The more he studied the photos in disbelief, the more he became "100% certain" that the photographs were of the same couple living in the adjacent apartment. He thought of them as a nice, retired couple, excellent tenants who always paid their rent on time; they were very quiet, discreet, and always kept to themselves.

As the agents worked to devise a plan to lure Bulger from his apartment, they sought the help of Bond, who was initially hesitant to have any part of it. The agents wanted the keys to #303 and planned a forced entry with a SWAT team, but as they weighed the options, they decided that it would be best to take Bulger alone, outside the apartment, to ensure that Catherine wouldn't be harmed. The agents had already set up a series of surveillance posts, and they were closing in fast on the fugitives. On the door of the apartment, Catherine frequently posted a note that read in all caps:

PLEASE DO NOT KNOCK ON THIS DOOR AT THIS TIME.
THANK YOU

FBI agents, U.S. Marshals, Santa Monica Police and Los Angeles police SWAT teams lured Bulger into the basement garage area where Bulger, unarmed, surrendered after being a fugitive for 16 years.

Bond explained that "Carol" had been telling everyone that Charlie had heart and other health problems, and that he slept during the day and asked not to be disturbed. The agents set up in a room at the Embassy that had a good view of the balcony of #303. Entering from the rear alley, Garriola followed Bond to his apartment, which shared a wall next door to the Gasko's in #304. In fact, Bond's living room shared a common wall with the couple's bedroom.

Once inside the apartment, Garriola had Bond quietly draw a detailed diagram of the apartment layout. It was during this planning that they devised a clever ruse to lure Bulger into the basement garage area. As part of the plan, Bond would call Charlie Gasko and explain that their locker had been burglarized. After careful review of the plan, Bond went to his office at the Embassy and awaited the cue from the FBI agents. When the agent gave Bond the go ahead, he called the Gasko's phone and let it ring several times, but there was no answer. The agent asked if he'd be willing to go over and knock on the door and lure them in person, but then the office phone rang and it was Carol. Bond explained that their storage locker had been broken into, and he offered that he could either call the police, or "Charlie" could meet him in the garage to examine the damage and survey for missing property. They talked it over and then she said that Charlie would meet him in the garage area in about five minutes. Bond later recalled:

> "I went down into the courtyard of the Embassy and as I was standing there across the street, I notice Carol come out onto her balcony. She looked over at me and then looked down towards the garage and then back at me...I could see that she looked worried...And she looked back in and then I got a call from the agent, and he said we got him..."

As Bulger emerged from the garage elevator, he was surrounded by FBI agents, U.S. Marshals and a Los Angeles police SWAT team. After a brief stand-off with Bulger refusing to comply with the directive to get down on cement with fresh oil stains, he was taken into custody by Garriola. The agent later stated that Bulger's demeanor changed when the agent asked if he needed to call a SWAT team to get Greig out of the apartment. He said Bulger offered to tell her to surrender and didn't want her to be harmed. Greig was arrested without incident and Bulger was charged with "murder, conspiracy to commit murder, extortion, narcotics distribution and money laundering." Agents found "more than $800,000 in cash, thirty firearms and fake IDs" at the apartment. Bulger was arraigned in federal court on July 6, 2011. He pled not guilty to forty-eight charges, including nineteen counts of murder, extortion, money

The apartment garage area where Bulger was surrounded and arrested.

laundering, obstruction of justice, perjury, narcotics distribution and weapons violations.

Garriola remembered about the arrest in the garage of the Princess Eugenia. "We just rushed him...I gave the words 'FBI—GET YOUR HANDS UP!' and they went up right away...At that moment, we told him to get down on his knees, and he gave us [laughing], 'I'm not getting down on my fucking knees...' Wearing white and seeing the oil on the ground, I guess he didn't want to get his pants dirty in the oil. I asked him to identify himself and that didn't go over very well...He asked me to identify my fuckin' self, which I did...And then I asked him, are you Whitey Bulger? He said yes...then Janice Goodwin, who lived just down the hall in apartment #309, attempted to intervene. She was coming down to do her laundry. She said 'Excuse me; I think I can help you, this man has dementia. If he's acting oddly, that could be why...' Oh my God, I just arrested an 81-year-old man who thinks he's Whitey Bulger. What is he going to tell me next? He's Elvis? 'Do me a favor, this woman over here says you have a touch of Alzheimer's...' "Don't listen to her, she's fucking nuts...I'm James Bulger." As he signed the consent form to search the apartment, he said, "That's the first time I signed that name in a long time." When I asked him, "Hey Whitey, aren't you relieved that you don't have to look over your shoulder anymore? He just looked and me and said, "Are you fucking nuts?" Bond recalled seeing Bulger handcuffed as he left the building:

> I went back to my apartment to change my clothes and then as I was leaving, I walked past the garage and outside there was police vehicles and Suburbans from the FBI everywhere. I looked over and there was Charlie handcuffed and surrounded by agents. He looked like he was relieved...He looked like he was laughing and telling stories to the agents. I glanced over and noticed Carol who also handcuffed and standing next to an agent. She looked at me and said, "Hi Josh..." I couldn't speak...I just waved at her...

Bulger indicated that the story provided by Special Agent Garriola was not entirely accurate. He remembered the events:

> I remember almost every word that was said in the garage that day. Some were omitted by the FBI on purpose. On that last morning, my neighbor Josh was asked by the FBI to call my apartment and to say that someone broke into my locker in the basement garage.
>
> When I entered the elevator, I kind of hesitated...I stood there for a minute after the doors closed and stared at the button. It's odd today to think about it, but my memory of those very last moments was standing in the elevator and looking intently at the worn buttons on the panel. I gathered my thoughts but was thinking I didn't want the cops called or have this turn into anything big. My plan was to just say it was no big deal, they didn't get away with anything and that I just used it for junk storage. I have that memory of reaching over and pressing the button and then the slow descent until the elevator finally stopped and the doors opened into the garage.
>
> When I got off the elevator and started to walk around a parked car, I could see my locker. I noticed that the door was hanging off. I knew something wasn't right...What first caught my eye was that I saw a few pieces of colored tape on the cement as if to mark positions like on a stage. There was a stillness that just seemed off. Hard to describe in words, but my instinct told me something was off. As I started walking toward my locker, a light was shined on me and quite a few men in full

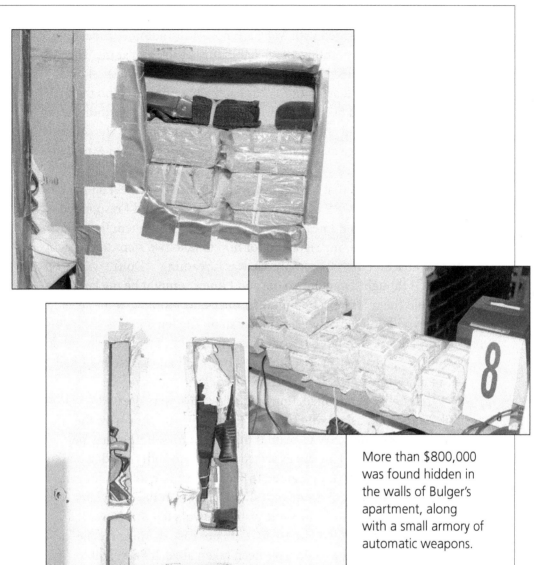

More than $800,000 was found hidden in the walls of Bulger's apartment, along with a small armory of automatic weapons.

combat gear and armed with M4 Carbines—fully automatic machine guns and a couple pointing Glock handguns—took aim at me. The agent in charge yelled "Who are you?" He quoted me as responding back "Who the fuck are you?" What I actually said was "Who the fuck are you, Homeland Security?" He said, "We're the FBI!" He didn't want to repeat what I said about Homeland Security. I felt I was the calmest person in the garage at that moment. Things were so tense I expected they may kill me...

They demanded that I kneel down and I refused to kneel on the oily garage floor. They were screaming "We will shoot!" and I responded "Go ahead...I'm not kneeling down in the oil." I told them that there was a clean place to my right and for him to take two steps to the right to that area and then I'd comply. He was screaming" "Don't try it or I'll shoot!" I thought I'm going to die and I knew it might be my last step, but I told them "Here is step number one," and I took it, and I debated with myself; do I dare chance another step? The tension was rising, but I said, "Fuck it." I'm not backing down and I said, "Here's step number two." They screamed, "Don't or we'll shoot!!!" I had that feeling I had as a kid waiting to feel the bullet in my back...

While being handcuffed, I noticed a few guys were dressed differently and I asked who they were and they said they were the Los Angeles County SWAT team. I thought to myself, this may be why I am still alive. I always expected the Feds to shoot me down as they had others who they wanted to silence, just like John Dillinger. Melvin Purvis, the FBI agent who shot Dillinger in the head, later committed suicide with the same pistol. I always felt that it was his own conscience that led him to do it. It's not easy to kill someone in cold blood when they could have been taken alive. It's a weight he carried until the end.

From the Los Angeles jail we were transported by van. I was real sick by the time I got to the airport and vomited the minute I stepped out of the van. I was in serious pain because of how I was cuffed up. We flew to Boston in a real modern and luxurious private Gulfstream jet. Catherine was placed up front with a couple of Marshals, and me to the rear with armed Marshals and federal agents.

They tried to get answers. They asked things like where did you get all the guns? I answered, none of your business. I am for the Second Amendment and feel all people should have the right to own guns to defend themselves. Especially the elderly. If someone comes into their house that's not welcome, they should be armed and shoot the bastard.

Not have their bodies lying there in a crime scene for some cop to write his report and who only reacts after the fact, etc. I also told them I feel that every retired senior citizen should have a hobby so that they may live longer...My hobby was guns. I had a huge stack of cash that had lasted sixteen years and had $817,000 and 14 cents that the government seized. For the record, I didn't complain, and I had suggested to release it to the victims. I hadn't realized they would confiscate the home that Catherine owned, left to her by her parents, and feel that was a great injustice. I could have held up the distribution of those funds, but the victims' families had suffered enough. They never

James "Whitey" Bulger's mugshot taken in Los Angeles on June 22, 2011.

knew the truth and I didn't want to add to their pain. Prior to this, the government had confiscated millions from my bank accounts and safe deposit boxes. There was money from accounts in London, Paris, Dublin, and safe deposit boxes with cash.

The agents asked, or rather I told them, and repeated five times, "Your boss, John Morris, supervisor of the Boston Organized Crime Squad, was my paid FBI informant. I bought information. I didn't give information and never was responsible for putting a single person in prison. This included my enemies. Your boss tried to get me murdered using the term ‹killed by a Machiavellian plot,' clever, was a good try." I figured it out when I went on the run and called him in his FBI office and told him "I knew it was you who put that story out that I was an FBI informant to get me killed"—his answer was "I'm sorry, I made a mistake." Not "I didn't or it wasn't me"—"I told you motherfucker if I knew that back then I'd have blown your fucking head off. You figured you'd have me killed to silence me, but if I go down, you're coming down with me." I was screaming into the phone in a complete rage. He later claimed that he suffered a major heart attack after that call and was hospitalized. It's hard for me to look back and think for years that I paid Morris. He ruins my reputation, tries to get me killed and I protect him by keeping my mouth shut. He then turns on his own for an immunity deal; he frames and testifies against John Connelly who is now serving a forty-year sentence for murder. I've always known that a fair trial is out of the question. The Feds have lots of witnesses against me who were given deals to hang me. They are embarrassed about the corruption of their star agents being on my payroll. I'm guilty of many serious crimes, but not all. After we landed in the private jet at Logan Airport in Boston, there was a mass of federal agents with bullet proof vests and automatic weapons waiting to greet us. After we landed and headed for booking in Boston, things from here became somewhat of a blur.

I don't feel like the guy that they say killed so many people, robbed so many banks, was involved in extortion, gang wars, and arson, or who survived shootings, or was shot at so many times from about fourteen years old on. I can remember each time I ran and kept thinking they would get me in the back. Gunfire sounds different, and you feel really vulnerable when you're a kid and running with nothing to shoot back with. I had that very same feeling in Santa Monica when I was captured in the garage. All the Feds; the Los Angeles SWAT team with machine guns, rifles, and a couple of Glock handguns drawn on me. How did I ever drift into this lane? It's as if I ended up in the wrong story.

Bulger at Logan Airport under the heavy guard of U.S. Marshals while being transferred to the federal courthouse in Boston.

When we went on the lam, Catherine asked me to please not hurt anyone. I kept that promise. I kept that promise to her because of the fear that if I shot anyone she could and would be prosecuted. I felt protective and would give my life for her. Catherine kept me from violent acts of revenge. I offered to plead guilty to all charges in exchange for her freedom, but it was rejected.

Sadly, the months of degrading strip searches and special treatment kind of wiped out the Santa Monica years. Now I'm completely isolated with a guard sitting outside my cell on constant watch. Special iron plates were welded to the front section. There's a camera on me at all times. No contact; no one can talk to me; I can't talk to anyone; shackles and cuffs whenever I leave my cell; months of no fresh air or sunlight, cold food, the temperature is kept at freezing... All of the things I call psychological torture used in prisoner of war camps to break men down and make them confess...tactics taught in regimens in Central and South America by our CIA, which is documented. They've brought me back to hate and anger. If I end up in hell, at least I'll thaw out from this fucking refrigerator.

THE BOOKS, THE MOVIES, THE LIES

fter the indictment and Bulger miraculously vanishing into thin air to evade authorities, he would inspire several books and movies. The saga of Bulger's adventurous criminal exploits morphed into legend. As one example, Martin Scorsese's cinematic masterpiece, *The Departed*, won an Academy Award for Best Picture and featured an elite Hollywood all-star cast that included Jack Nicholson, Leonardo DiCaprio, Matt Damon and Mark Wahlberg. Scorsese later explained the factors that help frame the essence of the characters and acknowledged Bulger's influence:

> In no way do we say that Francis Costello, played by Jack Nicholson, is directly patterned after Whitey Bulger, but let me put it this way, we

Each day during his trial, Bulger was transported by a motorcade of U.S. Marshals that included armored vehicles to and from the jail facility. Spectators lined the streets hopeful to catch a glimpse of the Boston crime mogul.

felt comfortable in the character; we felt comfortable in the situation, because we knew it to be true. We take that as a touchstone so to speak. In *The Departed*, Jack's character controls everything. He has the power of life and death over everybody around him, Leo, Matt, Queenan [the head of the police team trying to bring Nicolson down, played by Martin Sheen].

I was around a very powerful man growing up—a boss in the underworld in the old neighborhood in the fifties and sixties. At that point everything was changing in the world. I saw the effect this had on him when he started to fall apart. The first people he killed were his closest friends. They buried the bodies in a restaurant. People would come to my father to talk about it. They didn't know what to do... The fear was palpable. My father's younger brother, Joe—the one who "went wrong"—worked for this guy. I recall vividly him rushing into our apartment on a Sunday morning, out of breath, saying "I just almost got killed. He pulled a gun on me..." Then my father had to go and deal with certain people my uncle had been ostracized by.

My father always warned me, "Don't ever, ever, let them do a favor for you, because you'll never be able to pay it back. Stay away... Just smile, say hello, be respectful..." He was stuck in that world. He was oppressed by it. But he was apparently a person liked and listened to. My uncle, by the way, lived, but the boss was killed. Apparently, the police took the body out of the funeral parlor to determine the cause of his death. It wasn't natural.

That boss had been very nice to me. I was close friends with his nephew. I would play around his house all the time. But when he turned bad, so to speak, the people around him went down fast. Ultimately, he was taken down by his own people. All that went into Jack's character. That was a center point in *The Departed*. Who was really culpable in this relationship? The FBI or the Gangster? It all blends together... It's all gray... This is also what made Bulger interesting as a criminal.

In Bulger's Words:

I just have to accept this part of my life will not be easy. Much has been written about me, the movies, inspiration of fictional characters; so much, that I could never defend myself. My problem is that I'd have to explain the lies told by past accomplices; two got freedom for their cooperation. It means I'd have to prove them as liars and, in the process, guilty of murder. I'm sick over the thought of having to defend myself against these lies but lies unanswered become the truth. I've offered to plead guilty to crimes I'm innocent of if they would let my Catherine free. I swear I never killed any women and never gave any info of any substance to the FBI. I bought info, not sold it... The boss supervisor of the FBI was my paid informant. Not the other way around.

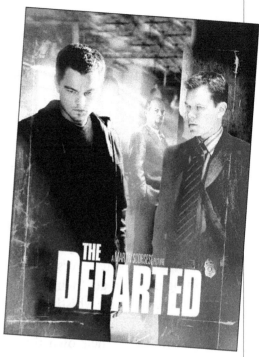

Since I was on the run, the books flowed, lies and more lies. These stories are full of part truth, mistruth and outright lies. If I were free to move about, no one would dare to fabricate this yarn. The books, news features, and everything else under the sun is inventive fiction. Even those that claim they cross checked against direct sources don't seem at all too interested in writing a balanced or accurate account of my life. I learned the hard way that dealing with journalists is like dancing with Dobermans. You don't know if they will lick your face or rip your throat out. What a nerve some of these reporters have writing after targeting me for so many years and not having any interest in the truth. They feel safe now that I'm caged. If they could interview me in this cell without shackles and a tether, I'd welcome it... then we are on equal terms. I could write pages about the flagrant errors. Even the basics reconstructed from the official records are flawed. As an example, I was never in a reformatory—wrong sequence of Air Force Bases—never stationed in Idaho—from Kansas transferred to Barksdale Field SAC in Shreveport Louisiana. In my life, I saw my father only drinking twice, my mother never did peoples' laundry and no twin sisters! The list of inaccuracies is voluminous even before delving into the criminal elements. Although I *was* a criminal, I was never as notorious as portrayed by the media. I was involved in twenty armed bank robberies, but I never fired a single shot in the bank, never hurt anyone and always grabbed the money and made a fast exit. Never like I was portrayed in books and movies, storming into banks with automatic weapons and firing into the air... never happened even once.

Looking back, I think Alcatraz was pretty good. Today the conditions here are dreary and depressing. It's much tougher that what I remember looking back at Alcatraz. Whenever I'm moved, they tightly secure leg irons around my ankles causing them to swell. Each step is so painful that it finally becomes too painful to even walk. My hands must be handcuffed behind my back. When my lawyer visits, I'm handcuffed in the front with leg irons and a tether. A strap goes from the cuffs to the leg irons. It's easier when I'm cuffed in the front as I can pull up the leg iron chains using the tether, reducing the weight on my leg irons. It makes it easier for me to walk. I've been told I will never leave this cell...I doubt I'll ever see television or a movie ever again. I expect that I will at least be here for years. So, if that means no television or movies, so be it. I've been stripped of everything except a pen and paper. My time now is spent writing family and a few friends. There's no dignity or pride in prisons today. At Alcatraz, you never had to worry about men reaching in and stealing personal items off your bed. You didn't have to hide anything or keep things out of reach. Now it's a complete reversal. You have these low life junkies, and they'll steal anything they can get their hands on. Once you had only a few low lives, weirdos and ass-kissing whistle blowers, now they are the majority, and all have one thing in common—drugs. The minority are the old timers and non-users just trying to do their own time quietly. The noise is the most insufferable. This place is populated by the lowest of the low. There's screaming, hollering, laughing at the television or sports games, and they slam dominoes down on the tables all day long. Had I known this is what it would be like, I would have gotten a job and stayed out of trouble.

A lot of these guys are happy and right at home in this environment. It's more like a mental institution. The mess hall here is chaos and I dread going there. No structure. It's just a bunch of yelling and you can't talk with the others at the table because it's so loud. I'll take the old system of bread and water diets; regular meals every third day, sitting on cold hard concrete in silence. That was easier time. I wish the Rock was still open and I could do my time there. You can't think straight with all the noises here. At my age, I can't really take advantage of the recreation yard that often. Most days are too hot and the heat is dangerous. There's no shade or anywhere to escape the heat.

> My cell is always kept freezing cold. I'm bundled up—thermal underwear, t-shirt, sweatshirt, orange jumper and turban made from long sleeve thermal underwear, pants, socks and sneakers, and I'm still freezing. This pod system is unlike the tier system of open front barred cells of Alcatraz. My cell is freezing cold and my writing pen doesn't function too well. Last night I quit trying to write. Tonight, I put two pens in a cup of hot water...So far so good. These pens are just thin ink inserts that look like they were made to go inside a

Bulger has inspired a series of major motion pictures and documentaries, including The Departed and Black Mass, which were both loosely based on Bulger. The Departed won four Academy Awards including Best Picture and Best Director for Martin Scorsese in 2007.

solid pen. These are considered safe and can't be used as a weapon for suicide. The rules here are nothing like Alcatraz. No nail clippers or razors and I'm only allowed to purchase one emery board per month. Haircuts are do it yourself using a community pair of clippers shared by over a hundred guys. It's filthy. My cell is the "outside cell." Concrete walls are cold. They installed a surveillance camera in my cell that monitors my every move. I guess extra security for one of their highest profile prisoners. They lag-bolted and welded with the help of a hoist device twenty large heavy thick sheets of steel to cover the outside of my cell, and also the interior walls for added security. It's all the media hype that creates this "Myth of Whitey!" The noise here is driving me crazy. I lie in bed and then hear a loud scream and realize it's me. What I fear the most is losing my sanity. The recycled air, pod type cells, food, etc., makes me look back at Alcatraz with nostalgia. The air in the cellblock at Alcatraz was pure, and sea air is best for me. I love the ocean salt air—the water is calming. That is why I settled in Santa Monica for fifteen years... This is what it's to be for years of trial—nineteen murders—extortion—sub-machine guns—silencers—and bribery of police and FBI and more charges to come. Two states have submitted paperwork for execution (Florida and Oklahoma). One is known as "Old Sparky" and "Ride the Thunderbolt," and the other is called the "Horizontal Crucifixion," death by needle. Me being a traditionalist, I favor "Ride the Thunderbolt" as being the best way to travel.

The one who sunk the lowest and really hurt me was Kevin Weeks. Honor has become a foreign word in this age, and I think discussing him is pointless. I will only go on record to say that we were close and I considered him my best friend. His father was a real nice guy who endured a hard life. After suffering a stroke and feeling like he was about to cash in, he pleads to me to look out for Kevin. I give him my word, tell him I'd watch over him, and I kept that promise. I protected him and a few years after I fled Boston, I hear the news that Kevin's been indicted and arrested. I explained to Catherine that I'm old and maybe it was time to lay down my cards and negotiate a surrender. I'd agree to plead guilty to all charges and take the death penalty in return for her and Kevin's freedom. I love Catherine and would sacrifice everything for her. She was crying and it took a lot to calm her. Within days, I see Kevin on television pointing out different spots (supposed crime scenes and burial locations of victims) to the FBI. This was all on television! He joins the choir and points everything back at me. I couldn't believe it.

Not many years later, he's out of prison, writes a book that he dedicates to prosecutor Fred Wyshak and members of the State Police. What a fucking joke...Now he's a celebrity doing book tours and college lectures telling students things like "After we killed someone we would go out and have a big meal." He cashed in on all these lies. I still can't get over that Kevin sunk as low as he did. He knows the truth and has to live with himself. That chapter is closed—I seek no revenge and would do nothing to change the deals they made. It would require me to testify—never have and never will. Honor still means something to me. This has been a complex trial and a set up—the Titanic was sinking and these passengers had dangled in front of them escape from certain death—the price for a seat in a lifeboat is way too steep for me.

As I mentioned, John Morris, the Supervisor of the Organized Crime Squad in Boston (John Connolly's boss) was on my payroll. The government wouldn't accept my offer for a plea deal because they are desperate to get even with the person who corrupted one of the top men in the FBI. Morris pled guilty, but he was not punished (part of his plea deal) and during the trial he admitted, after much prodding, that he took money from a criminal racketeer they called Mr. "X" to protect his identity. He has since passed away, but he was a bookmaker that paid us and the Mafia "rent" money, a term we used for taking a percentage of the profit in these types of rackets. I have all of the transcripts from that trial here in my cell. Morris required fourteen debriefings before he finally admitted to receiving money from him. He was such a fucking liar. Mr. X was also given immunity from prosecution for his testimony. They protected his identity, and again, no punishment or penalty because of Morris cooperating to prosecute John Connelly, his fellow agent, who is now serving a life sentence and is accused of receiving $250,000 from me. I paid John Connelly and his boss John Morris for information on cases that were being worked by the FBI that were related to our dealings, and for the names of anyone leaking information to the Feds, on us or any of our friends. Morris became the head of the Los Angeles FBI office when I went on the run. He gave a part-truth confession and was given one year probation. He'd already transferred out of Boston by the time all this came to light. Paperwork that was completely unknown to me was put in by Morris to enhance my image and value as if I was a good source. Allegedly this was done to protect me from being targeted. Again, this was all unknown to me and was done to ensure that "Santa Claus" stays free and keeps the presents flowing.

I tried to sabotage the FBI operation that was intended to destroy the Italian Mafia with illegal wire taps and bugs in their offices. So here is the most important point. This is the one thing that no one seems to really understand and needs to be in bold print. My motives were selfish—if the Italian Mafia went down, my friends and I would be the only organized group in Boston and would be the number one target of the FBI. That is the truth. I think the Italian Mafia would have played it the same way.

The Mafia are dangerous people and the FBI played both sides as pawns, figuring it was a win for them, regardless of who and what organization fell. They put it out there that we were hit men for the Mafia and that we rubbed out an Italian gang for them. The Feds placed a bug in their headquarters and heard plenty, including Larry the Consigliere plainly saying, "We get Whitey & Stevie, they will kill anyone; they will crash the door in and kill them." They wanted to kill a guy who owned a trucking company and another guy who was mad and revengeful over his brother's murder. This is all on tape and I'm quoting them here. I tried hard to sabotage the wiretap because if they were wiped out, the focus by the Feds would be on us. I tipped off an insider to quietly get word to them that they were being surveilled by the Feds, but the guy I tipped off and trusted, secretly wanted them to go down and didn't pass it along. He kept a good distance and watched his every word when he was close to the areas being recorded. It was ironic that he survived, only to later die of throat cancer.

So, all the rumors that we were working to take out the Italians is bullshit. I never passed along anything of any substance whatsoever and behind the scenes worked to protect them for my own advantage. Later I learned that the special agent in charge of the Boston FBI during the 1970's and 80's, Lawrence Sarhatt, was starting to figure out that I wasn't acting in any genuine role as an informant and he later wrote a memo that I should be subjected to an investigation. I agreed to meet with him in secret at a hotel on the grounds of the Logan Airport, but I didn't reveal anything to him, and it illustrates the depth of deception by the Feds. I was always careful and knew I was being watched by various agencies. Back in the day, I knew my phone was tapped and was the target of every police agency and the IRS. I always paid cash so there was no paper trail, but I also paid about $90,000 a year in taxes, and an extra $20,000 for unearned income. This would give me a cushion to fall on for whatever they uncovered, but I never had any problems with the IRS and didn't give them an opportunity to make me an easy target.

I was always aware of the wiretapping and surveillance efforts by the Feds. I kept a low profile and unless I called the location, I expected the Feds were listening in and there would be efforts to lure me into a trap. I also had suspicions of others who might have been working with state and federal agents. I didn't trust anyone outside my circle and it was a dangerous and complex world we lived in. Case in point, we were killers for the Boston Mafia. They had a problem with a gang member who killed one of the Mafia's friends, and we buried him. We were told in no uncertain terms they had planned to wipe out the local Boston Mafia and take over. So, enter the Winter Hill Gang. We in time wipe out this renegade gang—many were killed and wounded and the two brothers who were the bosses, they were both eliminated. The gang (us) have problems with the law and one guy goes to prison and another on the run for fourteen years.

We move off Winter Hill and into a garage in Boston's North End on Lancaster Street. We have paid sources rooted deep in the FBI, State and Boston Police force. I soon get word that State Police has big plans to trap us and bug the garage with wire taps. They've also set up film surveillance from across the street and they're watching everyone who enters and exits. They film all of the Mafia bosses and soldiers coming and going, and film us talking. Larry Zannino, (aka

Larry Baione the Consigliere of the Boston Mafia and the second highest-ranking figure in the Boston faction of the Patriarca family) is on film more than once. I've known him since the 1940's, and he's a very volatile and dangerous person who's killed many people through the years. Larry was half Italian and half Syrian. I knew him for years back when he was the driver for the Boss of the Mafia. Back then, Larry was a sharp dresser and ran a club on the edge of Boston's China Town. I respected the Italians. They were powerful, smart, and protective of their people and neighborhoods. This particular day, we are in the office, Larry (along with his driver, who is a big drug dealer and someone I knew in prison), asks me to kill a guy named Angelo Patrizzi who's supposed to be hiding out in my neighborhood. I tell him okay... He also says to me, "If you're going to kill any Italians in the future, it needs to be cleared with me," as if he was my boss. I ask him, "Who clears it with me if you are going to kill any Irishmen?" That kind of put him off balance and he replies, "Oh come on Whitey; we're pals here." He tried to lessen the seriousness of it and changed the subject but didn't answer my question. Later I mentioned it to my partner, who is Italian. I told him what Larry had said and ended it with, "Well, in the future, *after* we kill any Italians we will clear it with him," and we laughed about it. I never forgot this. Larry was loose lipped. I later learn that this whole conversation was caught on tape by the agents doing surveillance and the whole conversation is recounted back to me and is now making its rounds! At one point, on orders from New York, Larry orders us to kill some Jewish guy who is right in their midst. I tell Steve, fuck him; let them handle it. This one episode is recorded by the Feds and the guy survives as a result of the tapes. Later, they get Larry on tape saying, "Whitey and Stevie will kill anyone on orders, etc., etc..." On another tape he's telling another member that "Whitey's with us a thousand percent..." I never once discussed business this way and was never captured on tape. Later, Larry finds out and is cursing Jeremiah O'Sullivan, head of the New England Organized Crime Strike Force, and is again caught on tape threatening him saying, "We're not going to sit back and take this from that Irish motherfucker."

Larry had ordered the bombing of a lawyer who was representing Joe Barboza, who had turned against the Mafia for killing two of his guys. Barboza was isolated in prison with a $100,000 bail amount set. Despite this, he's still connected and sends out men to collect money from other Mafia figures. He expects the Mafia to bail him out, but to them, he's now nothing more than a liability and of no value. Barboza sends his men to various night spots, including Larry's club, to collect. They collect $65,000 in cash, a charity really, so Larry and his crew shoot the two guys, take their cash, and put their bodies in a car and park it in my neighborhood. Next, he orders the bombing of the lawyer's car, but he survives despite losing his leg. Barboza frames four in the Mafia that he doesn't like and they each do thirty-two years in prison. The government later pays $111 million in a settlement for false imprisonment. The US Attorney O'Sullivan took part in the framing and keeping them in prison. Larry is recorded discussing the fate of O'Sullivan and I don't find much of this out until later when I'm back in prison. Another FBI Agent Paul Rico helped frame these men and he's later convicted of a murder and dies in prison. There was a lot of corruption and blurred lines.

I know it will be hard for some to believe or understand, but I also used my influence for good cause. In one case, it was how the deal with the FBI was set. As an example, there was a priest in my neighborhood who got in touch and asked me for a favor, and I said sure. Usually, he would ask me to offer some type of aid to some elderly person in my neighborhood, help a poor family or donate funds to the homeless. He's a nice old guy and I was happy to help... He tells me someone is living in fear of being killed and wants me to meet him and see if I can help solve his problem. The priest tells me, "He's a decent family man, etc., but is facing serious trouble." I was asked to meet him on a bench in the Boston Public Garden by Charles Street and Beacon. "He'll be in a blue suit and tie, holding a leather briefcase in his lap and will be alone." I met this person who had the same last name as my best friend who was murdered in front of his house as his wife and six kids watched it through an upstairs window.

Turns out it is United States Attorney Jeremiah O'Sullivan. I sat next to him and we introduced ourselves to each other. I was armed and had on a dark blue jogging suit. I went alone because I was told this was top-secret. I didn't mention it to anyone but was ready for anything. A strange request and meeting downtown instead of my neighborhood. We talked at length. He was really scared. He told me of the tapes, and that he's being discussed by Larry, who everyone knew was dangerous and had ordered the killing of Barboza's lawyer and the Mafia's hatred of him. I listened and told him I can't understand why you want to talk with me—you have the full weight of the government behind you. He explained yes, they will assign five people to protect me; then it will be four; then two; then one; then weekends. The Mafia has a long memory, extraordinary patience and will wait, then strike. We talked about judges being killed, Dutch Schultz and how the Mafia ordered these killings. He then tells me the Feds know more about me than I suspected; how they're tracing my every move, and how the Mafia will soon order the hit. He feels I will be the one asked to rub him out and that is why he reached out and is appealing to me as one Irishman to another for help, and with my ties to the Irish Gang in New York with Tom Devaney, etc. I thought back to Larry's attitude towards the Irish and found myself saying, well here's one for the Irish! I told him here's the condition...I'm no spy...I'll not report back to you, ask advice or your permission. It's a one-time affair, a favor for the priest and only involves me keeping you alive. My

United States Attorney Jeremiah O'Sullivan.

call on methods and actions. I'm in your corner and you'll be under my umbrella. I'll try to settle this without violence, but if it gets to a critical point, I'll short circuit the whole thing and you'll have nothing to worry about and there's no debt. Issue handled. I knew if Larry was behind this, he would want to see me one-on-one. Because especially of the need for absolute secrecy, he would only discuss it face to face and with no one else present—that would be convenient to say the least. Confusion would reign, believe me, and people would be looking at one another. Not complicated and very simple to put together. We parted as friends and he felt real good to fight "fire with fire." I reassured him that that he was under my protection now and he could feel assured that I'd take care of him for as long as I was around. I told him there was no need to talk again, but his welfare was safeguarded from now on. He died years later of natural causes. I didn't find out that he'd passed away until I was captured. I had never told anyone of this in the criminal world back then. Larry and I stayed on reasonable terms and had many talks during those years. We always discussed the blowback on rash acts and I always used balance and measure in how I approached issues.

Larry could be turned around and we could reason with each other. As an example, he once asked me to kill Hobart Willis, a person I liked. I let Larry blow off some steam and he explained why Willis had to go. Then I said, I have a good idea. Why don't I turn this into money for you? I'll get him to pay you $50,000, he lives and doesn't cause you problems in the future. Larry agrees, but also said if I give him my word it holds. He agrees and two days later he has $50,000 in hand and no more problems from Hobart. He lives for many years and dies of natural causes while I'm on the run. My lawyers later requested files from O'Sullivan's office regarding our conversation and agreement. They told us, "No record" and the federal judge forbids them to discuss it further and bans it from the trial. My attorneys did a masterful job calling out O'Sullivan. The truth was that I met secretly with Jerry. He was convinced that he'd been targeted for murder and he needed my help. I agreed to offer him my protection. He assured me that he'd always be in my corner and not to worry; I'd never need to be concerned about prosecution for any federal crimes and he'd always protect me in that regard. It was a handshake arrangement that we'd protect one another. It had absolutely nothing to do with being a so-called informant. Again, I provided nothing. My deal was an exchange of protection, not selling out friends or adversaries.

Another example of falsities and the biased media coloring a story was with Stephen 'Stippo' Rakes, the original owner of Columbia Wine and Spirits. This was the liquor store that he and the media say I forced him out of. We were stand-up men, and we never would have marched in and strong-armed honest and hardworking people out of their business. It's sickening how all this was portrayed. The true story is not at all complicated. His sister says to Kevin Weeks, "If you're interested, my brother wants to sell his store." We responded and met him at his house. His wife was in the kitchen and his children were in and out of the room we were in (Steve Flemmi, Kevin, Stippo and I). We bought the store. No haggling. We took him at his word. Paid him $75,000— cash in paper bag—he explained he wanted little bills here and there for the outstanding amount. I told him no problem we'll take good care of him. Well, he gives his wife $65,000 and says that's what he sold the store for ($10,000 hidden). We find all of the expensive booze gone, no cash in store—bills not up to date—owes everyone—some guy comes in and tells us you still owe more than $20,000 for the building and walk-in refrigerator. I tell him okay, we'll pay the regular bills and pay every bill as they keep coming. No problem really. I want the store as an office for my business, etc. Stippo's father and mother live around the corner in a nice little house (Jenkins Street), the father a nice guy, hangs around the store (retired elderly), always involved in neighborhood events. The mother is quiet and has had a life of problems with her children! Stippo appears to be a quiet person, but we know better.

Stippo also had a store in the building before the liquor store. He lit it on fire for an insurance scam, and an elderly woman died in the fire. No prosecution. After we buy the store, Stippo buys a three-story tower house, moves it from one street to a vacant lot on 9th street, converts it into three condos (big money in South Boston for condos), he sells the three of them later. Later he gets his mother to help him— he has a business deal in the works but needs collateral to show the bank, etc. Finally, he wears her down and she signs her house over to him. He takes a mortgage loan on "his" house and in a few months' time, hands her the payment book and tells her he's broke! Stippo's brother is a fugitive for a murder charge. This is one of many examples of how the media twisted the truth without seeking the facts.

South Boston Liquor Mart.

So many of these guys are liars and embellishing stories to profit, and a couple of them lied their way right to their grave. One guy I barely knew, only from him coming into my liquor store, writes a book that he was an enforcer with the Irish Mafia as part of my crew. This book comes out and there's all these claims that he's in my gang and how we would walk around Castle Island together plotting. He claimed that I'd give him a big envelope with a picture of the target, car, plate number, their habits, etc., and he would beat these individuals within an inch of death. I barely knew who he even was. My memory of him was that he robbed an elderly woman and took a collection of Hummel ceramic figurines that she treasured. Word got to me that she was devastated, so I sought out who was responsible and set him straight. I grabbed him by the arm and made it painfully clear that he if robbed anyone again in South Boston, I'd kill him. When he would see me, he'd tremble. He was a complete coward, not an enforcer.

Lies sell and bottom line, I was off the scene and that made me an easy target. I had to consider Catherine and couldn't set the record straight or settle the score. It was no secret that I walked and handled business on Castle Island and I was photographed there frequently. I was under constant surveillance. Whenever we took walks along the trails, anyone in my company would be photographed, their license plates run by the Feds, and they'd attempt to conduct intelligence on our activities. The FBI, Boston Police, State Police, DEA and the FBI Taskforce all watched every move. It was also here that I conducted my business with the FBI. Castle Island was located on the coastal edge of Boston. It had benches, two war memorials, and a huge fortress surrounded by grass and water on the Boston Harbor. It was my favorite place in Boston, and I went there and sat for a few hours every day to handle business matters.

I never tolerated crimes against the elderly and the hardworking people in my neighborhood trying to make an honest living. I'd keep folded $100 bills and pass them when I'd shake hands. I'd tell them to buy their pet (I always knew their names) a nice meal on me. Some I'd give two bills if I knew they were struggling. I know it helped them. I can remember one woman was poor and had rescued two greyhounds that they were about to put down. She had kids and little means to support her family. She was a good-hearted woman and there were many like her in my neighborhood. So many elderly struggled in my town.

For years I couldn't chance combating the lies, etc., but now it's my number one problem along with trying to free Catherine, who remains being held without bail and maliciously being subjected to isolation. Cruel revenge by an agency that in its haste opened itself to multi-million-dollar lawsuits. In the past, I was the last man tried, when all the others had already been tried and convicted. I was on the run and captured, and I agreed to plead guilty to participation in bank robberies. By pleading that way, guys already in prison could change their plea and I could always be called by the defense. But it didn't happen, and they got less time than me. Being the last man standing is not so good at times. He usually gets the extra heat, as evidenced by me.

I would take a lie detector test if they would be willing to do the same regarding the truthfulness of what they wrote in their books. Use of a lie detector would prove the truth, that's exactly why it hasn't been used. Also, I will refuse to testify in court against them. I have no desire to send people back to prison, just prove them as liars. I want to firmly reiterate that I never killed a woman or child; I never caused a person to go to prison, and I never gave info. I bought it and can prove it. I traveled in dangerous waters with people who killed their best friends, killed out of boredom, or wanted to up their score. All I want is the truth to come out. I don't expect any breaks in life, nor will I sell out anyone for leniency or a deal. I'm doomed and there is no hope. None of this bothers me and I accept all that. In time, I feel the truth will all come out.

Back in my early prison days, if I had given up a name in Atlanta, it would have meant no Alcatraz and a positive parole in six years. They put on pressure, sent me to the hole in solitary and even made death threats. Still, that couldn't make me give anyone up, nor could systematic beatings in police stations, broken teeth, a fractured arm, a gun jammed down my throat and cocked by a drunken cop (McDonough, who was screaming that he would kill me after he fractured my arm by club) to make me give up a name.

AUTHOR'S NOTE: Stephen "Stippo" Rakes vehemently refuted Bulger's statement. In brief, he'd claimed that both Bulger and Weeks knocked on his door and strong armed him to take over the liquor store in 1984 by threatening to murder him if he didn't comply. He claimed it was never anything he'd agreed to willfully and was forced into the sale by the threat of death. During Bulger's trial in July of 2013, Rakes was found dead in Lincoln, Massachusetts. His death was ruled a homicide by poisoning.

THE END
OF THE TRAIL

I ALWAYS FEEL LIKE THAT SCULPTURE by James Earle Fraser. It's an Indian on horseback, weary and on a tired horse, named the "The End of the Trail." The horse and rider are bent forward, with a lance and bow. At the Santa Monica Pier, there was a Route 66 sign that read, "End of the Trail." Both of these images remained prominent in my mind. While we never looked over our shoulders and lived our lives day by day, that sign was always that reminder I carried like a ball and chain. I knew the truth sang in those words.

The story of my life is in extremes: to Europe on the Concorde flying at supersonic speeds, three hours and fifteen minutes from New York City or from Boston, to traveling cuffed and shackled on a prison bus. From eating in the finest restaurants and dining rooms in Paris, to eating cold food and every meal in this cold cell. I flew on the Concorde to Europe often. I never had to think twice about spending $18,000 for a roundtrip ticket.

Alcatraz is still a part of me and before going on the lam, I was able to visit and walk the old cellblocks and think back to all of the memories of life inside: the muffled sound of a passing seagull, the bell of the small buoy just off the Alcatraz shore, or the sound of a cell door racking, now by a park ranger rather than a prison guard.

At this point, I must face reality, this is the end of the trail, and it ends soon. In some cases, I'm guilty, in others, it's the guys who made deals. I was the last man standing when everyone else was arrested. They joined in the chorus of "Whitey's the Boss" and things like

"Whitey told me to do it." The bigger they make me, the bigger gangsters they make themselves to sell their books, movies, etc.

Most of my work over the course of my lifetime was that of a criminal. Came easy compared to legitimate work. As I've stated before, early on I packed in the idea that I'd ever be able to take on legit employment and faced the hard facts. I was a criminal and ultimately accepted this is my life. There's so much more to my life than what the press has fabricated. There are so many twists, turns, intrigue, double crosses, frame-ups, traps, assassination attempts against me, etc. That is the story left untold...

My time in prison was hard on my family. I struggled a lot with writing home. When I was on the Rock, I didn't want to embarrass my family with the prominent Alcatraz postmark. That postmark was a stigma. Everyone knew Alcatraz was designed to house the worst convicts and this would humiliate and place shame on my family. Coming from the South Boston housing projects, everyone knew, or had at least heard of me, including the mailman. It was a question of, do I write and try to make it easier on my parents with positive letters, or stay silent and suffer. I know they suffered. I've long felt immense guilt and especially for the pain I caused my mother. She placed blame on herself asking, "Where did I go wrong?" The lies of the media only made matters worse in the later years. A lie unchallenged becomes the truth. It is hard to challenge from the position I was in. All of the above is a bad dream. Looking back, I tried to come up with the answers of how I evolved into what I became, when the rest of my family is so different. I regret that my family became the target of the media. I played a rough game and accepted the rough treatment, but Catherine has been treated way too harshly. It's not justice when her only crime was being with me, and others who committed numerous murders served less time. I can't help but regret that our last day didn't end differently. If I had a crystal ball and saw this was to be Catherine's fate, I'd rather we died together in apartment #303. She lived a tough life and it's hard on her, considering she never hurt anyone in all her life, to be subjected to this treatment.

I consider myself a myth that has been created by the media and hungry reporters. These reporters would write stories that sounded like I had been tried and convicted of murder the way they reported some of the crimes. On a slow news day, blame "Whitey," and write anything that sells. I was a criminal, sure, but some of these crimes they pinned on me? I didn't rob the Isabella Stewart Gardner Museum in Boston and take those paintings. Good story for a slow news day. I think it's one of the faults of our society. What is seen as truth is painted by the media. The stories by the press made to be intriguing are often those that are mostly unimportant. Even the media-made stories of Alcatraz sometimes catch me off guard. Time marches on... It was always sobering, but also comical to see the old guys from Alcatraz show up on television. I saw Herbert "Lucky" Juelich (1190-AZ) in one of your books. He was talking about one of the early escape attempts. I knew him well and saw him on television when I was on the run; it kind of shocked me. On TV, he looked raggedy and like a little old homeless man. When I knew him, he was youthful and in good shape. He was a bit of an agitator and aggressive type in prison. The cellblocks at Atlanta were five tiers high and Lucky was terrified of heights. The guards knew this and tortured him by dragging him to his cell on the top tier. The more they taunted him the more aggressive he became. I didn't care for him at all. He was a cop killer and there wasn't anything about him that I saw as redeeming. I met Lucky's crime partner Lewis "Swede" Larson in Atlanta. The story was that the two of them were being transported to Atlanta Penitentiary by two Marshals to serve five years for a stolen car. Somewhere in Georgia they tried to make an escape, and, in the struggle, they were able to get one Marshal's pistol, shot one of them dead, and the other was taken as a hostage. A big chase ensured and led them deep into the woods. The hostage was in fear and figured he was next to be murdered. In the end, Lucky and Swede were captured. Both men were separated and questioned. The investigators

FEDERAL BUREAU OF I. TIGATION, UNITED STATES D. TMENT OF JUSTICE

UNITED STATES PENITENTIARY WASHINGTON, D. C.   UNITED STATES PENITENTIARY

Institution ......ALCATRAZ, CALIFORNIA......   Located at ......ALCATRAZ, CALIFORNIA......

Received ......JUL 23 1955......

From ......USP, ATLANTA, GA.......

Crime ......Murder & N&VTA......

Sentence: Life yrs. .... mos. .... days

Date of sentence ......8-6-53; 11-10-54......

Sentence begins ......Aug. 6, 1953......

Sentence expires ......Life......

Good time sentence expires ....

Date of birth ......6-5-28...... Occupation ....

Birthplace ......Minn....... Nationality ......USA......

F. B. I. NUMBER   611 346 A

Age ......27......   Comp. ......light......

Height ......5' 10"...... Eyes ......lt blue......

Weight ......170......   Hair ......dk brown......

Build ......med.......

Scars and marks ......Numerous tattoos on lower L. arm; ANN, BABY DOLL, DEAREST WIFE; 2 HEARTS & EAGLE on Lower R. arm; Anchor back of R hand

CRIMINAL HISTORY

NAME	NUMBER	CITY OR INSTITUTION	DATE	CHARGE	DISPOSITION OR SENTENCE
Herbert Eugene Juelich	73824-A	USP, ATLANTA, GA.	7-23-55	TRANSFERRED TO ALCATRAZ)	

(Please furnish additional criminal history and police record on separate sheet)   16—12593

Herbert "Lucky" Juelich

ask, "Which one of you shot the Marshal?" The authorities were completely shocked after they conclude their interviews. When the interviewers get together to compare notes, they're shocked that both men claim that they were the one who committed the murder. Both Lucky and Swede tried to confess to save the other. The Feds had never seen anything like this before. All of us in Atlanta had heard this story. I got to know Swede at Atlanta and Lucky at Alcatraz. He lived in C-Block on the tier below me.

Back to my original point, now you have cop killers as television personalities? The media has skewed and re-engineered some general values of societal decency. Let's keep in mind that some of the worst

394

cons at Alcatraz were friends of mine, just like you'd have in high school, but not people I necessarily admired. My heroes were men like my brothers. A cliché, but the men fighting the good fight. I'm not proud of my life. I hurt those who cared about me the most. There's only a small and very private circle of people that know the real me. I wish I had taken a different path. There's a saying that you should always look behind you to learn from your past, but for me, I was in too deep to change course. The persona of "Whitey Bulger" was written by people typing away on a keyboard with my Alcatraz mugshot in front of them crafting a fictional character, not the real me. I regret the path I took in crime, but I tried to keep honor and I can't take it back. All in all, this is my world now and I'm going to shut down all of my feelings that I can. There is something to the expression "Dead Man Walking." If I could choose my epitaph on my tombstone, it would be "I'd rather be in Alcatraz...1428-AZ." I look back to those years with nostalgia. It's all gone now. I feel like I've lived a life of unfinished things...

FINAL CURTAIN CALL

Whitey Bulger gave his life to the streets and his final years were spent alone and isolated in federal prison, paying the hard wages for his past sins. Long after Bulger ruled the streets of Boston, there were lingering questions relating to his convictions that came to light from one of the jurors who sat on his trial in 2013. Janet Uhlar, Juror #12, stated she was troubled by the fact that much of the evidence against him came through testimony by former criminal associates, who were also killers. They'd received reduced sentences in exchange for testifying against their former crime partner. Passages from a document she wrote (provided to me by Bulger) read in part:

> When Bulger was arrested in California, he surrendered without a fight and offered to plead guilty to all charges against him, accepting whatever punishment was deemed by the court—including a speedy execution. In return, he only asked for leniency for Catherine Greig.
>
> The US Attorney's Office gave FBI special agent Morris a free pass for accessory to murder. They gave serial killer Martorano approximately six months for each cold-blooded murder he committed. And, if Flemmi's testimony pleased the US Attorneys, it is highly probable that he will soon be back in town—released on what is known as a Rule 35

Motion (and it seems he will have plenty of money to live off—for the US Attorneys also saw to it that his approximate $2 million in assets were returned to Flemmi for his testimony).

Bulger's offer to plead guilty was denied, and the taxpayers will cough up the $2.6 million. But, on the positive side, Catherine Greig remains in prison—eight long years for harboring a fugitive. But wait—that reminds me of another witness in the trial—Martorano's girlfriend. Seems she harbored John for sixteen years, was involved in money laundering, and perjured herself in a grand jury hearing. How much time did she spend in jail? None. In fact, no charges were ever made.

I sat on the jury of the Bulger murder trial. I was involved in the deliberations. Now, I have questions. What was this trial really about -- and who holds the truth?

As the trial came to a close, his fate became increasingly clear. He commented:

My trial has been saturated with video of police surveillance showing grainy images of me with gang members, Mafia people outside of a garage that was reported to be the Mob headquarters. Against me are about eighty witnesses and after decades of imagination, the stories are filled with more fiction than truth. They paint the courtroom with crime scene photos of cars riddled in bullets, bodies that were mowed down with machine guns and photos of cash stashes. The family members, all innocent people, described the notifications of death, the effects, and the jury all assume that the dead people alleged to have been killed, were all victims of Whitey. Fellow gang members are like living family and all take the stand pointing at me to keep from compromising their own plea deals. They show the photos of these men with their families and the men from my alleged crew are all now like saints for their bravery in testifying against me, when they know the truth is that I didn't have any hand, or remote involvement in many of the crimes they claim I ordered. As a whole, it seems all so horrific, but each case examined one at time would reveal that so many of those dead were violent gangsters and killers. The victims' families have no voice, and none of those were ever on trial for their vicious crimes. They got away with murder. To hear the prosecutors, you would think they are pure and clean as driven snow. One murdered a father with several kids for $1,600. He took away their childhood. Another buried a victim in his cellar after hitting him in the face with an axe. Another shot my best friend in front of his wife

Bulger's path in some ways followed in the footsteps of Al Capone. In 1931, Capone's trial in Chicago was headline news with large crowds of spectators attempting a view of Capone as he was led to and from court. He would eventually be convicted to serve 11 years in federal prison and first served time at USP Atlanta, then was transferred to Alcatraz. Bulger would later read from some of the very same pages of books and digests from the prison library. He would pass one of Capone's first cells on his way to the mess hall and work assignment each day.

and six kids as they watched from their second-floor apartment. They watched in horror as it all unfolded. They see their father running for his life, but he is hit by a bullet and falls to the ground. The assailants approach him then shoot him in the back of the head. They all watched in horror as this murder unfolded. They were all screaming and crying as he was gunned down, and all were never the same. I could go on and on, but most of these men were violent men who lived by the sword and perished by the same. They knew the risks of living a life in crime.

Everyone is convinced I'm next and it becomes the fight for my life. I drove to Hell's Kitchen for machine guns and other arms. In New York, my best friend Bill, tough, dangerous and a killer, helps arm me to the hilt. The gang wars involved machine gun murders and car-to-car shootings in the streets, like Chicago in the 20s and 30s. It took only a few years to battle it out, but in the aftermath of the gang wars, so many dead. And I end up in control.

I'm driven to court each day in an armed motorcade that includes armored vehicles. What's not obvious is that behind that glass, Special Agents and U.S. Marshals are carrying automatic weapons and on-ready. It's a media circus and behind me in the courtroom are whispers that Robert Duvall, the actor who was in the *Godfather*, is sitting there watching me to research for a role. I can feel that every eye is locked on my every move.

I can feel the end of my time here will soon be over. Each day in court, I can see a tidal wave building to sweep over me. I feel like standing up and screaming "Free Catherine and end this charade; this side show; phony trial; necktie noose party. I'll agree to any punishment if they free Catherine. Let's face it, there's no justice in this court. It will be a ceremony and then guilty. On the good side, the truth is slowly coming out about me and the FBI who've been trying to brand me for years as an informant, but the truth has now surfaced, and my true role is clear. My lawyers have done a masterful job, but the trial has worn me down."

Bulger's brief note written on August 12, 2013, the night of the verdict:

It's late and a quiet night for a change so I thought I'd write a few lines. Today, the jury came back with its verdict. I was found guilty on 11 counts of murder, racketeering, illegal possession of more than fifty machine guns and other weapons. There were other counts I was convicted of… Money laundering, extortion, and I'm not even sure the total number. I lost count within a few minutes. As you know, I refused to testify. I told the court I was denied the right to relate certain facts and as such considered the trial to be a total sham. I'm not allowed to tell some of the most important aspects of the story to put everything in context? What a joke and injustice. Everyone should have the right to tell their side of the story. Home and my life with Catherine will only be a memory to me now.

Under secrecy and in the middle of the night following his trial, Bulger was transferred to various federal transfer centers including the Metropolitan Detention Center in Brooklyn, New York; Oklahoma City, and then finally to Tucson, Arizona, in early 2014. It would be the last time he'd ever see Boston. His new home was a maximum-security prison complex in the heart of the desert. Despite his advanced age, Bulger was mixed with the general population of convicts, many high profile and infamous prisoners convicted of horrific crimes. He later acknowledged an awareness that he'd be a prize kill for some cons trying to make a name for themselves. He kept mostly to himself, other than occasional visits to an art room where the focus was not telling stories and reliving their violent pasts, but rather of creative themes. Tucson was a welcome pace compared to Plymouth. Bulger, having remembered his early years in prison, maintained a keen awareness of those inmates from whom he should keep his distance.

On April 30, 2014, after a long period of no correspondence, Bulger wrote a letter that he asked to keep away from the media. He wanted to shield his family of any worry of his safety as long as he was in Tucson. His reason for not writing resulted from a failed murder attempt by another convict.

Bulger wrote from USP Tucson:

> I want to explain the most recent turn of events. I've told no one
> except my niece and her brother who came to visit a couple days ago.
> I want this kept secret until the Bureau of Prisons does a press release,
> since I don't want my family to be in fear for my safety. The media
> would blow it all out of proportion. I've already caused them so much
> grief that I don't want them to continue to be worried about me. This
> will all come out in due time, but I want to share what really happened
> before the press gets the story and turns it into some type of epic crime
> thriller!
>
> I was feeling under the weather and was in my cell alone. This
> prison has been laid back, and there's been no pressure on me. The
> guards never target anyone and the food is reasonably good. There's
> a big yard, good weather most always and I'm allowed long hours out
> of my cell if I choose. It's a major contrast to my isolation at Plymouth
> with cameras in the ceiling, a guard sitting in front of my cell 24-hours
> a day, thick steel plates welded to the exterior, and the multiple strip
> searches I was subjected to each day. In comparison, this place is like

heaven. The staff treats me good, my stress levels are way down and there are never any problems for me. Well…That all changed.

On this particular day, I was in bed asleep and everyone was in the mess hall eating breakfast. I was sound asleep. An unnamed "inmate" entered my cell and viciously stabbed me in the head with a makeshift knife, then made another attempt to cut my throat. I fought him off and then rolled out of my bed and squared off to fight. Now I'm ready to defend myself, but he ran out the door across the unit. I can't chase him in my condition. As he ran, I yelled out that he was a coward and I'd be waiting for him. He disappeared and I never saw him again. I felt pain and noticed I was bleeding. Using the force of his full body weight as he lunged in with the knife, he had stabbed me in the skull, but his attempt failed, and he didn't penetrate too deep. A little lower and he'd have got me good. I didn't talk and next thing I know after I get out of the hospital, they place me in the SHU (Special Housing Unit) in lockdown. Trust me, I welcomed it…I can only speculate the reason for the attack. The warden came to me wanting details. I explained that I wasn't looking to make a reputation and preferred to keep a low profile. It's impossible because of the media and their portrayal of me. Everyone knows who I am, and some young punk was looking to make a name for himself. There's hardly any honor in taking out an eighty-four-year-old with no weapon to fight back. He ran and went into hiding, which doesn't leave him any bragging rights…Back in the days of Alcatraz, the men didn't hide their identity when they made a hit. The attack was a small thing considering the life I'd led for so many years.

After the attempt on his life, Jim was keenly aware that he was a marked man. He was always having to look over his shoulder in population, once commenting to another convict who was an art instructor at the facility, "I hope they give it to me quick, because I gave it quick."

In February of 2015, reports surfaced that Bulger had inappropriately influenced a young female prison psychologist, who in turn extended him special privileges. The allegations were investigated by the Bureau of Prisons. They included secreting a cell phone, special writing privileges, and a private one-man cell. In return, she had allegedly taken signed photos and artwork. As a result of the allegations, and during their investigation, Bulger was transferred to USP Coleman, a high-security federal prison located in central Florida. It was the largest federal prison in the United States, and Bulger was stripped of all his freedoms. He wrote extensively that it had been such a gift to have had the privilege to write Catherine while at Tucson. He wrote her every day and commented the letters made him feel as though she was in the room. He treasured every page.

Though he mostly mingled with the older, more seasoned prisoners while at Coleman, his years there proved to be hard time. He suffered a series of health issues and complained frequently of harsh treatment. In the later years, his letters focused less on Alcatraz and his criminal past and shifted mostly to his memories of Catherine. He remembered their final moments together:

> Imprinted in my mind is the last time I saw Catherine being led away. I admit that in this moment, I was reminded how fragile and lucky I was to have had that time with her in Santa Monica. As I always knew it could happen...Deep down I knew it could someday...I watched her being led away...It was the last time I saw her...I felt as though life ended for me in that moment..."

In October of 2018, without any notice, Bulger was transferred to Hazelton Penitentiary in West Virginia, a maximum-security Federal prison nicknamed Misery Mountain. There were news reports that he had threatened prison staff, and had become a difficult prisoner, while other reports suggested he kept to himself and stayed clear of trouble. At the time of Bulger's transfer, Hazelton was considered the most violent prison in the Federal system, with nine prisoners being murdered between 2013 and 2018, more than at any other Federal penitentiary during that period.

James Bulger was brutally attacked and murdered within twelve hours of his arrival at Hazelton. News of his arrival had spread rapidly among the prisoners. It is almost unbelievable that Hazelton took no precautions. They surely knew that he would be a target. He was beaten so severely and with such violent force, he was left unrecognizable. He was placed back in his bed and posed to appear as if he was sleeping.

The alleged assailant, a known hitman for the Italian Mafia, purportedly entered Bulger's cell when it was first racked open in the early morning hours. Using a heavy steel padlock in a pillowcase as a weapon, he delivered a brutally violent ending to one of the most prominent crime figures of this era. In Bulger's final moments, when the reality of his fate became clear, he likely resigned himself to the consequence and brand of violence that was a trademark of his reputation.

Epilogue

I N THE WORLD OF ORGANIZED CRIME, loyalty and allegiance is everything. A misstep is a misdeed that leads to serious consequences. Whether it's breaking a deal, not keeping your word, or breaking your alliance, there's always a severe penalty. Regardless of whether the allegations against Bulger were true, rumored or only perceived, the stories of broken loyalty in the media made him a prime target in prison. James "Whitey" Bulger was eighty-nine years old at the time of his brutal murder. Despite knowing his purported affiliations in organized crime, the Bureau of Prisons served him a death sentence when they transferred him to Hazelton, where rival Mafia members lurked in wait and delivered a swift execution. Bulger, who once carried a notorious mob boss reputation for his willingness to use extremes of violence, became a frail victim in his final moments, unable to defend himself and ultimately suffered an unfathomable fate.

It should be noted that although individuals of the FBI were convicted or received plea deals to avoid prison, it does not reflect the character of the men and women of the agency as a whole. Most all approach their career with the purest of interests to preserve and protect the core values of goodness within our society. And there are still so many secrets that Bulger took with him to his grave. The mystery of the Isabella Gardner art heist. The allegation that he had more than $30 million when he fled Boston. Huge riches buried in old historic graveyards and stashed in safe deposit boxes around the world. Grand mysteries and curious questions that will likely forever go unanswered.

There is one redeeming story tangled in all the tales of violence and evasion. It was his love for Catherine and the desire to break free from a lifetime spent in the dark underworld of crime. His sixteen years living so near to the beach in beautiful Southern California, savoring the salt ocean breeze he'd grown to love at Alcatraz, being free to be in love at last, maybe even at peace. Maybe even savoring a world without murder, violence and revenge. What did Whitey Bulger leave behind? His name. His terrifying reputation as a stone-cold killer. His enemies. His family. His friends. His life... He felt lucky to have had those sixteen peaceful years with Catherine. Their quiet moments at night were filled with intimate talks, looking at the stars, sitting on the beach, listening to the soft crashing of the ocean waves, and showing compassion to stray cats and dogs. They were just a nice old retired couple, except for the $800K hidden in their walls, all the guns, and a secret past.

After his 2011 arrest, memories were all he carried with him. Catherine wrote in a letter, after she'd learned about Bulger's murder, and prior to her release from prison:

> "I miss him—desperately—my life will never be the same—but I'm comforted by wonderful memories. I'm reminded that many people live a lifetime and never experience the type of love we shared."

No words could ever comfort the victims and their families, but the memories and writings from Bulger show his human side, filled with regret, reflection, loss, and yes,
even love…

ACKNOWLEDGMENTS

I AM ETERNALLY GRATEFUL to so many I've been associated with through the Alcatraz connection. This project began only weeks following Bulger's capture and so many individuals were incredibly supportive, despite Bulger's reputation and past, to capture his memories of life on Alcatraz (an undertaking that took more than a decade). With that said, there are many listed in the acknowledgements who felt conflicted giving Bulger a voice and would have preferred no association. Acknowledging those who have helped me along the way is always so important, but I wanted to recognize those who still provided support on a subject they felt at odds with. So many of the people listed here were very much a part of this long journey to see it through to print and others inspired me years ago during my first interviews relating to the island's history. I owe special thanks to Kelly Rabe, Frankie Eld, Suzanne Roth, Candace Lind Jones, James Zach and John Reinhardt who all offered advice through various stages of the project on the content and structure, along with such gracious support. I can't express my gratitude to them enough…My family has continued supporting me over the years, and I am deeply grateful to James Bulger who shared his perspectives with the interest of preserving the great history of this National Historic Landmark.

My sincere and deepest appreciation to the following people:

Jamie Clark, Robert Schibline, Devik Wiener, Mary Hurley, Richard Tuggle, Catherine Greig, Josh Bond, Larry Hankin, Benny Batom, Charlie Hopkins, Al Blank, Alcatraz City Tours, Angelita Cecilio, Robert Lieber, Anthony Anderson, Art Owen, Art Roderick, Chris Warren, Chuck Stucker, Colin Fairbairn, Craig Glassner, Dan Cook, Dan Unger, Darwin Coon, David Clark, David Widner, Denise Rasmussen, Donna Spinola, Drew Morita, Emil Nicolas Gallina, Eric Begley, Gennifer Choldenko, George DeVincenzi, George Durgerian, Glenn Mullin, Hank Brennan, Heather Paris, James Quillen, Lori Quillen, Mikki Routheau, Jason Herrera, Jayeson Vance, Jerry & Amanda Arend, Jim Breeden, Jim Nelson, Joe Carnes, John and Michele Moran, John Cantwell, John Donelan, Jon Forsling, Joseph Sanchez, Katherina Machwitz, Ken Widner, Lala Macapagal, Lisa Rene Crane, Lorelei Octavo, Lori Brosnan, Marc Stokes, Matt Hess, Michael Badolato, Michael Dyke, Pete Dracopoulos, Jolene Babyak,

Philip R. Bergen, Monica Ball, Rachel Lawton, Richard and Megan Dole, Rick Rosen, Rob and Tracy Sebastian, Robert and Ida Luke, Roger Goldberg, Sharlene Baker, Stan Cordes, Stephen Covey, Steven Cote, Terry MacRae, Tim and Ana Brazil, Todd Nunn, Tom Kent, Tom Ryan, Walter Page, Wendy Solis, my family at GMR, and finally, my friends and family of the National Park Service at Alcatraz Island. Thank you all…

PHOTOGRAPH
AND ILLUSTRATION CREDITS

Unless noted, all prisoner catalog photographs and documents are courtesy of the Federal Bureau of Investigation, National Archives and Records Administration, Department of Justice and/or Bureau of Prisons Archives. If available, specific source information for photographs has been included in the source index below.

ABBREVIATIONS:
t-top, b-bottom, m-middle/center, l-left, r-right

AC	Author's Collection (Indicates personal collection of historical photograph(s)/or photographed by the author)
ACME	ACME News Photo
AP	Associated Press Photo
BG	Boston Globe
BH	Boston Herald
BOP	Bureau of Prisons
CA	Collier's Archive
CHPA	California State Highway Patrol Museum Archives
CI	Custom Illustration: Toby Mikle
CN	Cleveland News Photo
DOJ	Department of Justice
ESP	Eastern State Penitentiary Museum Archives
FBI	Federal Bureau of Investigation Archives
GGNRA	Golden Gate National Recreation Area, Park Archives
INP	International News Photo Service
JB	James Bulger
LAT	Los Angeles Times
LC	Library of Congress Historical Photograph and Document Collection
LW	The Estate of Leigh Wiener
NYDN	New York Daily News
PARC	Park Archives and History Center, National Park Service
PPA	Polaris Photo Archive
RP	Reuters Press Photo
SFC	San Francisco Chronicle
SFCB	San Francisco Call Bulletin
SFE	San Francisco Examiner

SFPL   San Francisco Public Library, History Center Archives
UPI   United Press International
USAO   United States Attorney's Office
USMS   United States Marshal Service
USNCL   Unknown Source – No Credit Listed - Press Photograph
WWP   Wide World Photo Service

XII AC; XV PPA; XXV AC; XXXVI AC; 1 DOJ; 2 DOJ; 3 Bill Greene/The Boston Globe via Getty Images; 5 USNCL; 6 DOJ; 8 Monogram Pictures; 9 WB; 11 AC; 12 AC; 13 Bostonian May 1941; 14 AC; 15 DOJ/Boston Police Dept;16 DOJ; 18 (t) from a photo postcard (non-credited), (b) AC; 19 (l) UPI (r) Bill Delargy/UPI; 22 DOJ/ Frankie Eld (Researcher); 24 DOJ/Miami Police Dept; 26 Miami Daily News/Moeser; 28 PPA; 30 (t)(b) BOP; 31 UPI; 35 INP; 43 Decca Records; 44 NYDN; 52 (t) SFCB/J. Dehane, (b) WWP; 53 AC; 55 (t) SFPL, (b) CA; 58 (t) AC, (b) AP; 59 (t) SFPL, (b) AP; 61 (t) FBI (b) AC; 64 INP ; 66 (t) CN (b) ACME; 67 (l) Ernest Lageson,(r) AC; 71 (t) (m) BOP, (b) National Archives RG129; 77 West Point Archives; 79 AP; 90 ACME; 91 UPI Telephoto; 96 BOP; 98 AC; 99 JB; 102 (t) AC, (b) ACME; 103 LW/Courtesy of Devik Wiener and the Estate of Leigh Wiener; 105 AC; 107 Candace Lind Jones; 110 (t) SFCB, (b) USNCL; 111 (t)(b) AP, 112 National Archives RG129; 113 PARC; 114 (t) CI, (b) National Archives RG129; 118 (t) Matt Hess, (b) AP; 119 (t)(l) INP, (t)(r) CA, (b) AC; 121 (t) AC, (m) INP, (b) AP; 123 (t) INP (m)(b) UPI; 124 (t) SFE/Fred Pardini, (b) UPI; 125 BOP; 128 AP; 130 UPI; 131 (t) Patrick Burke, (b) AP Archives; 132 (t) AC, (b) SFC; 133 (t)(m)(b)AC; 147 (r) Robert Lieber GGNPC, (b) AC; 160-161 AC; 163 AC; 166 UPI; 173 AP; 175 DOJ; 176 INP; 199 CHPA; 200 (t) CHPA,(b) AP; 201 (t), (m) UPI, (b) AP; 203 CHPA; 205 Santa Clarita Valley Signal; 207 (t) The Milwaukee Journal, (m)(b) UPI; 208 UPI; 211 Reuters/Tim Wimborne, Alamy Stock Photo; 214-215 AP; 220 (t) UPI, (b) AC; 222 SFE/Fred Pardini; 224 Newspaper Archive/Drew Morita; 225 BOP/Larry Quilligan; 228 AP; 229 INP; 230 AP; 231 (l) AP, (r) LA Times; 235 (t) LA Times/LAPD, (b) CSU Archives; 238 LAPD; 239 UPI; 240 INP/Dick Fallon; 244-245 AP; 250 SFPL; 257 AP; 261 CA; 265 (t) SFPL, (b) SFE/Fred Pardini; 267 (t) AC, (b) FBI; 276 Newspaper Archive/Frankie Eld (Researcher); 278 IDW Publishing; 279 AP; 282 ESP; 286 AP; 287 AC; 289 (l) Archive File Photo, (r) AC; 296 AC; 301 UPI; 302 AP; 303 (t) United Artists, (b) Hal Roach Studios; 304 AC; 306 AC; 312 UPI; 313 AP; 314 SFE/Fred Pardini; 315 INP; 316 AP; 319 (b) AC; 321 SFE/ Chris Kjobech; 322 BOP; 323 SFE/Fred Pardini; 327 (t) John Tlumacki/The Boston Globe via Getty Images, (b) DOJ; 328 DEA; 329 (t) DOJ, (b) AC; 331 (t) USNCL, (l) BH/Arthur Pollock, (r) USNCL; 332 BH/Nancy Lane; 333 BH/Ted Fitzgerald; 334 JB; 336 FBI File Photo; 338-339 DOJ; 342 (t) Newport Daily News, (inset) AC; 343 USAO; 347 JB; 348 AC; 349 (t) JB, (m) DOJ; 350 AC; 352-355 DOJ; 356 (t) Boston Globe/ John Tlumacki, (b) JB; 357-358 AC; 359 USAO; 360 USMS; 361 (t) AC, (b) DOJ; 363 Yoon S. Byun/The Boston Globe via Getty Images; 364 AC; 365 AP; 367 AC; 369 DOJ; 371 USMS; AP/ Bill Converse; 375 AP/Charles Krupa; 377-379 Warner Bros; 385 AP/David Tenenbaum; 387 BG/John Tlumacki; 392 Michael Cola; 397 LC; 402 Raphael Rivest.

ABOUT THE AUTHOR

MICHAEL ESSLINGER is a historical researcher and bestselling author; his work has appeared in numerous film and television documentaries, including segments on the Discovery, National Geographic, Travel and History Channels. From the elusive crew of Apollo 11 to prisoners of Alcatraz, he has interviewed icons and others who have shaped history and continues to write on subjects that explore a vast spectrum of historical subjects.

He was the co-author of *Escaping Alcatraz: The Untold Story of the Greatest Prison Break in American History*, winner of the 2018 International Book Award (sponsored by the American Book Festival) in the True Crime category. His other works, *Alcatraz: The History of the Penitentiary Years* and *Letters from Alcatraz* continue as best-selling references chronicling the island's rich historical past. He is the co-author of the movie memoir: *I Want It Now! A Memoir of Life on the Set of Willy Wonka and the Chocolate Factory*, a magical memoir written with Julie Dawn Cole, the original "Veruca Salt" in the classic motion picture starring Gene Wilder. Current projects include a detailed chronicle of the 1946 Battle of Alcatraz, and a comprehensive history of the Apollo 11 Mission titled *Apollo 11: From Launch to Recovery*, documenting mankind's first lunar landing, and based on first person interviews with the Apollo 11 astronauts and mission support personnel including Neil Armstrong, Buzz Aldrin, and Michael Collins.

INDEX

ESCAPING
ALCATRAZ
The Untold Story of the
1962 Great Escape from Alcatraz
WANTED BY FBI
JOHN WILLIAM ANGLIN
WANTED BY FBI
FRANK LEE MORRIS
WANTED BY FBI
CLARENCE ANGLIN
Winner of the 2018 International Book Award in the True Crime category, Escaping Alcatraz: The Untold Story of the Greatest Prison Break in American History by Michael Esslinger and David Widner, offers one of the most detailed and historical accounts of the 1962 famed prison break of Frank Morris and John & Clarence Anglin. This comprehensive account is illustrated with hundreds of photographs, FBI and Bureau of Prisons investigative notes, original source documents from the Anglin family library, inmate casefile records, interviews with key convicts, officers, and first person accounts of officials who investigated the escape to produce one of the most detailed narratives of the famed prison break.
INTERNATIONAL BOOK AWARDS WINNER
ESCAPING
ALCATRAZ
INTERNATIONAL BOOK AWARDS WINNER
MICHAEL ESSLINGER & DAVID WIDNER
Available in Print and Audio